CATECHIST MANUAL

AGE 3

God Made Me

AUTHORS
Sisters of Notre Dame
Chardon, Ohio

LoyolaPress.
A JESUIT MINISTRY
Chicago

Imprimatur: Reverend John F. Canary, S.T.L., D. Min., Vicar General, Archdiocese of Chicago, September 17, 2008

In accordance with c. 827, permission to publish in the Archdiocese of Chicago has been granted by the Very Reverend John F. Canary, Vicar General, on September 17, 2008. This means that the material has been found free from doctrinal or moral error, and does not imply that the one granting this permission agrees with the content, opinions, or statements expressed therein. Nor is any legal responsibility assumed by the Archdiocese of Chicago by granting this permission.

God Made Me of the *God Made Everything* Series
found to be in conformity

The Ad Hoc Committee to Oversee the Use of the Catechism, United States Conference of Catholic Bishops, has found the doctrinal content of this manual, copyright 2010, to be in conformity with the *Catechism of the Catholic Church.*

ACKNOWLEDGMENTS

Excerpts from the *New American Bible* with Revised New Testament and Psalms. Copyright © 1991, 1986, 1970 Confraternity of Christian Doctrine, Inc., Washington, DC. All rights reserved. No portion of the *New American Bible* may be reprinted without permission in writing from the copyright holder.

Excerpts from the English translation of *The Roman Missal* © 1973, International Committee on English in the Liturgy, Inc. (ICEL). All rights reserved.

Excerpts from *Catechism of the Catholic Church*. English translation of the *Catechism of the Catholic Church* for the United States of America copyright © 1994, United States Catholic Conference, Inc.—Libreria Editrice Vaticana.

Excerpt from *Economic Justice for All: A Pastoral Letter on Catholic Social Teaching and the U.S. Economy.* Copyright © 1986 United States Conference of Catholic Bishops, Inc., Washington, DC. No portion of this text may be reproduced by any means without written permission from the copyright holder.

Loyola Press has made every effort to locate the copyright holders for the cited works used in this publication and to make full acknowledgment for their use. In the case of any omissions, the publisher will be pleased to make suitable acknowledgments in future editions.

MUSIC 'N MOTION CD CREDITS

Track 1: "I Am Wonderfully Made," words and music by Jack Miffleton. Copyright © 1978, World Library Publications, Franklin Park, IL 60131-2158. www.wlpmusic.com. From the recording *Sing a Song of Joy,* ℗© 1999, World Library Publications. All rights reserved. Used by permission.

Track 2: "Helping," words and music by Jack Miffleton. Copyright © 1978, World Library Publications, Franklin Park, IL 60131-2158. www.wlpmusic.com. From the recording *Sing a Song of Joy,* ℗© 1999, World Library Publications. All rights reserved. Used by permission.

Track 3: "Peace in My Heart," words and music by Mary Ann Renna. Copyright © 2004, World Library Publications, Franklin Park, IL 60131-2158. www.wlpmusic.com. All rights reserved. Used by permission. From the recording *Kids Sing for Jesus,* ℗© 2004, AvilaRose, Inc. All rights reserved. Used by permission.

Track 4: "Jump Up, Get Down," words and music by Mary Ann Renna. Copyright © 2004, World Library Publications, Franklin Park, IL 60131-2158. www.wlpmusic.com. All rights reserved. Used by permission. From the recording *Kids Sing for Jesus,* ℗© 2004, AvilaRose, Inc. All rights reserved. Used by permission.

Track 5: "You Are the Light," words and music by Michael Mangan. Copyright © 2004, Litmus Productions. Exclusive licensing agent in North America: World Library Publications, Franklin Park, IL 60131-2158. www.wlpmusic.com. From the recording *Forever Will I Sing,* ℗© 2004, Litmus Productions. All rights reserved. Used by permission.

Track 6: "Come Together," words and music by Michael Mangan. Copyright © 1993, Litmus Productions. Exclusive licensing agent in North America: World Library Publications, Franklin Park, IL 60131-2158. www.wlpmusic.com. All rights reserved. Used by permission.

Track 7: "Stand Up!," words and music by Michael Mangan. Copyright © 2001, Litmus Productions. Exclusive licensing agent in North America: World Library Publications, Franklin Park, IL 60131-2158. www.wlpmusic.com. From the recording *Setting Hearts on Fire,* ℗© 2001, Litmus Productions. Exclusive licensing agent in North America: World Library Publications. All rights reserved. Used by permission.

Track 8: "Windy Days," words and music by Jack Miffleton. Copyright © 1979, World Library Publications, Franklin Park, IL 60131-2158. www.wlpmusic.com. From the recording *Sing a Song of Joy,* ℗© 1999, World Library Publications. All rights reserved. Used by permission.

Track 9: "Praise and Glorify," words and music by Julie Howard. Copyright © 1995, World Library Publications, Franklin Park, IL 60131-2158. www.wlpmusic.com. From the recording *Here I Am, God!,* ℗© 1995, World Library Publications. All rights reserved. Used by permission.

Track 10: "Care for Life," words and music by Michael Mangan. Copyright © 1997, Litmus Productions. Exclusive licensing agent in North America: World Library Publications, Franklin Park, IL 60131-2158. www.wlpmusic.com. From the recording *True Colors Shine,* ℗© 2007, Litmus Productions. Exclusive licensing agent in North America: World Library Publications. All rights reserved. Used by permission.

Track 11: "When the Saints Go Marching In," traditional.

Track 12: "No Place to Stay," music by Mary Beth Kunde-Anderson. Music copyright © 2008, World Library Publications, Franklin Park, IL 60131-2158. www.wlpmusic.com. All rights reserved. Used by permission.

Track 13: "Easter Alleluia," words and music by Michael Mangan. Copyright © 1993, Litmus Productions. Exclusive licensing agent in North America: World Library Publications, Franklin Park, IL 60131-2158. www.wlpmusic.com. From the recording *This Is the Time,* ℗© 2005, Litmus Productions. Exclusive licensing agent in North America: World Library Publications. All rights reserved. Used by permission.

Track 14: "Thank You, Jesus," words and music by Mary Ann Renna. Copyright © 2004, World Library Publications, Franklin Park, IL 60131-2158. www.wlpmusic.com. All rights reserved. Used by permission. From the recording *Kids Sing for Jesus,* ℗© 2004, AvilaRose, Inc. All rights reserved. Used by permission.

Track 15: "God Is Love," words and music by James V. Marchionda, O.P. Copyright © 1988, World Library Publications, Franklin Park, IL 60131-2158. www.wlpmusic.com. From the recording *Let the Children Come to Me,* ℗© 1988, World Library Publications. All rights reserved. Used by permission.

Track 16: "Happy Birthday! It's Your Day" (age 3), traditional melody.

Track 17: "Happy Birthday! It's Your Day" (age 4), traditional melody.

Track 18: "God Is Great," words and music by Michael Mangan. Copyright © 1998, Litmus Productions. Exclusive licensing agent in North America: World Library Publications, Franklin Park, IL 60131-2158. www.wlpmusic.com. All rights reserved. Used by permission.

ART CREDITS

Art credits are supplied in sequence, left to right, top to bottom. Page positions are abbreviated as follows: (t) top, (c) center, (b) bottom, (l) left, (r) right.

Illustration **T175, T247** Susan Tolonen, **T249**(t) ©iStockphoto.com/John Woodcock, **T249**(b) ©iStockphoto.com/Marguerite Voisey, **Cutouts** Phyllis Pollema Cahill, Renée Daily, Diana Magnuson, and Robert Masheris

Acknowledgments continued on page T316

LOYOLAPRESS.
A JESUIT MINISTRY

3441 N. Ashland Avenue
Chicago, Illinois 60657
(800) 621-1008
www.loyolapress.com

Designer: Kathleen M. Burke
Art Director: Judine O'Shea
Cover Artist: Susan Tolonen

Project Editor: Catherine T. M. Joyce
Catechetical Consultant: Susan Anderson

ISBN 10: 0-8294-2801-1, ISBN 13: 978-0-8294-2801-8

Copyright © 2010 Loyola Press, Chicago, Illinois.

All rights reserved. No part of this book may be reproduced, stored in a retrieval system, or transmitted in any form or by any means, electronic, mechanical, photocopying, recording, or otherwise, without the prior permission of the publisher.

Manufactured in China.
10 11 12 13 14 RRD 10 9 8 7 6 5 4 3 2

DEDICATION

THE SISTERS OF NOTRE DAME GRATEFULLY REMEMBER
PERSONS FROM THEIR PAST WHOSE MINISTRY
OF CATECHESIS THEY ARE PRIVILEGED TO CONTINUE
IN THE PRESENT.

Sister Maria Aloysia Wolbring (1828–1889) foundress of the Sisters of Notre Dame of Coesfeld, Germany, and the first sisters of this new community, were formed in the spiritual and pedagogical tradition of Reverend Bernard Overberg. God, our loving and provident Father, was presented not only as caring for persons more than anyone else ever could, but also as challenging them to a responsible love for themselves, for all other people, and for creation. One of Sister Aloysia's students recalled: "Her religious instructions meant more to us than the sermons preached in church. She spoke from deepest conviction and tried to direct our hearts to God alone. Best of all, she did not require too much piety of us. 'Children,' she would say, 'always follow the golden middle way—not too little, not too much.'"

Reverend Bernard Overberg (1754–1826) began his life work of shaping teacher formation and catechesis in 1783 in the diocese of Munster, Germany. Reverend Overberg sought to present the Church's faith and teaching in such a way as to lead children and adults toward a deep, mature relationship with God in Jesus Christ. Faith, experienced through the lens of salvation history and related to everyday life, was to touch both the mind and the heart, calling forth reflection, prayer, and active response. His approach to catechesis was the way the Coesfeld Sisters of Notre Dame were led to know God in their childhood, and how they were later formed as catechists.

Saint Julie Billiart (1751–1816), foundress of the Sisters of Notre Dame de Namur, was the source of the Rule by which the Coesfeld Sisters of Notre Dame were formed. With Christian education designated as the main work of the congregation, the sisters had a framework within which to continue the mission they had begun as lay teachers. As they learned more about Julie, the sisters were inspired by the story of how this simple French woman became a remarkable catechist who helped renew the people's faith after the chaos of the French Revolution. As a young girl, Julie's deep faith and love impelled her to share the Good News with others. During a 12-year period in which she suffered a crippling illness, Julie devoted herself to catechizing women and children. Julie's confidence in the goodness and provident care of God remained unshaken in the face of misunderstandings on the part of some bishops, priests, and even her own sisters. Always open to the Spirit, she courageously carried out her ministry and taught others to proclaim the Good News. The more the Coesfeld Sisters of Notre Dame came to know about Julie, the more they desired to make known God's goodness. "How good God is." Today they regard her as their spiritual mother.

Contents

God Made Me

Program Overview OV-3
Planning Calendar OV-14
Introduction T1

Unit 1: God Made Me Live

1. **I Can Hear** T4
   God's creation of us as special. The gift of hearing. The Bible.

2. **I Can See** T12
   The gift of vision. God's love.

3. **I Can Smell** T18
   The gift of smell. Showing God's love.

4. **I Can Touch** T24
   The gift of touch.
   Thanking God for goodness and love.

5. **I Can Taste** T30
   The gift of taste. Celebrating our wonderful gifts.

Unit 2: God Made Me Good

6. **I Can Help** T38
   Helping like Jesus. Ways to help.

7. **I Can Care** T46
   Caring for things and ourselves.
   Thanking God for the earth.

8. **I Can Clean** T52
   Using water to wash things. Washing ourselves.

9. **I Can Share** T58
   The joy of sharing. How to share like Jesus.

10. **I Can Smile** T64
    The meaning of a smile.
    The happiness Jesus brings.

Unit 3: God Made Me Happy

11. **I Can Talk** T72
    The gift of speech. Speaking politely.

12. **I Can Pray** T78
    Ways to talk to God. When to talk to God.

13. **I Can Sing** T84
    The joy of singing. Singing as praise.
    The song of Mary and of the angels.

14. **I Can Laugh** T90
    Jesus' care. Thanking God for laughter.
    The story of Abraham and Sarah.

15. **I Can Celebrate** T96
    Celebrating with food.
    Celebrating the color green.

Unit 4: God Made Me Active

16. **I Can Move** T106
    The ability to move. Dancing to praise God.

17. **I Can Play** T112
    The joy of playing. Sharing and being kind.

18. **I Can Work** T118
    Ways to work at home. How Jesus worked.

19. **I Can Make Things** T126
    God's creation. Making things and being creative.

20. **I Can Grow** T132
    Signs of growth. Jesus' growth.

God Made Me OV-1

Unit 5: God Made Me Special

- **21 I Can Feel** T142
  Types of feelings. Jesus' feelings.
- **22 I Can Wish** T148
  People's wishes. Best wishes and blessings.
- **23 I Can Learn** T156
  Learning facts and skills. Learning about God.
- **24 I Can Pretend** T162
  The fun of pretending. Thanking God for life.
- **25 I Can Love** T168
  Being loved. Showing love for others.

Special Seasons and Days   T174

Liturgical Calendar T175

- **1 Halloween/Feast of All Saints** T176
  Celebrating the saints. Saint Paul.
- **2 Advent** T182
  Preparing for Jesus. Gifts for Jesus.
- **3 Christmas** T188
  The story of Christmas. Celebrating Christmas.
- **4 Lent** T194
  How seeds grow. Growing in God's love.
- **5 Easter** T200
  New life. Celebrating the life of Jesus.
- **6 Pentecost** T206
  Importance of air. The gift of the Holy Spirit.
- **7 Thanksgiving** T212
  God's gift of food. Thanking God for everything.
- **8 Valentine's Day** T218
  God's love for us. Giving valentines.
- **9 Mother's Day** T224
  Mothers. Mary, our mother in heaven.
- **10 Father's Day** T230
  Fathers. God our Father.
- **11 Birthdays** T236
  Celebrating the gift of life. Wonderful things we can do.
- **12 Last Class/Summer** T242
  Summer fun. Review of the preschool classes.

Music 'n Motion   T247

Catechist's Handbook   T277

Parent-Catechist Meeting T298
Music List T302
Homemade Materials T308
Directory of Suppliers T311

Indexes

Scripture Index T313
Topical Index T314

Cutouts

Scripture Cards

GUIDING THE CHILD

Helping Young Children Know That...

God Made Everything

The *God Made Everything* series is a comprehensive early childhood program complete with all the components and catechist support you need to nurture and enrich the faith and spiritual lives of children ages three, four, and five. Each developmentally appropriate curriculum is carefully planned so that at completion, the children are ready to continue their faith journey into first grade and beyond.

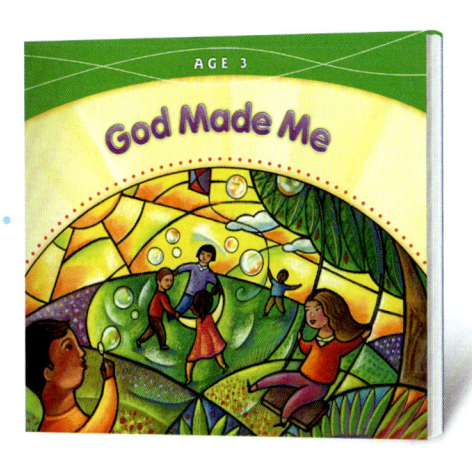

God Made Me
Child's Book for Pre-K, Age 3
Through this curriculum, three-year-olds understand that God created them and made them good, happy, active, and special. The children's own abilities serve as the central springboard for each chapter.

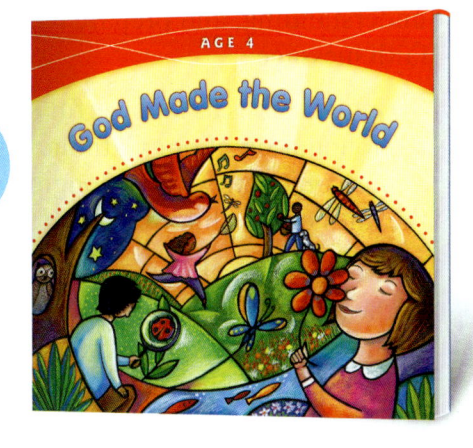

God Made the World
Child's Book for Pre-K, Age 4
In this curriculum, four-year-olds learn that God made living things, including people, holy things, the earth, and other wonderful surprises. A unique aspect of God's creation is the main focus of each chapter.

God Loves Us
Student Book for Kindergarten
Five-year-olds explore God's love as they are introduced to God's goodness shown through words, actions, feelings, people, places, and things. Learning, growing, sharing, and celebrating provide the foundation for each chapter. One special aspect of God's goodness is the focus of each chapter.

Program Overview   OV-3

GUIDING THE CHILD

God Made Me

Child's Book and Materials

Created especially for three-year-olds, *God Made Me* helps our youngest faithful grow and develop with lessons and activities suited just for them.

- The Child's Book includes **lessons and activity pages** for five units with five chapters in each unit.

- Life and faith are celebrated as children have fun learning about **special seasons and days with activities** for Halloween/Feast of All Saints, Advent, Christmas, Lent, Easter, Pentecost, Thanksgiving, Valentine's Day, Mother's Day, Father's Day, Birthdays, and Last Class/Summer.

- **Appealing illustrations and photographs** serve as a springboard for discussion and an introduction to the faith theme.

- **Discussion of the art** helps the children tap prior knowledge, develop ideas and understanding, and prepare to hear the faith message.

- **Scripture** serves as a powerful tool to explain the foundation of our Catholic faith, create a sense of identity and belonging, and enrich the faith of the children.

- **Active learning** reinforces chapter concepts as the children talk, move, play games, color, cut, glue, draw, or create to express themselves and their ideas.

- **Prayer** coincides with active learning to guide the children to reflect upon ideas and grow in their faith.

- Once the chapter is complete, the children take home their page and are invited to engage in **Family Time** with their loved ones.

- **Perforated cards** provide additional activity opportunities.

GUIDING THE CHILD

Music 'n Motion CD

Music 'n Motion provides a setting for young children to imagine, dream, mime, move, and express their ideas and emotions. Exercise of the creative imagination through movement, music, and drama helps lay the groundwork for development of the religious imagination.

Eighteen engaging songs introduce and reinforce important concepts from *God Made Me* and *God Made the World*.

Fun rhythms and melodies invite the children to sing, dance, and move with their catechist as guide.

Special-occasion songs are provided for Halloween/Feast of All Saints, Thanksgiving, Christmas, Valentine's Day, Easter, Birthdays, and Last Class/Summer.

Research-Based!

"... music in the lives of young children is a highly effective means of delivering vital information ..."

MENC: The National Association for Music Education, National Association for the Education of Young Children, and the U.S. Department of Education, and supported by Texaco, Inc. Washington D.C., June 14–16, 2000.

Program Overview   OV-5

GUIDING THE FAMILY

Child's Book and Materials *continued*

Living and experiencing faith at home is key to a child's faith formation. **Family Time** provides essential tools to help parents guide their child and live their faith together as a family.

Family Time

Chapter 5: I Can Taste ①
In this lesson the children learned about their sense of taste. They talked about their favorite food and were encouraged to eat a variety of foods. As a culmination of their study of the five senses, they had a party to celebrate themselves. Ask your child to show you the right order of the four pictures of a pizza. ②

Your Child
Children need a balanced diet. Keep snacks as healthful as possible and limit sugar, fat, and salt in your child's diet. Children have food preferences. You need not insist that your child eat foods that he or she strongly dislikes. You might serve your child's favorite meal sometime this week. Begin this meal with a short prayer of thanks to God.

Reflect ③
Learn to savor how good the Lord is[.] (Psalm 34:9)

Pray ④
Loving God, we praise you for your goodness and love.

Do ⑤
- Let your child go with you when you shop for food.
- Visit a farm and talk about the food it produces. Comment how good and wise God was in planning our food.
- Take your child to an ice-cream store and let him or her choose a flavor for a cone.
- Once in a while serve a new food to your child.
- Read to your child *Bread and Jam for Frances* by Russell Hoban. Discuss why it is nice to try and enjoy a variety of tastes. Thank God for the sense of taste and for good foods to eat. ⑥

For more family resources, refer to the Family Activity Booklet and visit www.loyolapress.com/preschool. ⑦

© LOYOLAPRESS.

---

① **Chapter background** is provided to set the stage for an enriching, positive experience.

② **Age-specific developmental stages and milestones** are discussed to help parents frame information in an understandable, appropriate way.

③ **The link to Scripture** provides a strong context for daily living.

④ **Prayer** flows from Scripture, deepens the experience, and guides families to worship.

⑤ **A variety of activities** are provided to meet the needs of every family.

⑥ **Children's storybooks** are suggested for special read-aloud and prayer time to reinforce the ideas of the chapter.

⑦ Families are invited to visit www.loyolapress.com/preschool to find even more opportunities for developing faith together. **Spanish translations** are available online in the section titled "Tiempo en familia."

The **Family Activity Booklet** is sent home at the beginning of the year for additional support and family-time fun. Family members can reference the activities, poems, and songs learned in the preschool program.

OV-6   God Made Me

GUIDING THE CATECHIST

God Made Me Catechist Manual

Catechist Manual and Materials

Ample background, support, and clear direction provide success for catechists of every experience level.

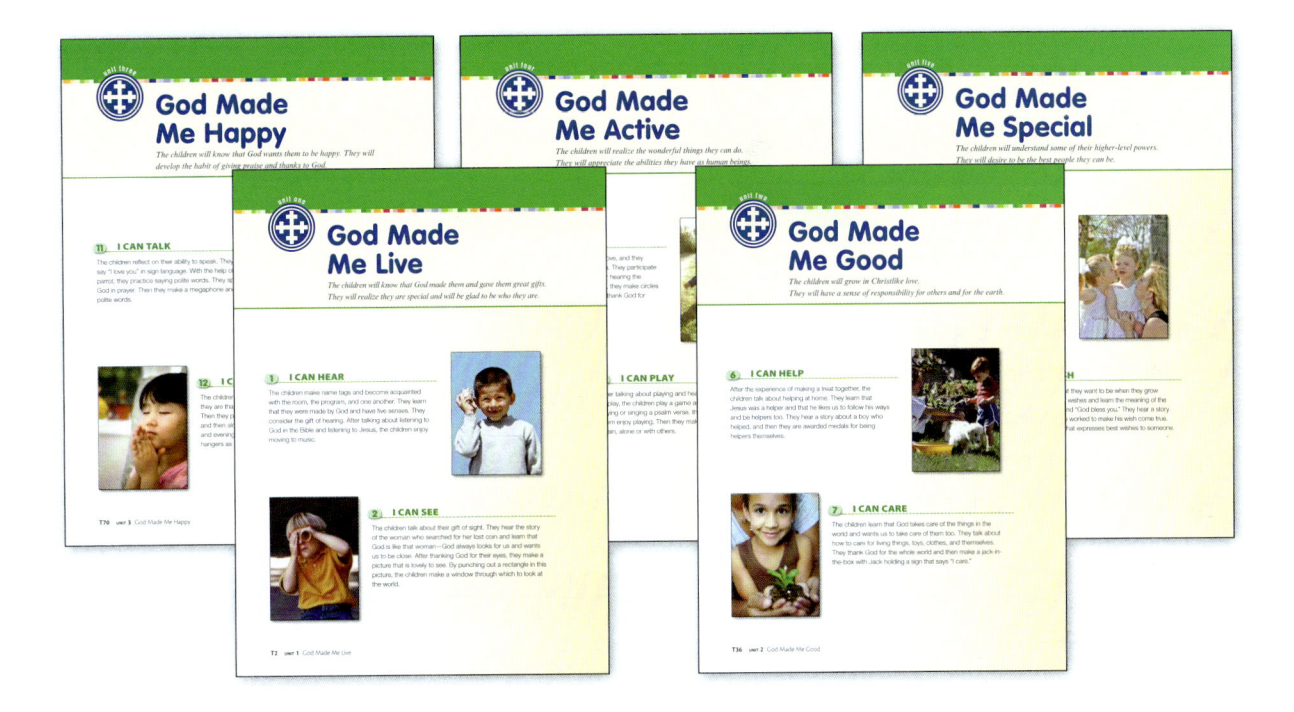

Five Units of Five Chapters Each

The Catechist Manual follows the Child's Book with five units of five chapters each. Each chapter includes the following elements:

- **Catechist preparation** through listening, reflecting, and responding to Scripture

- **Comprehensive lesson plan** that includes references to Scripture and the *Catechism of the Catholic Church*, materials list of program components and classroom supplies, preparation tips, music references, extension ideas to enrich the faith experience, children's storybook suggestions, and snack ideas

- **Alternative scheduling options** offer flexibility

- Clear **learning outcomes** and **child development background** for teaching success

- **Step-by-step lesson plans** that follow an easy three-step model

- **Checkpoints** to assess and gauge learning

- **Enriching the faith experience** with suggestions for additional activities

Program Overview **OV-7**

GUIDING THE CATECHIST

Teaching as Easy as 1, 2, 3

The three-step teaching method—Centering, Sharing, Acting—provides children with routine and repetition to aid in understanding the content and learning to pray.

Step-by-step directions clearly show the progression of each step in the chapter. These numbered steps guide new and experienced catechists through the chapter.

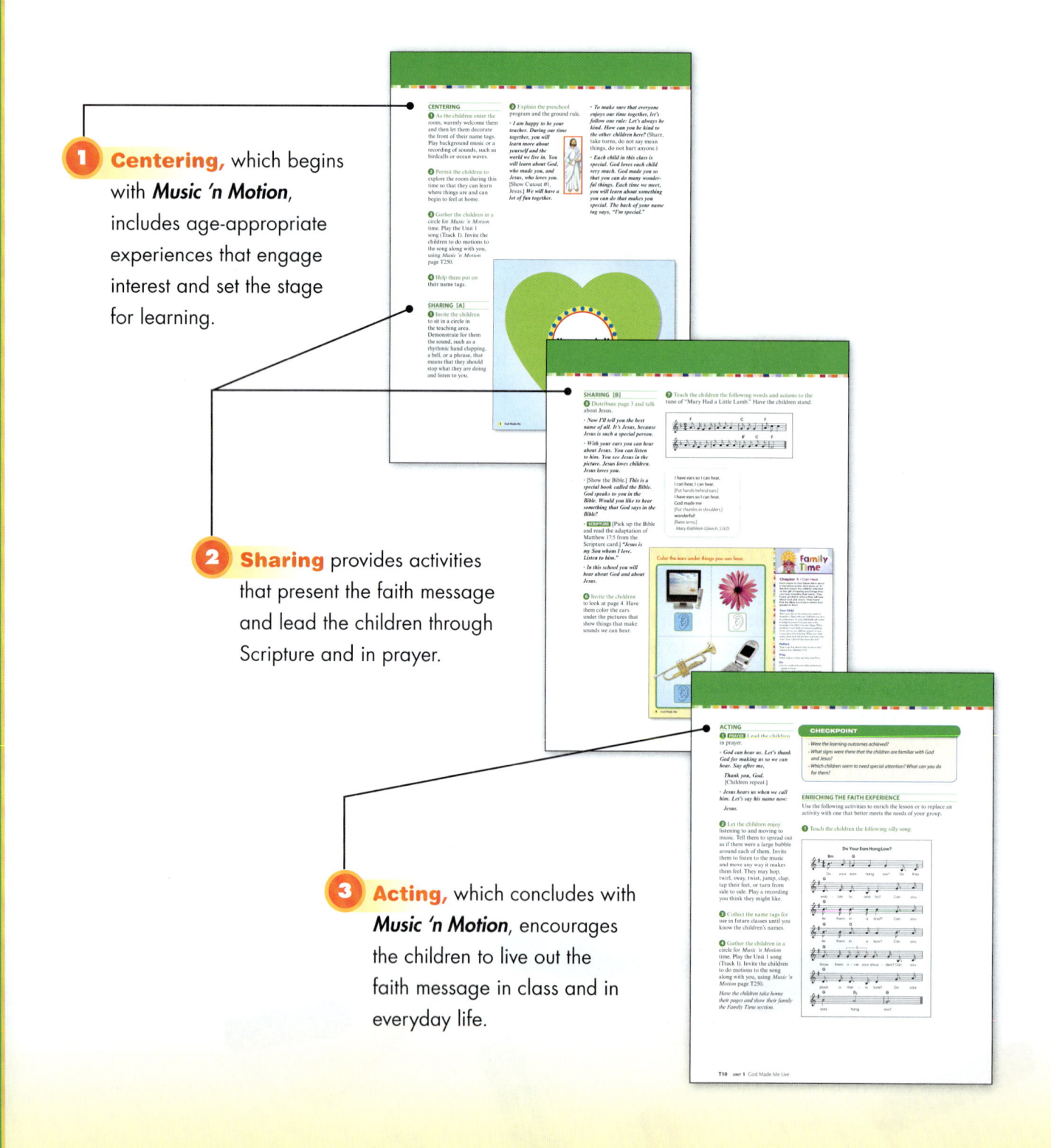

1 Centering, which begins with *Music 'n Motion*, includes age-appropriate experiences that engage interest and set the stage for learning.

2 Sharing provides activities that present the faith message and lead the children through Scripture and in prayer.

3 Acting, which concludes with *Music 'n Motion*, encourages the children to live out the faith message in class and in everyday life.

OV-8 *God Made Me*

GUIDING THE CATECHIST

Even More Ideas and Support

The Catechist Manual provides even more ideas and support for lively and effective catechesis.

Music 'n Motion *Support Materials*

The *Music 'n Motion* CD is supported with the following materials:

- **Professional-development** article by choreographer Nancy Marcheschi, nationally known for her leadership in the area of performing arts as prayer and ministry

- **Movement and motion guide** picturing key movements for songs on the CD

Additional Support

Additional lessons and supplements include the following elements to provide further background for teaching success:

- The **Special Seasons and Days** section provides additional lessons to celebrate important times throughout the year.

- Resources and support for a successful **Parent-Catechist Meeting**

- Comprehensive **Catechist's Handbook** with child development background, ideas for meeting individual needs, teaching methodology, and additional resources

- An **index** of Scripture passages, games, finger plays, poems, and songs

- **Scripture cards** that adapt Scripture to make it comprehensible to young children

- **Cutouts** to make learning interactive

Program Overview **OV-9**

GUIDING THE CATECHIST

Unit and Chapter Background

The *God Made Everything* series uses a holistic approach to early childhood faith formation. A variety of methods and techniques ensures that the Good News is conveyed in ways suited to different ages, learning styles, and teaching approaches.

Each chapter in *God Made Me* opens and ends with a song and dance or song and finger play from the *Music 'n Motion* CD. Additional music selections are provided for those who wish to include more music in their lessons.

Each unit has five chapters. The chapters are crafted to be taught once a week for approximately 60 minutes. Alternative program schedules are provided for each chapter in the **Preparing the Faith Experience** section. Activities from the **Enriching the Faith Experience** section at the end of the chapter can be used to adapt the chapter to better meet the children's needs.

Because young children need structure and delight in predictability, the weekly chapters have a similar pattern:

- **experiences** leading to a faith message
- presentation of **faith message** and **Scripture** readings
- developmentally appropriate **prayer** experiences to express and internalize the faith message
- **creative activities** to bring faith to life

The format of each chapter is generally the same. The chapter introduces the experiences from which the theme is drawn. Then the faith message is presented and extended or deepened through Scripture, activities, songs, and stories. The children are led in prayer at various times throughout the chapter.

"...young children are active learners who need to learn through a variety of hands-on activities."

"Preschool for All: A First-Class Learning Initiative."
California Department of Education, January 2005.

OV-10   *God Made Me*

GUIDING THE CATECHIST

Preparing for the Year

Complete the **Planning Calendar** on pages OV-12 and OV-13 to develop general plans based on your program calendar and the year's activities, liturgical seasons, and feasts.

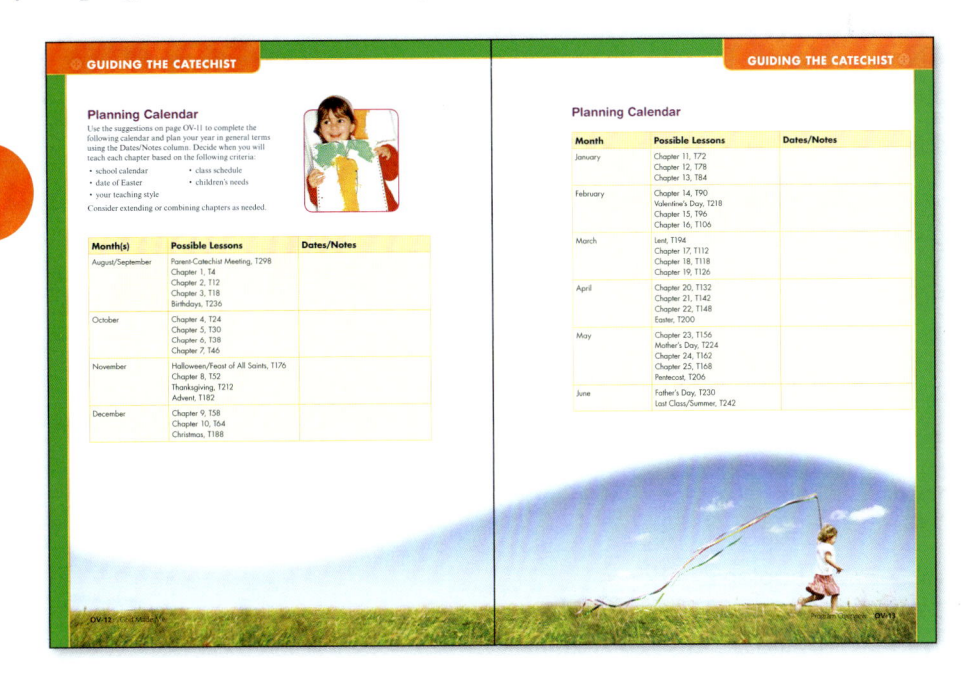

Consider the following recommendations as you plan:

1. Determine a day early in the year to schedule a **Parent-Catechist Meeting** to help parents effectively guide their children in living the Catholic faith. Record the date and planning notes on the Planning Calendar. See pages T298–T301 for meeting outline and planning tips.

2. Read the **Table of Contents** and review the **units** and **chapters** to determine the week during which you will teach each chapter. Determine how to incorporate these into your calendar.

3. Study the chapters for **Special Seasons and Days** on pages T174–T246 of this manual. The special season and feast day chapters can be taught on or near the appropriate date. Special Day chapters are optional. Determine how to integrate these into your calendar.

4. Detach and organize the **Scripture cards** and **cutouts,** placing them in a folder or envelope in order of use.

5. Remove the **perforated cards** from the Child's Book so they are ready for use.

Suggestions for Pacing

Your class may not meet enough times to cover all the chapters in this program. If so, some chapters can be combined so that you can focus on the most important material.

The following chapters are closely related in content and can be combined if necessary:

- 3 and 4
- 7 and 8
- 11 and 12
- 13 and 16
- 18 and 19

Program Overview   OV-11

GUIDING THE CATECHIST

Planning Calendar

Use the suggestions on page OV-11 to complete the following calendar and plan your year in general terms using the Dates/Notes column. Decide when you will teach each chapter based on the following criteria:

- school calendar
- class schedule
- date of Easter
- children's needs
- your teaching style

Consider extending or combining chapters as needed.

Month(s)	Possible Lessons	Dates/Notes
August/September	Parent-Catechist Meeting, T298 Chapter 1, T4 Chapter 2, T12 Chapter 3, T18 Birthdays, T236	
October	Chapter 4, T24 Chapter 5, T30 Chapter 6, T38 Chapter 7, T46	
November	Halloween/Feast of All Saints, T176 Chapter 8, T52 Thanksgiving, T212 Advent, T182	
December	Chapter 9, T58 Chapter 10, T64 Christmas, T188	

OV-12 God Made Me

GUIDING THE CATECHIST

Planning Calendar

Month	Possible Lessons	Dates/Notes
January	Chapter 11, T72 Chapter 12, T78 Chapter 13, T84	
February	Chapter 14, T90 Valentine's Day, T218 Chapter 15, T96 Chapter 16, T106	
March	Lent, T194 Chapter 17, T112 Chapter 18, T118 Chapter 19, T126	
April	Chapter 20, T132 Chapter 21, T142 Chapter 22, T148 Easter, T200	
May	Chapter 23, T156 Mother's Day, T224 Chapter 24, T162 Chapter 25, T168 Pentecost, T206	
June	Father's Day, T230 Last Class/Summer, T242	

Program Overview OV-13

PROGRAM STRUCTURE

Prepare and Teach

For each chapter, your manual presents material for preparation and personal reflection called **Preparing the Faith Experience**. This section is followed by the lesson plan for the chapter. It is important to consider carefully the lesson plans and ideas before and during teaching.

In Advance

1. Prayerfully read the **Listening** and **Reflecting** sections.

2. Consider the question found in the **Responding** section, perhaps writing your response in a prayer journal. Continue in prayer, using your own words or the suggested prayer.

3. Use the suggested Scripture references and the paragraphs from the *Catechism of the Catholic Church* for further insights or clarification.

4. Read the chapter and study the Child's Book pages.

OV-14   *God Made Me*

PROGRAM STRUCTURE

Before You Teach

1. Read the **Learning Outcomes** and lesson plan, including the **Comments,** which provide important background information on the content to be taught as well as helpful teaching tips.

2. Read **Enriching the Faith Experience** at the end of the chapter. Activities from this section can be substituted for activities found in the chapter or can be used to extend the lesson. Decide which options best meet the needs of the children.

3. Annotate your manual. Make notes that will help the flow of the lesson. Use a highlighter to set off sections you plan to use.

4. Familiarize yourself with the scripted teacher-talk in boldface italics so you can present the lesson in your own words as you teach. Avoid reading from the manual.

5. Gather necessary **Materials** for the chapter and review the preparation notes.

6. Review and gather **Books to Share** to incorporate into your lesson or to read aloud if you have extra time at the end of class. Visit www.loyolapress.com/preschool to find additional ideas for using storybooks in your lessons.

Teaching Tips

1. Follow tips from the **Catechist's Handbook.**

2. Prepare for each class as soon as possible after the previous class. Allow time to shape the lesson and to make it your own.

3. Pray frequently to the Holy Spirit, your partner and guide.

4. Write notes or an outline of your plan on a note card for easy reference.

Program Overview   OV-15

PROGRAM STRUCTURE

After You Teach

1. Evaluate your session using the **Checkpoint** at the end of the lesson to assess whether the outcomes of the lesson have been met.

2. Write follow-up comments on the lesson plan in your manual. Record ideas for improvement. Consult helpers, parents, and the children who participated in class to help determine which activities worked well and which could be improved.

3. Consider revisiting ideas and presenting information in a different way if children seemed to lack understanding at the end of the lesson.

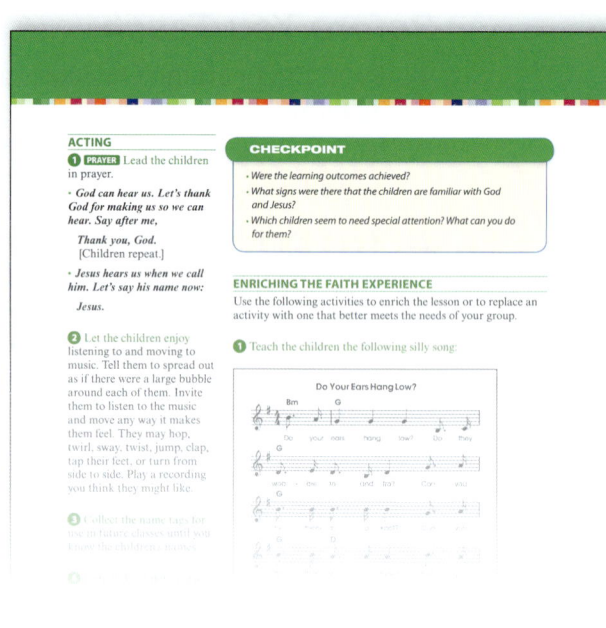

God Made Me

Introduction

The *God Made Me* preschool program is designed to lead three-year-old children, whose sense of identity is forming, to know and love God who made them. As the children awaken to the knowledge of their powers and skills, they come to realize that it is God's infinite goodness and love that makes them special. During the lessons, they delight in and develop their abilities and respond to God with joy, thanks, and praise. The goal of the program is to shape attitudes in the children that will prepare them to be committed Catholics who comprehend the truths of our faith and live by them. The lessons include a variety of activities geared to the learning styles and abilities of three-year-olds: play, games, sensory experiences, manipulative activities, stories, poems, and songs.

As they participate in the lesson activities, the children come to feel at home in a community, laying the foundation for a deeper life within the Christian community. References to God as good and loving, Jesus as our friend, the Bible, Christian symbols, and the importance of love are woven throughout the program, preparing the children for a more complete comprehension when they are older. The lessons evoke a response of prayer that frequently involves both song and ritual.

In **Unit 1** the children grow in appreciation for the five senses God has given them. In the process they learn that they are to listen to Jesus, that God speaks to them in the Bible, that God loves them and thinks they are precious, and that God desires their love. The unit concludes with a celebration of the wonderful things the children can do.

In **Unit 2** the children learn that they can use their powers for good. They are called to live like Jesus by helping others, sharing what they have, and making others happy. They become aware of their responsibility to care for the world God has given us.

In **Unit 3** the children explore some of the unique powers they have as human beings. They can speak, pray, and laugh. They practice using their voices in polite expressions and in prayers of thanks and praise. They learn that we can sing prayers, as Mary and the angels did. Because people laugh, talk, pray and sing at celebrations, the unit ends with a party celebrating the color green.

In **Unit 4** the children have opportunities to explore and develop their physical abilities. They thank God for being able to move, and they praise God in dance. They hear that God is always with them wherever they go. They learn that God likes them to play and be happy. Through activities they experience the satisfaction and joy of working and making things, and they ponder what God has made. Finally, they consider ways in which they are growing and what contributes to this growth.

In **Unit 5** the children study some of their higher-level characteristics. They are made aware of feelings, their own and others'. They learn about working to make wishes come true and hear about best wishes and blessings. They reflect on what they have learned and use their imaginations in pretending. The unit culminates in Jesus' commandment to exercise our greatest power: the power of love.

The **Special Seasons and Days** supplement offers twelve additional lessons with activities to help children learn about and celebrate the seasons and feast days of the Church year, as well as other special days.

unit one
God Made Me Live

The children will know that God made them and gave them great gifts.
They will realize they are special and will be glad to be who they are.

1 I CAN HEAR

The children make name tags and become acquainted with the room, the program, and one another. They learn that they were made by God and have five senses. They consider the gift of hearing. After talking about listening to God in the Bible and listening to Jesus, the children enjoy moving to music.

2 I CAN SEE

The children talk about their gift of sight. They hear the story of the woman who searched for her lost coin and learn that God is like that woman—God always looks for us and wants us to be close. After thanking God for their eyes, they make a picture that is lovely to see. By punching out a rectangle in this picture, the children make a window through which to look at the world.

T2 UNIT 1 God Made Me Live

3   I CAN SMELL

Through various experiences the children learn about their sense of smell and thank God for it and all the good smells in the world. They hear the story of the woman who put perfume on Jesus and are introduced to incense. They paint flowers to finish a picture and then add perfume to them.

4   I CAN TOUCH

After playing with clay or play dough, the children talk about their sense of touch. They touch things with various textures and give each other taps on the back. They thank God for the gift of being able to feel things. Then they make a collage using materials that have different textures.

5   I CAN TASTE

The children talk about the sense of taste and different kinds of foods, including their favorites. They praise God for food. After hearing that Jesus went to parties, they hold a celebration to celebrate themselves and their five senses.

Chapter 1
I Can Hear

FAITH FOCUS

God gave us ears to hear.

Matthew 13:3–9; Luke 11:28

PREPARING THE FAITH EXPERIENCE

LISTENING

"A sower went out to sow. And as he sowed, some seed fell on the path, and birds came and ate it up. Some fell on rocky ground, where it had little soil. It sprang up at once because the soil was not deep, and when the sun rose it was scorched, and it withered for lack of roots. Some seed fell among thorns, and the thorns grew up and choked it. But some seed fell on rich soil, and produced fruit, a hundred or sixty or thirtyfold. Whoever has ears ought to hear."

Matthew 13:3–9

REFLECTING

Because God created us with the ability to hear, we can wake up to bird song, sing or dance to a CD, enjoy a concert, and be delightfully surprised by the sound of a friend's voice on the phone. Hearing is a precious gift that we may take for granted until we begin to lose it.

Our five senses are channels that put us in touch with the world around us. Through them we also become aware of spiritual realities. Our sense of hearing plays a vital role in our faith. God is revealed through sound. Jesus, the Word made flesh, delivered his message orally. God the Father tells us to "listen to him." (Luke 9:35) Today the Bible, the written Word of God, is proclaimed to us each time we gather for the Eucharist.

The Good News resounds throughout the centuries. But like our human words, God's Word can be rejected, fall on deaf ears, be quickly forgotten, or be taken to heart, as the parable of the sower and the seed illustrates. Jesus praises people who hear God's Word, treasure it, and act on it. Even when it is difficult, they try to follow God's laws and live according to Jesus' instruction. The psalmist assures us that God returns the favor and listens to these people:

*When the just cry out,
the Lord hears
and rescues them
from all distress.*

Psalm 34:18

Mary, the Mother of Jesus, is one of these just ones. Attuned to God's slightest whispers, Mary was ready when God proposed a plan for her that would involve the salvation of the world. Mary truly heard God, responding yes with all her heart, and was faithful even to Calvary. Her last recorded words in the Bible can be taken as advice to us. Referring to her Son, Mary said, "Do whatever he tells you." (John 2:5) Interestingly, the word *obey* comes from the Latin word for "hear."

As Jesus once opened the ears of a deaf man, may he open our ears so that we can hear loud and clear the news of our salvation and the story of God's love for us. May we hear and obey God's laws, hear God's will for us, hear our call in life, and hear God speaking in the silence of our hearts. And then may we, like Mary, proclaim the Good News with joy and enthusiasm by our voices and by our lives so that others too may hear.

RESPONDING

Having reflected upon God's Word, take some time now to continue to respond to God in prayer. You might wish to use a journal to record your responses throughout this year.

- Who and what have helped me hear God's Word?

Lord, open the children's hearts to your Word.

T4 UNIT 1 *God Made Me Live*

Catechism of the Catholic Church

The themes of this chapter correspond to the following paragraphs: 104, 356–357, 2666.

THE FAITH EXPERIENCE

Child's Book pages 1–4

SCRIPTURE IN THIS CHAPTER
- *Matthew 17:5*

MATERIALS
- Chapter 1 Scripture card
- Bible
- Cutouts: #1, Jesus; #2, ears
- Option: telephone
- 16-inch pieces of yarn or ribbon for each child
- Hole punch
- Recording of music or sounds for CENTERING #2
- Crayons or markers
- Recording of music for ACTING #2

PREPARATION
- Cut out the heart on each page 1 and write the children's names on the lines. Using the hole punch, make a hole 1/2 inch below the dip at the top of the heart. String yarn or ribbon through the hole in the heart so the children can wear the hearts around their necks.
- Write the children's names on page 3.
- Separate the Scripture cards in the back of this manual and put them in a folder for future use during the year.
- Place the Chapter 1 Scripture card for SHARING #5 in the Bible.
- Decide what signal (a bell, a rhythmic clapping of hands, a phrase) you will use to call the children's attention.

MUSIC 'N MOTION
Use *Music 'n Motion* page T250 and CD Track 1 "I Am Wonderfully Made" for this chapter. For a list of additional music, see page T302.

ENRICHING THE FAITH EXPERIENCE
Use the activities at the end of the chapter to enrich the lesson or to replace an activity with one that better meets the needs of your group.

BOOKS TO SHARE
The Listening Walk by Paul Showers (HarperTrophy, 2007)

A Child's Book of Miracles by Mary Kathleen Glavich (Loyola Press, 1994)

God Made Me by Dandi Daley Mackall (HarperTrophy, 1994)

The Quiet Way Home by Bonny Becker (Bill Martin Books, 1995)

SNACK
Suggestion: a crunchy snack, such as dry cereal or pretzels

ALTERNATIVE PROGRAMS

DAILY PROGRAM
Day 1: Centering, Sharing A
Day 2: Sharing B
Day 3: Acting #1, Enriching the Faith Experience choice
Day 4: Enriching the Faith Experience choice
Day 5: Enriching the Faith Experience choice, Acting #2 and #3

THREE-DAY PROGRAM
Day 1: Centering, Sharing A
Day 2: Sharing B
Day 3: Acting

1 I Can Hear

LEARNING OUTCOMES
The children will
- appreciate the gift of hearing.
- know that God made them.
- understand that God speaks in the Bible.
- know that Jesus loves them.

COMMENTS

1. It is normal development for three-year-olds to have an egocentric view of the world. They are, moreover, coming to realize what fascinating creatures they are. Through experience they are learning about themselves and their powers. Through their senses they come to know not only their world but also the good God who made them. The more the children delight in themselves, the more prepared they are to turn to their Creator with thanks and praise.

2. Our faith is largely an oral tradition. The stories that are now in Hebrew Scriptures once passed from generation to generation by word of mouth. Years before they were written down in the Gospels, stories about Jesus were recounted by the first Christians during the celebration of the breaking of the bread. We hear the Word of God proclaimed at Mass in the Liturgy of the Word.

3. Preschool is probably the three-year-olds' first experience of being away from home and away from their parents for any length of time. Consequently, the catechist's role as nurturer is very important. Keep in mind that it is natural at first for three-year-olds to manifest anxiety, which, in time, will disappear. You may wish to have the parents remain in the room during this first lesson or at least part of it. When the parents leave, let them say goodbye to their child and have them reassure him or her that they will return.

4. During the five lessons about the senses, be sensitive to the feelings of children in whom the sense being studied is impaired.

5. Children will grasp that the Bible is a sacred book by the reverent way you handle it. By reading from the Bible whenever a Scripture passage is used in the lesson, you will reinforce that God speaks to the children through this book. The Scripture cards showing adapted Scripture texts are a resource for including the Bible in the lessons. These cards are located in the back of this manual.

1 God Made Me

T6 UNIT 1 *God Made Me Live*

CENTERING

1 As the children enter the room, warmly welcome them and then let them decorate the front of their name tags. Play background music or a recording of sounds, such as birdcalls or ocean waves.

2 Permit the children to explore the room during this time so that they can learn where things are and can begin to feel at home.

3 Gather the children in a circle for *Music 'n Motion* time. Play the Unit 1 song (Track 1). Invite the children to do motions to the song along with you, using *Music 'n Motion* page T250.

4 Help them put on their name tags.

SHARING [A]

1 Invite the children to sit in a circle in the teaching area. Demonstrate for them the sound, such as a rhythmic hand clapping, a bell, or a phrase, that means that they should stop what they are doing and listen to you.

2 Explain the preschool program and the ground rule.

• *I am happy to be your teacher. During our time together, you will learn more about yourself and the world we live in. You will learn about God, who made you, and Jesus, who loves you.* [Show Cutout #1, Jesus.] *We will have a lot of fun together.*

• *To make sure that everyone enjoys our time together, let's follow one rule: Let's always be kind. How can you be kind to the other children here?* (Share, take turns, do not say mean things, do not hurt anyone.)

• *Each child in this class is special. God loves each child very much. God made you so that you can do many wonderful things. Each time we meet, you will learn about something you can do that makes you special. The back of your name tag says, "I'm special."*

I'm special!

2 God Made Me © LOYOLAPRESS.

I Can Hear **CHAPTER 1** **T7**

3 Talk about sounds we hear.

• *Guess what we will talk about today? I'll give you a few hints. You have two of them. They're on your head. Maybe they hold up your hat or cap.* (Ears) [Show Cutout #2, ears.]

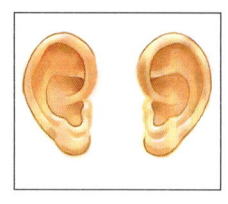

• *What sounds have you heard since you came into this room?* (Talking, music, signal)

• *What are some things you like to hear?* [Option: Show the phone.] (Music, friends' voices)

• *God made us with ears. God is good to give us ears so that we can hear.*

4 Play "Name Game."
Introduce it:

• *One of the nicest things to hear is someone saying your name. Let's learn one another's names. I'll whisper someone's name and point to the child. Then we will all say the child's name aloud and clap for him or her. When I say your name, you may stand—because you are special—and bow if you wish. I'll start with my name.* [Stand, say your name, and bow.]

Name _____

3 God Made Me

T8 UNIT 1 God Made Me Live

SHARING [B]

5 **Distribute page 3 and talk about Jesus.**

• *Now I'll tell you the best name of all. It's Jesus, because Jesus is such a special person.*

• *With your ears you can hear about Jesus. You can listen to him. You see Jesus in the picture. Jesus loves children. Jesus loves you.*

• [Show the Bible.] *This is a special book called the Bible. God speaks to you in the Bible. Would you like to hear something that God says in the Bible?*

• **SCRIPTURE** [Pick up the Bible and read the adaptation of Matthew 17:5 from the Scripture card.] *"Jesus is my Son whom I love. Listen to him."*

• *In this school you will hear about God and about Jesus.*

6 **Invite the children** to look at page 4. Have them color the ears under the pictures that show things that make sounds we can hear.

7 Teach the children the following words and actions to the tune of "Mary Had a Little Lamb." Have the children stand.

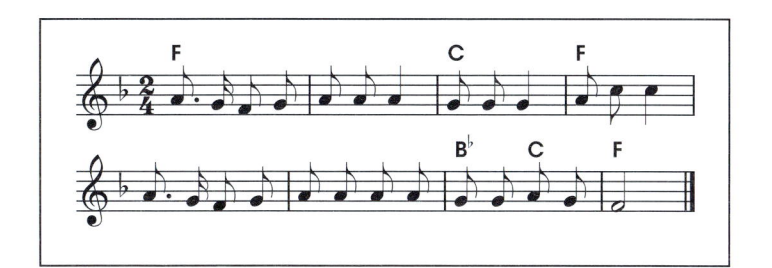

I have ears so I can hear,
I can hear, I can hear.
[Put hands behind ears.]
I have ears so I can hear.
God made me
[Put thumbs in shoulders.]
wonderful!
[Raise arms.]
   Mary Kathleen Glavich, S.N.D.

Color the ears under things you can hear.

Family Time

Chapter 1: I Can Hear
Each lesson in *God Made Me* is about a marvelous power God gives us. In this first lesson the children reflected on the gift of hearing and things they can hear, including their name. They found out that in school they will hear about God and Jesus. They heard that the Bible is a book in which God speaks to them.

Your Child
Three-year-olds are becoming more aware of themselves. Share with your child how you chose his or her name. As your child builds self-esteem by using the powers God gave him or her, encourage your child to try new things. When speaking to your child, use attention-grabbing words, such as *new*, *different*, *surprise*, or *secret* to keep him or her listening. When your child speaks, listen with full attention and look at him or her. Your child will then learn this skill.

Reflect
"Jesus is my Son whom I love. Listen to him." (adapted from Matthew 17:5)

Pray
Father, help us to hear and obey your Word.

Do
• Go for a walk with your child and listen for sounds of nature.
• Fill glasses with varying levels of water and have your child tap the sides with a spoon.
• Use modeling clay to form your child's initial.
• Use your child's name in songs.
• Read to your child *The Listening Walk* by Paul Showers. After a moment of quiet, encourage your child to identify sounds he or she heard. Thank God for giving us ears and good things to hear.

For more family resources, refer to the Family Activity Booklet and visit www.loyolapress.com/preschool.

ACTING

1 **PRAYER** Lead the children in prayer.

• *God can hear us. Let's thank God for making us so we can hear. Say after me,*

> Thank you, God.
> [Children repeat.]

• *Jesus hears us when we call him. Let's say his name now:*

> Jesus.

2 Let the children enjoy listening to and moving to music. Tell them to spread out as if there were a large bubble around each of them. Invite them to listen to the music and move any way it makes them feel. They may hop, twirl, sway, twist, jump, clap, tap their feet, or turn from side to side. Play a recording you think they might like.

3 Collect the name tags for use in future classes until you know the children's names.

4 Gather the children in a circle for *Music 'n Motion* time. Play the Unit 1 song (Track 1). Invite the children to do motions to the song along with you, using *Music 'n Motion* page T250.

Have the children take home their pages and show their family the Family Time section.

CHECKPOINT

- *Were the learning outcomes achieved?*
- *What signs were there that the children are familiar with God and Jesus?*
- *Which children seem to need special attention? What can you do for them?*

ENRICHING THE FAITH EXPERIENCE

Use the following activities to enrich the lesson or to replace an activity with one that better meets the needs of your group.

1 Teach the children the following silly song:

Do Your Ears Hang Low?

Do your ears hang low? Do they wobble to and fro? Can you tie them in a knot? Can you tie them in a bow? Can you throw them over your shoulders? Can you pluck a merry tune? Do your ears hang low?

T10   UNIT 1   God Made Me Live

❷ **Lead the children in a** cheer of thanks to God for the gift of hearing. Have one child hold Cutout #2, ears, in front of the class.

• *We can talk to God. Talking to God is praying. Let's thank God for giving us ears to hear with. Please stand. Say what I say and do what I do:*

> God who's near,
> You gave me ears
> [Point to ears.]
> so I can hear.
> I give some cheers:
> Thank you! Thank you! Thank you!
> [Raise arms three times.]
>   Mary Kathleen Glavich, S.N.D.

❸ **Make a toy phone out of** two paper or plastic cups. Poke a hole in the bottom of each cup. Insert one end of a two-foot piece of string through each hole and knot it. Let the children converse. Keep the phone in the toy section of the room.

❹ **Record various sounds** from home and have the children identify them. Possible sounds: a door closing, a running washing machine, a phone or a doorbell ringing, water running, popcorn popping.

❺ **Have the children do** various things with their names: sing them, say them very slowly, clap them, shout them, whisper them.

❻ **Call on children to choose a card from Cutouts #7 to 16,** animals, and make the sound of the animal pictured. Have the other children try to guess the animal being imitated.

I Can Hear CHAPTER 1 T11

Chapter 2
I Can See

FAITH FOCUS

God gave us eyes to see.

Luke 18:35–42

PREPARING THE FAITH EXPERIENCE

LISTENING

[A] blind man was sitting by the roadside begging, and hearing a crowd going by, he inquired what was happening. They told him, "Jesus of Nazareth is passing by." He shouted, "Jesus, Son of David, have pity on me!" The people walking in front rebuked him, telling him to be silent, but he kept calling out all the more, "Son of David, have pity on me!" Then Jesus stopped and ordered that he be brought to him; and when he came near, Jesus asked him, "What do you want me to do for you?" He replied, "Lord, please let me see." Jesus told him, "Have sight; your faith has saved you."

Luke 18:35–42

REFLECTING

The blind beggar at the roadside begged Jesus for the gift of sight. Most of us do not need to ask for physical sight, but we might be suffering from other visual impairments. So we beg for 20/20 Christian vision:

Lord, let us see clearly the truths you teach. May our own pride and selfish desires and the values and priorities of our culture not blur our vision.

Lord, keep us from being nearsighted, unwilling to consider the future and living just for the present. Keep us from being farsighted. Let us notice those nearby so that we do not overlook their needs and hurts.

Lord, let us see what is really there rather than mirages of false gods or dangerous, tempting illusions. Remove from our eyes any cataracts of fear and doubt that cloud our sight and make us afraid to act.

Lord, protect us from double vision, the compulsions to have more, to do more, to be more. Replace our tendency to make things more complex with a tendency to strive for holy simplicity.

Lord, keep us from having tunnel vision, seeing things from only our own narrow point of view. Expand our sight and our hearts to encompass the world. Sharpen our peripheral vision so that we are aware of the troubled people we may tend to overlook in our workplaces and in our families. May we recognize them, show interest in them, affirm them, and make them blossom.

Lord, give us x-ray vision to read the hearts of others so that we reach out to them with your love and compassion. Give us insight to solve problems peacefully and justly and hindsight to learn from our mistakes.

Lord, keep us focused on you, the light that helps us discern the safest ways to go. Finally, Lord, help us see others and ourselves as you see us and to see you in others. May we live and love so that someday we may enjoy the beatific vision, seeing God face-to-face, as a friend.

RESPONDING

God's Word calls us to respond in love. Respond to God now in the quiet of your heart and perhaps through your journal.

- In what way do I need improved spiritual vision?

Gracious God, open the children's eyes to your great love for them.

T12 UNIT 1 *God Made Me Live*

Catechism of the Catholic Church

The themes of this chapter correspond to the following paragraphs: 218, 1023.

THE FAITH EXPERIENCE

Child's Book pages 5–6

SCRIPTURE IN THIS CHAPTER
- *Luke 15:8–10*

MATERIALS
- Cutouts: #3, eyes; #17–26, ten coins
- Option: sunglasses
- Things to look at or with: picture books, magazine pictures, photo albums, kaleidoscope, magnifying glass, binoculars, telescope
- Crayons or markers
- Background music for ACTING #2
- Option: colored cellophane and tape
- Perforated Card A

PREPARATION
- Write the children's names on page 5 and on perforated Card A.
- Hide Cutouts #17–25.

MUSIC 'N MOTION
Use *Music 'n Motion* page T250 and CD Track 1 "I Am Wonderfully Made" for this chapter. For a list of additional music, see page T302.

ENRICHING THE FAITH EXPERIENCE
Use the activities at the end of the chapter to enrich the lesson or to replace an activity with one that better meets the needs of your group.

BOOKS TO SHARE
Can You See What I See? by Walter Wick (Cartwheel, 2002)

1 Hunter by Pat Hutchins (Harper Trophy, 1986)

Have You Seen My Duckling? by Nancy Tafuri (HarperTrophy, 1991)

Planting a Rainbow by Lois Ehlert (Voyager Books, 1992)

SNACK
Suggestion: vanilla wafers or round crackers

ALTERNATIVE PROGRAMS

DAILY PROGRAM
Day 1: Centering, Sharing A
Day 2: Sharing B, Acting #1
Day 3: Enriching the Faith Experience choice
Day 4: Enriching the Faith Experience choice
Day 5: Acting #2–3

THREE-DAY PROGRAM
Day 1: Centering, Sharing A
Day 2: Sharing B
Day 3: Acting

2　I Can See

LEARNING OUTCOMES

The children will
- know that God gave them eyes to see.
- thank God for the gift of sight.
- know the story of the lost coin.

COMMENTS

1. Three-year-old children are fascinated by the world around them. As they explore their environment, they already have a sense of the power and goodness of the One who created such marvelous sights as dew on a spider web, light reflecting off a pond, a sleek horse, or a garden full of color. Pointing out the wonders of nature to the children and letting them draw our attention to these wonders deepen their spirituality and ours as well. In time they will come to know that "What is essential is invisible to the eye." (*The Little Prince* by Antoine de Saint-Exupéry)

2. At this age children do not perceive things as adults do. A picture of a woman at the edge of a page, for instance, may provoke tears in a child who thinks the woman has no arm. Three-year-olds also tend to focus on one characteristic of an object at a time, usually the most obvious one. Keep in mind that some children may have impairments in perceiving colors (color blindness).

CENTERING

❶ Gather the children in a circle for *Music 'n Motion* time. Play the Unit 1 song (Track 1). Invite the children in a circle to do motions to the song along with you, using *Music 'n Motion* page T250.

❷ Invite the children to look at picture books, pictures, and other items and to use various instruments for seeing.

SHARING [A]

❶ Call the children to you and comment:

- *We talked about how we can hear. We can hear beautiful sounds. We can hear about God who made us so wonderful. Today let's talk about something you use to look at picture books and to see where you're going. What are they?* (Eyes) [Show Cutout #3, eyes.]

❷ Distribute page 5 and talk about the picture.

- *What are the children in the picture seeing with their eyes?* (Circus: bear, clown, elephants, lion tamer, lion, tightrope walker)

- *What are some things that you like to see with your eyes?*

T14　UNIT 1　*God Made Me Live*

- *How do your eyes help you?* (They keep me from danger. They show my feelings. They help me learn. They help me find things.) [Option: Show sunglasses and explain that they protect our eyes from the sun.]

- *God is very good to give us eyes. We can't see God, but someday we will.*

3 **SCRIPTURE** Tell the story of the woman and the lost coins. (Luke 15:8–10) Show the Bible.

- *Sometimes we use our eyes to look for things that are lost.*

- *Listen to this story that Jesus told about someone who used her eyes. This story is in the special book, the Bible. Once there was a woman who had 10 coins. One day one of them was missing. What do you think she did?* (She looked for it.) *She lit a lamp and looked and looked. She swept her house. She looked in all the corners and under things. And she found her lost coin.* [Show Cutout #26, coin.] *The woman was so happy that she invited her friends over to celebrate.*

- *God is like that woman. God always looks for us and wants to keep us close.*

4 Have the children stand and act out the story with you, using the following motions:

> Once a woman had 10 coins.
> [Hold up 10 fingers.]
> One day one was missing.
> [Fold a thumb over.]
> She looked and looked.
> [Hold hand above eyes and look from side to side.]
> She swept her house.
> [Make sweeping motions.]
> She found her coin.
> [Hold up hand.]
> The woman ran to get her friends.
> [Run in place.]
> And they celebrated.
> [Jump up and down waving arms in air.]

SHARING [B]

5 Have the children name and then write an *X* on the circular objects pictured on page 6. Introduce the activity:

- *A circle is round.* [Show Cutout #26.] *Coins have the shape of a circle. What can you find in the picture that is round like a coin? Write an X on each circle you see.* [Demonstrate.]

6 Play "Find the Coins." Show Cutout #26 and tell the children to use their eyes to find other paper coins hidden in the room. Celebrate with a snack.

Family Time

Chapter 2: I Can See

In this lesson the children studied the precious gift of vision that God gave them. They talked about how their eyes help them and named things they like to see. They made a beautiful picture in class to give joy to anyone who sees it. Ask your child to tell you the Bible story about the woman who used her eyes to find her coin (Luke 15:8–10). Comment that God values us and keeps us in sight.

Your Child
Our vision is a source of delight. Call your child's attention to lovely sights (a flower, a sunrise, a field, clouds) and make it a practice to thank God for what you see as well as the ability to see.

Reflect
My eyes are upon you, O God, my Lord[.] (Psalm 141:8)

Pray
God, open our eyes to the beauty of your creation.

Do
- Point out various shapes to your child.
- Teach your child the names of colors. Finish a meal with a colorful dessert, such as rainbow sherbet or layered gelatin.
- Look out a window with your child, especially when it is raining or snowing.
- Let your child use a magnifying glass or binoculars.
- Display your child's work.
- Take your child to the zoo or to a garden to see God's creations.
- Read to your child *Can You See What I See?* by Walter Wick. Talk about the pictures to guide his or her appreciation of the gift of sight. Thank God for giving us eyes and beautiful things to see.

For more family resources, refer to the Family Activity Booklet and visit www.loyolapress.com/preschool.

© LOYOLAPRESS.

Write an **X** in each circle.

6 God Made Me

I Can See CHAPTER 2 T15

7 Teach the children the following words and actions to the tune of "Mary Had a Little Lamb":

> I have eyes so I can see, I can see, I can see.
> [Point to eyes.]
> I have eyes so I can see.
> God made me
> [Put thumbs in shoulders.]
> wonderful!
> [Raise arms.]
> Mary Kathleen Glavich, S.N.D.

ACTING

1 **PRAYER** Lead the children in a prayer of thanks. You might prompt ideas by displaying pictures or showing slides.

•*Let's thank God for our eyes. We will name things we can see. After someone names something, we'll all say "Thank you, God." Raise your hand to let me know when you would like to name something. After I tap your shoulder, you may say it. I'll start.*

I can see blue skies.
(Thank you, God.)

2 Invite the children to design pictures on perforated Card A that are lovely to see. Encourage them to use many different colors and to fill the whole card. Play music as they work and suggest that they make their crayons or markers dance to the music as they draw on the card.

When the children are finished, tell them you have a surprise for them. Punch out for the children the three sides of the rectangle on the back of the card and fold it back to make a magic window. Suggest that they look through their windows in various directions to see what they can see. If you wish, tape colored cellophane over the windows.

3 Gather the children in a circle for *Music 'n Motion* time. Play the Unit 1 song (Track 1). Invite the children to do motions to the song along with you, using *Music 'n Motion* page T250.

Have the children take home their pages and show their family the Family Time section.

CHECKPOINT

- Were the learning outcomes achieved?
- Do any children need to have their eyes examined?
- What signs showed that the children were responsive during the prayer?

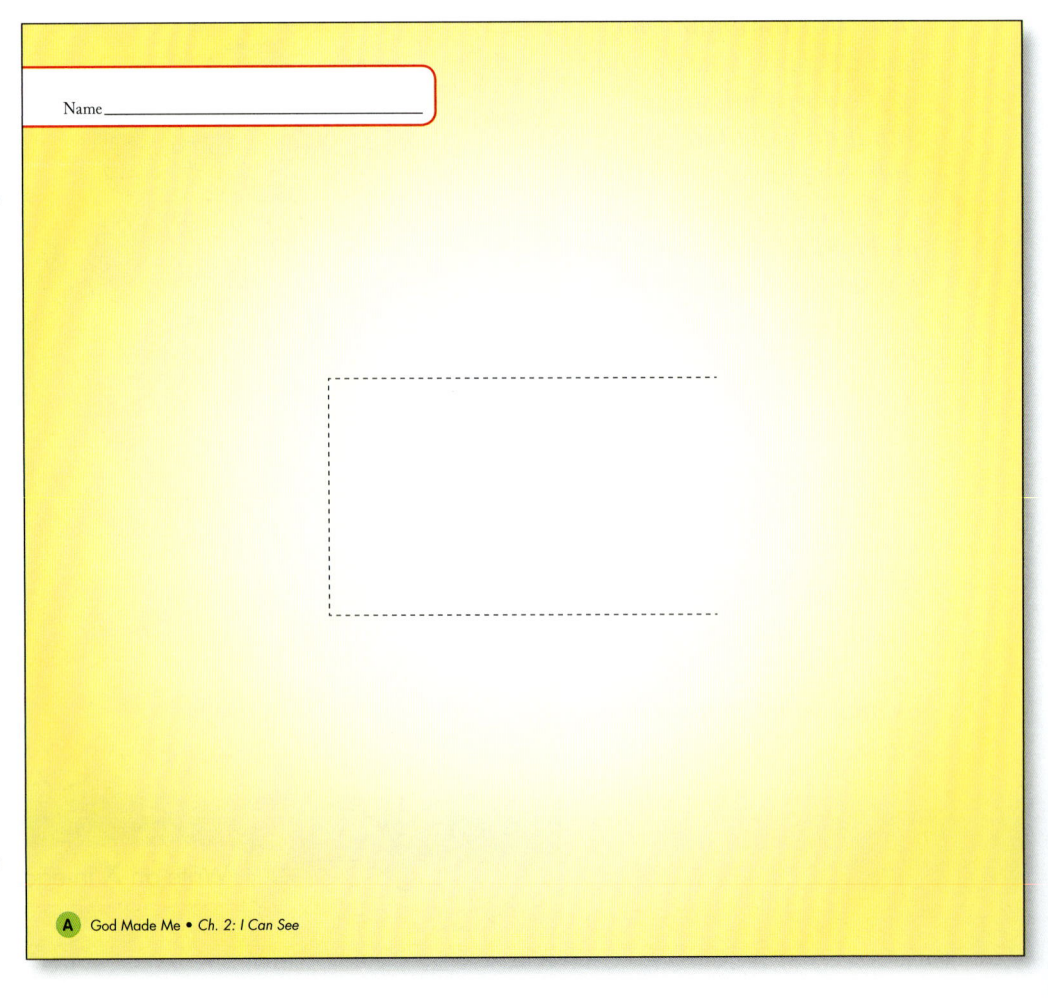

Name _____

A *God Made Me* • Ch. 2: I Can See

T16 UNIT 1 *God Made Me Live*

ENRICHING THE FAITH EXPERIENCE

Use the following activities to enrich the lesson or to replace an activity with one that better meets the needs of your group.

❶ Take the children outside. Have them look in front of them, behind them, to the left, to the right, up, and down. Each time, invite them to thank God for something they see. If you wish, have them use the windows made in Acting #2 for this activity.

❷ Draw pictures of simple objects on the board or on a large pad of paper and have the children guess what you are drawing.

❸ Play "I Spy." Place five or six objects in front of the children and describe one object until a child guesses what it is.

❹ Play "What's Different?" Stand behind a door or folding screen and make changes in your appearance, such as putting on a sweater or rolling up your sleeves. Each time you return, ask the children to tell what is different.

❺ Show the children a tray of objects. Hide the tray and ask them to name all the things on the tray they can remember. Start with three objects and add more gradually. You might instead remove one object from a tray of objects and ask the children which one is missing.

❻ Teach the children the song "The Bear Went Over the Mountain."

The Bear Went Over the Mountain

The bear went over the mountain, the bear went over the mountain, the bear went over the mountain to see what he could see. And all that he could see, and all that he could see was the other side of the mountain, the other side of the mountain, the other side of the mountain was all that he could see.

I Can See CHAPTER 2 **T17**

Chapter 3
I Can Smell

FAITH FOCUS

God gave us noses to smell.

Corinthians 2:15

PREPARING THE FAITH EXPERIENCE

LISTENING

[We] are the aroma of Christ for God among those who are being saved . . .

2 Corinthians 2:15

REFLECTING

One spring as two friends drove to Washington, D.C., through the hills of Pennsylvania and West Virginia, they became aware of one scent after another. As the fragrance of honeysuckle was replaced by the smell of lilacs, one friend commented, "We could make this journey by our noses."

God has filled the world with fragrances that delight us. We enjoy smelling a wide variety of flowers, each with its distinctive scent. In some areas one may experience the crisp smell of leaves in autumn. We like to make ourselves more pleasing by putting on cologne. Some people are even identified by the scents they wear. And everyone knows how the smell of food whets the appetite and enhances taste. Particular odors—the musty smell of books; the sharp, clean smell of a swimming pool; or the indescribable smell of a school—evoke memories and have the power to induce certain emotions.

Saint Paul tells us that we are the aroma of Christ. In us Christians, people ought to detect the presence of Christ. How can we describe the fragrance of Christ? It must be something like

- the wholesome smell of freshly baked bread. It is the *goodness* that makes others feel comfortable and at home, the goodness that nourishes them and inspires them to grow.

- the heady fragrance of newly mown grass. It is an *enthusiasm and zest* for life that invigorates others and gives them confidence.

- the gentle scent of lilacs. It is a *peacefulness* that steadies and calms others, offering them a refuge when their lives are full of turmoil.

- the fragrance of roses, a *joy* sprung from faith, a joy that fosters hope and courage in the hearts of others, dispelling pessimism, discontent, competition, and envy.

- the alluring fragrance of perfume, a *love* that entices others to respond with a similar love and to surrender their lives and all they have and are to God, who is love.

- the thick, heavy odor of incense, a scent of *sacredness,* a reminder to others that this world and we are holy, that there is a spiritual dimension to our being, and that we are made for another world.

Let us pray with John Henry Cardinal Newman:

Lord Jesus, help me to spread your fragrance everywhere. Flood me with your spirit and life; penetrate and possess my whole being so completely that my life may only be a radiance of yours. Shine through me, and be so in me that everyone with whom I come into contact may feel your presence within me. Let them look up and no longer see me, but only you, Jesus.

RESPONDING

Having been nourished by God's Word, we are able to respond to God's great love for us. In prayer respond to God's call to you to share his Word with others. You may also wish to respond in your prayer journal.

- What quality of Christ do I especially show?

Holy Spirit, help me and the children be the aroma of Christ in the world.

T18   UNIT 1   *God Made Me Live*

Catechism of the Catholic Church

The themes of this chapter correspond to the following paragraph: 1189.

THE FAITH EXPERIENCE

Child's Book pages 7–10

SCRIPTURE IN THIS CHAPTER
- Mark 14:3–9

MATERIALS
- Cutouts: #1, Jesus; #4, nose
- Option: flowers
- Items with a strong odor: orange, lemon, cinnamon, banana, pickle, chocolate candy, bath powder, pine needles
- Several small jars or boxes
- Perfume
- Option: hand cream
- Paint
- Sponges
- Clip clothespins
- Option: objects for printing and a blow dryer
- Cotton balls
- Glue

PREPARATION
- Write the children's names on pages 7 and 10.
- Place the items to be smelled in separate jars or boxes. If the items are visible in the jars, tape paper around the jars. Poke holes in the lids or tops.
- Protect the painting area with newspapers.
- Have old shirts or aprons for the children to wear.

MUSIC 'N MOTION
Use *Music 'n Motion* page T250 and CD Track 1 "You Are Wonderfully Made" for this chapter. For a list of additional music, see page T302.

ENRICHING THE FAITH EXPERIENCE
Use the activities at the end of the chapter to enrich the lesson or to replace an activity with one that better meets the needs of your group.

BOOKS TO SHARE
Little Bunny Follows His Nose by Katherine Howard (Golden Books, 2004)

The Biggest Nose by Kathy Caple (Houghton Mifflin, 1988)

The Nose Book by Al Perkins (Random House Books for Young Readers, 1969)

God Made You Nose to Toes by Leslie Parrott (Zonderkidz, 2002)

SNACK
Suggestion: graham crackers

ALTERNATIVE PROGRAMS

DAILY PROGRAM
Day 1: Centering, Sharing A
Day 2: Sharing B
Day 3: Acting
Day 4: Enriching the Faith Experience choice
Day 5: Enriching the Faith Experience choice, Acting

THREE-DAY PROGRAM
Day 1: Centering, Sharing A
Day 2: Sharing B
Day 3: Acting

3 I Can Smell

LEARNING OUTCOMES

The children will
- recall good fragrances.
- thank God for their gift of smell.
- know that pleasant-smelling things can be given as gifts.

COMMENTS

1. God is ingenious in filling our world with delights. As the children talk and think about their sense of smell, they come to appreciate their own powers and the good, loving God who gave them.

2. Whenever the children do a creative activity, as they usually do in Acting, process is more important for them than product. By manipulating the media and equipment and by expressing themselves through color and lines, the children are learning to cope with the world and are developing their creative potential.

3. For centuries, sweet-smelling incense has been used in our worship. The use of incense involves our whole bodies in adoration. The altar, the Gospel book, the crucifix, the priest, and the holy people of God may be incensed at Mass. The Blessed Sacrament is incensed during Eucharistic devotion. Incense for private prayer has recently increased in popularity.

Name _____

7 God Made Me

CENTERING

1 Gather the children in a circle for *Music 'n Motion* time. Play the Unit 1 song (Track 1). Invite the children to do motions to the song along with you, using *Music 'n Motion* page T250.

2 Invite the children to come up to the boxes or jars that contain fragrant things and identify them by their aromas. Comment:

• *Let's have some sniff tests and see how good your noses are.*

SHARING [A]

1 Talk about the gift of smell. Show Cutout #4, nose.

• *God gave us noses so that we could enjoy good smells. We like to smell good things. Close your eyes and in your head think of the smell of perfume . . . the smell of fresh air . . . the smell of turkey roasting in the oven . . . the smell of newly cut grass.*

• *Our noses help keep us safe too. They tell us when something is burning.*

2 Distribute page 7 and talk about the picture. [Option: Let the children smell flowers.]

• *What is the girl doing?*

• *What do you think the flowers smell like?*

• *What things do you like to smell?*

3 Have the children circle things on page 8 that smell good.

4 Play "Follow Your Nose." Tell the children that "follow your nose" means to go straight. Line up the children across one end of the room and have them "follow their noses" and run to you at the other end. Then have them run back.

Circle the things that smell good.

Family Time

Chapter 3: I Can Smell

In this lesson the children reflected on their sense of smell. They practiced identifying various aromas. They heard the story of the woman who gave Jesus the gift of perfume (Mark 14:3–9), and they learned about the use of incense in church. Admire your child's picture of flowers made in class. Ask your child to sing for you the song that begins "I've a nose," sung to the tune of "Mary Had a Little Lamb."

Your Child
Lead your child to appreciate our sense of smell by pointing out the aromas of certain foods cooking, flowers, and just-cut grass. Make your child aware of the smell of certain places: a barn, a bakery, a library, a beach.

Reflect
For we are the aroma of Christ for God among those who are being saved . . . (2 Corinthians 2:15)

Pray
Holy Spirit, help us to be the aroma of Christ in the world.

Do
- Let your child put on cologne and then enjoy the fragrance together.
- With your child, plan a meal of foods that smell especially good.
- Have your child close his or her eyes and identify certain foods that have distinctive smells: toast, orange slices, pizza, strawberries, popcorn.
- Visit a garden with your child and smell the flowers.
- Read to your child *Little Bunny Follows His Nose* by Katherine Howard. Ask your child to name other things they like to smell. Thank God for our sense of smell.

For more family resources, refer to the Family Activity Booklet and visit www.loyolapress.com/preschool.

© LOYOLAPRESS.

8 God Made Me

I Can Smell **CHAPTER 3** **T21**

SHARING [B]

5 **SCRIPTURE** Tell the story of the woman who put perfume on Jesus. (Mark 14:3–9) Show the Bible and Cutout #1, Jesus.

> Once a woman wanted to show Jesus that she loved him very much. Do you know what she did? When Jesus was at a party, the woman broke open a beautiful jar of perfume and put it on him. Everyone there saw what she did and enjoyed the perfume. Its lovely smell filled the room. The woman's act of love made Jesus happy.

- *We like to give people good-smelling things as gifts. What are some gifts that smell nice?* (Flowers, perfume, soap, hand lotion, bath powder, after-shave lotion)

- *Sometimes in church we burn something that smells good as a gift to God. It's called incense. It makes smoke. Have you ever smelled it?*

6 Teach the children the following words and actions to the tune of "Mary Had a Little Lamb."

> I've a nose so I can smell, I can smell, I can smell.
> [Point to nose.]
> I've a nose so I can smell.
> God made me
> [Put thumbs in shoulders.]
> wonderful!
> [Raise arms.]
>   *Mary Kathleen Glavich, S.N.D.*

ACTING

1 Put perfume on each child's wrist. [Option: give each child a dab of hand cream.]

2 **PRAYER** Lead the children in prayer.

> *Let's thank God for noses and good smells. Close your eyes and smell your perfume (or hand cream).* [Pause.] *Thank God quietly in your heart, and God will know what you say.*

Page 10 is blank.

UNIT 1 God Made Me Live

❸ Help the children make the flowers on page 9, following these directions:

•*Paint flowers on the stems, using sponges held with clip clothespins dipped in paint.* (Or print with objects such as lids, cookie cutters, spools, or old toothbrushes.)

•*We will blow the paint dry with a blow dryer if necessary.*

•*Glue cotton balls in the center of the flowers.*

•*Add perfume to the cotton balls.*

❹ Gather the children in a circle for *Music 'n Motion* time. Play the Unit 1 song (Track 1). Invite the children to do motions to the song along with you, using *Music 'n Motion* page T250.

Have the children take home their pages and show their family the Family Time section.

CHECKPOINT

- *Were the learning outcomes achieved?*
- *Were the children familiar with incense?*

ENRICHING THE FAITH EXPERIENCE

Use the following activities to enrich the lesson or to replace an activity with one that better meets the needs of your group.

❶ Burn some incense for the children or light a scented candle and pray a prayer of thanks to God for the gifts of sight, hearing, and smell. Use a mild incense, such as one with a natural scent. Check your local fire codes to see whether this activity is permissible.

❷ Spray air deodorizer some distance from the children and have them jump up and down when the smell reaches them.

❸ Make popcorn for the class and enjoy its smell as well as its taste.

❹ Read this poem to the children:

My Nose

With my nose I smell things
   like these:
Bacon, popcorn, and
   Christmas trees,
Babies, roses, and apple pie;
And this is probably the
   reason why
My nose has such an
   important place—
Right in the middle of my
   face.
   Mary Kathleen Glavich, S.N.D.

I Can Smell CHAPTER 3 T23

Chapter 4
I Can Touch

FAITH FOCUS

God gave us bodies that can touch and feel.

Matthew 19:13–15

PREPARING THE FAITH EXPERIENCE

LISTENING

And people were bringing children to him that he might touch them, but the disciples rebuked them. When Jesus saw this he became indignant and said to them, "Let the children come to me; do not prevent them, for the kingdom of God belongs to such as these. Amen, I say to you, whoever does not accept the kingdom of God like a child will not enter it." Then he embraced them and blessed them, placing his hands on them.

Mark 10:13–16

REFLECTING

Our sense of touch is a source of delight, pleasure, and comfort. We enjoy soaking in a warm bath, petting a cat or dog, and being cooled by a breeze on a hot day. We use touch to communicate. A handshake conveys welcome and acceptance and sometimes seals agreements. We find the most joy in touch, however, when it conveys love. Jesus used touch often.

Frequently, the touch of Jesus expressed affection. He embraced the children brought to him. His touch brought blessings to them. Notice that Jesus was not embarrassed to display affection in front of his 12 companions. It is a grace to be able to express love freely and spontaneously through touch. A quick hug or a pat on the back declares to another "I accept you," "I cherish you," or "I love you." By bestowing these signs of affection, we are loving as Jesus loved.

The touch of Jesus healed. Repeatedly, he touched those who were blind, deaf, and paralyzed—even lepers—in order to heal them. He took Peter's mother-in-law by the hand, and the fever left her. He took Jairus's daughter by the hand, and she came back to life. Sick people seeking a cure thronged to Jesus in hope of touching him or even just his clothing. Our touch too can be healing. It can soothe a worried brow, stop tears, lessen pain, and ease a heart that is longing to be forgiven. When President Reagan was recovering from being shot, a nurse held his hand. He later located this nurse whose touch had comforted him during his ordeal.

The touch of Jesus imparted strength and empowered others. When Peter was sinking in the water, Jesus stretched out his hand to save him. Our touch can encourage: a steadying hand on a child learning to swim or ride a bike, a quick hug for someone laboring over a paper or project, a kiss at the beginning of a loved one's hard day.

Although we cannot feel Jesus' touch physically, we can pray for him to touch us through his Spirit and bring us his love, healing, and strength.

RESPONDING

God's Word moves us to respond in word and action. Let God's Spirit work within you as you prayerfully consider how you are being called to respond to God's message to you today. Responding through your journal may help strengthen your response.

- Which sign of affection do I give my loved ones that shows that I care about them? What sign of affection makes me feel loved or peaceful?

Jesus, may the children give and receive many kind and loving signs of affection.

T24 UNIT 1 *God Made Me Live*

Catechism of the Catholic Church

The themes of this chapter correspond to the following paragraph: 364.

THE FAITH EXPERIENCE

Child's Book pages 11–14

SCRIPTURE IN THIS CHAPTER
- *Luke 5:12–13*

MATERIALS
- Cutout #5, hands
- Option: live pet or a stuffed animal
- Clay or play dough (See homemade recipes on page T308.)
- Red crayons or markers
- Materials of various shapes, sizes, and textures: felt, foil, yarn, cotton, silk, corduroy, construction-paper scraps, foam pieces, sandpaper, wallpaper
- Glue

PREPARATION
Write the children's names on pages 11 and 14.

MUSIC 'N MOTION
Use *Music 'n Motion* page T250 and CD Track 1 "I Am Wonderfully Made" for this chapter. For a list of additional music, see page T302.

ENRICHING THE FAITH EXPERIENCE
Use the activities at the end of the chapter to enrich the lesson or to replace an activity with one that better meets the needs of your group.

BOOKS TO SHARE
My Hands by Aliki (HarperTrophy, 1991)

Hand, Hand, Fingers, Thumb by Al Perkins (Random House Books for Young Readers, 1969)

Eyes, Nose, Fingers, and Toes: A First Book All About You by Judy Hindley (Candlewick, 2002)

Hands Are Not for Hitting by Martine Agassi, Ph.D. (Free Spirit Publishing, 2000)

SNACK
Suggestion: gelatin figures

ALTERNATIVE PROGRAMS

DAILY PROGRAM
Day 1: Centering, Sharing A
Day 2: Enriching the Faith Experience choice
Day 3: Sharing B
Day 4: Enriching the Faith Experience choice
Day 5: Acting

THREE-DAY PROGRAM
Day 1: Centering, Sharing A
Day 2: Sharing B
Day 3: Acting

4 I Can Touch

LEARNING OUTCOMES
The children will
- realize the advantages of their ability to feel.
- know that God made the many textures in the world.
- be grateful to God for their sense of touch.

COMMENTS

1. Young children can be helped to become sensitive to the beauty and variety in the world around them and to perceive its gifts as signs of God's love.

2. Researchers have found proof of something that we know intuitively: touching promotes well-being. Babies who are held and cuddled are healthier than babies who are deprived of human touch. Three-year-olds need the encouragement, reassurance, and love that a hug or a pat on the head conveys.

3. God reaches us and speaks to us through our senses, including the sense of touch. This is obvious when we consider the sacraments. We join the Church through Baptism, during which we come into contact with water that refreshes and cleanses and oil that heals and soothes. During the Anointing of the Sick, the priest lays his hands on the person and anoints the person's forehead and hands.

4. Explain to the children that Jesus touched people only to show love and to heal them. Jesus wants us to touch others in a gentle way. Others should not touch us in a way that makes us feel uncomfortable or scared.

5. Be aware of any child who seems uncomfortable with the topic of touching. It is recommended to report concerns to your school's or program's administration.

T26 UNIT 1 *God Made Me Live*

CENTERING

❶ **Gather the children in a** circle for *Music 'n Motion* time. Play the Unit 1 song (Track 1). Invite the children to do motions to the song along with you, using *Music 'n Motion* page T250.

❷ **Invite the children to make** balls or snakes out of clay or play dough. Point out that their hands tell them whether the clay or play dough is too crumbly or too sticky and whether there is something in it that does not belong. Their hands also help by feeling when the balls they make are round and the snakes are smooth.

SHARING [A]

❶ **Show Cutout #5,** hands, and talk about the sense of touch.

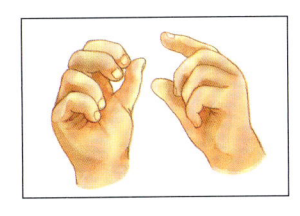

• *Your hands helped you make things with the clay (or play dough) because you can feel with them. God made us so that we can feel things. We can feel not only with our hands but also with our whole body.*

• *When you go outside barefoot on a warm, sunny day, what might you feel?* (The sun's warm rays, a breeze, the warm sidewalk, grass that tickles) [Option: Let the children pet the live or stuffed animal.]

❷ **Distribute page 11 and talk** about the picture.

• *What can the girl in the picture feel?* (The dog's fur; the dog's wet, rough tongue; the grandmother's hug; the soft blanket)

• *God made things so that they feel different from one another. Some things are rough and some are smooth. Some are hard and some are soft. Some are wet and some are dry.*

• *What are some things you like to feel?*

• *Isn't God good to make us so that we can feel all these wonderful things? God must love us very much.*

Color the boxes red under the hot things.

Family Time

Chapter 4: I Can Touch

In this lesson the children focused on their sense of touch. They played with clay or play dough and identified the way objects in the room felt. They also made collages from material with various textures. Ask your child to tell you how pieces of his or her collage feel.

Your Child
Our actions communicate our love. Your child needs to be assured frequently of your love by signs such as holding, cuddling, snuggling, back-rubbing, tickling, hand-holding, squeezing, and hugs and kisses.

Reflect
At sunset all who had people sick with various diseases brought them to [Jesus]. He laid his hands on each of them and cured them. (Luke 4:40)

Pray
Jesus, may we know your healing presence in our lives.

Do
- Let your child help make cookies by mixing dough, forming shapes, or using a cookie cutter.
- Provide clay, play dough, or a sandbox for your child.
- Call attention to things in nature that feel good: the sun's rays, a breeze on a hot day, grass under bare feet, or mud squishing between toes.
- Make your child "goop" to squeeze and hold: Mix three tablespoons of cornstarch and two tablespoons of cold water.
- Read to your child *My Hands* by Aliki. Ask your child to name five things we can do with our hands. Thank God for hands and the gift of touch.

For more family resources, refer to the Family Activity Booklet and visit www.loyolapress.com/preschool.

12 God Made Me © LOYOLAPRESS.

I Can Touch **CHAPTER 4** **T27**

3 **PRAYER** Lead the children in prayer.

- *Look at your hands and think of some things you have touched today. [Pause.] We can thank God for letting us feel. Let's stand and raise our hands and pray*

   Thank you, God, for your goodness and love.
   [Children repeat.]

4 On page 12 have the children identify hot things and color the boxes under them red. Ask the children what happens when they touch something hot.

5 **SCRIPTURE** Tell the story of the healing of the leper. (Luke 5:12–13) Show the Bible.

- *Listen to this story from the Bible. One day a man asked Jesus to heal him from a skin disease. Jesus wanted to help the man. When Jesus touched the man, he was healed.*

SHARING [B]

6 Give the children the following commands:

- *Touch your hand to your elbow,*
- *your nose to your knee,*
- *your hand to your shoulder,*
- *your chin to your chest,*
- *your palm to your cheek,*
- *your ear to your shoulder,*
- *your elbow to your knee,*
- *your thumb to your ankle,*
- *your foot to your knee.*

7 Teach the children the following words and actions to the tune of "Mary Had a Little Lamb":

> I've two hands so I can feel, I can feel, I can feel.
> [Hold out hands.]
> I've two hands so I can feel.
> God made me
> [Put thumbs in shoulders.]
> wonderful!
> [Raise arms.]
>   Mary Kathleen Glavich, S.N.D.

13 God Made Me

Page 14 is blank.

T28   UNIT 1   *God Made Me Live*

ACTING

1 Have the children tap one another on the back. Form a line with the children. Join the beginning and end of the line to make a circle so that each child is behind someone. Have each child tap on the back of the child in front of him or her.

2 Help the children make collages on page 13. Give them pieces of materials of various shapes, sizes, and textures to choose from. Have the children arrange the pieces as they wish and glue them to the page.

3 Gather the children in a circle for *Music 'n Motion* time. Play the Unit 1 song (Track 1). Invite the children to do motions to the song along with you, using *Music 'n Motion* page T250.

Have the children take home their pages and show their family the Family Time section.

CHECKPOINT

- Were the learning outcomes achieved?
- Which children need special attention to make them feel comfortable in the group?

ENRICHING THE FAITH EXPERIENCE

Use the following activities to enrich the lesson or to replace an activity with one that better meets the needs of your group.

1 Let the children help you make cookies by mixing the dough and then forming the individual cookies.

2 Make a puppet named Smiley on the side of your hand. Make a fist. Draw two eyes and a mouth so that the "upper lip" is on your forefinger and the "lower lip" is on your thumb. Introduce Smiley to the children and let him teach parts of the lesson. As the children work on their collages, you might ask whether any of them want Smiley on one of their hands. Use washable markers to draw the Smileys.

3 Show and name for the children five or six objects. (These might be religious items: cross, medal, book, rosary, candle, statue.) Put them in a bag. Let the children take turns putting a hand in the bag and naming an item they touch. Have them pull out the item to see whether they are right.

4 Fill two bags with six or seven identical items, such as a paper clip, a spool of thread, an eraser, a cup, a piece of clay, a crayon, and an orange. Have the children take turns pulling an item from one bag and then, without looking, finding a matching one in the other bag.

5 Recite this poem for the children:

> Fuzzy Wuzzy was a bear.
> Fuzzy Wuzzy had no hair.
> Fuzzy Wuzzy wasn't fuzzy,
>   was he?

6 Play "Hot Potato." Have the children pass a beanbag or a ball from one to the other, pretending that it is a hot potato.

7 Have the children go on a scavenger hunt to find things in the room that are rough, smooth, hard, soft, cold, and warm.

Chapter 5
I Can Taste

FAITH FOCUS

God gave us mouths to taste and made delicious food.

Psalm 23:5; John 6:53–57

PREPARING THE FAITH EXPERIENCE

LISTENING

Jesus said to them, "Amen, amen, I say to you, unless you eat the flesh of the Son of Man and drink his blood, you do not have life within you. Whoever eats my flesh and drinks my blood has eternal life, and I will raise him on the last day. For my flesh is true food, and my blood is true drink. Whoever eats my flesh and drinks my blood remains in me and I in him. Just as the living Father sent me and I have life because of the Father, so also the one who feeds on me will have life because of me."

John 6:53–57

REFLECTING

How ingenious and kind of God to make our process of nourishment such an enjoyable experience. God could have created us to be nourished in an efficient way that brought no pleasure, such as intravenous feeding. Instead, eating is one of life's delights. Our foods vary in color, taste, texture, and aroma. God has provided us with a tremendous smorgasbord: succulent steak; crisp, fresh salad; spicy salsa; crunchy corn on the cob; sweet, juicy strawberries—to name only a few of our many choices.

Eating plays an important role in relationships. We celebrate special occasions by dining out, at times conduct business over a meal, build family spirit around the dining-room or kitchen table, and develop intimacy in a shared meal for two. No wonder that in Jesus' parables and in our minds, heaven is compared to a banquet.

How wise of God to choose a meal as the means of filling us with divine life. As we journey toward the heavenly banquet, we are nourished at the Eucharist and our spiritual life grows. There we who hunger and thirst for the Lord are satisfied. When we gather around the table of the Lord, we are fed with the Body and Blood of Christ. The Eucharist is a meal in which Jesus enters us and where we are gradually transformed into him. Normally, our food becomes us; in the Eucharist we become more like Jesus. Moreover, when we are united with Christ, we are united with every member of his Body, the Church. The Eucharist is a shared meal in which God's people grow in love and in unity.

Jesus promised to be our food and drink after he had performed the miracle of the multiplication of loaves and fishes. (John 6) He fulfilled this promise when he instituted the Eucharist at the Last Supper the night before he died. For the past 2,000 years, people have been coming together for this sacred banquet. At Mass we can pray with the psalmist

Learn to savor how good the Lord is[.]

Psalm 34:9

RESPONDING

Having reflected upon God's Word, take some time now to continue to respond to God in prayer. You might also wish to respond in your personal journal.

- What does the Eucharist mean to me?

Lord, give the children a taste for what is good.

T30   UNIT 1   God Made Me Live

Catechism of the Catholic Church

The themes of this chapter correspond to the following paragraphs: 294, 356.

THE FAITH EXPERIENCE

Child's Book pages 15–18

SCRIPTURE IN THIS CHAPTER
- *Genesis 1:29–30*

MATERIALS
- Bible
- Chapter 5 Scripture card
- Cutouts: #2, ears; #3, eyes; #4, nose; #5, hands; #6, mouth
- Option: your favorite food
- Decorations: crepe paper, decorations, balloons
- Table decorations: place mats, napkins, centerpiece
- Masking tape
- Crayons or markers
- Glue
- 8 1/2 x 11 sheets of paper
- Option: precut magazine pictures of food
- Lollipop or other edible gift for each child

PREPARATION
- Place the Chapter 5 Scripture card in the Bible for Sharing #1.
- Write the children's names on page 15.
- Separate the pictures on page 17. Cut the 8 1/2 x 11 paper lengthwise and tape the short ends together to make one long strip for each child. Write childrens' names on the strips.
- Display Cutouts #2–6.
- Put pieces of rolled tape on wall decorations.

MUSIC 'N MOTION
Use *Music 'n Motion* page T250 and CD Track 1 "I Am Wonderfully Made" for this chapter. For a list of additional music, see page T302.

ENRICHING THE FAITH EXPERIENCE
Use the activities at the end of the chapter to enrich the lesson or to replace an activity with one that better meets the needs of your group.

BOOKS TO SHARE
Bread and Jam for Frances by Russell Hoban
 (HarperTrophy, 1986)

Growing Vegetable Soup by Lois Ehlert
 (Harcourt Big Books, 1991)

The Line Up Book by Marisabina Russo
 (HarperTrophy, 1986)

That Tickles! The Disney Book of Senses by Cindy West
 (Disney, 1993)

SNACK
Suggestion: muffins

ALTERNATIVE PROGRAMS

DAILY PROGRAM
Day 1: Centering, Enriching the Faith Experience #3, Sharing A
Day 2: Sharing B, Acting #1 and #2
Day 3: Enriching the Faith Experience choice
Day 4: Enriching the Faith Experience choice
Day 5: Acting #3–5

THREE-DAY PROGRAM
Day 1: Centering, Enriching the Faith Experience #3, Sharing A
Day 2: Sharing B, Acting #1 and #2
Day 3: Acting #3–5

5 I Can Taste

LEARNING OUTCOMES
The children will
- know that God gave them the sense of taste.
- be grateful for the sense of taste.
- enjoy a celebration.

COMMENTS
1. Celebrations are an integral part of life and worship. Each sacrament is a celebration. We celebrate the Eucharist together on the Lord's Day or every day. Children, especially three-year-olds, love to celebrate. Take advantage of this by planning a party for any occasion. Experiencing celebrations develops social skills and prepares the children to understand Church celebrations later.

2. Three-year-olds are aware of the rich variety of foods and flavors God has provided for us. These children have good appetites and are able to eat most foods. They already have their favorite foods and need to be encouraged to have a balanced diet.

CENTERING
Gather the children in a circle for *Music 'n Motion* time. Play the Unit 1 song (Track 1). Invite the children to do motions to the song along with you, using *Music 'n Motion* page T250.

SHARING [A]
1 SCRIPTURE Show Cutout #6, mouth, and talk about the sense of taste. Read the adaptation of Genesis 1:29–30 from the Scripture card in the Bible.

- We've been talking about things we can do that make us special. What are they? (See, hear, smell, touch)

- Today we'll talk about how God gave us taste. Then we will have a party to celebrate how wonderful we are.

- Why do we have to eat? (To grow and be strong)

- *The Bible tells us that God made food for us to eat. When God created the world, he said "I give you food to eat." God was good to us. God made it fun to eat. In the world God put many different things for us to eat with many different tastes.*

Name_____

15 God Made Me

T32   UNIT 1   God Made Me Live

❷ **Distribute page 15 and** discuss the picture.

- *What are the children in the picture eating?* (Watermelon)
- *Do you like watermelon?*
- *What are some other things you like to eat?*
- *What do you like to drink?*
- *What would happen if all you ate was candy?* (I would get sick.)
- *To be healthy, we eat different kinds of food—especially fruit, vegetables, meat, milk, and bread.*

❸ Have the children pretend to be popcorn. Limit the jumping area.

- *How many of you like popcorn? Let's pretend you are kernels of popcorn sitting in a bag in a microwave oven. Spread out in the room and squat. Someone turns the heat on and you're getting warm. One by one you pop up and jump around. Pop, pop, pop! How high can you jump?*
- *Now come back and sit down.*
- *Popcorn is dried corn, which grows on a plant. God planned that some of our foods grow on trees.*

❹ Help the children circle foods that grow on trees on page 16.

SHARING [B]

❺ **Teach the children the** following words and actions to the tune of "Mary Had a Little Lamb":

> I've a mouth so I can taste, I can taste, I can taste.
> [Point to mouth.]
> I've a mouth so I can taste.
> God made me
> [Put thumbs in shoulders.]
> wonderful!
> [Raise arms.]
>   Mary Kathleen Glavich, S.N.D.

❻ Give the children the four pictures from page 17. Have the children glue them in sequence onto the strip of paper to show the correct order of making a pizza.

Family Time

Chapter 5: I Can Taste

In this lesson the children learned about their sense of taste. They talked about their favorite food and were encouraged to eat a variety of foods. As a culmination of their study of the five senses, they had a party to celebrate themselves. Ask your child to show you the right order of the four pictures of a pizza.

Your Child
Children need a balanced diet. Keep snacks as healthful as possible and limit sugar, fat, and salt in your child's diet. Children have food preferences. You need not insist that your child eat foods that he or she strongly dislikes. You might serve your child's favorite meal sometime this week. Begin this meal with a short prayer of thanks to God.

Reflect
Learn to savor how good the LORD is[.] (Psalm 34:9)

Pray
Loving God, we praise you for your goodness and love.

Do
- Let your child go with you when you shop for food.
- Visit a farm and talk about the food it produces. Comment how good and wise God was in planning our food.
- Take your child to an ice-cream store and let him or her choose a flavor for a cone.
- Once in a while serve a new food to your child.
- Read to your child *Bread and Jam for Frances* by Russell Hoban. Discuss why it is nice to try and enjoy a variety of tastes. Thank God for the sense of taste and for good foods to eat.

For more family resources, refer to the Family Activity Booklet and visit www.loyolapress.com/preschool.

Circle foods that grow on trees.

I Can Taste CHAPTER 5 T33

ACTING

1 **PRAYER** Invite the children to praise God for food. You might have them choose pictures of their favorite food from magazines. Explain:

•*Praising God means telling how great and wonderful we think God is. Let's praise God for all the good, delicious foods in the world. When I touch you on the shoulder, you may stand if you wish and say your favorite food* (and hold up your picture). *We'll all say "We praise you, God, for . . ." and name your favorite food.*

•*I'll start.* [Name (and show) your favorite food.]

We praise you, God, for [your favorite food].

2 Tell the children about Jesus and parties.

•*Jesus went to many parties. He loved to be with people. He liked to celebrate and eat together with his family and friends. Jesus likes to see you having a good time at parties.*

•*Let's have a party now to celebrate the wonderful things we can do.*

3 Let the children help you decorate the room for a party. Put up balloons and crepe-paper streamers. Let the children put up wall decorations. If the snack table is not needed for the craft activity, set it with place mats. Unfold the napkins and insert them in the juice glasses at each place. If the children ask what they are celebrating, tell them, "You!"

4 Hold the celebration. Have the children sing the five verses of the song they learned about their senses. Enjoy the snack at the decorated table. Give each child a lollipop or other edible gift to take home.

5 Gather the children in a circle for *Music 'n Motion* time. Play the Unit 1 song (Track 1). Invite the children to do motions to the song along with you, using *Music 'n Motion* page T250.

Have the children take home their pages and show their family the Family Time section.

CHECKPOINT

- Were the learning outcomes achieved?
- What indications are there that the children eat nutritious meals?

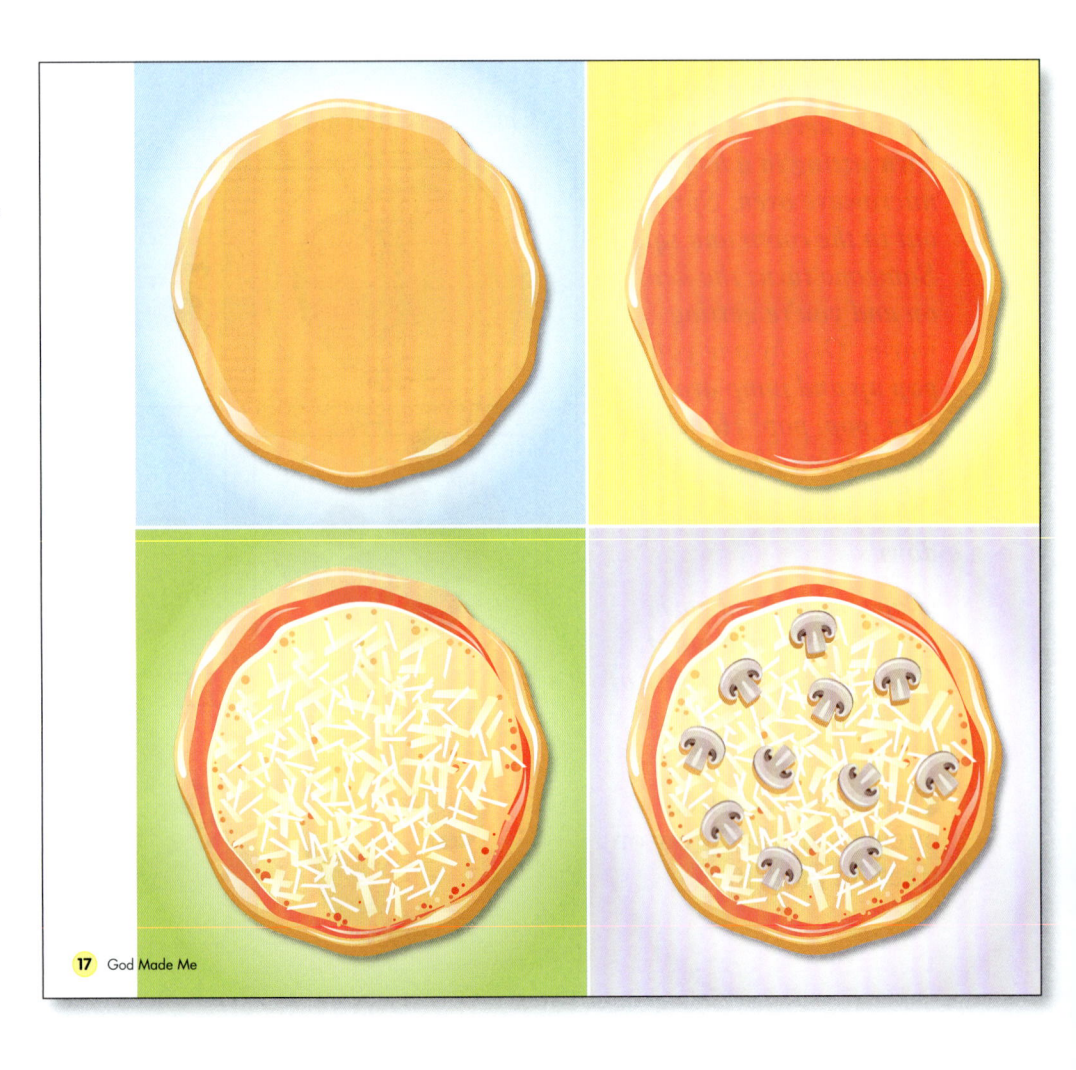

17 God Made Me

T34   UNIT 1   God Made Me Live

ENRICHING THE FAITH EXPERIENCE

Use the following activities to enrich the lesson or to replace an activity with one that better meets the needs of your group.

1 Let the children play in small groups, pretending to cook a meal.

2 Let the children press their forefingers or thumbs on a wad of paper towels soaked with paint and make prints of their own special fingerprints on a sheet of paper. Display the designs in the room with the children's names.

3 Give the children bits of various foods and talk about the differences. You might have them sample a pretzel, a piece of fruit, chocolate candy, a piece of lemon, and a cheese curl.

4 Make lemonade with the children: Mix 6 cups water, 1 cup lemon juice, 1 cup sugar. Chill and serve with ice cubes.

5 Teach the children the following finger play. Then ask the children what other fruit could be in a tree and have them repeat the poem with it.

> Away up high in the apple tree,
> [Raise arms.]
> Two red apples smiled at me.
> [Make a circle with each hand.]
> I shook that tree as hard as I could,
> [Shake hands in air.]
> And down came those apples.
> [Drop hands to side.]
> Yummmmmm. They were good!
> [Rub tummy.]

I Can Taste CHAPTER **5** **T35**

unit two

God Made Me Good

The children will grow in Christlike love.
They will have a sense of responsibility for others and for the earth.

6   I CAN HELP

After the experience of making a treat together, the children talk about helping at home. They learn that Jesus was a helper and that he likes us to follow his ways and be helpers too. They hear a story about a boy who helped, and then they are awarded medals for being helpers themselves.

7   I CAN CARE

The children learn that God takes care of the things in the world and wants us to take care of them too. They talk about how to care for living things, toys, clothes, and themselves. They thank God for the whole world and then make a jack-in-the-box with Jack holding a sign that says "I care."

T36   UNIT 2   God Made Me Good

8   I CAN CLEAN

After playing with soapy water, the children talk about washing and cleaning things, taking a bath, and washing their hands. They thank God for water to use in washing. Then they put together a picture puzzle of toys put away on shelves.

9   I CAN SHARE

The children talk about sharing and learn that God wants us to share because we are all like brothers and sisters. After hearing that sharing brings happiness, they share their talents by painting a picture for someone they love.

10   I CAN SMILE

The children learn that a smile is a sign of happiness that makes them look good and makes others happy. They hear that Jesus made others happy, and they listen to the story of the man with the shriveled hand whom Jesus healed. They pray psalm verses about joy. Then they make a smiling face appear on a card to take home as a reminder to smile.

God Made Me Good UNIT 2   T37

Chapter 6
I Can Help

FAITH FOCUS

Jesus wants us to help others.

Matthew 25:31–46; Luke 10:29–37

PREPARING THE FAITH EXPERIENCE

LISTENING

"A man fell victim to robbers as he went down from Jerusalem to Jericho. They stripped and beat him and went off leaving him half-dead. . . . a Samaritan traveler who came upon him was moved with compassion at the sight. He approached the victim, poured oil and wine over his wounds and bandaged them. Then he lifted him up on his own animal, took him to an inn and cared for him. . . . Go and do likewise."

Luke 10:30,33–34,37

REFLECTING

We read about Good Samaritans in the news: a man scales a high fence to save a child from three fierce dogs; an Olympic athlete donates blood to her brother right before the games; a man plunges into an icy river to save victims of a plane crash. Helpful acts we have experienced may be big news in our personal lives. How grateful we are to the driver next to us who signals that something is wrong with our car and then changes the tire for us, or the friend who watches our children so that we can have some free time.

True Christians do not hide behind phrases such as "I don't want to get involved," "That's not my problem," or "Let someone else do it." Instead, they pattern their lives on Christ, the divine helper, who came to the rescue of all humanity. Jesus made it clear that his followers are to show compassion for others. We are to be like Mary, a perfect model of discipleship, who, after she conceived Jesus, hurried to help her older cousin, who was also pregnant.

Each Spiritual and Corporal Work of Mercy is a way to help others. Matthew 25:31–46 contains Jesus' parable about the sheep who will be invited into the kingdom. They are the people who feed the hungry and clothe the naked. A modern parable echoes this message. A man had a vision of hell. He saw long tables laden with food, but the people seated there were silent and not partaking of the banquet. The only way they could eat was to use yard-long chopsticks. Then the man had a vision of heaven. There too he saw tables and yard-long chopsticks. But the people were enjoying themselves as they fed one another using the chopsticks. People who have a habit of serving others will be at home in heaven.

Generously helping others flows from the understanding that we are the Body of Christ, as Saint Paul points out in 1 Corinthians 12:24–27. We are more closely related to others than brothers and sisters: we are one. Therefore, we share responsibility for others. When we help others, we are being Christ for them. God helps others through us. As Christians, we should have the reputation of being people others can count on for help.

RESPONDING

God's Word calls us to respond in love. Respond to God now in the quiet of your heart, and perhaps through a journal that you are keeping this year.

- When has someone shown the love of Christ by offering me help?

Jesus, fill the children with the love that reaches out to others.

T38　UNIT 2　*God Made Me Good*

Catechism of the Catholic Church
The themes of this chapter correspond to the following paragraphs: 1917, 1932.

THE FAITH EXPERIENCE
Child's Book pages 19–24

SCRIPTURE IN THIS CHAPTER
- Matthew 20:30–34

MATERIALS
- Ingredients and tray or plate for CENTERING #2
- Bible
- Cutout #1, Jesus
- Crayons or markers
- Option: pencils
- Hole punch
- 20-inch piece of ribbon for each child
- Option: medal

PREPARATION
- Write the children's names on pages 19 and 21.
- Fold pages 21–22 for the children.
- Write the children's names on the medals on page 23. Cut out the medals, punch holes at the top, and string the medals on ribbons.

MUSIC 'N MOTION
Use *Music 'n Motion* page T251 and CD Track 2 "Helping" for this chapter. For a list of additional music, see page T302.

ENRICHING THE FAITH EXPERIENCE
Use the activities at the end of the chapter to enrich the lesson or to replace an activity with one that better meets the needs of your group.

BOOKS TO SHARE
Herman the Helper by Robert Kraus (Prentice Hall, 1987)

Wolf's Favor by Fulvio Testa (Puffin, 1990)

My Mama Needs Me by Mildred Pitts Walter (Walter, 1983)

Katy and the Big Snow by Virginia Lee Burton (Houghton Mifflin, 1974)

SNACK
Suggestion: cheese and crackers
Put one square of cheese on each cracker and then place crackers on a tray or plate.

ALTERNATIVE PROGRAMS

DAILY PROGRAM
Day 1: Centering
Day 2: Sharing A
Day 3: Sharing B
Day 4: Enriching the Faith Experience choice
Day 5: Acting

THREE-DAY PROGRAM
Day 1: Sharing A
Day 2: Sharing B
Day 3: Acting

6 I Can Help

LEARNING OUTCOMES
The children will
- know that Jesus helped people.
- be aware of ways they can help others.
- desire to be of help.

COMMENTS

1. In the footsteps of Christ, Christians are called to manifest love for others by acts of service. At the end of each Eucharist, we are sent to go and to love and serve the Lord. Christ assured us in Matthew 25 that we serve God when we serve others. We try to live the words we sing: "They will know we are Christians by our love."

2. Three-year-old children naturally enjoy being helpers. This tendency can be cultivated so that it becomes a lifelong habit. Whenever you can, enlist the children's help in lesson preparation and in the lessons themselves. Acknowledge their help and thank them. Encourage them to be helpers at home.

CENTERING

❶ Gather the children in a circle for *Music 'n Motion* time. Play the Unit 2 song (Track 2). Invite the children to do motions to the song along with you, using *Music 'n Motion* page T251.

❷ Let the children help you prepare the cheese and crackers. One child can place crackers neatly on the tray or plate, and another child can place a square of cheese on each cracker. Point out how easy it is to make something when everyone helps.

SHARING [A]

❶ Distribute page 19 and talk about the picture.

- *What is the girl doing?* (Helping in the kitchen)
- *What do you think she is helping her father make?* (A salad)
- *How is she helping?* (Mixing the salad)
- *What else could she do to help?* (Add more ingredients to the salad, pour dressing, wash the salad bowl and utensils when they're done using them)
- *How do you help at home?*
- *Do you like to help?*

T40   UNIT 2   *God Made Me Good*

2 SCRIPTURE Present Jesus as a helper. Show Cutout #1, Jesus, and the Bible. Tell the story of how Jesus healed the two men who were blind, adapted from Matthew 20:30–34.

• The Bible tells us about Jesus. It tells us that Jesus liked to help others. Listen to this story about how Jesus helped two men who were blind.

• One day, two men called out to Jesus while he was passing by. They asked Jesus to help them because they were blind. Jesus stopped and asked, "What do you want me to do for you?" The men asked Jesus to make them see. Immediately, Jesus touched their eyes and they received their sight.

• The Bible tells many stories like this. When people needed help, Jesus came and helped. He helped people who were in trouble. He helped people who were hungry and people who were sick. He helped people do their work. When Jesus was a boy, he helped his mother and his foster father the way you help people in your own family.

• Jesus wants us to be like him. He wants us to come running when people need help.

3 Have the children stand and sing the following verses to the tune of "Here We Go 'Round the Mulberry Bush" and act out the ways to help:

1. This is the way we pick up our toys . . . so early in the morning.
2. This is the way we carry the package . . .
3. This is the way we set the table . . .
4. This is the way we rock the baby . . .

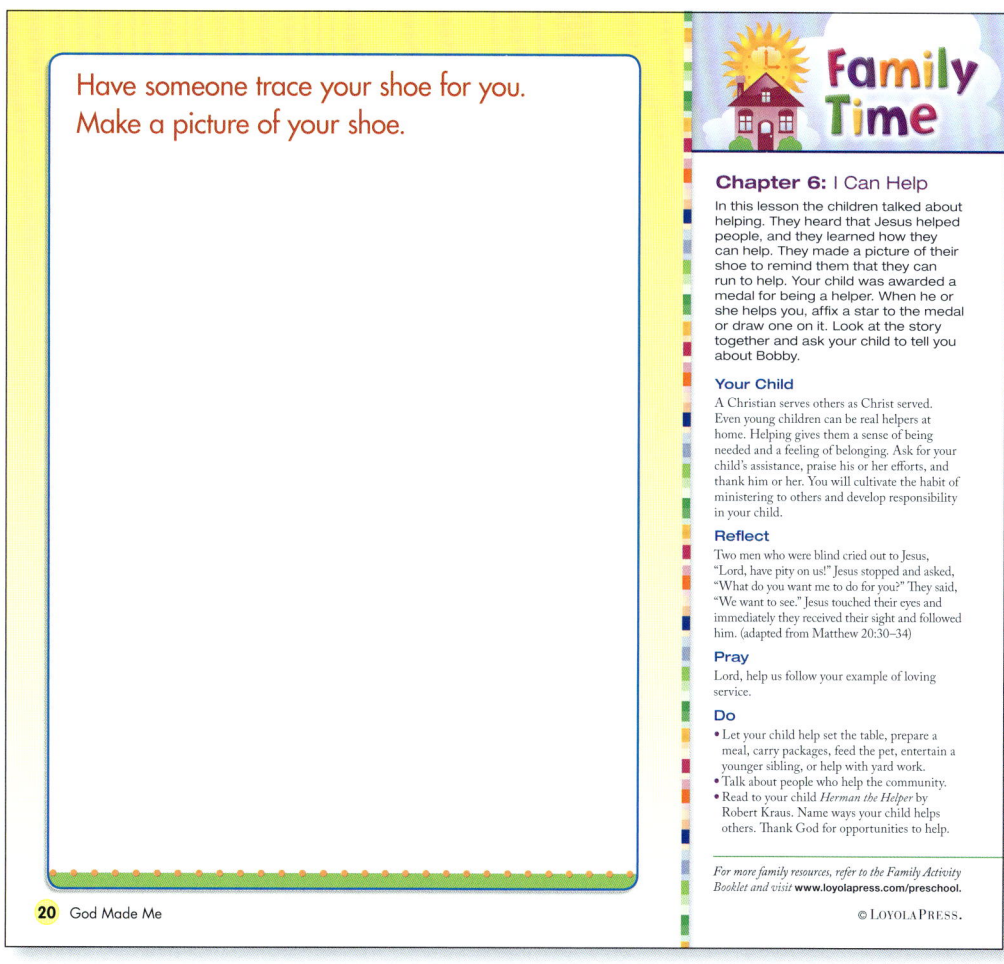

Have someone trace your shoe for you.
Make a picture of your shoe.

Family Time

Chapter 6: I Can Help

In this lesson the children talked about helping. They heard that Jesus helped people, and they learned how they can help. They made a picture of their shoe to remind them that they can run to help. Your child was awarded a medal for being a helper. When he or she helps you, affix a star to the medal or draw one on it. Look at the story together and ask your child to tell you about Bobby.

Your Child
A Christian serves others as Christ served. Even young children can be real helpers at home. Helping gives them a sense of being needed and a feeling of belonging. Ask for your child's assistance, praise his or her efforts, and thank him or her. You will cultivate the habit of ministering to others and develop responsibility in your child.

Reflect
Two men who were blind cried out to Jesus, "Lord, have pity on us!" Jesus stopped and asked, "What do you want me to do for you?" They said, "We want to see." Jesus touched their eyes and immediately they received their sight and followed him. (adapted from Matthew 20:30–34)

Pray
Lord, help us follow your example of loving service.

Do
• Let your child help set the table, prepare a meal, carry packages, feed the pet, entertain a younger sibling, or help with yard work.
• Talk about people who help the community.
• Read to your child *Herman the Helper* by Robert Kraus. Name ways your child helps others. Thank God for opportunities to help.

For more family resources, refer to the Family Activity Booklet and visit www.loyolapress.com/preschool.

20 God Made Me

© LoyolaPress.

I Can Help **CHAPTER 6** **T41**

❹ **Help the children draw** one of their feet (with shoe on) on page 20. Have them stand on the card so that you or a helper can trace their shoe. Explain:

• *You may make a picture of one of your feet that can run to help others. Color the shoe on the card to look like your own shoe.*

SHARING [B]

❺ **Distribute pages 21–22** and have the children follow along as you read aloud the story "Bobby the Helper."

❻ **Talk about the story.**

• *How did Bobby help others?* (He buttered toast, helped with shopping and the laundry, helped the baby go to sleep, and helped wash the car.)

• *Who was Bobby acting like when he helped others?* (Jesus)

• *We show others we love them when we help them as Jesus did.*

• *Whom have you helped? How did you help the person?*

• *We can help others by using the wonderful bodies God gave us. How can we help others with our eyes?* (Look for lost things) *Our ears?* (Listen for the telephone or doorbell) *Our mouth?* (Sing for the baby) *Our hands?* (Set the table) *Our feet?* (Go to get something)

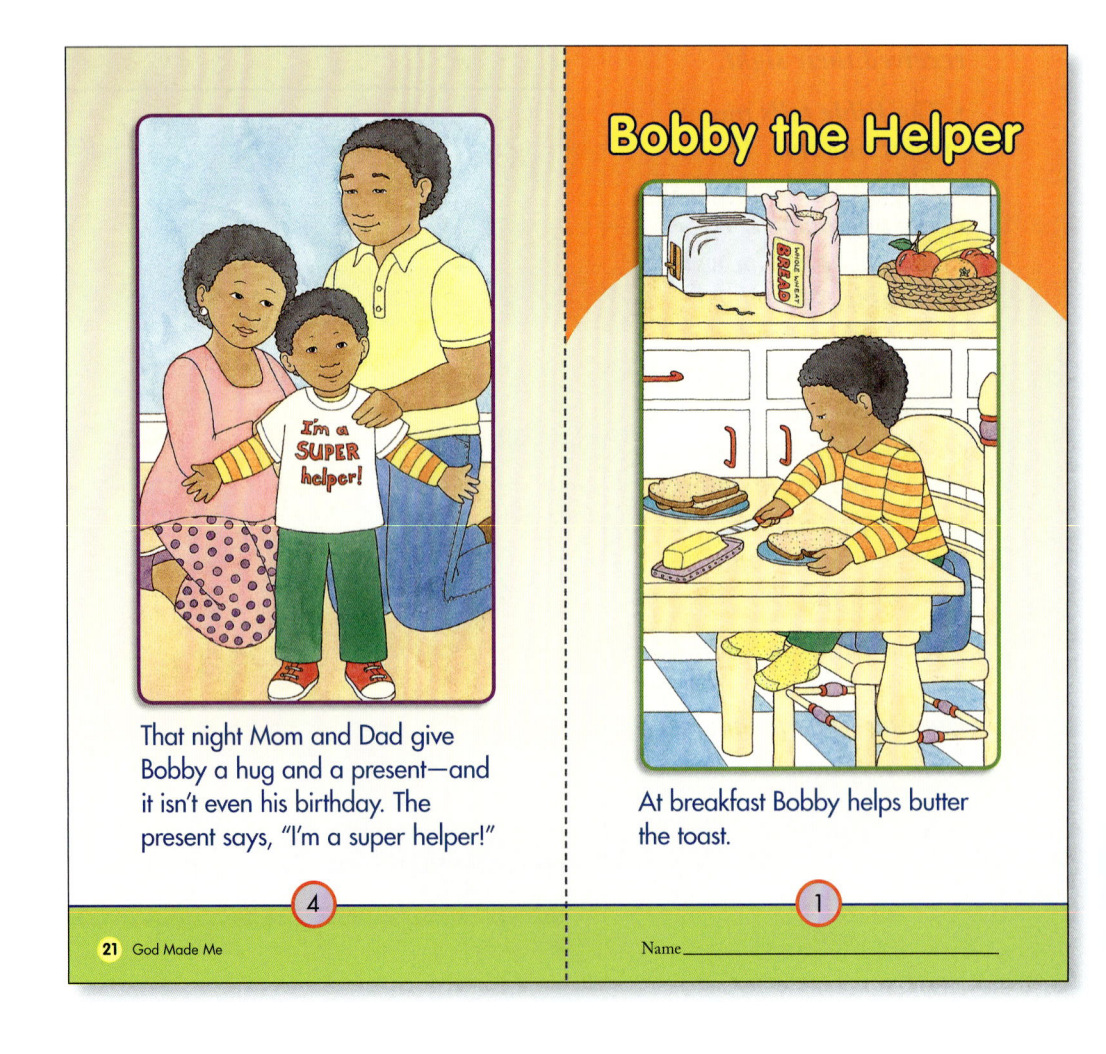

That night Mom and Dad give Bobby a hug and a present—and it isn't even his birthday. The present says, "I'm a super helper!"

4

21 God Made Me

Bobby the Helper

At breakfast Bobby helps butter the toast.

1

Name _____

T42 UNIT 2 *God Made Me Good*

ACTING

1 PRAYER Lead the children in an action prayer of thanks. Teach them the words and actions to the following song.

- *Let's thank God for giving us bodies that can help others. Let's sing a song as a gift to God.*

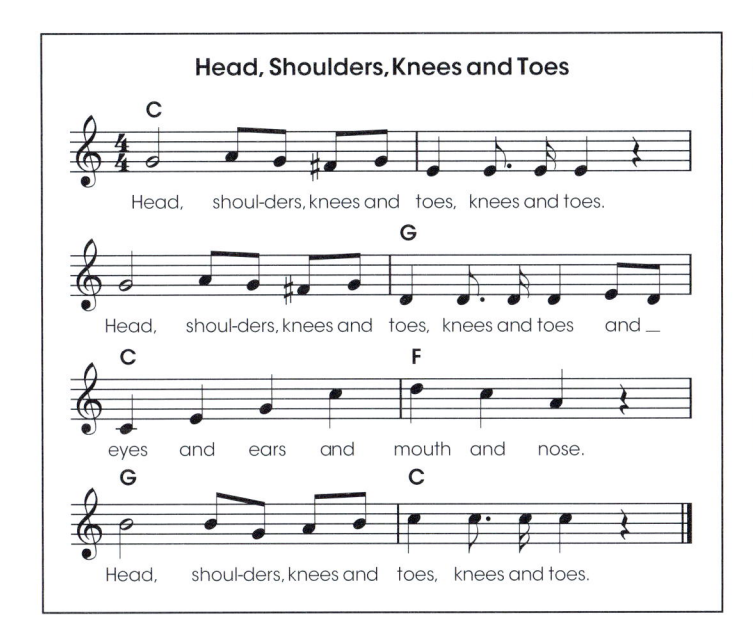

Head, Shoulders, Knees and Toes

Head, shoul-ders, knees and toes, knees and toes.
Head, shoul-ders, knees and toes, knees and toes and __
eyes and ears and mouth and nose.
Head, shoul-ders, knees and toes, knees and toes.

Head, shoulders, knees and toes, knees and toes.
[Touch hands to respective parts.]
Head, shoulders, knees and toes, knees and toes
[Touch hands to respective parts.]
and eyes and ears and mouth and nose.
[Point to respective parts.]
Head, shoulders, knees and toes, knees and toes.
[Touch hands to respective parts.]

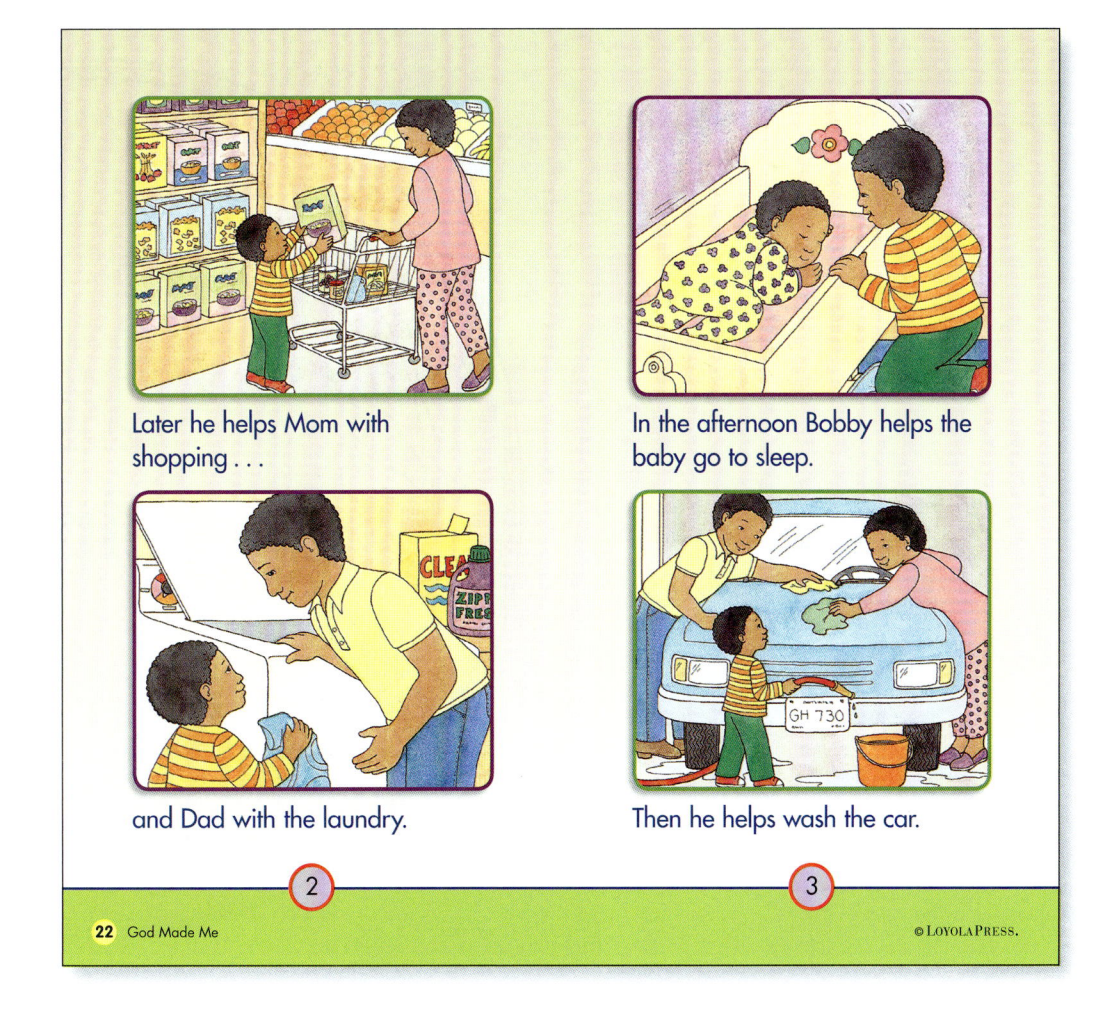

Later he helps Mom with shopping . . .

In the afternoon Bobby helps the baby go to sleep.

and Dad with the laundry.

Then he helps wash the car.

2   3

22 God Made Me © LOYOLAPRESS.

I Can Help **CHAPTER 6** **T43**

2 Show the medals made from page 23. [Option: Show a real medal.] Explain:

- *A medal is given to someone who has done something great. These medals are for helpers. They say your name and "#1 helper." On the other side they say ". . . like Jesus." Because you are all good helpers, I will give you each a medal.* [Call the children one by one and give each a medal.]

3 Gather the children in a circle for *Music 'n Motion* time. Play the Unit 2 song (Track 2). Invite the children to do motions to the song along with you, using *Music 'n Motion* page T251.

Have the children take home their pages and show their family the Family Time section.

CHECKPOINT

- Were the learning outcomes achieved?
- In what ways are the children attempting to be more helpful to one another and to you?

#1 Helper

23 God Made Me

T44 UNIT 2 God Made Me Good

ENRICHING THE FAITH EXPERIENCE

Use the following activities to enrich the lesson or to replace an activity with one that better meets the needs of your group.

❶ **Have the children trace or** make prints of their hands, using a pad of paper towels soaked with tempera paint. Write "Helping Hands" on each child's paper. Suggest that the children hang their papers in their rooms as a reminder to be helpers.

❷ **Trace around the children's** hands and cut out the shapes. Make a tree trunk on a large sheet of paper. Post it in the room and put the cutout hands at the top to make a Helping Hands Tree.

❸ **Carry out a class** project in which everyone helps. You might make a train out of cartons or make a mural of flowers for the wall.

❹ **Talk about people** who are helpers in stores, on the street, in the neighborhood, and in church.

❺ **Make puppets from** Cutout #7, dog, and Cutout #8, cat, by taping them to a ruler or pencil. Tell the children that the dog and cat will be speaking to each other, and after they talk, the children are to respond "yes" if the animal was being a good helper or "no" if it was not. Make the puppets engage in dialogues, such as the following:

1. Dog: Would you bring me that bone over there?
   Cat: Sure. I'm not doing anything anyway. (Yes.)

2. Cat: Would you get that sock for me?
   Dog: No. Can't you see I'm busy? (No.)

3. Dog: Would you tell me when my favorite show is on TV?
   Cat: I'd be glad to. (Yes.)

4. Cat: Would you hold the door open for me?
   Dog: Sure thing. (Yes.)

5. Cat: The birds in the yard are bothering me. Would you chase them away?
   Dog: Do it yourself. (No.)

6. Dog: I'm sick. Would you come here and hold my paw?
   Cat: I'll be right there. (Yes.)

...like Jesus

24 God Made Me

I Can Help CHAPTER **6** **T45**

Chapter 7
I Can Care

FAITH FOCUS

We can help care for the world.

Genesis 2:15

PREPARING THE FAITH EXPERIENCE

LISTENING

The LORD God then took the man and settled him in the garden of Eden, to cultivate and care for it.

Genesis 2:15

REFLECTING

In the *Catechism of the Catholic Church*, we read: "There is a solidarity among all creatures arising from the fact that all have the same Creator and are all ordered to his glory." (344) Our relationship with creation requires that we have "a religious respect for the integrity of creation." (2415)

After creating the earth, God pronounced it good and set us over it to care for and develop it. We enjoy the earth, stand in awe of its wonders, and delight in delving into its mysteries. This is as it should be, for the earth was created for us. But let us not forget that we also are responsible for the earth. God has entrusted creation to us and made us its caretakers.

Christ's redemption encompassed all creation, promising that all creation will be made new. In Scripture we read, "For creation awaits with eager expectation the revelation of the children of God; . . . We know that all creation is groaning in labor pains even until now[.]" (Romans 8:19,22) With this understanding that all creation is holy, we should not dare to exploit and destroy any facet of creation. To harm the earth is to show contempt for God, who created it and loves it. Water, air, rain forests—all are precious, all are a gift, and all are in danger from those who don't care.

Saint Francis of Assisi held the earth in great esteem and we can learn much from his example. He addressed the various creatures as his brothers and sisters: Brother Sun, Sister Water, Brother Wind. They spoke to him of God. Flowers revealed God's beauty; fire revealed God's light. It is said that Francis so loved all creation that he moved earthworms off the road and avoided stepping into water on the ground.

This is how Saint Francis explained why he wrote his famous poem "Canticle of the Sun": "I want to compose a new hymn about the Lord's creatures, of which we make daily use, without which we cannot live, and with which the human race greatly offends its creator."

If we share Saint Francis's view of our relationship to creation, we will be more careful and less wasteful. We will recycle, try to use less water, and accept our responsibility for keeping or making our air clean. By our daily acts we can acknowledge that the earth is God's gift, and we can express our gratitude for it.

RESPONDING

Having been nourished by God's Word, we are able to respond to God's great love for us. In prayer, respond to God's call to you to share his Word with others. You may also wish to respond in your prayer journal.

- How can I be a better steward of the earth?

Holy Spirit, instill in the children a reverence for the earth.

UNIT 2 God Made Me Good

Catechism of the Catholic Church

The themes of this chapter correspond to the following paragraphs: 301, 2218, 2280, 2402, 2415.

THE FAITH EXPERIENCE

Child's Book pages 25–26

SCRIPTURE IN THIS CHAPTER
- *Psalm 104:13–14*

MATERIALS
- Chapter 7 Scripture card
- Bible
- Toys
- Option: jack-in-the-box
- Crayons or markers
- Perforated Card B

PREPARATION
- Write the children's names on page 25.
- Place the Chapter 7 Scripture card for SHARING #2 in the Bible.
- Separate the strip on perforated Card B. Fold the large section and make a slit in the middle as indicated.

MUSIC 'N MOTION
Use *Music 'n Motion* page T251 and CD Track 2 "Helping" for this chapter. For a list of additional music, see page T302.

ENRICHING THE FAITH EXPERIENCE
Use the activities at the end of the chapter to enrich the lesson or to replace an activity with one that better meets the needs of your group.

BOOKS TO SHARE
Harry the Dirty Dog by Gene Zion (HarperCollins, 1976)

Don't You Feel Well, Sam? by Amy Hest (Candlewick, 2007)

Sam Who Never Forgets by Eve Rice (HarperTrophy, 1987)

Let's Get a Pup! Said Kate by Bob Graham (Rebound, 2003)

SNACK
Suggestion: crispy rice treats

ALTERNATIVE PROGRAMS

DAILY PROGRAM
Day 1: Centering, Sharing A
Day 2: Sharing B
Day 3: Enriching the Faith Experience choice
Day 4: Enriching the Faith Experience choice
Day 5: Acting

THREE-DAY PROGRAM
Day 1: Centering, Sharing A
Day 2: Sharing B
Day 3: Acting

I Can Care CHAPTER 7 T47

7 I Can Care

LEARNING OUTCOMES
The children will
- know that God cares for the world.
- realize their responsibility to care for the things of nature.
- take care of themselves.

COMMENTS
1. God entrusts us with the care of the world. We are to exercise good stewardship of our planet so that we, as well as future generations, may enjoy its riches. Keeping our air and water clean and preserving forests and wildlife are no longer just the concern of a few environmentalists. All of us are increasingly aware that the resources of the earth are not infinite. We are accepting responsibility for our environment and taking action against pollution and the depletion of our natural resources.

2. Three-year-old children can learn to put things away, to take care of belongings, and to show respect for their things and for those of other people. They can begin to care for themselves and to practice habits of personal hygiene and good nutrition. This lesson will reinforce what they are learning at home about caring for themselves and their possessions.

CENTERING
1 Gather the children in a circle for *Music 'n Motion* time. Play the Unit 2 song (Track 2). Invite the children to do motions to the song along with you, using *Music 'n Motion* page T251.

2 Let the children engage in free play with toys in the room, such as building blocks, picture books, and trucks.

SHARING [A]
1 Talk about the free-play session.

- *Did you enjoy playing with the toys?*

- *You were able to enjoy them because other children have taken good care of them. They did not lose them or break them or ruin them.*

- *God made many things for us to enjoy in the world. God takes care of them and wants us to take care of them too.*

T48 UNIT 2 God Made Me Good

❷ **SCRIPTURE** Distribute page 25 and talk about the picture. Discuss how God wants us to help care for things.

- *What are some things in the picture that the children are enjoying?* (Grass, flowers, water, boat, birds, kitten)

- **SCRIPTURE** *God's book, the Bible, says that God takes care of many things. Listen:* [Read the adaptation of Psalm 104:13–14 from the Scripture card in the Bible.] *"God gives the earth rain. God makes grass grow. God gives food to birds and other animals."*

- *God wants us to help care for things.*

- *How can we care for grass and flowers?* (Plant them, water them, avoid stepping on them, don't throw litter on them)

- *How can we care for animals?* (Play with them, feed them, give them water, pet them)

- *How can we care for our clothes?* (Don't get good clothes dirty, put clothes away)

- *How can we care for our toys?* (Put them away, be gentle with them, don't leave them outside)

❸ Play a simple version of "Jack-in-the-Box" with the children.

- *Let's pretend you are a jack-in-the-box. A jack-in-the-box is a box with a funny little man named Jack inside. When you press the button, Jack jumps up.* [Option: Show a jack-in-the-box.]

- *Squat as if you are in a box. When I say "Jack out of the box," jump up. When I say "Jack into the box," squat again.*

❹ Talk about caring for oneself.

- *God takes care of you. Your parents or other grownups who love you take care of you. God also wants you to take care of yourself.*

- *What are some things you do to take care of yourself so that you stay well and strong?* (Brush my teeth, eat good food, dress for the weather, get enough sleep, exercise)

SHARING [B]

❺ On page 26 have the children color the heart by the thing or things that have been cared for in each pair of pictures.

Color the hearts by things that have been cared for.

Family Time

Chapter 7: I Can Care

In this lesson the children learned that God expects us to care for the gifts of this world. They talked about ways to care for grass and flowers, animals, their own things, and themselves. Ask your child what the jack-in-the-box made in class helps him or her remember (to care for things and themselves).

Your Child
Continue to train your child to practice healthful habits, such as eating good foods, brushing teeth regularly, washing hands, and dressing for the weather. Three-and-a-half-year-old children may balk at routines. During this phase, someone other than the primary caregiver may have more success with the child at mealtimes or when the child is getting dressed.

Reflect
God gives the earth rain. God makes grass grow. God gives food to birds and other animals. (adapted from Psalm 104:13–14)

Pray
God, help us to care for the earth and all of creation.

Do
- Teach your child not to run water unnecessarily.
- Let your child help plant or water flowers.
- Give your child a special responsibility at home: caring for a plant, dusting a table, straightening the newspapers.
- Read a bedtime story to your child to entice him or her to go to bed on time.
- Read to your child *Harry the Dirty Dog* by Gene Zion. Discuss ways we care for ourselves and others. Thank God for his love and care.

For more family resources, refer to the Family Activity Booklet and visit www.loyolapress.com/preschool.

26 God Made Me © LOYOLAPRESS.

6 Teach the children the following poem:

> I'm glad the sky is painted blue
> And the earth is painted green,
> With such a lot of nice fresh air
> All sandwiched in between.

ACTING

1 **PRAYER** Lead the children in prayer. Invite them to repeat each line after you.

Dear God, I like your earth.

I like your flowers and grass.

I like your rivers and lakes.

I like your animals, and I like myself.

I will take care of your wonderful world.

I will take care of myself.

2 Help the children make a jack-in-the-box from perforated card B. Have them decorate the front of the box. Show them how to insert Jack in the slit and move him up and down. Explain:

- *Jack is holding a sign that says "I care." When you see him, remember to care for things and for yourself.*

3 Gather the children in a circle for *Music 'n Motion* time. Play the Unit 2 song (Track 2). Invite the children to do motions to the song along with you, using *Music 'n Motion* page T251.

Have the children take home their pages and show their family the Family Time section.

CHECKPOINT

- Were the learning outcomes achieved?
- How are the children being more careful with the things in the classroom?

B God Made Me • Ch. 7: I Can Care

T50 UNIT 2 God Made Me Good

ENRICHING THE FAITH EXPERIENCE

Use the following activities to enrich the lesson or to replace an activity with one that better meets the needs of your group.

1 Have the children make lunch bags into litter bags for the family car. Fold down the tops about one inch. Have the children decorate the bags. Then tape the two ends of a piece of yarn to each side as a handle.

2 Clean up an area with the children. Wash the classroom tables or straighten the toy shelves.

3 Talk more about the importance of brushing teeth and how to do it.

4 Give each child a little plant to care for. The children might plant seeds in a portion of an egg carton.

5 Teach the children this song with motions:

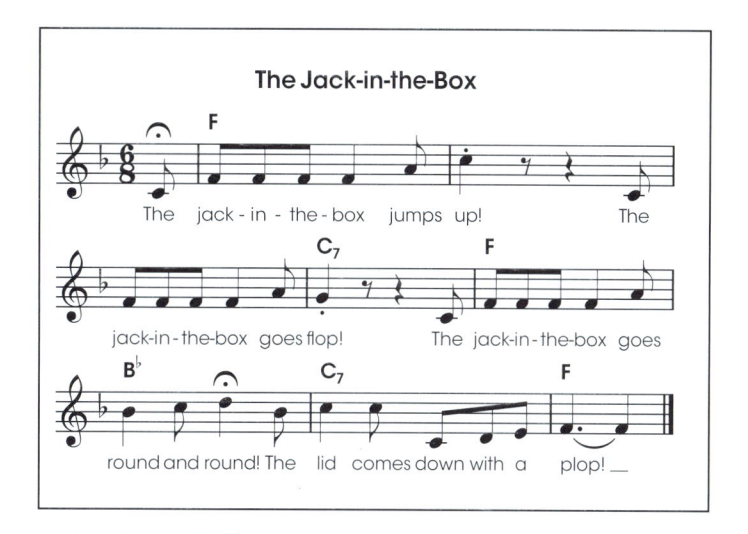

The Jack-in-the-Box

The jack-in-the-box jumps up! The jack-in-the-box goes flop! The jack-in-the-box goes round and round! The lid comes down with a plop!

Begin bent over with hands covering head.
On *up*, jump and reach up.
On *flop*, bend over with fingers touching floor.
On *round and round*, stand and spin.
On *plop*, squat and cover head with hands for a lid.

I Can Care CHAPTER 7 T51

Chapter 8
I Can Clean

FAITH FOCUS

God wants us to clean and be clean. Psalm 51:9; John 9:1–11

PREPARING THE FAITH EXPERIENCE

LISTENING

. . . Christ loved the church and handed himself over for her to sanctify her, cleansing her by the bath of water with the word, that he might present to himself the church in splendor, without spot or wrinkle or any such thing, that she might be holy and without blemish.

Ephesians 5:25–27

REFLECTING

In the Bible we hear the story of how God saved Noah and his family from the great flood. When the flood ended, God gave the rainbow as a sign of his covenant with Noah and his descendants. In the story of the flood, we see a sign of Baptism and our salvation in Christ. God sent his only Son to wash the world clean of sin. By his death on the cross and his Resurrection, Jesus made us new creatures. In the prayer *Anima Christi*, we pray "Water from the side of Christ, wash me."

When we are joined to Christ's Death and Resurrection in the waters of Baptism, we are filled with divine life. Because of our Baptism by water, the expression "Cleanliness is next to godliness" takes on new meaning. Baptism is our bath, or rebirth, in which we are washed by the Holy Spirit, our sins are buried in the water, and we are reborn as sons and daughters of God. The white robe presented to us at Baptism symbolizes the pure life we have been given.

Keeping ourselves shining with baptismal innocence—the pure beauty and goodness God intended for us—is not easy. Despite our best intentions and resolutions, sin and our failings tarnish our lives every day. Over and over we find we need to scrub and polish our spiritual selves by an act of contrition or the Sacrament of Penance and Reconciliation. Once a year during the season of Lent, we do intense spring cleaning, trying to sweep out the cobwebs—our faults. We may be disappointed in ourselves but not discouraged. Jesus, the living water, has saved us and is always ready to save us again. We believe that purgatory is the final purification that makes us worthy of enjoying divine love forever.

At the Last Supper after Jesus had washed Peter's feet, Peter cried out, asking Jesus to wash his hands and head as well. Only by being clean would Peter be able to share Jesus' inheritance. Like Peter, we desire to be with Jesus and share his life, so we pray with the psalmist:

Wash away all my guilt;
from my sin cleanse me.

Cleanse me with hyssop, that I may be pure;
wash me, make me whiter than snow.

Psalm 51:4,9

RESPONDING

God's Word moves us to respond in word and action. Let God's Spirit work within you as you prayerfully consider how you are being called to respond to God's message to you today. Responding through your journal may help to strengthen your response.

- Which fault(s) do I most desire to be made clean?

Loving Father, may the children always trust in your mercy.

T52 UNIT 2 *God Made Me Good*

Catechism of the Catholic Church

The themes of this chapter correspond to the following paragraphs: 2288, 2415.

THE FAITH EXPERIENCE

Child's Book pages 27–28

SCRIPTURE IN THIS CHAPTER
- *Ezekiel 36:25*

MATERIALS
- Chapter 8 Scripture card
- Bible
- Basins of soapy water
- Option: aprons
- Water toys, such as cups, detergent bottles, funnels, sieves, corks, bulb basters, and sponges
- Deck of cards
- Crayons or markers
- Rinse water
- Towels
- Option: washcloth
- Envelope for each child
- Perforated Card C

PREPARATION
- Write the children's names on page 27.
- Place the Chapter 8 Scripture card for SHARING #1 in the Bible.
- Separate the puzzle pieces for perforated Card C and put them in an envelope, one for each child.

MUSIC 'N MOTION
Use *Music 'n Motion* page T251 and CD Track 2 "Helping" for this chapter. For a list of additional music, see page T302.

ENRICHING THE FAITH EXPERIENCE
Use the activities at the end of the chapter to enrich the lesson or to replace an activity with one that better meets the needs of your group.

BOOKS TO SHARE
How Do Dinosaurs Clean Their Rooms? by Jane Yolen (Blue Sky Press, 2004)

Count Down to Clean Up by Nancy Elizabeth Wallace (Houghton Mifflin, 2001)

King Bidgood's in the Bathtub by Audrey Wood (Harcourt Big Books, 1993)

Maisy Cleans Up by Lucy Cousins (Candlewick, 2002)

SNACK
Suggestion: fruit, such as grapes or berries
Have the children help you rinse the fruit.

ALTERNATIVE PROGRAMS

DAILY PROGRAM
Day 1: Centering, Sharing A
Day 2: Sharing B
Day 3: Enriching the Faith Experience choice
Day 4: Enriching the Faith Experience choice
Day 5: Acting

THREE-DAY PROGRAM
Day 1: Centering, Sharing A
Day 2: Sharing B
Day 3: Acting

I Can Clean CHAPTER **8** T53

8 I Can Clean

LEARNING OUTCOMES

The children will
- know that we care for things by cleaning.
- learn ways that they can clean.
- desire to help clean things.

COMMENTS

1. Keeping the world clean is one way of making a better, more beautiful world. The act of cleaning shows respect for things, for others, and for oneself.

2. Three-year-olds love to play with water and in it. Bath time is enjoyable, and the only thing the children may resist is getting out of the tub. Because the 10 best ways to spread germs are at the ends of our hands, it is important to stress the washing of hands with the children.

3. Water, the primary cleaning agent, makes a fitting symbol for Baptism. Through Baptism God refreshes us, cleanses us from sin, and brings new life. This lesson prepares the children for a later understanding of this sacrament.

CENTERING

❶ Gather the children in a circle for *Music 'n Motion* time. Play the Unit 2 song (Track 2). Invite the children to do motions to the song along with you, using *Music 'n Motion* page T251.

❷ Let the children engage in free play with soapy water. If possible, provide aprons.

SHARING [A]

❶ **SCRIPTURE** Distribute page 27 and talk about the picture.

- *What is happening in the picture?* (The dog is getting a bath.)
- *How do you think the dog feels?*
- *Why does the dog need a bath?* (To be clean, to smell good, to be healthy)
- *We take baths too. Do you like to take a bath?*
- *We use soap and water to wash dogs and ourselves. What else do we wash?* (Clothes, dishes, the car)

T54 UNIT 2 God Made Me Good

- *We try to keep things fresh and clean. When we wash things, they become almost like new.*

- *Sometimes God cleans the whole world. How?* (With rain)

- *Do you like to go outside after a rain? What is the world like?* (Fresh and clean)

- *Listen to what God says to us in the Bible:* [Read the adaptation of Ezekiel 36:25 from the Scripture card in the Bible.] *"I will sprinkle clean water to cleanse you."*

2 Talk about cleaning at home.

- *What do people in your family do to keep your house clean?* (Pick up things and put them where they belong, vacuum, wash windows, dust)

- *How do people in your family keep your yard and sidewalk neat and clean?* (Rake leaves, shovel snow, pick up litter, mow the lawn)

- *God wants you to help keep the world clean. How do you help clean at home?*

3 Play "52 Pickup." Hold half a deck of cards in each hand and throw them into the air. Have the children scramble to pick up all the cards.

4 Guide the children in making lines to connect the things that go together on page 28.

SHARING [B]

5 Talk about caring for personal things.

- *How do you keep your toys and clothes clean?* (By putting them away, being careful with them, not touching them with dirty hands)

6 Talk about washing hands.

- *It is important to keep our hands clean. When should you wash your hands?* (Before you eat, after going to the bathroom, when you are sick)

Draw lines to connect things that are used together to clean.

Family Time

Chapter 8: I Can Clean

In this lesson the children talked about keeping things and themselves clean. They told how they helped clean at home and learned that washing their hands is important. They played with water and thanked God for this creation that enables us to clean. Have your child work the puzzle made in class.

Your Child
Preschoolers are capable of learning how to clean. In fact they enjoy cleaning things. Make use of this characteristic to occupy your child, provide exercise, and take care of small chores.

Reflect
I will sprinkle clean water to cleanse you. (adapted from Ezekiel 36:25)

Pray
Merciful God, cleanse us from sin and make us holy.

Do
- Make bath time an even happier experience by providing toys, bath crayons, sponges cut in shapes, and colorful scented soap.
- Let your child do small tasks as you clean your house, yard, garage, or car.
- With your child, watch cleaners at work: street cleaners, window cleaners, people at a car wash.
- Go for a walk in the rain with your child.
- Teach your child to put away his or her toys and clothes.
- Read to your child *How Do Dinosaurs Clean Their Rooms?* by Jane Yolen. Discuss how your child can pick up toys and other belongings. Thank God for all the ways we keep ourselves clean and respect our belongings.

For more family resources, refer to the Family Activity Booklet and visit www.loyolapress.com/preschool.

© LOYOLAPRESS.

7 PRAYER Lead the children in prayer. Pour water on each child's hands over a basin. As the water is poured, invite each child to say "Thank you, God, for water." Have the children dry their hands.

ACTING

1 Have the children pretend to wash their faces. Demonstrate and then guide them in pretending to rub soap on the cloth and then wash their foreheads, inside their ears, behind their ears, their noses, their cheeks, around their mouths, and under their chins. Comment:

- *Now you look fresh and new and clean. Do you feel better too?*

2 Have the children put together the puzzle from perforated Card C. Explain:

- *You are going to clean up toys in a picture by putting the puzzle together. When you are finished, all the toys will be on the shelves where they belong.*

3 Gather the children in a circle for *Music 'n Motion* time. Play the Unit 2 song (Track 2). Invite the children to do motions to the song along with you, using *Music 'n Motion* page T251.

Have the children take home their pages and show their family the Family Time section.

CHECKPOINT

- Were the learning outcomes achieved?
- Do the children like to help clean at home and at school?

C God Made Me • Ch. 8: I Can Clean

T56   UNIT 2   *God Made Me Good*

ENRICHING THE FAITH EXPERIENCE

Use the following activities to enrich the lesson or to replace an activity with one that better meets the needs of your group.

1 Make soap in shapes. Mix soap flakes with water until the mixture has the consistency of play dough. Pat out the dough and let the children cut shapes with cookie cutters. Let the shapes harden.

2 Let the children help clean the classroom. They might wash the blocks they play with, wash the board, shine wood after you have sprayed polish on it, and straighten the toy shelves.

3 Have the children play with large soap bubbles. See page T308 for homemade recipes.

4 For an action break have the children pretend to be washing machines, churning a load of clothes.

5 Have the children sing and act out the following verses to "Here We Go 'Round the Mulberry Bush."

1. This is the way we sweep the floor . . . so early in the morning.
2. This is the way we dust the table . . .
3. This is the way we vacuum the room . . .
4. This is the way we wash our hands . . .

Chapter 9
I Can Share

FAITH FOCUS
We are to share what we have.
1 Kings 17:7–16; Matthew 25:31–46

PREPARING THE FAITH EXPERIENCE

LISTENING

"Have dominion over the fish of the sea, the birds of the air, and all the living things that move on the earth." God also said: "See, I give you every seed-bearing plant all over the earth and every tree that has seed-bearing fruit on it to be your food; and to all the animals of the land, all the birds of the air, and all the living creatures that crawl on the ground, I give all the green plants for food." And so it happened. God looked at everything he had made, and he found it very good.

Genesis 1:28–31

REFLECTING

The Second Vatican Council stated:

> God destined the earth and all it contains for all men and all peoples so that all created things would be shared fairly by all mankind under the guidance of justice tempered by charity.
>
> *Pastoral Constitution on the Church in the Modern World,* No. 69

People have exhausted natural resources throughout the world, making international relations tense and competitive. Admitting negligence in the use of God's gifts, some people are trying to conserve and renew the earth's resources for future generations. People and nations must take responsible action to prevent exploitation, which stems from avarice and leads to materialism.

Those who accept their social responsibilities and trust in God's help will reap their reward:

> Trust in the LORD and do good
> that you may dwell in the land and live secure.
> *Psalm 37:3*

The People of God are called to work together to establish a kingdom of peace, justice, and love. The kingdom is characterized by solidarity, rather than competition, and special concern for those who are poor. The United States bishops' pastoral letter *Economic Justice for All* raises hard questions: Does our economic system emphasize profits at the expense of human needs and human dignity? Is it right to sell poor countries weapons when food, medicine, and schools are needed so much more? The letter states, "Misuse of the world's resources or appropriation of them by a minority of the world's population betrays the gift of creation." (*Economic Justice for All,* 34)

There is a story about a woman who became disturbed at the sight of a poor little girl, undernourished and dressed in rags, playing with trash on a city street. The woman rebuked God, "Why did you let this happen? Why don't you do something about it?" God answered, "I did do something. I created you."

Children who are taught to share food and toys will be prepared for our interdependent society and global village and also for the Kingdom of Heaven.

RESPONDING

Having reflected upon God's Word, take some time now to continue to respond to God in prayer. You might wish to use your journal to record your responses.

- Have I ever given someone something that I treasured or that was the last one I had?

Gracious Father, give the children generous hearts.

Catechism of the Catholic Church

The themes of this chapter correspond to the following paragraphs: 2446–2449.

THE FAITH EXPERIENCE

Child's Book pages 29–32

SCRIPTURE IN THIS CHAPTER
- *Matthew 25:35–36*

MATERIALS
- Bible
- Chapter 9 Scripture card
- Cutout #27, chipmunks
- Option: book
- Music for SHARING #3
- Crayons or markers
- Tempera paint

PREPARATION
- Write the children's names on pages 29 and 32.
- Place the Scripture card for SHARING #2 in the Bible.
- You might fold page 31 in half for the children.
- Practice telling the story in CENTERING #2.

MUSIC 'N MOTION
Use *Music 'n Motion* page T251 and CD Track 2 "Healing" for this chapter. For a list of additional music, see page T302.

ENRICHING THE FAITH EXPERIENCE
Use the activities at the end of the chapter to enrich the lesson or to replace an activity with one that better meets the needs of your group.

BOOKS TO SHARE
The Rainbow Fish by Marcus Pfister (North-South Books, 1996)

The Selfish Giant by Oscar Wilde (Longman, 2001)

I Can Share by Karen Katz (Grosset & Dunlap, 2004)

Will Sheila Share? by Elivia Savadier (Roaring Book Press, 2008)

SNACK
Suggestions: graham crackers or another snack that can be broken and shared

---

ALTERNATIVE PROGRAM

DAILY PROGRAM
Day 1: Centering, Sharing A
Day 2: Enriching the Faith Experience choice
Day 3: Sharing B
Day 4: Enriching the Faith Experience choice
Day 5: Acting

THREE-DAY PROGRAM
Day 1: Centering, Sharing A
Day 2: Sharing B
Day 3: Acting

9 I Can Share

LEARNING OUTCOMES
The children will
- be willing to share with others.
- know that Jesus wants them to share.
- experience the benefits of sharing.

COMMENTS

1. God shares divine life with us. God made the world and shares it with us too. Now we are to take the goods of this world—its beauties, its natural resources, land, and food—and share these gifts with our brothers and sisters in the family of God.

2. Three-year-olds are less selfish than two-year-olds. They do not hang onto their possessions and hoard them quite so much. They are not too young to learn how to share. If they share small things now, such as toys, they will be more apt to share more significant things later. They will be better Christians, whose hallmark is love.

CENTERING

1 Gather the children in a circle for *Music 'n Motion* time. Play the Unit 2 song (Track 2). Invite the children to do motions to the song along with you, using *Music 'n Motion* page T251.

2 Gather the children and read aloud "Chippy and His Friends."

Chippy and His Friends

Chippy Chipmunk lived with his parents in a hole in the ground near a river. One night there was a big storm. As it rained, the river got higher and higher, coming closer and closer to the Chipmunks' home. Chippy and his father and mother scampered from their hole and hurried to Chippy's cousin's home, which was farther away from the river. The next morning Chippy's family couldn't even find their home. The river had covered it up! [Show Cutout #27, chipmunks.]

Chippy's father soon found another place to live on higher ground. But the trouble was that Chippy had no toys. They were all under water.

One day Peter Squirrel came by. "Hey, Chippy!" he called. "Let's play ball. Go get your bat and ball."

Chippy said, "I have no bat or ball or any other toy. I lost them in the flood. Let's just play tag." So they did.

That afternoon Chippy's doorbell rang. There was Peter Squirrel with a bat and ball, and Sarah Skunk with a teddy bear. Rosa Rabbit was pulling a wagon. Behind them were Georgie Groundhog on a tricycle and Molly Mouse with a basketball. Timothy Turtle held a kite. Each of Chippy's friends had brought him a toy. Now Chippy had more toys than before.

Every day the animal children have a wonderful time in Chippy's yard playing with all his toys. [Turn around Cutout #27 to show the animal children playing.]

T60 UNIT 2 *God Made Me Good*

SHARING [A]

1 Talk about sharing.

- *Chippy was happy because his friends shared. Do you think his friends were happy too?*

- *What did Chippy do with his new toys?* (He shared them.)

- *It is good to share all kinds of things: toys, food, TV, books.* [Option: Show the book.]

- *Did anyone ever share something with you? Tell us about it.*

- *Did you ever share something? Tell us about it.*

2 **SCRIPTURE** Explain that God wants us to share.

- *God gave us all the wonderful things in the world and wants us to share them. Jesus told us this.* [Read the adaptation of Matthew 25:35–36 from the Scripture card in the Bible.]

> If someone is hungry, share your food.
> If someone is thirsty, share your drink.
> If someone has no clothes, share your clothes.

- *We share with one another because we are like brothers and sisters in a family. God made us all. We belong to God's family.*

3 Play "Partners." Have the children find partners and hold hands. Tell them to walk along together swinging hands. When you say "change," they are to find another partner. If there is an uneven number of children, let one child be the one to call "change." Play music as the children walk.

SHARING [B]

4 Distribute page 29 and talk about the picture.

- *What are the children in the picture sharing?* (Popcorn, pail, shovel, ball)

- *Suppose one boy kept the ball all to himself and wouldn't let anyone else play with it. How would the other child feel?* (Unhappy)

- *The boy would be selfish. Do you think he would be happy?* (No.)

5 Have the children color the bread and the juice pitcher on page 30. Give each child only one crayon so that everyone must share.

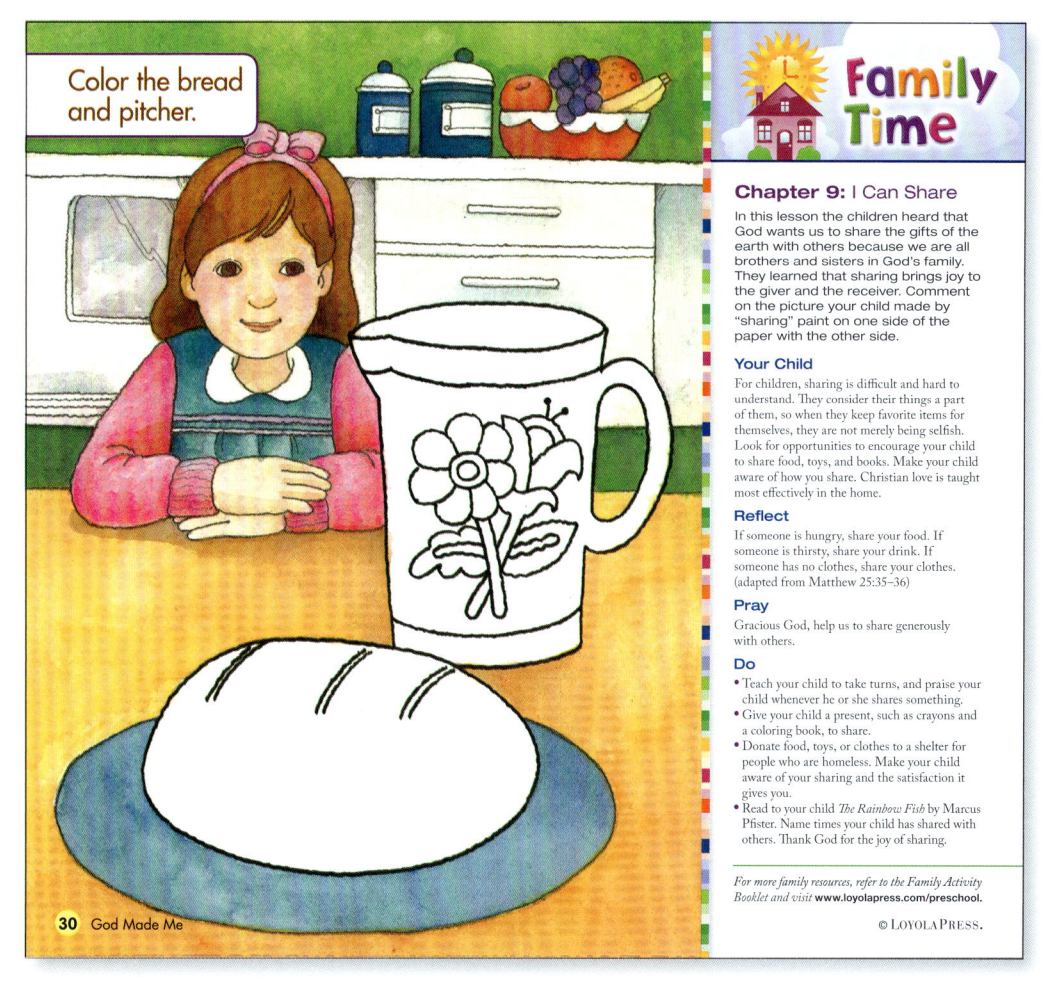

Family Time

Chapter 9: I Can Share

In this lesson the children heard that God wants us to share the gifts of the earth with others because we are all brothers and sisters in God's family. They learned that sharing brings joy to the giver and the receiver. Comment on the picture your child made by "sharing" paint on one side of the paper with the other side.

Your Child
For children, sharing is difficult and hard to understand. They consider their things a part of them, so when they keep favorite items for themselves, they are not merely being selfish. Look for opportunities to encourage your child to share food, toys, and books. Make your child aware of how you share. Christian love is taught most effectively in the home.

Reflect
If someone is hungry, share your food. If someone is thirsty, share your drink. If someone has no clothes, share your clothes. (adapted from Matthew 25:35–36)

Pray
Gracious God, help us to share generously with others.

Do
- Teach your child to take turns, and praise your child whenever he or she shares something.
- Give your child a present, such as crayons and a coloring book, to share.
- Donate food, toys, or clothes to a shelter for people who are homeless. Make your child aware of your sharing and the satisfaction it gives you.
- Read to your child *The Rainbow Fish* by Marcus Pfister. Name times your child has shared with others. Thank God for the joy of sharing.

For more family resources, refer to the Family Activity Booklet and visit www.loyolapress.com/preschool.

© LOYOLAPRESS.

ACTING

1 **PRAYER** Lead the children in prayer. Tell them to close their eyes, be very quiet, and say in their hearts what you say.

Dear God, you give me many wonderful things. Thank you for sharing your world with me. Please keep me from being selfish. Help me be a kind, loving person who shares.

2 Have the children paint a picture on page 31 to give to someone as a gift. Have them drop tempera paint on only one side of the line. Then have them fold over the empty side of the paper onto the paint and press down so that the paint is "shared" with the empty half. Point out the beauty of the designs.

3 Gather the children in a circle for *Music 'n Motion* time. Play the Unit 2 song (Track 2). Invite the children to do motions to the song along with you, using *Music 'n Motion* page T251.

Have the children take home their pages and show their family the Family Time section.

CHECKPOINT

- Were the learning outcomes achieved?
- How open were the children to the idea of sharing?

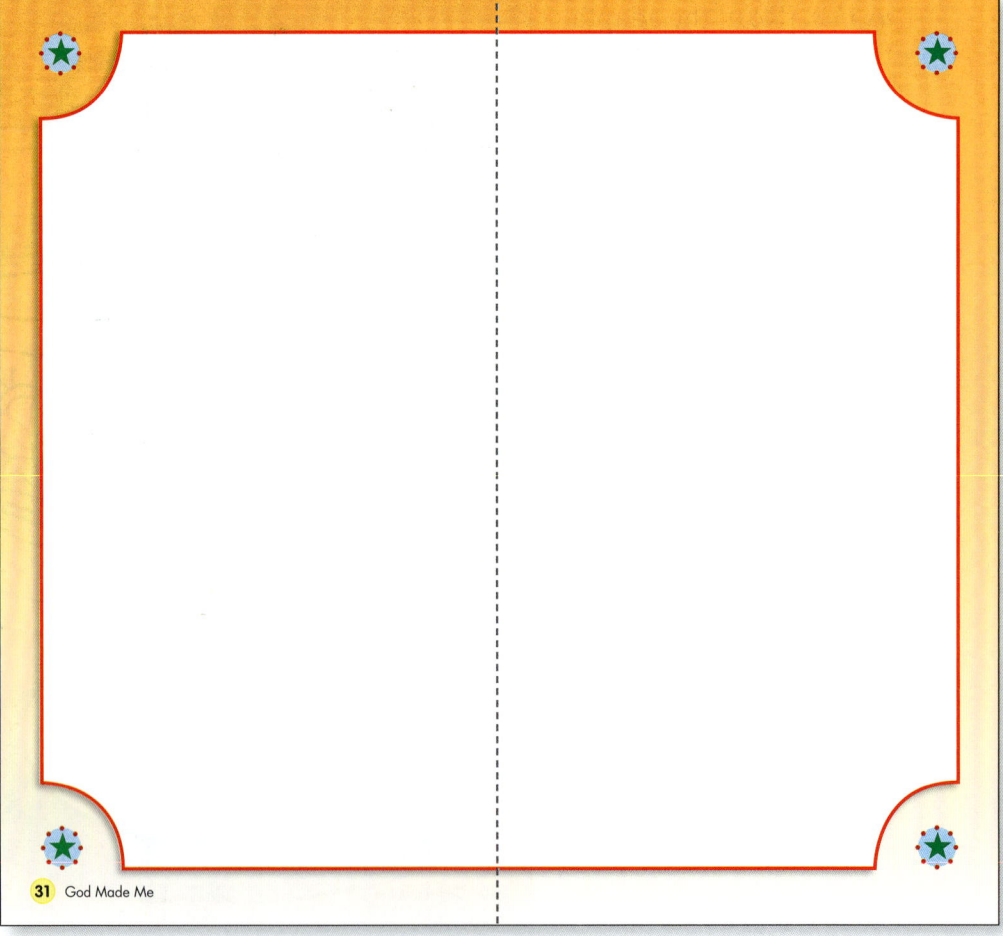

31 God Made Me

Page 32 is blank.

T62 UNIT 2 God Made Me Good

ENRICHING THE FAITH EXPERIENCE

Use the following activities to enrich the lesson or to replace an activity with one that better meets the needs of your group.

❶ Have the children bring in canned goods or toys to give to children who are in need.

❷ Hold a penny collection and donate the money to an organization that works for those who are poor.

❸ Tell the story from 1 Kings 17:7–16 of the widow who shared.

The Widow Who Shared

In the Bible there is a story about a woman who shared. Her husband had died, and she lived with her son. One year there was no rain where she lived. People were starving because no crops had grown. Finally, the woman had only a handful of flour left and a little oil. She was going to make bread for her son and herself. After that was gone they would have no food at all.

As the woman went to get sticks for a fire, she met an old man. He asked her for a cup of water and some bread. She made him some bread with her flour and oil. Do you know what happened after that? From that day on she never ran out of flour and oil. Whenever she needed some, they were there.

❹ Have the children recite "Sharing Poem" with you. Have them say "We share" twice at the right times, patting their thighs on each word and clapping twice afterwards.

Sharing Poem

When we're munching on a treat,
And our friend has none to eat,
What do we do?
We [Pat] share. [Pat] [Clap, clap]
We [Pat] share. [Pat] [Clap, clap]

When we're paging through a book,
And our sister wants a look,
What do we do?
We [Pat] share. [Pat] [Clap, clap]
We [Pat] share. [Pat] [Clap, clap]

When we're watching the TV,
And there's a show Dad wants to see,
What do we do?
We [Pat] share. [Pat] [Clap, clap]
We [Pat] share. [Pat] [Clap, clap]

When we're bouncing a new ball,
And someone's playing not at all,
What do we do?
We [Pat] share. [Pat] [Clap, clap]
We [Pat] share. [Pat] [Clap, clap]

When we're playing with a toy,
And here comes a girl or boy,
What do we do?
We [Pat] share. [Pat] [Clap, clap]
We [Pat] share. [Pat] [Clap, clap]

Mary Kathleen Glavich, S.N.D.

Chapter 10
I Can Smile

FAITH FOCUS

God made us to be happy.

Psalm 100:1–2; Mark 3:1–6

PREPARING THE FAITH EXPERIENCE

LISTENING

. . . I will see you again, and your hearts will rejoice, and no one will take your joy away from you.

John 16:22

REFLECTING

Perhaps you have heard the old riddle "What is the longest word in the dictionary?" The answer is *smiles*, because there is a mile in the middle. Smiles do go a long way. They brighten others' days, lighten dreary or tense tasks, and can change attitudes in a split second.

What a difference a smile makes. We look our best when we smile, which is why we smile for pictures. Smiles are one of our most effective nonverbal means of communication. They radiate joy, peace, encouragement, and love. A smiling face indicates a happy heart.

Christians possess a deep-seated joy born of the fact that we are loved by God. Buoyed up by God's love and care, we can endure worry, concern, and pain and still smile. We are assured that our problems in this world are nothing compared to the fullness of joy that awaits us in the next life. We believe that God works everything out for the good.

Joy is one of the Fruits of the Holy Spirit. Those who live as God's children have light steps, shining eyes, and smiles on their faces. They believe the words of Julian of Norwich that "All shall be well." The *Catechism* reminds us that "the future of humanity is in the hands of those who are capable of providing the generations to come with reasons for life and optimism." (1917)

Stereotypical images of saints might portray them as grim and serious—people intent on being perfect, who frowned on all those who weren't. Some saints, however, such as Lawrence, Don Bosco, Philip Neri, and Julie Billiart were known to be lighthearted and playful. They knew that faith is more a matter of love than of law. Saint Teresa of Jesus prayed, "Lord, may we be saved from sour-faced saints!"

Smiles are infectious, thus the saying "If you see someone without a smile, give that person yours." Bestowing a smile on someone is a gift of love. It doesn't cost anything and requires fewer muscles than frowning. It also makes us feel good.

There are many kinds of smiles. Some smiles are pasted on for the sake of duty or as a means to an end. Other smiles are spontaneous and sincere. They reach the eyes and create little lines in their corners. These are the smiles that make a face glow.

RESPONDING

God's Word calls us to respond in love. Respond to God now in the quiet of your heart, and perhaps through the journal that you are keeping this year.

- Whose smile stands out in my mind?

Jesus, give the children the joy that never ends.

T64 UNIT 2 *God Made Me Good*

Catechism of the Catholic Church

The themes of this chapter correspond to the following paragraphs: 1718, 2247, 2548.

THE FAITH EXPERIENCE
Child's Book pages 33–36

SCRIPTURE IN THIS CHAPTER
- *Mark 3:1–6*

MATERIALS
- Toys for CENTERING #2
- Option: camera
- Child-safe mirror
- Chapter 10 Scripture card
- Bible
- Crayons or markers

PREPARATION
- Write the children's names on pages 33 and 36.
- Place the Chapter 10 Scripture card for ACTING #1 in the Bible.

MUSIC 'N MOTION
Use *Music 'n Motion* page T251 and CD Track 2 "Healing" for this chapter. For a list of additional music, see page T302.

ENRICHING THE FAITH EXPERIENCE
Use the activities at the end of the chapter to enrich the lesson or to replace an activity with one that better meets the needs of your group.

BOOKS TO SHARE
Where's Your Smile, Crocodile by Claire Freedman (Peachtree Publishers, 2001)

Smile, Maisy! by Lucy Cousins (Candlewick, 2004)

The Happy Lion by Louise Fatio (Knopf Books for Young Readers, 2004)

I Like Me! by Nancy Carlson (Puffin, 1990)

Silly Sally by Audrey Wood (Harcourt Big Books, 1994)

SNACK
Suggestion: round cookies with smiling faces

ALTERNATIVE PROGRAMS

DAILY PROGRAM
Day 1: Centering, Sharing A
Day 2: Sharing B
Day 3: Enriching the Faith Experience choice
Day 4: Acting 1, Enriching the Faith Experience #3
Day 5: Enriching the Faith Experience choice, Acting #2 and #3

THREE-DAY PROGRAM
Day 1: Centering, Sharing A
Day 2: Sharing B
Day 3: Acting

I Can Smile CHAPTER 10 T65

10 I Can Smile

LEARNING OUTCOMES

The children will
- know that God wants them to be happy.
- desire to make others happy.

COMMENTS

1. We are made for happiness. Gradually, we learn that our true joy lies in being close to God. As we meet the challenges of life in this shadow land the best we can, we look forward to happiness without end in heaven where we will behold the beatific vision.

2. Three-year-olds are just beginning to know their own feelings. They should be encouraged to be aware of times when they are happy and times when they are sad. They know that it is good to be happy and can try to make others happy. In general three-year-olds can be described as happy and friendly. They enjoy others and delight in pleasing them.

CENTERING

1 Gather the children in a circle for *Music 'n Motion* time. Play the Unit 2 song (Track 2). Invite the children to do motions to the song along with you, using *Music 'n Motion* page T251.

2 Tell the children they may play with the toy that makes them happiest.

SHARING [A]

1 Distribute page 33 and talk about the picture.

- *How do you know that the children in the picture are happy?* (They are smiling.)
- *Why do you think they are happy?*
- *What makes you happy?*
- *God wants us to be happy. God made us so we can smile.*

2 Talk about smiling.

- *You smile when you get your picture taken.* [Option: Show the camera.] *You want to look your best. You look good when you smile. Your face looks brighter. God made you to be happy.*

Name _____

33 God Made Me

T66 UNIT 2 God Made Me Good

3 Hold up the mirror and let the children look in it individually to see what they look like when they smile.

4 Have the children smile at one another. Comment:

- *A smile is catching. When you smile at someone, that person usually smiles back. You make that person happy.*

- *Sometimes we don't feel like smiling. We might wake up in a bad mood and feel grumpy and grouchy. If we smile anyway, we feel better and other people feel better too.*

5 Play "Photographer." Have a child pretend to hold a camera while the rest of the children move about the room. Tell the class that when the photographer says "freeze," they are to hold their pose and smile until he or she says "click." Give several children a chance to be the photographer.

SHARING [B]

6 SCRIPTURE Tell the children how Jesus made people happy.

- *Jesus liked to make people happy. In the Bible (Mark 3:1–6) there is a story about a man Jesus made happy.* [Show the Bible.] *This man had something wrong with one of his hands. It was smaller than the other and had shriveled up. He couldn't use it. One day Jesus saw him. He called the man to him and told him to stretch out his hand. The man did as Jesus said, and Jesus healed his hand. The man was very happy. He went away smiling. All his family and friends were happy too.*

- *Jesus likes to make you happy too. We know that Jesus loves us. That makes us happy.*

7 Have the children circle the smiling children on page 34.

Circle the children who are smiling.

Family Time

Chapter 10: I Can Smile
In this lesson the children reflected on being happy. They learned that God wants them to be happy, and they were encouraged to try to make others happy. Ask your child what Jesus did to make others happy. Decide where your child could display the smiling face received in class.

Your Child
Children are sensitive to your moods. Try to maintain your child's natural happiness and peace by smiling and being cheerful, especially when you do not feel like it. Enjoy your child's lightheartedness by joining in with his or her silly talk, jokes, and games. Use humor to smooth over difficult events and to persuade your child to obey.

Reflect
Sing joyfully to God, all people. Live for God with gladness. Come before God with joyful song. (adapted from Psalm 100:1–2.)

Pray
God, may we praise you with joy forever.

Do
- In the mornings greet your child cheerfully.
- Make smiling face cookies with your child.
- Spend a day with your child. Do what makes him or her happy.
- Greet your neighbors and smile.
- With your child, plan a surprise for a family member that will make him or her happy.
- When you and your child have had a happy experience, thank God aloud.
- Before your child goes to bed, recall the day's happy events.
- Read to your child *Where's Your Smile, Crocodile?* by Claire Freedman. Name ways to spread happiness. Thank God for all the people who share happiness with others.

For more family resources, refer to the Family Activity Booklet and visit www.loyolapress.com/preschool.

34 God Made Me © LOYOLAPRESS.

ACTING

1 **PRAYER** Lead the children in praying an adaptation of Psalm 100:1–2, reading from the Scripture card in the Bible:

- **In the Bible there is a prayer about being happy. Let's pray it together. Say each part after me:**

  Sing joyfully to God, all people.

  Live for God with gladness.

  Come before God with joyful song.

2 Have each child draw a picture of his or her smiling face in the circle on page 35, using crayons or markers. Tell the children to display the face at home where it will remind them to smile.

3 Gather the children in a circle for *Music 'n Motion* time. Play the Unit 2 song (Track 2). Invite the children to do motions to the song along with you, using *Music 'n Motion* page T251.

Have the children take home their pages and show their family the Family Time section.

CHECKPOINT

- Were the learning outcomes achieved?
- Are any children unusually sad? Why?

35 God Made Me

Page 36 is blank.

T68 UNIT 2 God Made Me Good

ENRICHING THE FAITH EXPERIENCE

Use the following activities to enrich the lesson or to replace an activity with one that better meets the needs of your group.

❶ Teach the children the following song with the appropriate actions:

If You're Happy and You Know It (sheet music)

1. Stamp your feet.
2. Nod your head.
3. Do all three.

❷ Invite the children to thank God for the things that make them happy. Let them take turns naming these in a litany.

❸ Have the children draw their own smiling faces on paper plates. Give them yarn to glue on for hair. Pass out red glitter pens, yarn, red licorice, or cinnamon candies to glue on for a smile.

❹ Take pictures of the children and display them. Put a picture of Jesus in the middle and add the caption "Jesus makes us smile."

unit three

God Made Me Happy

The children will know that God wants them to be happy. They will develop the habit of giving praise and thanks to God.

11 I CAN TALK

The children reflect on their ability to speak. They learn to say "I love you" in sign language. With the help of a paper parrot, they practice saying polite words. They speak to God in prayer. Then they make a megaphone and repeat polite words.

12 I CAN PRAY

The children make a prayer book of pictures of things for which they are thankful. They talk about prayers of thanks and praise. Then they pray from their prayer books, first quietly alone and then aloud with the group. After hearing that morning and evening are good times for prayer, they make doorknob hangers as prayer reminders.

13   I CAN SING

After enjoying singing together, the children talk about singing and learn that it can be a prayer. They hear about Mary's song of joy and the angels' song on the night Jesus was born. They sing a prayer and then make a stand-up angel.

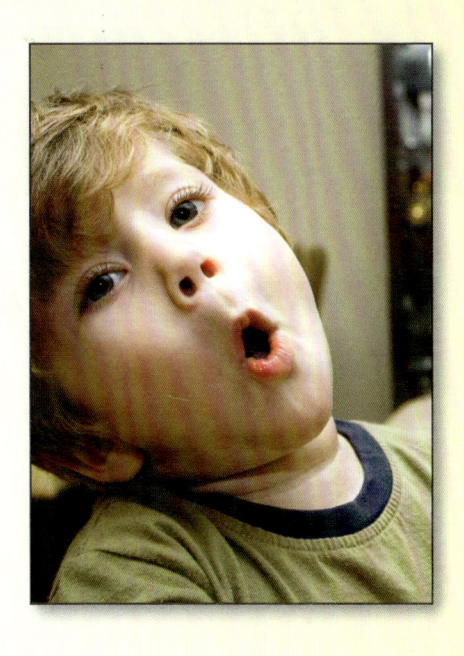

14   I CAN LAUGH

The children talk about laughing and being happy. They learn that God wants us to be happy and that because Jesus cares for us, we can be happy. They hear the story of Abraham and Sarah having a son, Isaac, whose name means "he laughs." They thank God for the gift of laughter and then make tube heads with laughing faces.

15   I CAN CELEBRATE

The children help decorate the room in green and then talk about celebrating. They hear about Jesus' picnic, for which Jesus provided food. Then they make party hats and have a picnic to celebrate green and God's goodness to them.

Chapter 11
I Can Talk

FAITH FOCUS

God gave us the gift of speech.

Ephesians 4:25–32; James 3:1–10

PREPARING THE FAITH EXPERIENCE

LISTENING

If anyone does not fall short in speech, he is a perfect man, able to bridle his whole body also. If we put bits into the mouths of horses to make them obey us, we also guide their whole bodies. It is the same with ships: even though they are so large and driven by fierce winds, they are steered by a very small rudder wherever the pilot's inclination wishes. In the same way the tongue is a small member and yet has great pretensions.

James 3:2–5

REFLECTING

The power of speech is a great gift unique to human beings. Because we can talk, we can communicate with others. We can let one another know what we think and how we feel.

Through speech we can teach, inspire, encourage, entertain, warn, motivate, affirm, and pray. Like our other gifts, however, speech can be used for good or for evil. Through speech we can also curse, ruin reputations, tempt people, lie, insult God, and hurt others. Someone aware of the negative side of speech observed that God gave us two eyes and two ears, but only one mouth.

The Word of God is powerful. According to Genesis, God created the universe by words alone. The Son of God is known as the Word, the Revelation of God. Jesus is the Word made flesh. This Word saved the universe.

Our words are also powerful. Once uttered, they can never be taken back. How often we have cause to regret foolish or hasty words. On the other hand, sometimes we regret not having spoken certain words, such as "I'm sorry" or "I love you." It is a wise person who can distinguish "a time to be silent, and a time to speak" (Ecclesiastes 3:7) and who knows precisely what words to say. Invoking the Holy Spirit for inspiration before a significant conversation, talk, or class is a good idea.

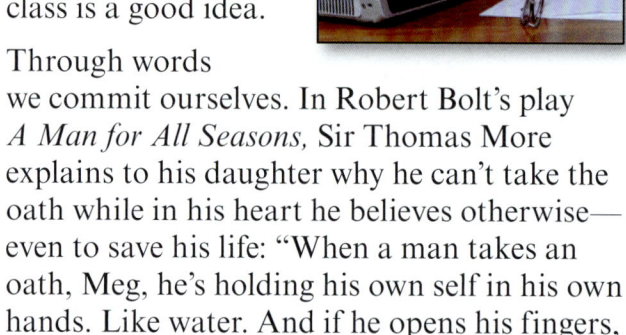

Through words we commit ourselves. In Robert Bolt's play *A Man for All Seasons,* Sir Thomas More explains to his daughter why he can't take the oath while in his heart he believes otherwise—even to save his life: "When a man takes an oath, Meg, he's holding his own self in his own hands. Like water. And if he opens his fingers, then—he needn't hope to find himself again."

Jesus is our model in the use of language. Study how he used words when he encountered the Samaritan woman, Zacchaeus, the Pharisees, the woman who anointed him, the woman accused of adultery, Pontius Pilate, and the apostles after the Resurrection. Christians should be masters of the language of love, the universal language.

RESPONDING

Having been nourished by God's Word, we are able to respond to God's great love for us. In prayer, respond to God's call to you to share his Word with others. You may also wish to respond in your prayer journal.

- What words have meant a great deal to me? What are my favorite words of Jesus?

Jesus, help the children speak only what is kind and true.

Catechism of the Catholic Church

The themes of this chapter correspond to the following paragraph: 2475.

THE FAITH EXPERIENCE

Child's Book pages 37–38

SCRIPTURE IN THIS CHAPTER
- *Psalm 51:17*

MATERIALS
- Cutout #28, parrot
- Option: microphone or megaphone
- Tape recorder
- Chapter 11 Scripture card
- Crayons or markers
- Stapler
- Perforated Card D

PREPARATION
- Write the children's names on page 37.
- Punch out the megaphone shapes on perforated Card D for the children and put their names on the megaphones.
- Place Chapter 11 Scripture card for SHARING #2 in the Bible.

MUSIC 'N MOTION
Use *Music 'n Motion* page T252 and CD Track 3 "Peace in My Heart" for this chapter. For a list of additional music, see page T302.

ENRICHING THE FAITH EXPERIENCE
Use the activities at the end of the chapter to enrich the lesson or to replace an activity with one that better meets the needs of your group.

BOOKS TO SHARE
Is Your Mama a Llama? by Deborah Guarino (Scholastic Inc., 2004)

Ask Mr. Bear by Marjorie Flack (Aladdin, 1971)

I Can Talk with God by Debby Anderson (Crossway Books, 2003)

My First Mother Goose by Blanche Fisher Wright (Cartwheel Books, 1996)

SNACK
Suggestion: crackers

ALTERNATIVE PROGRAMS

DAILY PROGRAM
Day 1: Centering, Sharing A
Day 2: Sharing B
Day 3: Enriching the Faith Experience choice
Day 4: Enriching the Faith Experience choice
Day 5: Acting

THREE-DAY PROGRAM
Day 1: Centering, Sharing A
Day 2: Sharing B, Enriching the Faith Experience choice
Day 3: Acting

11 I Can Talk

LEARNING OBJECTIVES
The children will
- thank God for the gift of speech.
- desire to speak with kindness.
- use polite expressions.

COMMENTS
1. Our gift of speech is a powerful means of communication. It enables us to convey our thoughts and feelings clearly and efficiently. Our words can be kind, noble, and loving—or cruel, crude, and deceitful. Jesus pointed out that it is what comes out of a person's mouth that can destroy. Three-year-olds already know that words can hurt or heal. This is a good time to teach the children polite expressions.

2. Three-year-olds have a vocabulary of about 1,200 words. They delight in talking, but not necessarily with others. As they talk to themselves, they are refining their language skills. Incorrect usage can be changed by using the correct expression immediately after a child's mistake, rather than by pointing out the error. At this age, children talk for fun and enjoy language play: coined words, rhyming words, and long words. Their play with others sometimes consists of quiet conversations.

3. Children tend to stutter at this age. Rather than calling attention to the stuttering by having the child repeat the words, simply ignore this normal developmental phase.

CENTERING
❶ Gather the children in a circle for *Music 'n Motion* time. Play the Unit 3 song (Track 3). Invite the children to do motions to the song along with you, using *Music 'n Motion* page T252.

❷ Record the children's voices on a tape recorder and let them listen to themselves. First tape each child individually saying his or her name and completing a sentence that begins "I like . . . " Then tape the children reciting a poem or singing a song together. If a tape recorder is not available, you might have the children pair off and hold pretend phone conversations.

SHARING [A]
❶ Distribute page 37 and talk about the picture.

- *What is the girl doing?* (Talking on the phone)
- *Whom do you think she is speaking to?*
- *Whom do you like to talk to?*
- *God gave us the power to speak. Animals make sounds, but they can't really talk.*

T74   UNIT 3   *God Made Me Happy*

2 **SCRIPTURE** Talk about our gift of speech. [Show Cutout #28, parrot.]

• *We have a surprise visitor today. This is Polly. What is Polly?* (Parrot)

• *Some parrots can say words, but they don't talk the way we do. They can't tell how they're feeling. They can't tell us a story.*

• *We can use the voice God gave us in different ways. We have a normal speaking voice—the one I'm using now. We have a whispering voice. Say "I love you" in a whisper.* [Pause.] *We have a shouting voice. Shout "I love you."* [Pause.] *We also have a singing voice. Sing after me: "I love you."* [Sing on one note.]

• *To make our voice louder, we sometimes use a microphone and speaker or a megaphone.* [Option: Show a microphone or megaphone.]

• [Read the adaptation of Psalm 51:17 from the Scripture card in the Bible.] *The Bible tells us another way we can use our voice: God, I will speak words of praise to you.*

3 Have the children pretend to be parrots and "fly" around the room. Introduce the activity:

• *Birds like Polly can't talk as we do, but they can do something we can't do. What is it?* (Fly)

4 Direct the children to look at page 38 and teach them the sign language there.

• *Some people can't hear. We can talk to them by making signs with our hands. Here you can see how to say "I love you" in sign language. Let's try it.*

SHARING [B]

5 Have the children practice saying polite words with the parrot, Cutout #28, talking to them.

• *God wants us to use our voices in good ways. We can use our voices to say kind, polite things. Let's play the game "What Do You Say?" with Polly.*

• [Polly speaks.] *What if you're walking down the street and you see me in a tree. What do you say?* (Hi, hello)

• *I ask "How are you?" and what do you say?* (I'm fine, thank you.)

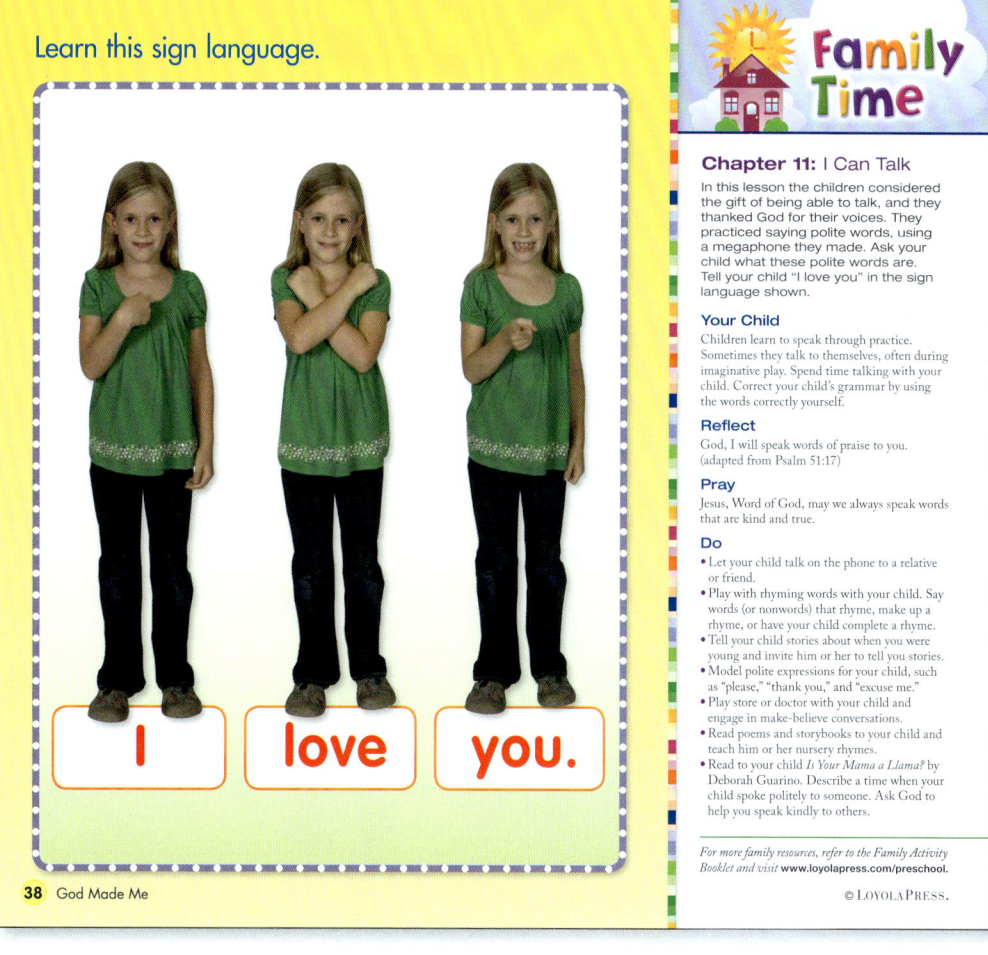

Learn this sign language.

I love you.

38 God Made Me

Family Time

Chapter 11: I Can Talk

In this lesson the children considered the gift of being able to talk, and they thanked God for their voices. They practiced saying polite words, using a megaphone they made. Ask your child what these polite words are. Tell your child "I love you" in the sign language shown.

Your Child
Children learn to speak through practice. Sometimes they talk to themselves, often during imaginative play. Spend time talking with your child. Correct your child's grammar by using the words correctly yourself.

Reflect
God, I will speak words of praise to you. (adapted from Psalm 51:17)

Pray
Jesus, Word of God, may we always speak words that are kind and true.

Do
• Let your child talk on the phone to a relative or friend.
• Play with rhyming words with your child. Say words (or nonwords) that rhyme, make up a rhyme, or have your child complete a rhyme.
• Tell your child stories about when you were young and invite him or her to tell you stories.
• Model polite expressions for your child, such as "please," "thank you," and "excuse me."
• Play store or doctor with your child and engage in make-believe conversations.
• Read poems and storybooks to your child and teach him or her nursery rhymes.
• Read to your child *Is Your Mama a Llama?* by Deborah Guarino. Describe a time when your child spoke politely to someone. Ask God to help you speak kindly to others.

For more family resources, refer to the Family Activity Booklet and visit www.loyolapress.com/preschool.

© LOYOLAPRESS.

I Can Talk CHAPTER **11** T75

- *All of a sudden I sneeze.*
- *What do you say?* (God bless you.)
- *I'm eating my favorite food—crackers—and you would like one. What do you say?* (May I please have one?)
- *I give you a cracker, and what do you say?* (Thank you.)
- *You eat the cracker and burp. What do you say?* (Excuse me.)

ACTING

1 **PRAYER** Lead the children in prayer.

- *Let's use our voices now to talk to God.*

    Use your whispering voice to thank God now for giving you your voice. [Pause.]

    Tell God what you like about your voice. [Pause.]

    Ask God to help you say kind things. [Pause.]

    Sing "I love you" to God.

2 Have the children make megaphones from perforated Card D. Let them decorate the megaphones. Then staple the ends together for them. Caution the children not to use their megaphone to shout in someone's ear.

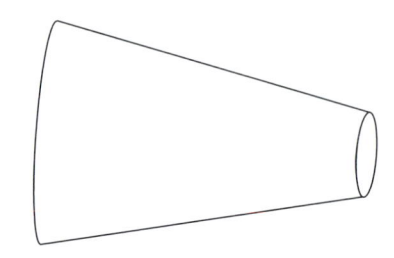

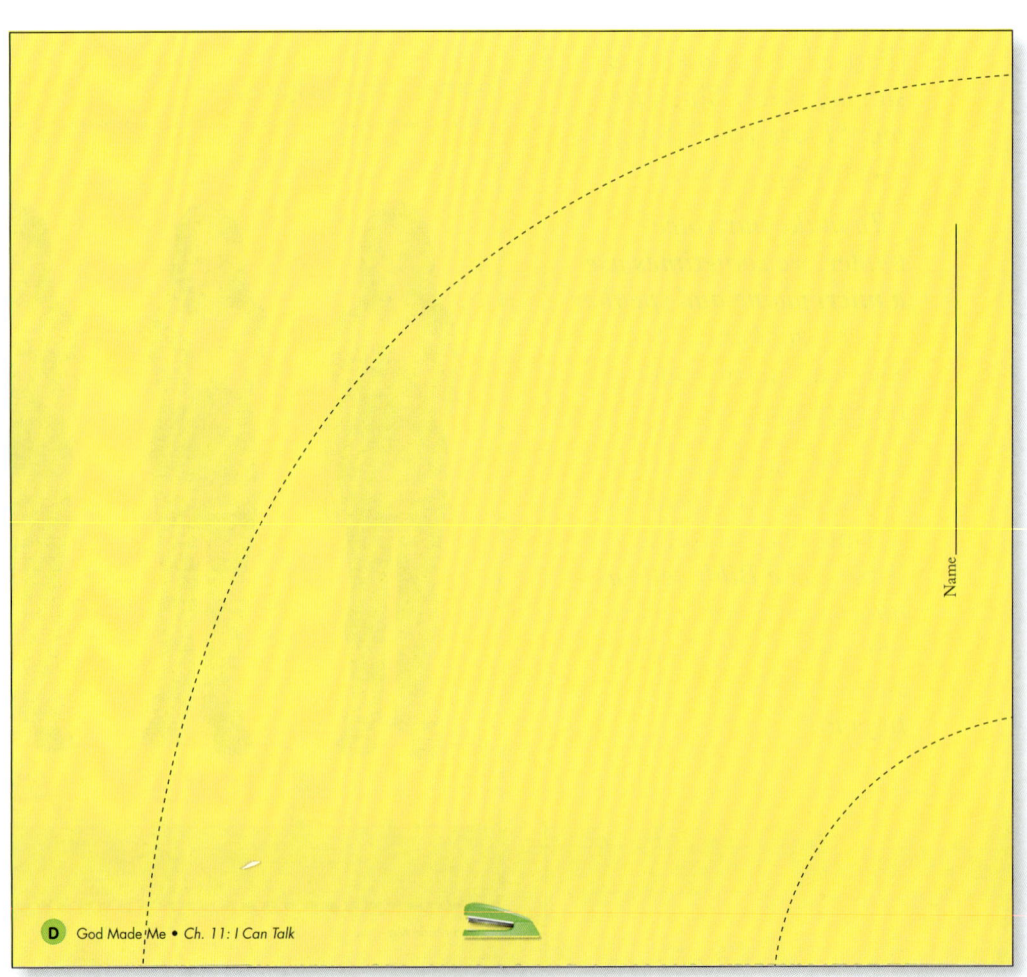

3 Let the children use their megaphones to repeat polite words after you, such as "thank you," "please," "pardon me," "excuse me," and "God bless you."

4 Gather the children in a circle for *Music 'n Motion* time. Play the Unit 3 song (Track 3). Invite the children to do motions to the song along with you, using *Music 'n Motion* page T252.

Have the children take home their pages and show their family the Family Time section.

CHECKPOINT

- Were the learning outcomes achieved?
- Do the children need more practice in using polite expressions?

D God Made Me • Ch. 11: I Can Talk

T76 UNIT 3 God Made Me Happy

ENRICHING THE FAITH EXPERIENCE

Use the following activities to enrich the lesson or to replace an activity with one that better meets the needs of your group.

❶ Show Cutouts #7–16, animals, one by one and have the children imitate the sound that each animal makes.

❷ Have the children use their voices to tell the following story with you. Tell them to raise their hands when they have an idea about what to say.

> Once upon a time I was going to _____. I was wearing _____. On the way I met _____ who was carrying _____. I said, _____. Then I _____ and went home because _____.

❸ Challenge the children to recite a nursery rhyme as fast as they can.

❹ Have the children practice saying their last names. Have them pretend to not know where they are and tell a police officer their names and where they live. Appoint one child as the police officer and let him or her wear a badge.

Chapter 12
I Can Pray

FAITH FOCUS
God hears us when we pray.

Matthew 6:5–6

PREPARING THE FAITH EXPERIENCE

LISTENING

*"This is how you are to pray:
 Our Father in heaven,
  hallowed be your name,
  your kingdom come,
  your will be done,
   on earth as in heaven.
  Give us today our daily bread;
  and forgive us our debts,
   as we forgive our debtors;
  and do not subject us to the final test,
   but deliver us from the evil one."*

Matthew 6:9–13

REFLECTING

Prayer is as essential to our lives as breathing. It is communication with God, the source and destiny of our being. Tradition defines prayer as "the lifting of the mind and heart to God." Saint Teresa of Jesus calls it "a conversation with one whom you know loves you."

Why pray? God does not need our prayers. Nor do prayers change God's mind. We pray because Jesus told us to. He himself prayed and taught us how to pray. We pray because we need to pray. The *Catechism* describes the kinds of prayer, which are all contained in the Eucharist, the ultimate prayer.

We need prayers of *adoration*. An inner urge impels us to acknowledge God's greatness in words and in reverential silence. We find fulfillment in praising our Creator. We bless God for having blessed us, and our prayers result in more blessings.

We need prayers of *petition*. We call upon an all-wise and all-loving God for help and are saved from despair. Prayers of petition keep us mindful of needs and spur us to action. Saint Ignatius advised, "Pray as though everything depends on God, but work as though everything depends on you." The foremost prayer of petition is *asking forgiveness*. When we sin, we damage our relationship with God and harm ourselves as well. When we admit our guilt, express sorrow, and ask forgiveness, we are restored to peace and wholeness. Another form of petition is prayer of *intercession*—asking for something for another person. When we pray intercessory prayer, we pray as Jesus, who intercedes for all people. As we pray for others, we strengthen and express the Communion of Saints.

We need prayers of *thanksgiving*. When someone shows kindness to us, we want to reciprocate. While we cannot repay God, who has given us everything and who has saved us, the least we can do is voice our thanks.

We need prayers of *love*. We are made for an intimate relationship with God, who is love. Prayer deepens that relationship. The more we pray, the more we become like God—good, kind, patient, forgiving, and compassionate. In other words, more Christlike.

RESPONDING

God's Word moves us to respond in word and action. Let God's Spirit work within you as you prayerfully consider how you are being called to respond to God's message to you today. Responding through your journal may help to strengthen your response.

- How much time do I devote to prayer each day?

God, give the children the gift of prayer.

T78　UNIT 3　*God Made Me Happy*

Catechism of the Catholic Church

The themes of this chapter correspond to the following paragraphs: 2559, 2565, 2639.

THE FAITH EXPERIENCE

Child's Book pages 39–40

SCRIPTURE IN THIS CHAPTER
- Matthew 6:6

MATERIALS
- Bible
- Chapter 12 Scripture card
- Perforated Card E
- Cutout #29, heart
- Option: prayer book
- Crayons or markers
- Option: magazine pictures and glue
- Option: glitter or glitter pens, yellow disks of felt, and glue

PREPARATION
- Write the children's names on page 39.
- Separate the two parts of perforated Card E. The "Thank You God" part will be used for CENTERING #2.
- Split the line and punch out the circle on the doorknob hangers on perforated Card E.
- Place the Chapter 12 Scripture card for SHARING #3 in the Bible.

MUSIC'N MOTION
Use *Music 'n Motion* page T252 and CD Track 3 "Peace in My Heart" for this chapter. For a list of additional music, see page T302.

ENRICHING THE FAITH EXPERIENCE
Use the activities at the end of the chapter to enrich the lesson or to replace an activity with one that better meets the needs of your group.

BOOKS TO SHARE
Teach Me to Pray by Pennie Kidd (Loyola Press, 1999)

I Can Pray! by Jennifer Holder and Diane Stortz (Standard Publishing Company, 2002)

Prayer Is . . . for Me! by Christine Tangvald (Bethany House, 2001)

Play and Pray: Toddler Prayers by Deb Lund (Morehouse Publishing, 2002)

SNACK
Suggestion: curved pretzels (like praying hands)

ALTERNATIVE PROGRAMS

DAILY PROGRAM
Day 1: Centering, Sharing A
Day 2: Sharing B
Day 3: Acting
Day 4: Enriching the Faith Experience choice
Day 5: Enriching the Faith Experience choice

THREE-DAY PROGRAM
Day 1: Centering, Sharing A
Day 2: Sharing B
Day 3: Acting

I Can Pray CHAPTER 12 T79

12 I Can Pray

LEARNING OBJECTIVES
The children will
- know that God hears prayers.
- begin the habit of praying.
- pray alone and with others.

COMMENTS

1. Prayer is not just an obligation but a joy. Just as two people who love each other enjoy being together, we enjoy spending time in prayer with God, who made us and loves us. Through prayer we strengthen our relationship with God.

2. Prayer shared with others unites us as the People of God. Saint John Vianney said, "Private prayer is like straw scattered here and there; if you set it on fire, it makes a lot of little flames. But gather these straws into a bundle and light them, and you get a mighty fire, rising like a column into the sky; public prayer is like that."

3. Prayers of petition and intercession are difficult for young children to comprehend and can often lead to misunderstanding. If, for example, they pray for rain and it does not rain, the children might conclude that either God does not love them or that God is not all-powerful. On the other hand, young children easily understand and delight in prayers of adoration, thanksgiving, and praise. They are also quite open to forms of prayer involving their bodies, such as singing, dancing, and motioning.

CENTERING

1 Gather the children in a circle for *Music 'n Motion* time. Play the Unit 3 song (Track 3). Invite the children to do motions to the song along with you, using *Music 'n Motion* page T252.

2 Help the children make prayer books from perforated Card E, following the directions here. [Option: Show the prayer book to introduce the activity and tell the children they will make their own.]

- *Tell the children to place their hands on the card with their fingers together and with the dotted line between their thumbs. Trace or have helpers trace each child's hands.* (Or the children might make handprints, using tempera paint-soaked paper towels as an ink pad.)

- *On the back of the card, have the children draw or glue pictures of several things for which they are thankful.*

- *Fold or have the children fold the card along the dotted line to form praying hands.*

T80 UNIT 3 God Made Me Happy

SHARING [A]

❶ **Distribute page 39 and talk** about praying.

- *What is the family in the picture doing?* (Praying)
- *Where are they?* (In church) *Have you ever been to church?*
- *We talk to God in church. Where else can we talk to God?* (At home, outside, anywhere)
- *God is everywhere. God always sees us and knows what we say and do.*

❷ **Tell the children about** prayers of thanks and praise.

- *For all the things God has made, we can say "I praise you, God." This means we think God is great and wonderful. God hears us.*
- *For making us and for giving us everything in the world, we can say "I thank you, God." And God hears us.*

❸ **SCRIPTURE** Read an adaptation of Matthew 6:6 from the Scripture card in the Bible:

- *Jesus tells us to pray to God, our Father. In the Bible he says "Pray silently in your heart in secret. Your Father will hear you."*

❹ **PRAYER** Invite the children to pray silently as they look at page 40.

- *Let's pray to God silently now. Turn over* the picture with the family on it. Here are things you can praise God for. You may spread out in the room so you can be alone and talk to God. Touch each thing in the picture and say to God, "I praise you." You can tell God other things too.

SHARING [B]

❺ **PRAYER** Call the children to come together again and pray.

- *We can pray alone. We can also pray together.*
- *Let's thank God together for the wonderful things on your picture.*
- *If you wish, you may stand when I whisper your name, show us one of the pictures you have in your prayer book, and say what it is. We will all say "Thank you, God."*

❻ **Introduce morning and** evening prayer.

- *We can pray in the morning as soon as we wake up and at night before we fall asleep.*
- *God always thinks about us. God likes it when we talk to him. God likes to hear us say "I love you."* [Show Cutout #29, heart.]

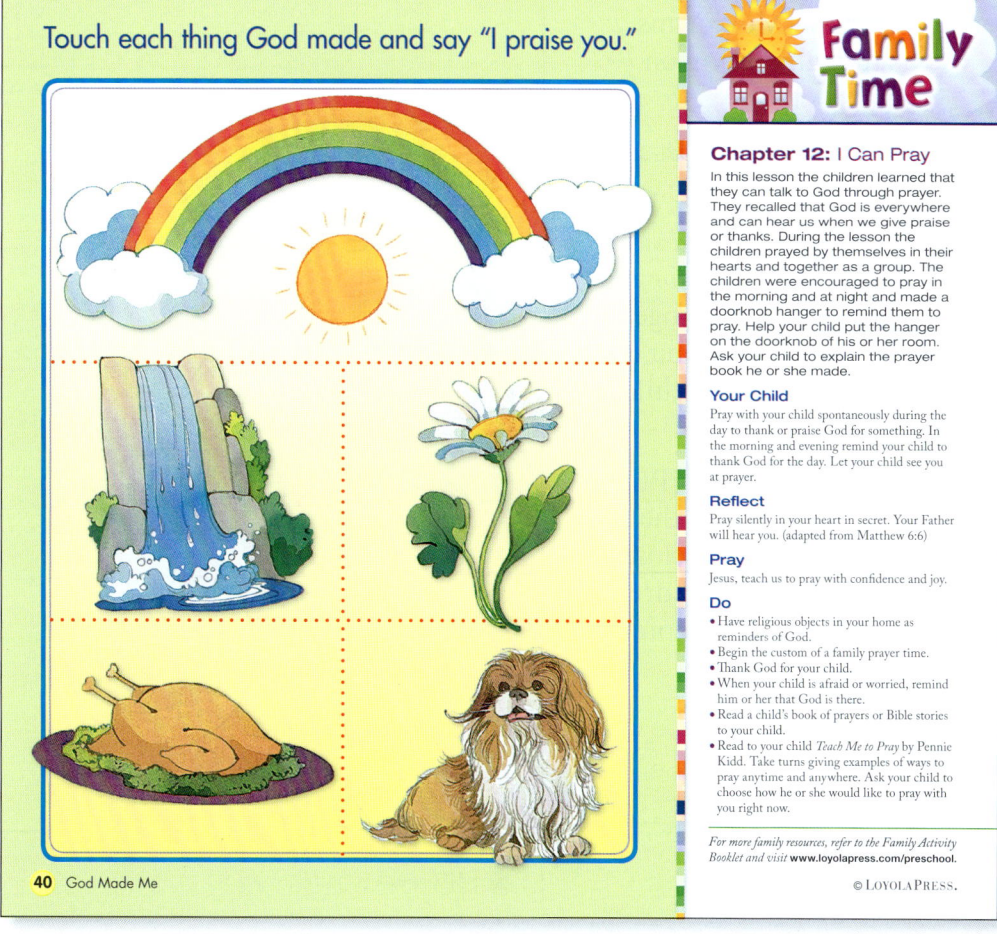

I Can Pray CHAPTER **12** T81

7 PRAYER Have the children pantomine praying.

- **Let's practice praying in the morning and at night. Do what I do.**

  It's morning. I wake up and rub my eyes. [Rub eyes.]

  I stretch and yawn. [Stretch and yawn.]

  I praise God for a new day. [Put hands together and say "I praise you, God, for a new day!" The children repeat.]

  During the day, whenever I see something good or when something good happens, I say "Thank you, God!" [Put hands together and say "Thank you, God!" The children repeat.]

  At night I put on my pajamas. [Move arms as though putting on pajamas.]

  I brush my teeth. [Brush teeth.]

  I jump into bed and say "Thank you, God, for the day!" [Put hands together and say "Thank you, God, for the day!" The children repeat.]

  Then I go to sleep. [Put hands together at the side of your head and close your eyes. The children will enjoy it if you pretend to snore.]

ACTING

1 PRAYER Invite the children to pray by singing the following song after you:

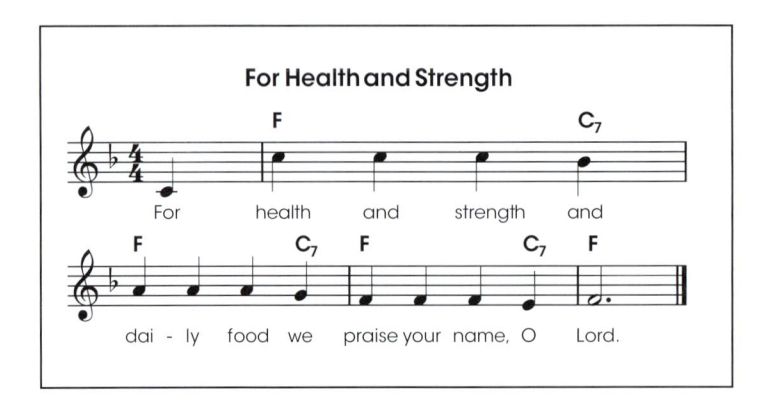

For Health and Strength

For health and strength and daily food we praise your name, O Lord.

2 Give the children the doorknob hangers from perforated Card E. Read the words ("I love you") and tell the children that the doorknob hanger will remind them to pray in the morning and at night. Show how to hang one on a doorknob. Mention that the hanger may be taped to a wall instead.

T82   UNIT 3   *God Made Me Happy*

❸ Have the children color the sun on the doorknob hanger or glue a yellow felt disk in the circle. They might also add glitter to the stars with glitter pens or a little glue and some help.

❹ Gather the children in a circle for *Music 'n Motion* time. Play the Unit 3 song (Track 3). Invite the children to do motions to the song along with you, using *Music 'n Motion* page T252.

Have the children take home their pages and show their family the Family Time section.

CHECKPOINT

- Were the learning outcomes achieved?
- Are there signs that the children are familiar with praying?
- How will you reinforce this chapter?

ENRICHING THE FAITH EXPERIENCE

Use the following activities to enrich the lesson or to replace an activity with one that better meets the needs of your group.

❶ Take the children to church. Tell them that we can show respect in church by being very quiet. Have them sit in one of the aisles. Let them sing the song in Acting #1 and talk to God in their hearts. Help them experience the church through their senses. Point out statues and stained-glass windows. Hold an unlit candle to their noses to smell. Play the organ. Ring the bell. Have them feel the smoothness of the wooden pews.

❷ **PRAYER** Teach the children to pray before their snacks:

*God is great. God is good.
So we thank God for our food.
Yeah, God!*

❸ Have the children practice being silent. Ask them what sounds they can hear when it is quiet.

❹ Use the following poem, with the appropriate movements, as a settling activity, especially to prepare the children for prayer:

> I wiggle my fingers.
> I wiggle my toes.
> I wiggle my shoulders.
> I wiggle my nose.
> Now all the wiggles are out of me,
> and I can sit so quietly.

I Can Pray **CHAPTER 12** **T83**

Chapter 13
I Can Sing

FAITH FOCUS

We can sing to praise God.

Luke 1:26–31; Luke 2:8–14; Ephesians 5:18–20

PREPARING THE FAITH EXPERIENCE

LISTENING

Come, let us sing joyfully to the Lord;
  cry out to the rock of our salvation.
Let us greet him with a song of praise,
  joyfully sing out our psalms.

Psalm 95:1–2

REFLECTING

Singing and worship go together. Singing lifts our spirits and praises God. It involves more energy than merely saying the words of the prayers. Perhaps this explains Saint Augustine's claim that "Singing well is praying twice." At our liturgies we join our voices in song to praise and thank God. Singing together helps create unity.

Many of the greatest musical compositions, such as Handel's *Messiah,* were inspired by faith. Gregorian chant, which has soothed and stirred hearts for centuries, can be heard on CDs. One recording, *Chant,* by the Benedictine Monks of Santo Domingo de Silos even reached the Top Ten! Among the most revered religious songs are the psalms in the Bible. Although the original melodies of these songs have been lost, the psalms have been set to music by composers. We sing them at Mass, in the Liturgy of the Hours, on retreats, or perhaps when working around the house.

Psalms express our deep feelings toward God in our various moods and situations—

When we are overwhelmed by the greatness of God's creation: *"[H]ow awesome is your name through all the earth!"* (8:2)

When we need help: *"Hear my words, O Lord; / listen to my sighing."* (5:2)

When we are moved to tell God of our love: *"I love you, Lord, my strength, / Lord, my rock, my fortress, my deliverer."* (18:2–3)

When we are in danger: *"Do not stay far from me, / for trouble is near, / and there is no one to help."* (22:12)

When we need to know what to do: *"Guide me in your truth and teach me. . ."* (25:5)

When we need forgiveness: *"Have mercy on me, God, in your goodness; / in your abundant compassion blot out my offense."* (51:3)

When a prayer has been answered: *"I love the Lord, who listened / to my voice in supplication, / Who turned an ear to me / on the day I called."* (116:1–2)

Memorizing psalm verses enables us to pray them as a mantra (a short prayer repeated over and over). As did other Jewish people, Jesus prayed and sang the psalms often. In this tradition Saint Paul exhorts us, "[B]e filled with the Spirit, addressing one another [in] psalms and hymns and spiritual songs, singing and playing to the Lord in your hearts. . ." (Ephesians 5:18–19)

RESPONDING

Having reflected upon God's Word, take some time now to continue to respond to God in prayer. You might wish to use your journal to record your responses.

- What are my favorite hymns?

God, may the children always sing praise to you.

T84 UNIT 3 God Made Me Happy

Catechism of the Catholic Church

The themes of this chapter correspond to the following paragraphs: 1061–1065, 1156–1158, 2642.

THE FAITH EXPERIENCE

Child's Book pages 41–44

SCRIPTURE IN THIS CHAPTER
- *Luke 1:46–47*
- *Luke 2:14*

MATERIALS
- Bible
- Chapter 13 Scripture card
- Cutouts: #30, Mary; #31, angel
- Option: song book from church
- Crayons or markers
- Option: glitter or glitter pens, glue, and cotton

PREPARATION
- Place Chapter 13 Scripture card for SHARING #5–6 in the Bible.
- Write the children's names on pages 41 and 44.

MUSIC 'N MOTION
Use *Music 'n Motion* page T252 and CD Track 3 "Peace in My Heart" for this chapter. For a list of additional music, see page T302.

ENRICHING THE FAITH EXPERIENCE
Use the activities at the end of the chapter to enrich the lesson or to replace an activity with one that better meets the needs of your group.

BOOKS TO SHARE
All God's Critters Got a Place in the Choir by Bill Staines (Puffin, 1993)

Sing-Along Song by JoAnn Early Macken (Viking Juvenile, 2004)

The Baby Chicks Are Singing/Los Pollitos Dicen by Ashley Wolff (L.B. Kids, 2005)

Mary Wore Her Red Dress by Merle Peek (Clarion Books, 2006)

SNACK
Suggestion: drinkable yogurt

ALTERNATIVE PROGRAMS

DAILY PROGRAM
Day 1: Centering, Sharing A
Day 2: Sharing B
Day 3: Enriching the Faith Experience choice
Day 4: Enriching the Faith Experience choice
Day 5: Acting

THREE-DAY PROGRAM
Day 1: Centering, Sharing A
Day 2: Sharing B
Day 3: Acting

I Can Sing CHAPTER 13 T85

13   I Can Sing

LEARNING OUTCOMES

The children will
- know that a song can be a prayer.
- thank God for the gift of song.
- become acquainted with Mary and the angels.

COMMENTS

1. In many cultures throughout the centuries, worship has included singing. The *Catechism* states, "The musical tradition of the universal Church is a treasure of inestimable value, greater even than that of any other art. The main reason for this preeminence is that, as a combination of sacred music and words, it forms a necessary or integral part of solemn liturgy." (1156) Teaching children to enjoy their own singing voices and the experience of singing together will help ensure their active participation in liturgical celebrations later.

2. Three-year-old children are not yet shy about singing solos in public. They invent their own songs spontaneously. Take advantage of these things and encourage them to sing as they participate in appropriate activities and games. Make up little poems, especially poems about the children themselves. Sing them to the tunes of nursery rhymes and familiar children's songs.

CENTERING

❶ Gather the children in a circle for *Music 'n Motion* time. Play the Unit 3 song (Track 3). Invite the children to do motions to the song along with you, using *Music 'n Motion* page T252.

❷ Hold a short sing-along, selecting some of the children's favorite songs.

SHARING [A]

❶ Distribute page 41 and talk about the picture.

- *What is happening in the picture?* (The family is singing together while the grandfather plays the piano.)
- *Who is singing?* (Mother, father, children, grandfather, dog, and bird)
- *Do you like to sing?*
- *What songs do you sing at home?*

T86   UNIT 3   *God Made Me Happy*

- *When do you sing?* (In the bathtub, in church, in school, in the car)
- *Sometimes we sing because we are happy.*
- *It's fun to sing together.*

2 Talk about singing as a form of praise.

- *We can sing to praise and thank God for everything. Our singing can be a prayer.*
- *People sing in church as a prayer to God.* [Option: Show a song book from church.]

3 PRAYER Have the children sing "Head, Shoulders, Knees and Toes" with the actions that they learned in Chapter 6. [See page 43.] Introduce the activity:

- *Let's praise and thank God for our wonderful bodies by singing "Head, Shoulders, Knees and Toes." First, in your heart, say "This song is for you, God."*

4 Direct the children to find and circle the five hidden singing birds on page 42.

SHARING [B]

5 SCRIPTURE Tell about Mary's song of joy.

- *Do you know who this is?* [Show Cutout #30, Mary.] (Mary, the Mother of Jesus)
- *Do you know who this is?* [Show Cutout #31, angel.] (Angel) *Angels live with God. They are God's messengers.*
- *Before Jesus was born, an angel came to Mary with a message. The angel told Mary that she was going to have a baby named Jesus.*
- *Mary was very happy to hear this. She went to visit her relative Elizabeth, and when she saw her, Mary sang a song about how good God is. Mary's song was a prayer.*
- [Read the adaptation of Luke 1:46–47 from the Scripture card in the Bible.] *Listen to Mary's prayer: "I sing praise to the Lord; I rejoice in God my savior."*

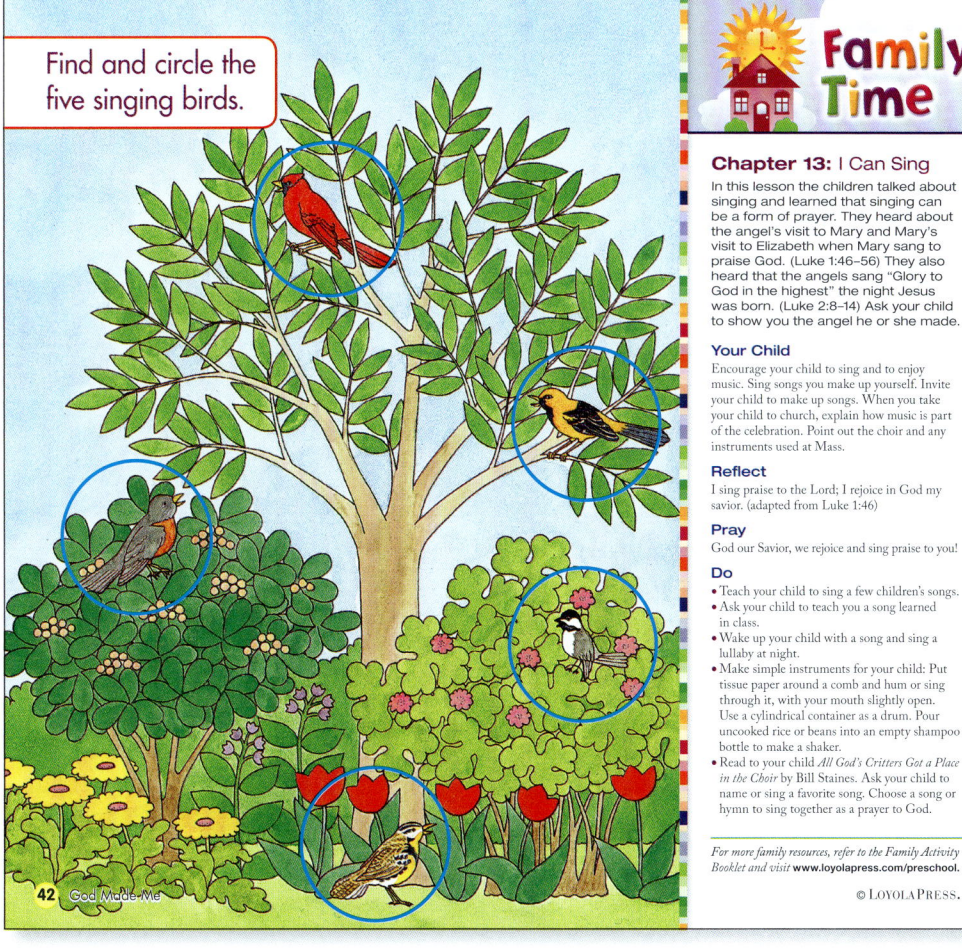

Find and circle the five singing birds.

Family Time

Chapter 13: I Can Sing

In this lesson the children talked about singing and learned that singing can be a form of prayer. They heard about the angel's visit to Mary and Mary's visit to Elizabeth when Mary sang to praise God. (Luke 1:46–56) They also heard that the angels sang "Glory to God in the highest" the night Jesus was born. (Luke 2:8–14) Ask your child to show you the angel he or she made.

Your Child
Encourage your child to sing and to enjoy music. Sing songs you make up yourself. Invite your child to make up songs. When you take your child to church, explain how music is part of the celebration. Point out the choir and any instruments used at Mass.

Reflect
I sing praise to the Lord; I rejoice in God my savior. (adapted from Luke 1:46)

Pray
God our Savior, we rejoice and sing praise to you!

Do
- Teach your child to sing a few children's songs.
- Ask your child to teach you a song learned in class.
- Wake up your child with a song and sing a lullaby at night.
- Make simple instruments for your child: Put tissue paper around a comb and hum or sing through it, with your mouth slightly open. Use a cylindrical container as a drum. Pour uncooked rice or beans into an empty shampoo bottle to make a shaker.
- Read to your child *All God's Critters Got a Place in the Choir* by Bill Staines. Ask your child to name or sing a favorite song. Choose a song or hymn to sing together as a prayer to God.

For more family resources, refer to the Family Activity Booklet and visit www.loyolapress.com/preschool.

© LOYOLAPRESS.

6 **SCRIPTURE** Tell about the angels' song.

• *Later, when Jesus was born, angels came to some shepherds. Shepherds are people who take care of sheep. The angels told the shepherds that Jesus was born. Then the angels sang a song to praise God.* [Read Luke 2:14 from the Scripture card in the Bible.] *They sang, "Glory to God in the highest."*

• [Show the Bible.] *The stories about Mary and the angels are in the Bible.*

7 Teach the children to sing "Glory to God in the highest" on one note.

• *Let's sing the prayer the angels sang. Repeat after me.* [Sing.] *Now when you sing "glory," put your arms straight out at your side. When you sing "highest," put your arms up.* [Demonstrate.]

ACTING

1 **PRAYER** Lead the children in a litany. Invite them to add prayers.

• *Let's sing a prayer to God now. I'll say something great that God did, and we'll all sing "Glory to God in the highest." We'll try to make our song beautiful like Mary's song and the angels' song.*

God made us wonderful . . .

God gave us voices . . .

God made us able to sing . . .

God gave us Mary . . .

God sent Jesus . . .

2 Have the children decorate the angel's robe on page 43. With help, they might glue cotton balls on the clouds or glue glitter or use glitter pens on the robe. Show the children how to fold back the sides of the card so that the angel stands.

3 Gather the children in a circle for *Music 'n Motion* time. Play the Unit 3 song (Track 3). Invite the children to do motions to the song along with you, using *Music 'n Motion* page T252.

Have the children take home their pages and show their family the Family Time section.

CHECKPOINT

• Were the learning outcomes achieved?

• What indication is there that the children enjoy singing?

Page 44 is blank.

T88　UNIT 3　*God Made Me Happy*

ENRICHING THE FAITH EXPERIENCE

Use the following activities to enrich the lesson or to replace an activity with one that better meets the needs of your group.

1 Teach or pray with the children these psalm verses about singing:

> *The promises of the LORD I will sing forever*[.] (Psalm 89:2)
>
> *It is good to give thanks to the LORD,*
> *to sing praise to your name, Most High*[.] (Psalm 92:2)

2 Teach the children "I'm Gonna Sing When the Spirit Says Sing." Add verses by substituting words for *sing*, such as *dance*, *hop*, *jump*, *spin*, and *clap*.

I'm Gonna Sing When the Spirit Says Sing

(musical score: I'm gon-na sing when the spi-rit says sing; I'm gon-na sing when the spi-rit says sing; I'm gon-na sing when the spi-rit says sing, and o-bey the spi-rit of the Lord.)

3 Teach the children to sing "Amen." Tell them it is a prayer word that means "yes." Read verses such as the following and have the children sing "Amen" as shown.

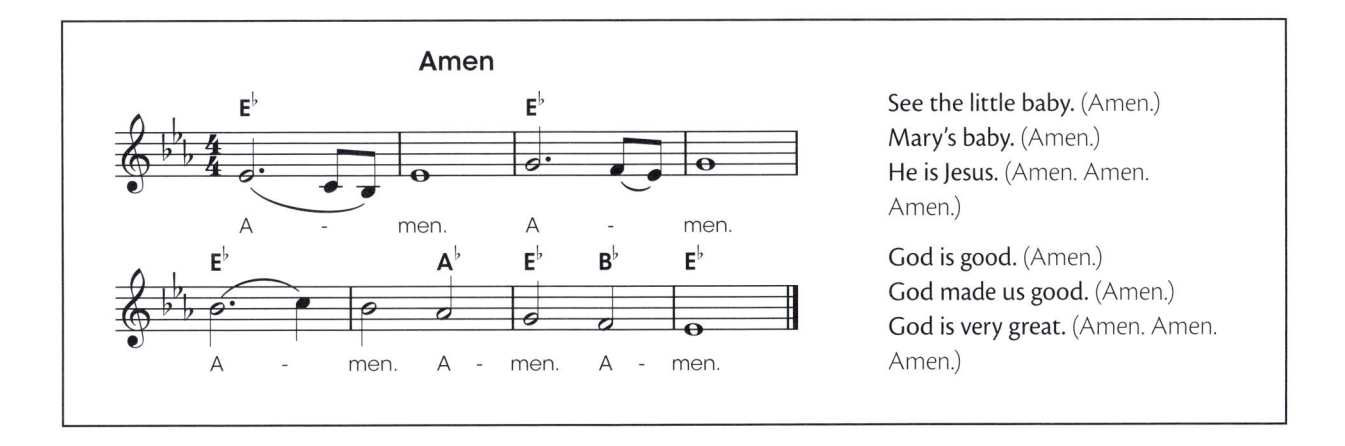

Amen

(musical score: A-men. A-men. A-men. A-men. A-men.)

4 Make maracas for the children to shake in time to a song. Put uncooked rice or beans inside a plastic or paper drinking cup and tape another cup to it, brim to brim. Or use a long-necked plastic ketchup, vinegar, or shampoo bottle.

5 Invite a singer to sing for and with the children.

See the little baby. (Amen.)
Mary's baby. (Amen.)
He is Jesus. (Amen. Amen. Amen.)

God is good. (Amen.)
God made us good. (Amen.)
God is very great. (Amen. Amen. Amen.)

I Can Sing CHAPTER **13** T89

Chapter 14
I Can Laugh

FAITH FOCUS
God gives us the gift of laughter.
Sirach 30:22

PREPARING THE FAITH EXPERIENCE

LISTENING

*A joyful heart is the health of the body,
but a depressed spirit dries up the bones.*
Proverbs 17:22

REFLECTING

Anyone who has visited a zoo knows that God has a sense of humor as well as a fantastic imagination. Monkeys, giraffes, and duck-billed platypuses reflect the lightheartedness of their Creator. If we who are made in God's image and likeness can laugh, then surely God can laugh too—in some spiritual way. No doubt we ourselves give God plenty to chuckle over.

Usually we take ourselves too seriously. Once we realize that we are fallible and imperfect and that God loves us despite our flaws, we can laugh at our mistakes. Instead of trying to impress people with our achievements and knowledge, we will entertain and delight them with stories of some silly or stupid things we have done, things with which everyone can identify.

Because Jesus was truly human, he laughed. Surely he laughed as he played with the children. He must have laughed to see Zacchaeus in the tree. Perhaps he even roared with laughter at Peter's face when this fisherman found money to pay taxes in a fish—a divine practical joke. During his conversation with the Samaritan woman at the well, Jesus must have had difficulty keeping in the laughter. He probably chuckled when she left her water jar behind and ran off to tell others about him. Certainly Jesus must have laughed with pleasure each time he saw the ecstatic joy of someone he cured.

Laughter is psychologically healthy. It is a wise person who can see humor in various situations—or can add it, when appropriate, thus possibly helping prevent ulcers and nervous breakdowns. A funny remark can reduce the tension during a somber meeting and in dangerous, awkward, or embarrassing circumstances. In addition, it has been proved that laughter is physically healthy, confirming what the Bible says: "Gladness of heart is the very life of man, / cheerfulness prolongs his days." (Sirach 30:22)

Even though the world may be in turmoil and our personal life a shambles, with the right perspective and priorities, we can still laugh, for Christ has redeemed us. His Resurrection justifies laughter. In *The Little Prince* by Antoine de Saint-Exupéry, the Little Prince leaves his friend the gift of laughter. Jesus gives us this gift, and we can pass it on.

RESPONDING

God's Word calls us to respond in love. Respond to God now in the quiet of your heart, and perhaps through the journal that you are keeping this year.

- Do people describe me as cheerful, sad, serious, or grumpy?

Holy Spirit, make the children merry.

T90 UNIT 3 *God Made Me Happy*

Catechism of the Catholic Church

The themes of this chapter correspond to the following paragraphs: 1718, 1723, 1829.

THE FAITH EXPERIENCE

Child's Book pages 45–48

SCRIPTURE IN THIS CHAPTER
- *Genesis 17:15–19; 18:1–15; 21:1–7*

MATERIALS
- Bible
- Cutout #32, baby
- Yarn or ribbon
- Crayons or markers
- Stapler

PREPARATION
- Write the children's names on pages 45 and 47.
- Cut strands of yarn or ribbon as hair for the heads on page 47. If you wish, curl the ribbon, using scissor blades.

MUSIC 'N MOTION
Use *Music 'n Motion* page T252 and CD Track 3 "Peace in My Heart" for this chapter. For a list of additional music, see page T302.

ENRICHING THE FAITH EXPERIENCE
Use the activities at the end of the chapter to enrich the lesson or to replace an activity with one that better meets the needs of your group.

BOOKS TO SHARE
Rosie's Walk by Pat Hutchins (Aladdin, 2005)

The Day the Goose Got Loose by Reeve Lindbergh (Puffin, 1995)

The Adventures of Curious George by H. H. Rey (Houghton Mifflin, 1995)

Animals Should Definitely Not Wear Clothing by Judi Barrett (Aladdin, 1988)

SNACK
Suggestion: animal crackers

ALTERNATIVE PROGRAMS

DAILY PROGRAM
Day 1: Centering, Sharing A
Day 2: Enriching the Faith Experience choice
Day 3: Sharing B
Day 4: Enriching the Faith Experience choice
Day 5: Acting

THREE-DAY PROGRAM
Day 1: Centering, Sharing A
Day 2: Sharing B
Day 3: Acting

I Can Laugh CHAPTER 14 T91

14   I Can Laugh

LEARNING OUTCOMES
The children will
- know that God is with them.
- appreciate being able to laugh.
- be familiar with the story of Isaac.

COMMENTS

1. Pictures of the laughing Christ are unusual because we do not often think of Jesus as laughing. Nowhere in Scripture does it mention that he laughed. But because Jesus was truly human, he must have laughed. Laughter is one of the gifts that distinguishes us from animals. Because of our intellect, we recognize the incongruous and respond with laughter.

2. Three-year-olds love to laugh. Oddly, they laugh most at human predicaments, such as people falling or things breaking. The producers of cartoon shows know this. Cultivate a sense of humor in the children by pointing out what is funny in certain situations. Join in the verbal horseplay that children this age delight in. Enjoy laughing frequently with the children.

CENTERING

❶ Gather the children in a circle for *Music 'n Motion* time. Play the Unit 3 song (Track 3). Invite the children to do motions to the song along with you, using *Music 'n Motion* page T252.

❷ Have the children play "Belly Laughs." Explain that they are going to play a funny game. Form a line of girls and a line of boys. Help the two lines lie on the floor so that the head of each child (except the first one in each line) rests on the stomach of another child. Tell the two children at the beginning of the lines to laugh. The laughter will ripple through the lines.

SHARING [A]

❶ Talk about laughing.

- *It's fun to laugh, isn't it? Laughing means we are happy.*
- *What makes you laugh?*
- *Who sometimes tickles you a little bit to make you laugh?*
- *God made us so that we can laugh. God likes to hear us laughing. Isn't God good?*

T92   UNIT 3   *God Made Me Happy*

2 Distribute page 45 and talk about Jesus.

• *How can you tell that the people in the picture are happy?* (They are laughing.)

• *Why do you think they are happy?* (They are friends. They like being with Jesus. They like being together.)

• *Jesus is with us too. We can't see him, but we know he is here and that he loves us. Jesus is our friend. We can laugh and be happy because Jesus cares for us.*

3 Guide the children in drawing lines from the laughing child to the animals on page 46. Talk about what the children find funny about the animals. Comment:

• *Some of the animals that God made do funny things that make us laugh.*

SHARING [B]

4 Play "Silly Race." Have the children line up across one side of the room. Tell them to run to the other side, do something silly, and then run back.

5 SCRIPTURE Tell the story of Isaac based on Genesis 17:15–19; 18:1–15; 21:1–7. Show the Bible.

• *In the Bible is a good story about how God made people laugh. You can help me tell the story. Whenever I say "laughed" or "laughs," say "Ho, ho ho."*

God Made People Laugh

Once upon a time there was a man named Abraham. He was married to Sarah. They didn't have any children although they wanted them very much. One day when they were very, very old, God told Abraham he would have a son. Abraham laughed. [Ho, ho, ho] He rolled on the floor he laughed so hard. [Ho, ho, ho] A while later some visitors told Abraham again that he would have a son. This time Sarah heard. Then she laughed. [Ho, ho, ho] She knew that she was too old to have a baby.

Then guess what happened. Sarah had a baby boy. [Show Cutout #32, baby.] Abraham named him Isaac. The name Isaac means "he laughs." [Ho, ho ho] God must have laughed too when Isaac was born. [Ho, ho, ho]

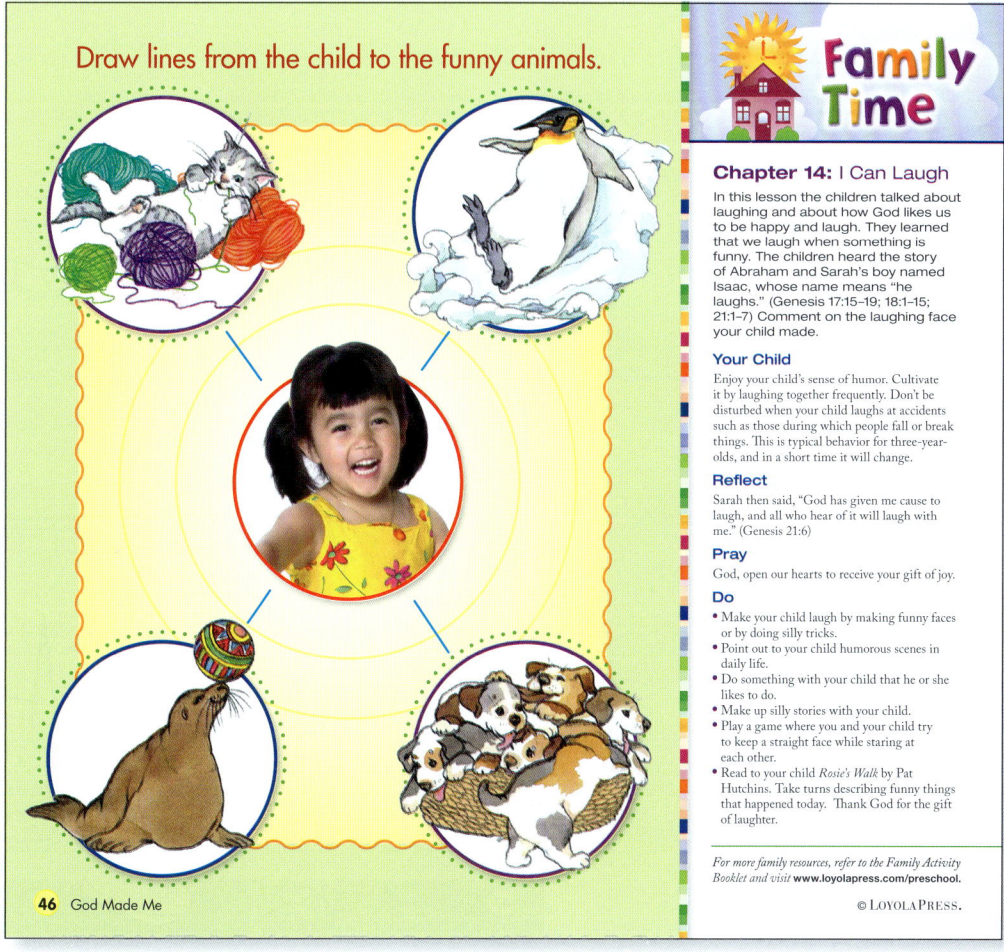

Draw lines from the child to the funny animals.

Family Time

Chapter 14: I Can Laugh

In this lesson the children talked about laughing and about how God likes us to be happy and laugh. They learned that we laugh when something is funny. The children heard the story of Abraham and Sarah's boy named Isaac, whose name means "he laughs." (Genesis 17:15–19; 18:1–15; 21:1–7) Comment on the laughing face your child made.

Your Child
Enjoy your child's sense of humor. Cultivate it by laughing together frequently. Don't be disturbed when your child laughs at accidents such as those during which people fall or break things. This is typical behavior for three-year-olds, and in a short time it will change.

Reflect
Sarah then said, "God has given me cause to laugh, and all who hear of it will laugh with me." (Genesis 21:6)

Pray
God, open our hearts to receive your gift of joy.

Do
• Make your child laugh by making funny faces or by doing silly tricks.
• Point out to your child humorous scenes in daily life.
• Do something with your child that he or she likes to do.
• Make up silly stories with your child.
• Play a game where you and your child try to keep a straight face while staring at each other.
• Read to your child *Rosie's Walk* by Pat Hutchins. Take turns describing funny things that happened today. Thank God for the gift of laughter.

For more family resources, refer to the Family Activity Booklet and visit www.loyolapress.com/preschool.

© LOYOLAPRESS.

46 God Made Me

I Can Laugh **CHAPTER 14** **T93**

ACTING

1 **PRAYER** Lead the children in prayer.

• *God is with us now. God sees us laughing together. Let's thank God for being able to laugh. Say after me:*

   Thank you, God, for laughter.

2 Help the children make laughing girls or boys from page 47. First have them complete the picture, add details, and color the child. Then have the children trace the smile using a red crayon or marker. Help them staple the sides of the cards to form long tube bodies. The children can glue or staple yarn or ribbon along the top as hair.

3 Gather the children in a circle for *Music 'n Motion* time. Play the Unit 3 song (Track 3). Invite the children to do motions to the song along with you, using *Music 'n Motion* page T252.

Have the children take home their pages and show their family the Family Time section.

Note: If you will teach Chapter 15 next, tell the children that they might like to wear something green next time they come to school because they will be celebrating the color green. If you wish, notify the parents.

CHECKPOINT

- Were the learning outcomes achieved?
- What signs were there that the children enjoyed this lesson?

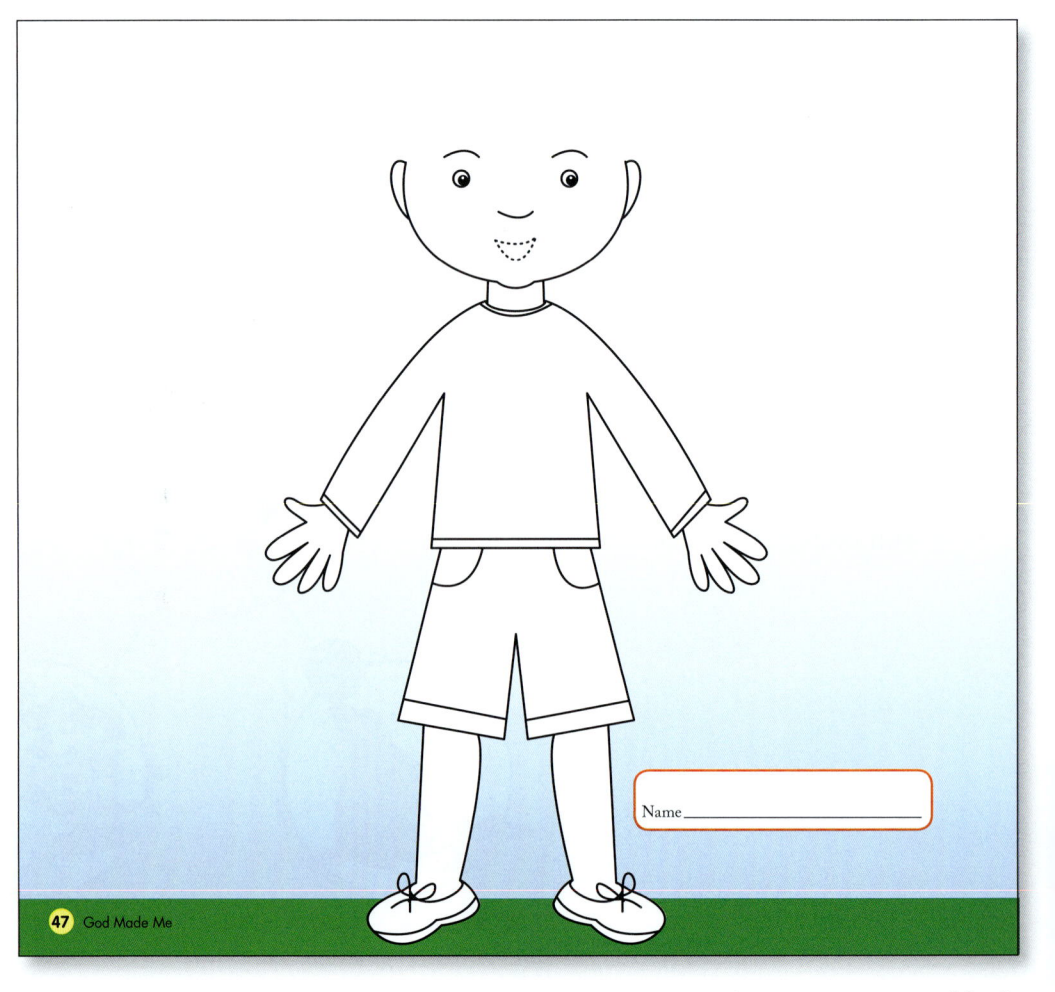

Page 48 is blank.

ENRICHING THE FAITH EXPERIENCE

Use the following activities to enrich the lesson or to replace an activity with one that better meets the needs of your group.

❶ Show an appropriate video to the children and enjoy laughing together.

❷ Read to the children the following poem:

Family Laughs

My mother usually giggles.
The baby squeals with glee.
My father laughs so his
   stomach shakes.
Aunt Rose just goes "Tee hee."

I laugh so much I hurt.
I laugh until I cry.
I laugh so hard I roll on the
   ground
And sometimes don't even
   know why.
   Mary Kathleen Glavich, S.N.D.

❸ Tape laughter and play it for the children, letting them laugh along with it.

❹ Teach the children the song "Animal Fair" or sing it for them.

Animal Fair

I went to the an-i-mal fair.
The birds and the beasts were there.
The big ba-boon, by the light of the moon,
was comb-ing his au-burn hair.
You ought to have seen the monk;
He climbed up the el-e-phant's trunk.
The el-e-phant sneezed and fell on her knees,
and what be-came of the monk?

I Can Laugh CHAPTER **14** **T95**

Chapter 15
I Can Celebrate

FAITH FOCUS

We celebrate good things from God.

Psalm 23:2; Matthew 22:1–14

PREPARING THE FAITH EXPERIENCE

LISTENING

*"Worthy are you, Lord our God,
to receive glory and honor and power,
for you created all things;
because of your will they came to be and
were created."*

Revelation 4:11

*"Worthy is the Lamb that was slain
to receive power and riches, wisdom and
strength,
honor and glory and blessing."*

Revelation 5:12

REFLECTING

What is celebration? It is rejoicing together because of something good, commemorating a wonderful happening, or honoring someone. We celebrate birthdays, weddings, anniversaries, and retirements. At a celebration, there is laughter, communication, music, and feasting. For good reason Jesus described heaven in terms of a banquet or feast. In heaven all creation celebrates the goodness of God in a celebration without end.

The Church on earth in her liturgy also celebrates the wonderful works of God—in particular the Paschal Mystery of Christ, which saved us. The *Catechism* states that those who celebrate liturgy "are already in the heavenly liturgy, where celebration is wholly communion and feast." (1136)

We are a people who have much to celebrate. The Eucharist and other sacraments are celebrations of the astonishing Christian mystery. We remember and celebrate that Jesus suffered, died, rose, and ascended, thereby restoring life to us. Each Sunday, the Lord's Day, the risen Lord invites us to his banquet. There we encounter him, recall the wonders he has done for us, enter into the Paschal Mystery, and give thanks to God. During the course of the liturgical year, we celebrate various aspects of the mystery of Christ, culminating in the great feast of Easter. We also celebrate in the yearly sanctoral cycle Mary and other saints in whom the Paschal Mystery has been realized.

Participating in liturgy is not so much an obligation as a privilege and a joy. In the liturgy we find hope and strength. We find true self-fulfillment and what our hearts most deeply desire. Bonded with people who share our beliefs and ideals, united with Christ our Savior, we pray and sing our thanks and praise to God. As we pray prayers such as "Holy, holy, holy Lord," we swell the prayer of the four living creatures who in John's vision of heaven represent universal creation:

*"Holy, holy, holy is the Lord God almighty,
who was, and who is, and who is to come."*

Revelation 4:8

RESPONDING

Having been nourished by God's Word, we are able to respond to God's great love for us. In prayer, respond to God's call to you to share his Word with others. You may also wish to respond in your prayer journal.

- How can I enhance my celebration of the Eucharist?

Jesus, may the children always remember what you have done for them.

UNIT 3 *God Made Me Happy*

Catechism of the Catholic Church

The themes of this chapter correspond to the following paragraph: 1141.

THE FAITH EXPERIENCE
Child's Book pages 49–52

SCRIPTURE IN THIS CHAPTER
- *Mark 6:34–44*

MATERIALS
- Cutouts #33–42, shamrocks
- Cutouts #43 and 44, two green strips
- Perforated Card F
- Option: green plant
- Green flowers, one for each child
- Option: pipe cleaners and green tissue paper
- Safety pins
- Tape to attach decorations
- Green crepe paper and green balloons
- Green construction paper, one sheet for each child
- Green crayons or markers
- Hole punch
- Two 10-inch pieces of yarn per child
- Green napkins
- Green gift for each child (pencil, eraser, toy, or sticker)

PREPARATION
- Write the children's names on pages 49 and 51.
- Punch out the party hats from perforated Card F and write the children's names on them.
- Fold page 51 in half to make a book.
- Roll pieces of tape for the backs of decorations.
- If you wish, make green carnations from tissue paper for the children. (Staple six green circles together in the center and fluff them up to make petals. Staple a green pipe cleaner to the flower. Insert a safety pin in the back.)
- Hide the 10 shamrocks in the room.

MUSIC 'N MOTION
Use *Music 'n Motion* page T252 and CD Track 3 "Peace in My Heart" for this chapter. For a list of additional music, see page T302.

ENRICHING THE FAITH EXPERIENCE
Use the activities at the end of the chapter to enrich the lesson or to replace an activity with one that better meets the needs of your group.

BOOKS TO SHARE
If You Give a Pig a Party by Laura Numeroff (Laura Geringer, 2005)

Miss Spider's Tea Party by David Kirk (Scholastic Press, 1997)

Mrs. Muddle's Holidays by Laura F. Nielsen (Farrar, Straus & Giroux, 2008)

Fancy Nancy & Bonjour Butterfly by Jane O'Connor (HarperCollins, 2008)

SNACK
Suggestion: green grapes and crispy rice cereal treats with green sugar sprinkles

---

ALTERNATIVE PROGRAMS

DAILY PROGRAM
Day 1: Centering #2, Sharing #1–2
Day 2: Sharing #3, Enriching the Faith Experience choice
Day 3: Acting 1
Day 4: Sharing #4–5
Day 5: Centering #3, Sharing #6, Acting #2–3

THREE-DAY PROGRAM
Day 1: Centering, Sharing #1–2
Day 2: Sharing #3, Acting #1
Day 3: Sharing #4–6; Acting #2–3

15 I Can Celebrate

LEARNING OUTCOMES

The children will
- enjoy a celebration.
- thank God for the color green.

COMMENTS

1. Christians are a celebrating people. Each year we celebrate the key events of our redemption with the feasts of Christmas and Easter as the highpoints. Each week we celebrate the Paschal Mystery in the Eucharistic celebration. We celebrate significant events in our personal lives with the sacraments. The celebration in this lesson not only will prepare children for liturgical celebrations but also will give them an appreciation of an aspect of creation: the color green, which stands for life.

2. In the previous class you might notify the parents and children to the celebration of green and suggest that the children wear something green to this class. Wear something green yourself.

CENTERING

❶ Gather the children in a circle for *Music 'n Motion* time. Play the Unit 3 song (Track 3). Invite the children to do motions to the song along with you, using *Music 'n Motion* page T252.

❷ Tell the children they will have a celebration.

- *We will do something different today. We will have a celebration. People celebrate good things. They do something special when they celebrate. Today we will celebrate the color green by having a picnic.*

❸ Decorate the room. Tell the children that whoever finds a shamrock [Cutouts 33–42] may post it as a decoration. Have all the children help decorate the room in green, using balloons and crepe paper. Give them green construction paper to put on the floor as place mats.

T98 UNIT 3 *God Made Me Happy*

SHARING [A]

❶ Distribute page 49 and talk about the picture.

- *What is the family doing?* (Having a picnic) *Maybe they are celebrating a family member's birthday.*

- *Outside you can see many things God made that are green. God must like the color green.*

- *Many living things are green.* [Option: Show a green plant.]

- *What green things do you see in the picture?* (Grass, plants, tree leaves, frog, snake, turtle, grasshopper)

❷ Have the children draw green lines to match the shapes on page 50.

❸ Play "Frog Hop." Place the two green strips (Cutouts #43 and 44) on the floor about six inches apart. Tell the children that they will pretend to be little green frogs, jumping across a stream. Have them form a line, jump the strips, and hop to the end of the line. Each time the first child is ready for another turn, move the strips a little farther apart. If a child steps in the "stream," comment that it is all right because frogs like water.

Draw green lines to match the shapes.

Family Time

Chapter 15: I Can Celebrate

In this lesson the children held a celebration and heard about Jesus' picnic for a crowd. (Mark 6:34–44) They celebrated the color green with green decorations, snacks, and flowers. On special occasions let your child wear the hat he or she made.

Your Child
Celebrating is characteristic of human beings. Celebrate birthdays and invite relatives and friends. Celebrate "ordinary" events: a child's losing the first tooth, a parent's new job, the arrival of a pet, or the first day of school. Include a prayer in the celebrations.

Reflect
The LORD is my shepherd;
   there is nothing I lack.
In green pastures you let me graze;
   to safe waters you lead me;
   you restore my strength. (Psalm 23:1–3)

Pray
Gracious God, we celebrate the wonder of your great love.

Do
- Celebrate anniversaries of sacraments. Establish rituals for the celebrations. Use special plates, sing a family song, or wear certain clothes.
- Celebrate holidays with a special meal or by getting together with relatives and friends.
- Celebrate whenever your child learns something new.
- Invite your child to suggest a reason for celebrating, especially on a gloomy day.
- Read to your child *If You Give a Pig a Party* by Laura Numeroff. Help your child to remember several recent family celebrations. Thank God for giving so many good reasons to celebrate.

For more family resources, refer to the Family Activity Booklet and visit www.loyolapress.com/preschool.

© LOYOLAPRESS.

SHARING [B]

4 SCRIPTURE Tell the children about Jesus' big picnic based on Mark 6:34–44.

• *Jesus once had a picnic for many, many families. The Bible tells us that Jesus had the people sit on the ground. They looked like flowers in the green grass. Then Jesus and his friends gave them all something to eat.*

• *Jesus likes people to have a good time together.*

• *God is with us here today as we celebrate. Let's give a cheer. Say the words after me:*

> God is here with us today,
> So we say "Hip, hip hooray!"
> [Raise arm three times on "Hip, hip, hooray."]

5 Let the children decorate the party hats from perforated Card F with green. They might cut shapes out of the green scraps of the card and glue them on the hats. Staple the hats together. Punch holes where the dots are and tie the pieces of yarn on the hats. You might staple green crepe paper streamers to the top of each hat. Tell the children they may wear the hats if they wish. (Some three-year-olds do not like to have anything on their heads.)

6 Give the children green flowers and help them pin them on.

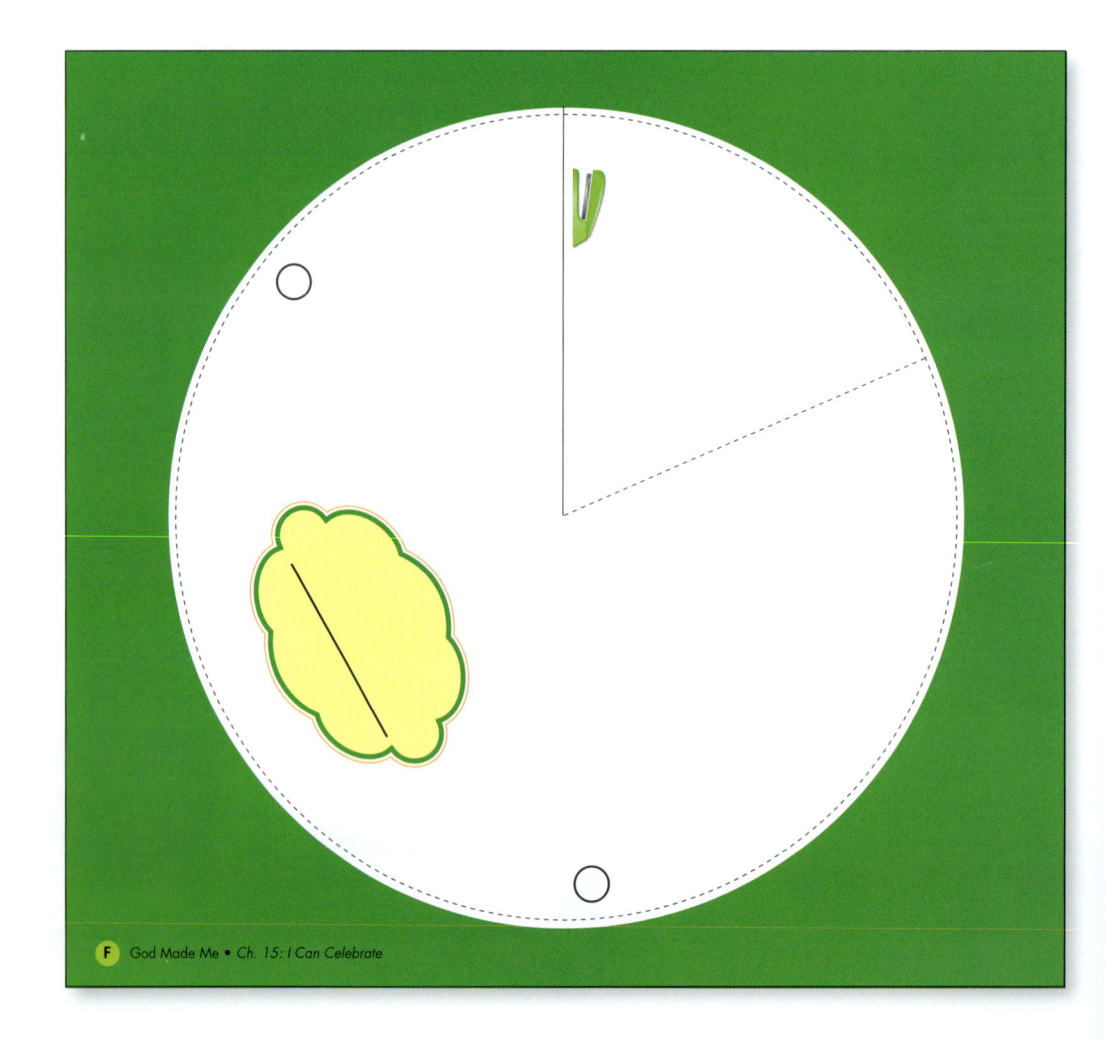

F *God Made Me* • *Ch. 15: I Can Celebrate*

T100   UNIT 3   *God Made Me Happy*

ACTING

1 Give the children page 51, which you folded into a book. Read aloud the poem. Have them find the hidden animals in the pictures.

2 PRAYER Hold a picnic on the floor with the children enjoying their snacks on the paper place mats. Use the green napkins. Give them green gifts. Before eating, pray:

Dear God, we thank you for all the gifts you give us. We especially thank you today for everything green. We celebrate how good you are to us.

[Sing the "Amen" if the children learned it in Chapter 13, page T89.]

Green Things I See

one bunch of grapes—green, juicy, and mine!

Three green frogs in green grass I see,

51 God Made Me

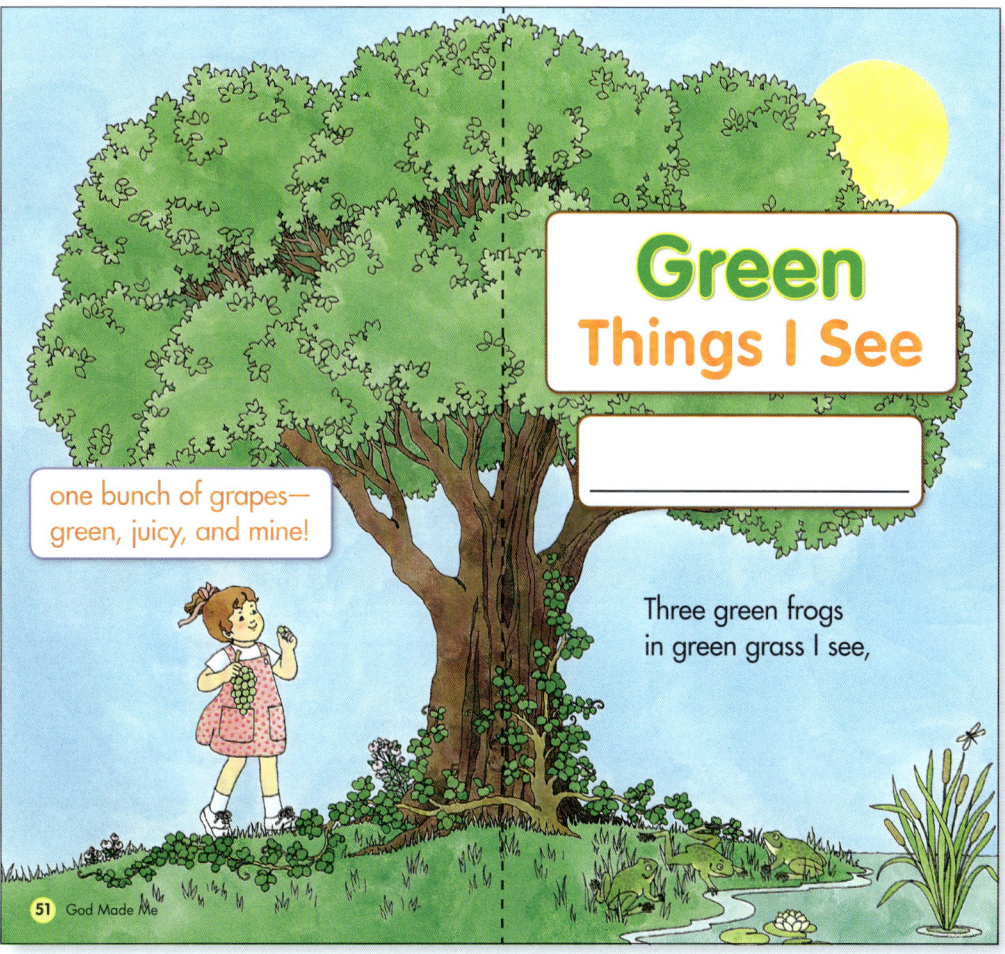

I Can Celebrate CHAPTER 15 T101

3 Gather the children in a circle for *Music 'n Motion* time. Play the Unit 3 song (Track 3). Invite the children to do motions to the song along with you, using *Music 'n Motion* page T252.

Have the children take home their pages and show their family the Family Time section.

CHECKPOINT

- *Were the learning outcomes achieved?*
- *How could the picnic have been improved?*

three green birds in a big green tree,

three green turtles near a dark green vine,

52 God Made Me © LOYOLA PRESS.

T102 UNIT 3 God Made Me Happy

ENRICHING THE FAITH EXPERIENCE

Use the following activities to enrich the lesson or to replace an activity with one that better meets the needs of your group.

❶ Guide the children in planting grass seeds in potting soil placed in an egg carton. Watch the seeds grow over the coming days.

❷ Have the children make pictures with green finger paint.

❸ Have the children make collages of green items, such as scraps of paper or fabric.

❹ Ask the children riddles about green things:

• *Sometimes I'm red, and sometimes I'm green. I grow on trees. You make pies out of me. What am I?* (Apple)

• *I spend my time in or near the water. I have a long tail and a great big mouth with many teeth. I have green scales. What am I?* (Alligator or crocodile)

• *I grow on soil, especially in yards. I am thin strips. You must mow me to keep me neat. What am I?* (Grass)

• *I grow on trees. I come in different shapes. In the fall I fall to the ground. What am I?* (Leaves)

• *I grow on vines. I'm sweet to eat. I'm green or red. I'm small and round. What am I?* (Grapes)

• *I live in a pond, lake, or river. I hop and croak. What am I?* (Frog)

unit four

God Made Me Active

The children will realize the wonderful things they can do. They will appreciate the abilities they have as human beings.

16 I CAN MOVE

The children talk about being able to move, and they discuss various means of transportation. They participate in activities that involve movement. After hearing the biblical story of Miriam dancing for God, they make circles and use them in a dance to praise and thank God for letting them move.

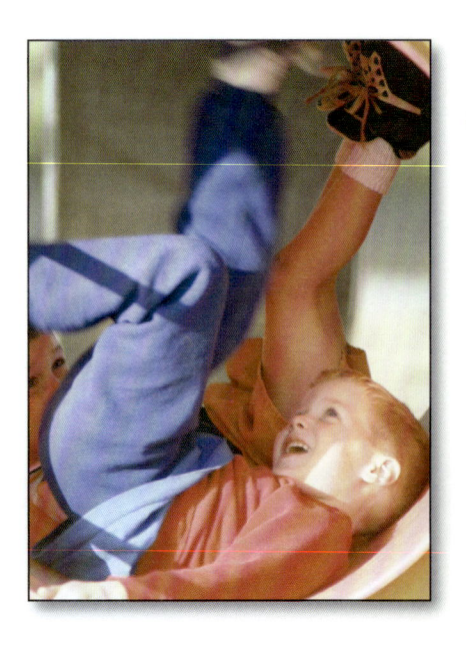

17 I CAN PLAY

After talking about playing and hearing that God likes them to play, the children play a game and learn a finger play. By saying or singing a psalm verse, they thank God for letting them enjoy playing. Then they make squirrel puppets and play again, alone or with others.

18   I CAN WORK

The children pretend to be workers. Then they talk about working, helping at home, and the importance of work. They learn that Saint Joseph was a carpenter and that Jesus probably helped him in his workshop. They hear a story about Busy Bee and Lazy Bee. Then they work hard to make a beautiful picture by gluing objects or paper squares on a card.

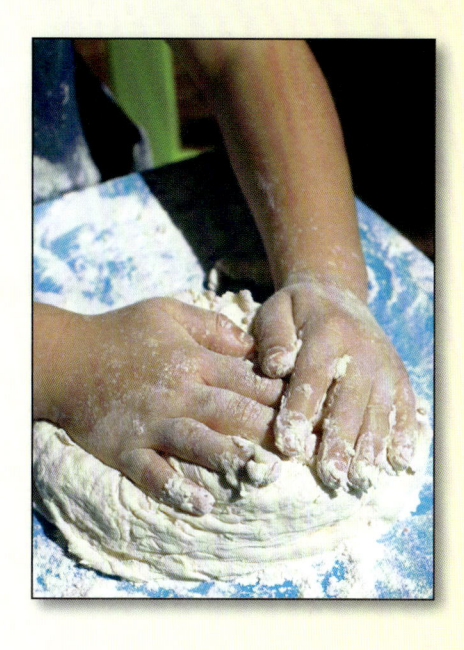

19   I CAN MAKE THINGS

The children make necklaces and then talk about the enjoyment that comes from making things. They learn that God made everything and lets us make things too. They thank God for the things in creation. Then they make a stand-up dog.

20   I CAN GROW

After pretending to take care of a baby, the children talk about their babyhood and the ways they have changed. They learn that all living things grow and that Jesus grew too. They recall what helps them grow and read a poem about their growth. Then they make a growth chart to be completed at home.

God Made Me Active UNIT 4   T105

Chapter 16
I Can Move

FAITH FOCUS

God made us able to move, and our movements can praise God. Psalm 150:4; Acts of the Apostles 3:1–8

PREPARING THE FAITH EXPERIENCE

LISTENING

[A] man crippled from birth was carried and placed at the gate of the temple called "the Beautiful Gate" every day to beg for alms from the people who entered the temple. When he saw Peter and John about to go into the temple, he asked for alms. But Peter looked intently at him, as did John, and said, "Look at us." He paid attention to them, expecting to receive something from them. Peter said, "I have neither silver nor gold, but what I do have I give you: in the name of Jesus Christ the Nazorean, [rise and] walk." Then Peter took him by the right hand and raised him up, and immediately his feet and ankles grew strong. He leaped up, stood, and walked around, and went into the temple with them, walking and jumping and praising God.

Acts of the Apostles 3:2–8

REFLECTING

The ability to move about, walk, run, swim, and dance, is a gift often taken for granted. Sometimes a sprained ankle or broken leg leads us to a greater appreciation of our mobility. The paralytic man cured by Peter and John in the name of Jesus became ecstatic when he was able to walk and jump.

As believers we know that in God "we live and move and have our being." (Acts of the Apostles 17:28) Our lives should give praise to our Creator. A song inspired by Blessed Teresa of Calcutta exhorts us, "Make all your life something beautiful for God. Make every moment a prayer—every movement of your hands joyful praise to his Name."

Liturgical movement, or dance, is not the only way to praise God by our movements. Any movement is holy and praises God when it is Christlike. A father who paces the floor with his crying infant, a mother who goes to the store for food, an office worker who helps a coworker— each is involved in a great dance of praise.

After World War II, soldiers found in a bombed church a crucifix with parts missing from the body of Christ. Posted below it was the following: "I have no feet but yours; I have no hands but yours. Yours are the eyes through which I look out over the world. Yours is the voice that speaks my Word. Yours is the heart that must bring my love to all."

Jesus still depends on us to be his hands and feet. He loves and works through us, his followers. Our hands are to serve, to soothe, and to heal. Our feet are to journey to spread the message of God's love, to run to the aid of those in trouble, and to march for the causes of truth, peace, justice, and life. We do not have to undertake great missionary journeys as Saint Paul did. Our actions can make an impact on people and have a ripple effect.

RESPONDING

God's Word moves us to respond in word and action. Let God's Spirit work within you as you prayerfully consider how you are being called to respond to God's message to you today. Responding through your journal may help to strengthen your response.

- How do my hands and feet praise God?

Jesus, may the children move to do good.

T106 UNIT 4 *God Made Me Active*

Catechism of the Catholic Church

The themes of this chapter correspond to the following paragraph: 2639.

THE FAITH EXPERIENCE

Child's Book pages 53–54

SCRIPTURE IN THIS CHAPTER
- *Exodus 15:19–21*

MATERIALS
- Bible
- Cutout #45, horse
- Option: tambourine
- Broom or yardstick
- Transportation toys for CENTERING #2
- Perforated Card G
- Crayons or markers
- Dance music
- Option: stapler and ribbon or crepe-paper streamers

PREPARATION
- Write the children's names on page 53.
- Punch out the circles on perforated Card G for the children.
- Tape or tack Cutout #45, horse, to a broom or yardstick.

MUSIC 'N MOTION
Use *Music 'n Motion* page T256 and CD Track 4 "Jump Up, Get Down" for this chapter. For a list of additional music, see page T302.

ENRICHING THE FAITH EXPERIENCE
Use the activities at the end of the chapter to enrich the lesson or to replace an activity with one that better meets the needs of your group.

BOOKS TO SHARE
Barn Dance! by Bill Martin Jr. and John Archambault (Henry Holt and Co., 1988)

George and Martha Encore by James Marshall (Houghton Mifflin, 1977)

The Foot Book by Dr. Seuss (Collins, 2004)

Go, Dog, Go by P. D. Eastman (Random House, 1961)

SNACK
Suggestion: round cookies made to look like wheels (draw spokes with frosting) or "wheel" round crackers (draw spokes with cheese)

ALTERNATIVE PROGRAMS

DAILY PROGRAM
Day 1: Centering, Sharing #1 and #2
Day 2: Sharing #3–5
Day 3: Enriching the Faith Experience choice
Day 4: Sharing #6, Acting #1
Day 5: Acting #2 and #3

THREE-DAY PROGRAM
Day 1: Sharing A
Day 2: Sharing B
Day 3: Acting

I Can Move **CHAPTER 16** **T107**

16 I Can Move

LEARNING OUTCOMES

The children will
- appreciate their ability to move.
- know that movements can praise God.
- enjoy moving and dancing.

COMMENTS

1. Three-year-olds are active. They are interested in what they can do with their bodies on equipment such as tricycles and jungle gyms. When they first use equipment, they need encouragement, help, and reassurance. Some children do not control their actions well. They tend to ride fast, bump into things, and upset objects.

2. Around age three and a half, children may regress in some areas of development, including physical ability. They may stutter, stumble, tremble, and become uncoordinated.

3. Children are getting used to the power of their bodies. Through exercise and play, they refine their coordination and motor skills.

4. In this lesson the children come to realize that their bodies can be used to praise God. This prepares them for liturgical rituals such as gestures, postures, processions, liturgical movement, and dance.

CENTERING

❶ Gather the children in a circle for *Music 'n Motion* time. Play the Unit 4 song (Track 4). Invite the children to do motions to the song along with you, using *Music 'n Motion* page T256.

❷ Invite the children to take turns "riding" the horse made from Cutout #45, horse. Let them engage in free play with trucks, trains, cars, planes, and boats.

SHARING [A]

❶ Distribute page 53 and discuss the picture.

- *What are the children doing?* (Dancing)

- *Do you like to dance?*

- *God gave us bodies that can move. Can a rock take a walk around the block?* (No.) *Can a flower run away from a rainstorm?* (No.) *Can a tree brush off a bee?* (No.)

- *Many things God made can't move as we can. We can walk, run, and move in many different ways. Isn't God good to make us with bodies that move?*

T108   UNIT 4   *God Made Me Active*

2 Have the children stand and move in different ways. Give these directions and demonstrate each movement for the class:

- Move your head from side to side.
- Move your eyes up and down.
- Swing your arms in large circles.
- Hop like a bunny.
- Run in place.
- Touch your toes.
- Swing your leg.
- Do a knee bend.
- Spin like a top and then sit down.

3 Talk about means of transportation.

- *When we want to go somewhere that's too far to walk, what do we do?* (Take a car, bus, train, boat, or plane)
- *No matter where we go or how far away, God is always there.*

4 Have the children add wheels to the things shown on page 54.

SHARING [B]

5 Play "Train." Have the children form a line and put their right hand on the shoulder of the child in front. Tell them to bend their left arm. Then demonstrate how they should take small steps on their toes and move their left hand in a circular motion at the side. Appoint one child to be the whistle and say "toot, toot!" while everyone else says "chug, chug, chug, chug" as the train moves around the room.

6 **SCRIPTURE** Talk about dancing as a way to praise God. Tell the story of Miriam, based on Exodus 15:19–21. Show the Bible.

- *We can use our bodies to praise God. We can dance for God.*
- *In the Bible is a story about a woman named Miriam who danced for God. God saved Miriam, her family, and friends. To show how happy and thankful she was, Miriam led the other women in a dance. As they danced, they played tambourines.* [Option: Show a tambourine and play it.]
- *Today people dance for God too. You can dance for God.*

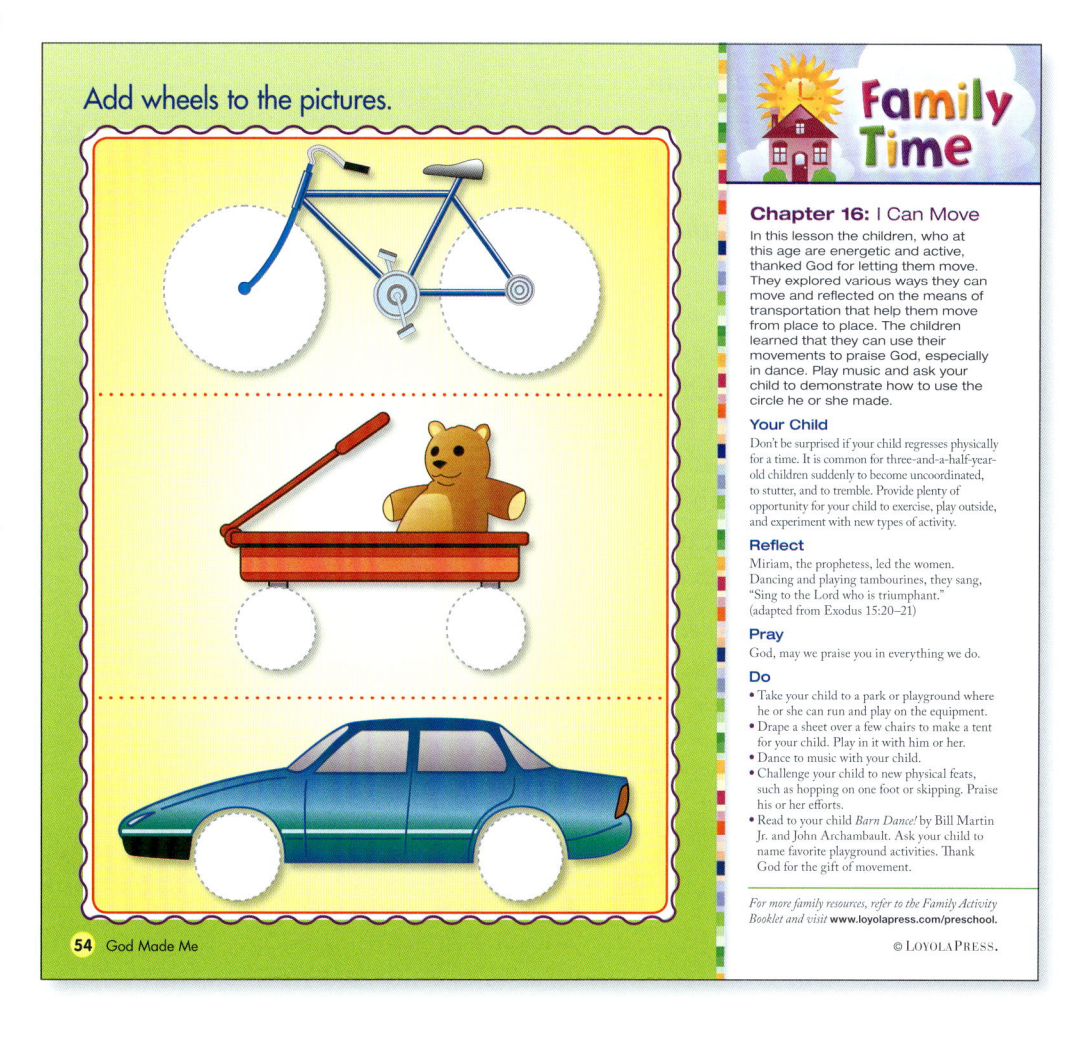

Add wheels to the pictures.

54 God Made Me

Family Time

Chapter 16: I Can Move
In this lesson the children, who at this age are energetic and active, thanked God for letting them move. They explored various ways they can move and reflected on the means of transportation that help them move from place to place. The children learned that they can use their movements to praise God, especially in dance. Play music and ask your child to demonstrate how to use the circle he or she made.

Your Child
Don't be surprised if your child regresses physically for a time. It is common for three-and-a-half-year-old children suddenly to become uncoordinated, to stutter, and to tremble. Provide plenty of opportunity for your child to exercise, play outside, and experiment with new types of activity.

Reflect
Miriam, the prophetess, led the women. Dancing and playing tambourines, they sang, "Sing to the Lord who is triumphant." (adapted from Exodus 15:20–21)

Pray
God, may we praise you in everything we do.

Do
- Take your child to a park or playground where he or she can run and play on the equipment.
- Drape a sheet over a few chairs to make a tent for your child. Play in it with him or her.
- Dance to music with your child.
- Challenge your child to new physical feats, such as hopping on one foot or skipping. Praise his or her efforts.
- Read to your child *Barn Dance!* by Bill Martin Jr. and John Archambault. Ask your child to name favorite playground activities. Thank God for the gift of movement.

For more family resources, refer to the Family Activity Booklet and visit www.loyolapress.com/preschool.

© LOYOLAPRESS.

ACTING

1 Have the children decorate the circle from perforated Card G to make pretend tambourines. Play music and suggest that they make their crayons or markers dance on the circle as they draw. Tell the children that their movements as they color can praise God. You might staple ribbons or crepe paper streamers to the children's tambourines.

2 **PRAYER** Invite the children to dance with their tambourines to give praise and thanks to God. Explain:

• *Let's dance to praise and thank God for letting us move. You can dance with the tambourines you have made.*

• *As you dance, you might lift your tambourines up high, twirl around with them, pass them from one hand to the other, or wave them through the air.*

3 Gather the children in a circle for *Music 'n Motion* time. Play the Unit 4 song (Track 4). Invite the children to do motions to the song along with you, using *Music 'n Motion* page T256.

Have the children take home their pages and show their family the Family Time section.

CHECKPOINT

- Were the learning outcomes achieved?
- Which children need more exercise?

ENRICHING THE FAITH EXPERIENCE

Use the following activities to enrich the lesson or to replace an activity with one that better meets the needs of your group.

1 Place large footprints or sheets of paper on the floor. Play music and have the children dance. Whenever the music stops, they are to run and stand on a footprint or sheet of paper.

UNIT 4 God Made Me Active

2 Teach the children the following songs, adding the appropriate motions:

The Bus

1. The people on the bus go up and down, up and down, up and down. The people on the bus go up and down all through the town.
2. The wheels on the bus go 'round and 'round, 'round and 'round, 'round and 'round. The wheels on the bus go 'round and 'round all through the town.
3. The horn on the bus goes "Toot! toot! toot!"
4. The wipers on the bus go "Swish! swish! swish!"
5. The driver on the bus says, "Move on back!"

Did You Ever See a Lassie?

Did you ever see a lassie, a lassie, a lassie, did you ever see a lassie go this way and that? Go this way and that way and this way and that way; did you ever see a lassie go this way and that?

(laddie, a laddie, a laddie,) (laddie) (laddie)

3 Play "Train," with the children holding the circles they made at their sides as wheels. Teach them the following poem to say as they move:

> Engine, engine number nine,
> Going down the railroad line.
> If the train goes off the track,
> Will I get my money back?

4 Have the children spread out and perform the following movements:

- fly like a bird
- hop like a frog
- slither like a snake
- swim like a fish
- waddle like a penguin
- gallop like a pony
- leap like a deer
- walk like a dinosaur

5 Call out hair color, shoe color, or clothing descriptions, such as jeans, blue shirts, and fuzzy sweaters. Have children with those features or clothing run to you when they hear a description that fits them.

I Can Move CHAPTER **16**   T111

Chapter 17
I Can Play

FAITH FOCUS

God wants us to enjoy playing

Proverbs 8:12,22,30–31; Isaiah 11:8

PREPARING THE FAITH EXPERIENCE

LISTENING

"I, Wisdom, dwell with experience, . . .
*The L*ORD *begot me, the firstborn of his ways . . .*
Then was I beside him as his craftsman,
 and I was his delight day by day,
Playing before him all the while,
 playing on the surface of his earth;
 and I found delight in the sons of men."

Proverbs 8:12,22,30–31

REFLECTING

The Book of Proverbs depicts Wisdom helping God plan the universe. It shows Wisdom playing like a child before God. This Wisdom is the Second Person of the Trinity, who millions of years later became a human being and actually played as a child on the face of the earth. Play is not something relegated only to childhood, when it is integral to our development into healthy human beings. As adults we still need to play in order to be well-balanced individuals.

Because Jesus was a perfect human being, he spent time playing and relaxing. He invited his apostles: "Come away by yourselves to a deserted place and rest a while." (Mark 6:31) In Cana when he turned water into wine, he was at a wedding. The Gospels also record that Jesus often went to dinner with friends.

Jesus, the Wisdom of God, taught us how to play the game of life. He taught us to play hard and well, to follow the rules, to play fair, and to be good sports. He taught us that life isn't a game of solitaire or, worse yet, Monopoly, in which we try to accumulate as much as we can for ourselves. A race once run at a camp for children who were mentally disabled exemplifies Christ's teaching of how to play the game of life.

At the camp, about 20 children began the race. Peter, who was taller and more agile than the others, had a big lead. As he approached the finish line, he glanced back and saw the other children behind him. Audrey, a large, awkward girl, was bringing up the rear. Peter paused and then began to run backwards. The other children stopped in their tracks and watched him. When Peter reached Audrey, he put his arm around her and said, "Come on. You can do it." The two ran up to the other children. Then with their arms around one another, the children continued to run. As they all stepped over the finish line together, Peter shouted, "We won! We won!"

RESPONDING

Having reflected upon God's Word, take some time now to continue to respond to God in prayer. You might wish to use your journal to record your response.

- Do I have a healthy balance of work and play in my life?

Father, may the children learn how to play well.

T112   UNIT 4   *God Made Me Active*

Catechism of the Catholic Church

The themes of this chapter correspond to the following paragraph: 2184.

THE FAITH EXPERIENCE

Child's Book pages 55–58

SCRIPTURE IN THIS CHAPTER
- *Psalm 111:1*

MATERIALS
- Bible
- Chapter 17 Scripture card
- Play dough or pieces of aluminum foil
- Crayons or markers
- Option: toy
- Stapler

PREPARATION
- Place the Chapter 17 Scripture card for SHARING #3 in the Bible.
- Write the children's names on page 55.
- Cut out the tails from pages 57 and 58. Staple the squirrels closed along the side and top to form a hand puppet. Then staple the tails to the puppet. (Make sure all staples are closed so that the children do not injure themselves when they put their hands inside the puppet.)

MUSIC 'N MOTION
Use *Music 'n Motion* page T256 and CD Track 4 "Jump Up, Get Down" for this chapter. For a list of additional music, see page T302.

ENRICHING THE FAITH EXPERIENCE
Use the activities at the end of the chapter to enrich the lesson or to replace an activity with one that better meets the needs of your group.

BOOKS TO SHARE
William's Doll by Charlotte Zolotow (HarperTrophy, 1985)

Where Is Sarah? by Bob Graham (Little, Brown and Company, 1988)

Changes, Changes by Pat Hutchins (Aladdin, 1987)

Lily Goes to the Playground by Jill Krementz (Random House Books for Young Readers, 1986)

SNACK
Suggestion: cookies

ALTERNATIVE PROGRAMS

DAILY PROGRAM
Day 1: Centering, Sharing A
Day 2: Sharing B
Day 3: Enriching the Faith Experience choice
Day 4: Enriching the Faith Experience choice
Day 5: Acting

THREE-DAY PROGRAM
Day 1: Centering, Sharing A
Day 2: Sharing B
Day 3: Acting

17 I Can Play

LEARNING OUTCOMES

The children will
- know that God wants them to be happy.
- enjoy playing.

COMMENTS

1. Through play and hands-on experience, children learn about themselves, others, and the world. They strengthen their bodies, increase their physical powers, practice social skills, and form attitudes. At the age of three, some children are moving from parallel play (playing next to but not with each other) to cooperative play. Some may still prefer to play alone, while others are beginning to share, to take turns, and to understand other children's feelings.

2. Observe the children as they play independently. Note the activities they like best and those they avoid. How do they solve problems? Do they share? Jot down your observations and address needs and issues with the children later.

3. Play, or recreation, is as necessary for adults as it is for children. "All work and no play makes Jack a dull boy" is indeed a wise saying. We need times of play as a respite from the stress of daily work. God established the gift of the Sabbath, commanding the Israelites to keep this day holy, set apart for worship and rest from daily work. Christians celebrate Sunday as the Lord's Day, the day of the Christ's Resurrection, as a day for worship, rest, and works of mercy. Heaven itself can be thought of as an eternal Sabbath.

CENTERING

❶ Gather the children in a circle for *Music 'n Motion* time. Play the Unit 4 song (Track 4). Invite the children to do motions to the song along with you, using *Music 'n Motion* page T256.

❷ Invite the children to make things from play dough or aluminum foil. Mention that they can make whatever they like and as many as they like.

T114   UNIT 4   God Made Me Active

SHARING [A]

1 **Distribute page 55** and talk about the different ways the children are playing in the picture. Ask:

- *What are the children doing?*
- *What do you like to play?*
- *What are your favorite toys?* [Option: Show the children the toy.]

2 **On page 56** have the children find and circle the five toys hidden in the picture.

3 **SCRIPTURE** Tell the children that God likes them to play. Read Psalm 111:1 from the Scripture card in the Bible.

- *God likes to see you playing happily and having fun. God loves you and wants all of you to enjoy life.*

- *God likes to see you sharing and being kind while you play so that everyone is happy. When we are kind and share with others, we give praise to God.*

- *Listen to this prayer from the Bible: "I will praise the L*ORD *with all my heart."*

SHARING [B]

4 **Play "Squirrel in a Tree."** Ask the children whether they have seen squirrels playing in the yard or in trees. Group the children in threes. In each group direct two children to hold hands to be the tree and the third child to be the squirrel standing inside their arms. When you (or a "leftover" child) say "change," all the squirrels (and the leftover child) go to another tree. (If there is a new leftover child, let him or her call "change.") As the game continues, let the children change roles.

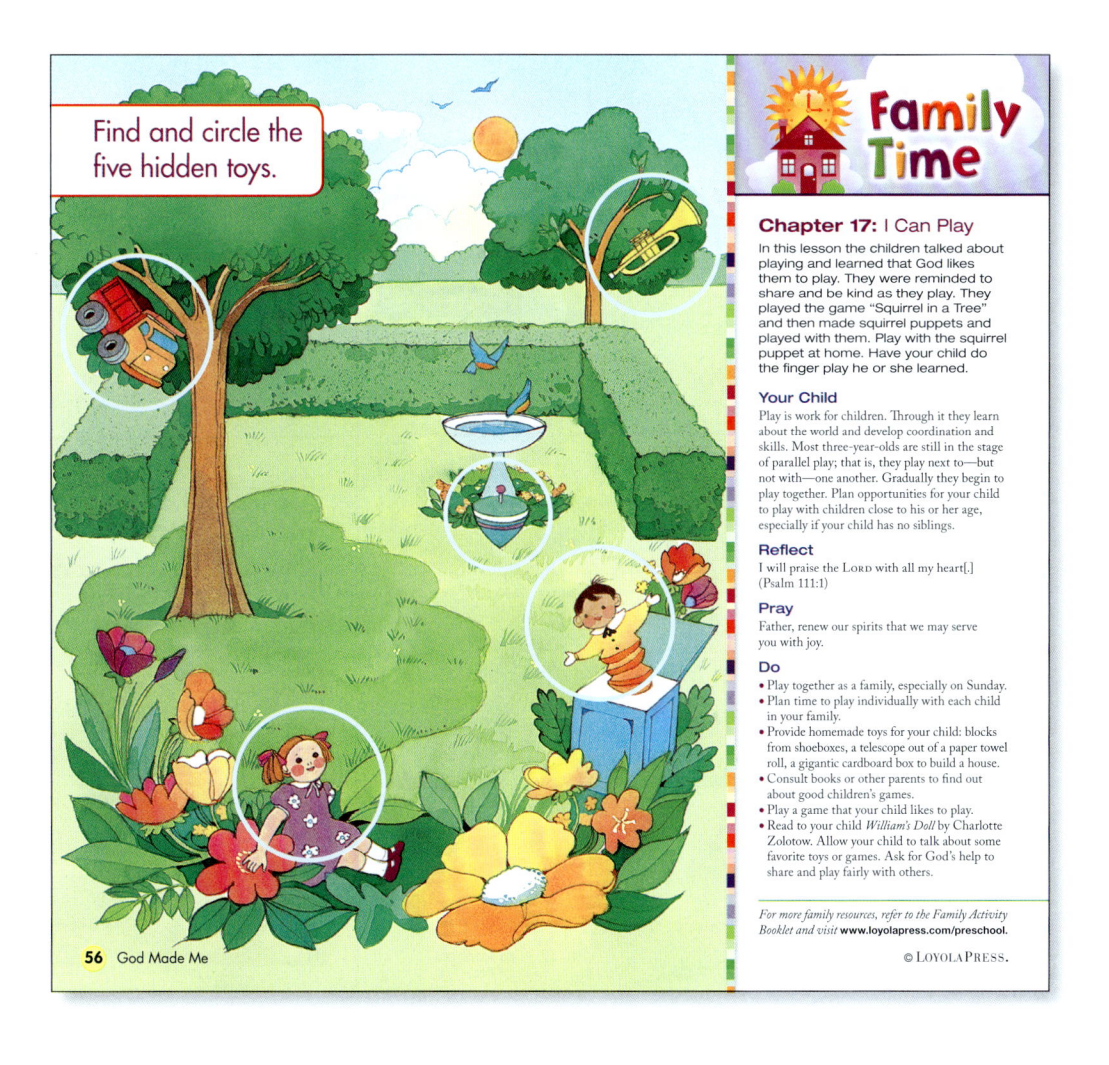

Find and circle the five hidden toys.

56 God Made Me

Family Time

Chapter 17: I Can Play

In this lesson the children talked about playing and learned that God likes them to play. They were reminded to share and be kind as they play. They played the game "Squirrel in a Tree" and then made squirrel puppets and played with them. Play with the squirrel puppet at home. Have your child do the finger play he or she learned.

Your Child
Play is work for children. Through it they learn about the world and develop coordination and skills. Most three-year-olds are still in the stage of parallel play; that is, they play next to—but not with—one another. Gradually they begin to play together. Plan opportunities for your child to play with children close to his or her age, especially if your child has no siblings.

Reflect
I will praise the LORD with all my heart[.] (Psalm 111:1)

Pray
Father, renew our spirits that we may serve you with joy.

Do
- Play together as a family, especially on Sunday.
- Plan time to play individually with each child in your family.
- Provide homemade toys for your child: blocks from shoeboxes, a telescope out of a paper towel roll, a gigantic cardboard box to build a house.
- Consult books or other parents to find out about good children's games.
- Play a game that your child likes to play.
- Read to your child *William's Doll* by Charlotte Zolotow. Allow your child to talk about some favorite toys or games. Ask for God's help to share and play fairly with others.

For more family resources, refer to the Family Activity Booklet and visit www.loyolapress.com/preschool.

© LOYOLAPRESS.

I Can Play CHAPTER 17 T115

5 Teach the children the following finger play. Have them call out the last line.

Playful Kittens

Five little kittens
Like to run and play.
[Move fingers on left hand.]
Five other kittens
Are not far away.
[Wiggle fingers on right hand.]

Ten little kittens meet,
[Move both hands in front of chest.]
Having loads of fun.
[Keep moving fingers.]
Along comes a dog.
See those kittens run!
[Move arms outward, fingers moving faster.]
Ten little kittens
Scamper up a tree.
[Move arms over head with fingers moving.]
Ten little kittens said,
"You can't catch me!"
Helen Kitchell Evans

ACTING

1 **PRAYER** Have the children thank God for letting them enjoy playing. Invite them to cross their hands on their hearts and repeat this psalm verse:

I will praise the Lord with all my heart . . .
(Psalm 111:1)

You might have the children sing the verse by singing "I will" on the same note (middle C) and then going up the scale for the other words.

2 Distribute the squirrel puppets from pages 57–58. Show how to fold the squirrel's head along the line.

Insert your hand and arm into the puppet and bend your hand to make it move. Let the children play with the puppets alone or with friends.

3 Gather the children in a circle for *Music 'n Motion* time. Play the Unit 4 song (Track 4). Invite the children to do motions to the song along with you, using *Music 'n Motion* page T256.

Have the children take home their pages and show their family the Family Time section.

57 God Made Me

T116   UNIT 4   *God Made Me Active*

CHECKPOINT

- Were the learning outcomes achieved?
- What can you do to help children who do not get along with others?

ENRICHING THE FAITH EXPERIENCE

Use the following activities to enrich the lesson or to replace an activity with one that better meets the needs of your group.

1 Hide nuts made out of paper and have the children find them.

2 Play a game that the children enjoyed previously.

3 Have the children play "Drop the Clothespin." Set a plastic wide-mouthed jar in back of a sturdy chair. Have the children kneel on the chair facing its back and try to drop clothespins into the jar.

4 Teach the following nursery rhyme and talk about what the children might want to play outside:

> Rain, rain, go away.
> Come again some
>   other day.
> Little children want to
>   play.

5 Teach the children the following song. Have them roll their arms on the words "they all rolled over." Or have 10 children act out the song on the floor.

Ten in a Bed

1. There were ten in a bed and the little one said, "Roll o-ver! Roll o-ver!" So they all rolled o-ver and one fell out!

2–9: There were nine . . . (eight, seven, six, and so on)
10: There was one in bed,
    And the little one said, [spoken] "Good night!"

I Can Play CHAPTER 17 T117

Chapter 18
I Can Work

FAITH FOCUS

Working is good.

Proverbs 6:6–11; 10:5

PREPARING THE FAITH EXPERIENCE

LISTENING

May the favor of the Lord our God be ours.
Prosper the work of our hands!
Prosper the work of our hands!

Psalm 90:17

REFLECTING

The three Persons of the Trinity know what it means to work. By the hand of God the universe was created. In Christ, God carried out the saving work of salvation. By the power of the Holy Spirit, God is constantly at work in us to make us holy. When we work, we who are made in God's image share in the activity of God. Work is ennobling.

Whatever we do—creating pieces of art, programming computers, fixing cars, or sorting chicken parts in an assembly line—we are participating in creation. We are contributing to the well-being of the world. As we develop our God-given gifts and talents and devote our time and energy to a particular labor, in some way we are serving the human community.

We can unite our work to Christ's work and make it redemptive. Work can be a cross that is carried faithfully. It can entail hardships, such as a very early rising; an irritable boss; a room that is too hot, too cold, or too noisy; or tedious, physically exhausting tasks. In the Morning Offering, we give to God all the works of the day. Our sufferings offered as a sacrifice bear fruit on the spiritual plane and benefit others as well as ourselves.

Work can lead to holiness. And because work is a duty, when we engage in it, we are doing what we are supposed to do. Work can be the means of perfecting ourselves as we exercise our gifts and practice discipline. Work can also be a way to bring Christ to certain people and activities.

Our work enables us to enjoy and appreciate leisure, rest, and recreation. In addition, work keeps us from being bored.

As with any good thing, work in excess can be dangerous. Our health and family life can be jeopardized if we allow work to consume us. The *Catechism* reminds us that "work is for man, not man for work." (2428) Let us pray:

God our Father,
you have placed all the powers of nature
under the control of man and his work.
May we bring the spirit of Christ to all
*   our efforts*
and work with our brothers and sisters at our
*   common task,*
establishing true love and guiding your
creation to perfect fulfillment.
We ask this through our Lord Jesus Christ,
*   your Son,*
who lives and reigns with you and the
*   Holy Spirit,*
one God, for ever and ever.

Opening Prayer
Mass for the Blessing of Human Labor

RESPONDING

God's Word calls us to respond in love. Respond to God now in the quiet of your heart and perhaps through your journal.

- What is my attitude toward my work?

God, instill in the children a love for work.

T118 UNIT 4 God Made Me Active

Catechism of the Catholic Church

The themes of this chapter correspond to the following paragraphs: 2427–2428.

THE FAITH EXPERIENCE

Child's Book pages 59–64

SCRIPTURE IN THIS CHAPTER
- *Psalm 90:17*

MATERIALS
- Bible
- Chapter 18 Scripture card
- Option: hammer
- Crayons or markers
- O-shaped cereal (or seeds, rice, or macaroni dyed with food coloring)
- Glue
- Option: colored tissue paper

PREPARATION
- Place the Chapter 18 Scripture card for SHARING #2 in the Bible.
- Write the children's names on pages 59, 61, and 64.
- Fold pages 61 and 62 to form a book.

MUSIC 'N MOTION
Use *Music 'n Motion* page T256 and CD Track 4 "Jump Up, Get Down" for this chapter. For a list of additional music, see page T302.

ENRICHING THE FAITH EXPERIENCE
Use the activities at the end of the chapter to enrich the lesson or to replace an activity with one that better meets the needs of your group.

BOOKS TO SHARE
The Very Busy Spider by Eric Carle
  (Grosset & Dunlap, 2006)

Oh, Were They Ever Happy! by Peter Spier
  (Trumpet Club, 1989)

Curious George Takes a Job by H.A. Rey
  (Houghton Mifflin, 1974)

Pigs at Work by Jon Buller and Susan Schade
  (Troll Communications, 1998)

Clifford Gets a Job by Norman Bridwell (Scholastic, 1985)

SNACK
Suggestion: homemade trail mix (raisins, chocolate chips, and dry cereal) Let the children help by adding ingredients and mixing them in a bowl.

ALTERNATIVE PROGRAMS

DAILY PROGRAM
Day 1: Centering, Sharing A
Day 2: Sharing B, Enriching the Faith
  Experience #1, Acting #1
Day 3: Enriching the Faith Experience choice
Day 4: Enriching the Faith Experience choice
Day 5: Acting #2 and #3

THREE-DAY PROGRAM
Day 1: Centering, Sharing A
Day 2: Sharing B, Enriching the Faith
  Experience #1, Acting #1
Day 3: Acting #2 and #3

I Can Work CHAPTER 18 T119

18 I Can Work

LEARNING OUTCOMES
The children will
- know that Jesus worked.
- desire to work well.
- appreciate what workers do for them.

COMMENTS
1. Saint Irenaeus, an early Doctor of the Church, stated, "The glory of God is a person fully alive." When we are fully alive, we use our powers to the best of our ability. We are meant to work with our heads and our hands to make the world a better place.

2. Like the rest of us, children take pride in their work. They can experience the satisfaction of a job well done even when they have no audience. They are also capable of admiring other children's work. Encourage good work by verbally affirming the children as they work hard and by displaying their masterpieces.

CENTERING
❶ Gather the children in a circle for *Music 'n Motion* time. Play the Unit 4 song (Track 4). Invite the children to do motions to the song along with you, using *Music 'n Motion* page T256.

❷ Suggest that the children pretend to work as a housekeeper, a cashier, a doctor, or a carpenter as they engage in free play. Encourage both girls and boys to try out all the roles.

SHARING [A]
❶ Distribute page 59 and talk about the picture.

- *What is the girl doing?* (Helping her mother in the garden)

- *Do you ever help in the garden? How?*

- *There is much work to be done at home. What work must your mother or father do at home?* (Cook, clean, make beds, repair things, wash clothes and dishes, mow the lawn, plant flowers, weed the garden)

- *How do you help with work at home?*

❷ **SCRIPTURE** Talk about the importance of work. Read the adaptation of Psalm 90:17 from the Scripture card in the Bible.

- *God gave us strong bodies and good brains so that we can work. Listen to this prayer from the Bible: "May God bless us and bless the work that we do."*

- *God wants us to work hard for ourselves and for other people.*

- *Who are some people who help you through their work?* (Parents, police officers, firefighters, doctors, nurses, teachers, priests, storekeepers)

- *We feel good when we do a good job.*

T120   UNIT 4   God Made Me Active

3 Have the children act out carpenters' work to verses of "Did You Ever See a Lassie?" (The music is on page T111.) Introduce the activity:

- *What is a carpenter?* (Someone who makes things out of wood)

- [Option: Show a hammer.] *What are some things carpenters make?* (Tables, chairs, houses, barns, toys)

- *How do carpenters make these things?* (They saw wood, pound nails, sand wood, glue parts, add paint or varnish.)

- *Let's pretend we are carpenters. Stand up and do what I do.* [Sing:]

4 Have the children look at the picture on page 60. Explain:

- *Joseph, known as the father of Jesus on earth, was a carpenter. Jesus probably helped Joseph in his workshop.*

- *Joseph and Jesus did their best work as they made things for others. God likes to see us doing our best.*

- *When Jesus grew up, he worked as a teacher. He taught people about God.*

5 Direct the children to color the picture on page 60. Encourage them to do their best work. Be sure to praise their efforts.

---

1. Did you ever see a
   carpenter, carpenter,
   carpenter?
   Did you ever see a
   carpenter saw wood
   like this?
   [Sawing motions]

   We saw wood and
   saw wood and saw
   wood and saw
   wood.

   Did you ever see a
   carpenter saw wood
   like this?

2. Pound nails
   [Pounding motions]
3. Sand wood
   [Sanding motions]
4. Paint wood
   [Painting motions]

Color Jesus and Joseph in the workshop.

60 God Made Me

Family Time

Chapter 18: I Can Work

In this lesson the children considered how people work. They recalled how they themselves work and learned that Jesus worked as a teacher and as a carpenter. They worked hard to finish coloring a picture and to make a lovely piece of art. Commend your child for good work. Display the art where it can be seen and admired. Ask your child to tell you the story of the bees on the story card he or she received.

Your Child
Although your child finds satisfaction in work—which is in itself a reward—you might also praise and sometimes reward him or her for a job well done, or at least for the effort made.

Reflect
May God bless us and bless the work that we do. (adapted from Psalm 90:17)

Pray
God, may our love for you show forth in the work we do.

Do
- Explain to your child what you do at work or the work required around the house.
- Enlist your child's help in doing work around the house.
- With your child, watch construction workers, police officers, farmers, crossing guards, and other people at work.
- Sing with your child while you work around the house or yard.
- Reward yourself and your child with a special treat after a task is finished.
- Read to your child *The Very Busy Spider* by Eric Carle. Acknowledge your child's contributions to work around the house. Together ask God to bless all the work that you do.

For more family resources, refer to the Family Activity Booklet and visit www.loyolapress.com/preschool.

© LOYOLAPRESS.

SHARING [B]

6 Distribute pages 61–62 and have the children follow along as you read the story-poem aloud. Ask:

• *Who would you want to work for you, Busy Bee or Lazy Bee?* (Busy Bee) *Why?* (He would get the work done.)

• *How do you think Busy Bee felt when he was finished working?* (Happy, tired)

• *What if all the flowers had died before Lazy Bee started working?* (He wouldn't have made any honey.)

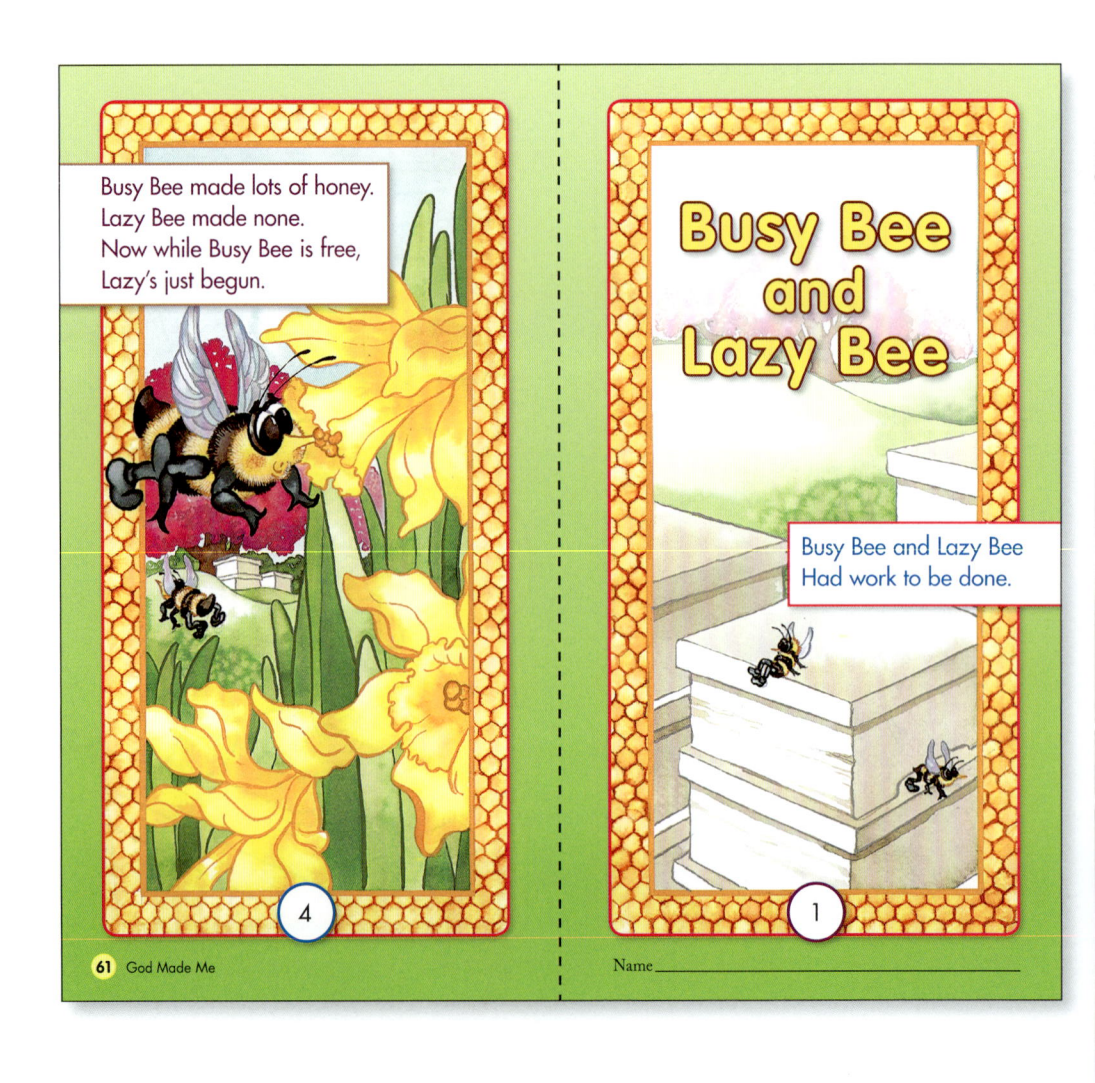

Busy Bee made lots of honey.
Lazy Bee made none.
Now while Busy Bee is free,
Lazy's just begun.

Busy Bee and Lazy Bee

Busy Bee and Lazy Bee
Had work to be done.

61 God Made Me

Name _____

T122 UNIT 4 *God Made Me Active*

ACTING

1 **PRAYER** Lead the children to prayer:

- *Close your eyes and think of some work you did this week. In your heart thank God for letting you work.*

2 Have the children make designs or a flower in the frame on page 63 by gluing on cereal, seeds, rice, or colored macaroni. Suggest that they work hard to make a beautiful picture. If you prefer, have the children use one-inch squares of colored tissue paper.

3 Gather the children in a circle for *Music 'n Motion* time. Play the Unit 4 song (Track 4). Invite the children to do motions to the song along with you, using *Music 'n Motion* page T256.

Have the children take home their pages and show their family the Family Time section.

CHECKPOINT

- Were the learning outcomes achieved?
- Were the children familiar with Saint Joseph?

Busy Bee got busy,
But Lazy Bee had fun.

Busy buzzed to many flowers
And worked on every one.
Lazy snoozed for hours and hours
In the nice, warm sun.

62 God Made Me

I Can Work **CHAPTER 18** **T123**

ENRICHING THE FAITH EXPERIENCE

Use the following activities to enrich the lesson or to replace an activity with one that better meets the needs of your group.

1 Let the children "buzz" about the room to music, pretending to be busy bees collecting nectar.

2 Discuss how animals work: birds build nests, beavers build dams, ants carry food, horses pull plows and wagons, lions and tigers perform in circuses, some dogs guide people who are blind.

3 Obtain small pieces of wood and have the children glue them together to create works of art.

4 Invite parents as guest speakers to tell the children about their work.

5 Provide toys that give the children the opportunity to hammer.

Page 64 is blank.

T124   UNIT 4   *God Made Me Active*

6 Teach this finger play. Substitute the children's names for "Johnny."

Johnny pounds with one hammer, one hammer, one hammer.
[Pound one fist on knee.]
Johnny pounds with one hammer. Then he pounds with two.
[Pound both fists on knees.]

Johnny pounds with two hammers, two hammers, two hammers.
Johnny pounds with two hammers. Then he pounds with three.
[Pound knees and tap a foot.]

Johnny pounds with three hammers, three hammers, three hammers.
Johnny pounds with three hammers. Then he pounds with four.
[Pound knees and tap both feet.]

Johnny pounds with four hammers, four hammers, four hammers.
Johnny pounds with four hammers. Then he pounds with five.
[Pound knees, tap feet, nod head.]

Johnny pounds with five hammers, five hammers, five hammers.
Johnny pounds with five hammers, Then sits down to rest.

Chapter 19
I Can Make Things

FAITH FOCUS

We can make things and contribute to the world God made.

Genesis 1:1–31

PREPARING THE FAITH EXPERIENCE

LISTENING

When I see your heavens, the work of your fingers,
 the moon and stars that you set in place—
What are humans that you are mindful of them,
 mere mortals that you care for them?
Yet you have made them little less than a god,
 crowned them with glory and honor.
You have given them rule over the works of your hands,
 put all things at their feet.

Psalm 8:4–7

REFLECTING

God delighted in making the universe and giving it to us. As God's children made in his image and likeness, we too like to make things and give them as gifts. Young children delight in drawing and presenting their pictures to others. Adults enjoy making a wide variety of things to give as gifts—crocheted afghans, carved figures, watercolors, and special meals.

Any gift signifies love. A handmade gift is especially valued because it has something of its maker within it. It shows the maker's taste, style, and abilities and will always remind us of the person who made it and bestowed it on us.

Similarly, creation reflects God. The *Catechism* states, "Light and darkness, wind and fire, water and earth, the tree and its fruit speak of God and symbolize both his greatness and his nearness." (1147) The beauty of flowers tells of God's beauty; the majesty of the mountains, of God's majesty; the power of the oceans, of God's power. Most of all, everything God has created shouts out God's love for us.

Just as God's creation was found good, what we make can usually be declared good. Our creative work brings us pride and satisfaction.

Yet as we construct buildings, design works of art, and invent new machines, we are mindful that God not only supplies the material but also inspires us and gives us our talents and creative abilities. We depend on God's help to make new creations, aware that "Unless the LORD build the house, / they labor in vain who build." (Psalm 127:1)

We pray to recognize the Creator's presence in the world:

God our Father,
open our eyes to see your hand at work
in the splendor of creation,
in the beauty of human life.
Touched by your hand our world is holy.
Help us to cherish the gifts that surround us,
to share your blessings with our brothers and sisters,
and to experience the joy of life in your presence.
We ask this through Christ our Lord.
Alternative Opening Prayer
17th Sunday in Ordinary Time

RESPONDING

Having been nourished by God's Word, we are able to respond to God's great love for us. In prayer, respond to God's call to you to share his Word with others. You may also wish to respond in your prayer journal.

- What homemade gifts have I recently given and received?

Holy Spirit, give the children joy in making things.

T126 UNIT 4 *God Made Me Active*

Catechism of the Catholic Church

The themes of this chapter correspond to the following paragraphs: 290, 293, 2501.

THE FAITH EXPERIENCE
Child's Book pages 65–66

SCRIPTURE IN THIS CHAPTER
- *Genesis 1:31*

MATERIALS
- Bible
- Chapter 19 Scripture card
- 20-inch piece of yarn for each child
- Transparent tape or glue
- Construction paper
- Tube-shaped pasta
- Option: vinegar, food dye, plastic bag
- Hole punch
- O-shaped cereal
- Option: flower
- Option: pictures of creation for ACTING #1
- Paint, crayons or markers
- Option: green construction paper
- Glue
- Perforated Card H

PREPARATION
- Place the Chapter 19 Scripture card for SHARING # 1 in the Bible.
- Write the children's names on page 65 and perforated Card H.
- Put tape around one end of the yarn or dip it in glue to make it easier for the children to string things. Make a large knot at the other end of the yarn.
- Cut construction paper into small shapes. Punch holes in the centers of the shapes. As an option, place a tablespoon of vinegar, food dye, and pasta in a plastic bag to color the pasta. Shake until pasta is colored.
- Punch out the dog parts from perforated Card H. Glue the head circles and tail circles together.

MUSIC 'N MOTION
Use *Music 'n Motion* page T256 and CD Track 4 "Jump Up, Get Down" for this chapter. For a list of additional music, see page T302.

ENRICHING THE FAITH EXPERIENCE
Use the activities at the end of the chapter to enrich the lesson or to replace an activity with one that better meets the needs of your group.

BOOKS TO SHARE
Maisy Makes Lemonade by Lucy Cousins (Candlewick Press, 2002)

Curious George Makes Pancakes by Margaret Rey (Houghton Mifflin, 1998)

Building a House by Byron Barton (HarperTrophy, 1994)

Let's Cook by Robert Crowther (Candlewick, 2004)

SNACK
Suggestion: cream cheese on crackers. The children can spread the cream cheese on the crackers.

ALTERNATIVE PROGRAMS

DAILY PROGRAM
Day 1: Centering
Day 2: Sharing A
Day 3: Sharing B
Day 4: Acting #1
Day 5: Acting #2 and #3

THREE-DAY PROGRAM
Day 1: Centering, Sharing A
Day 2: Sharing B
Day 3: Acting

I Can Make Things CHAPTER 19

19 I Can Make Things

LEARNING OUTCOMES
The children will
- understand that God made everything.
- experience the satisfaction of making things.

COMMENTS
1. God created everything out of nothing. Merely by willing their existence, God called all things into being. Now we, God's children, are the inheritors of God's handiwork. The universe and its treasures are ours to use and enjoy. Their care is in our hands. Whenever we beautify the world or make something with its materials, we share somewhat in God's great act of creation. We experience the joy of using our minds and bodies to bring about something new.

2. Through making things, children become familiar with the extent of their powers. They also perfect their physical skills, such as hand-eye coordination and fine and gross motor skills. Perhaps most importantly, by producing original creations, the children are able to express their feelings and thoughts and demonstrate their unique talents.

CENTERING

❶ Gather the children in a circle for *Music 'n Motion* time. Play the Unit 4 song (Track 4). Invite the children to do motions to the song along with you, using *Music 'n Motion* page T256.

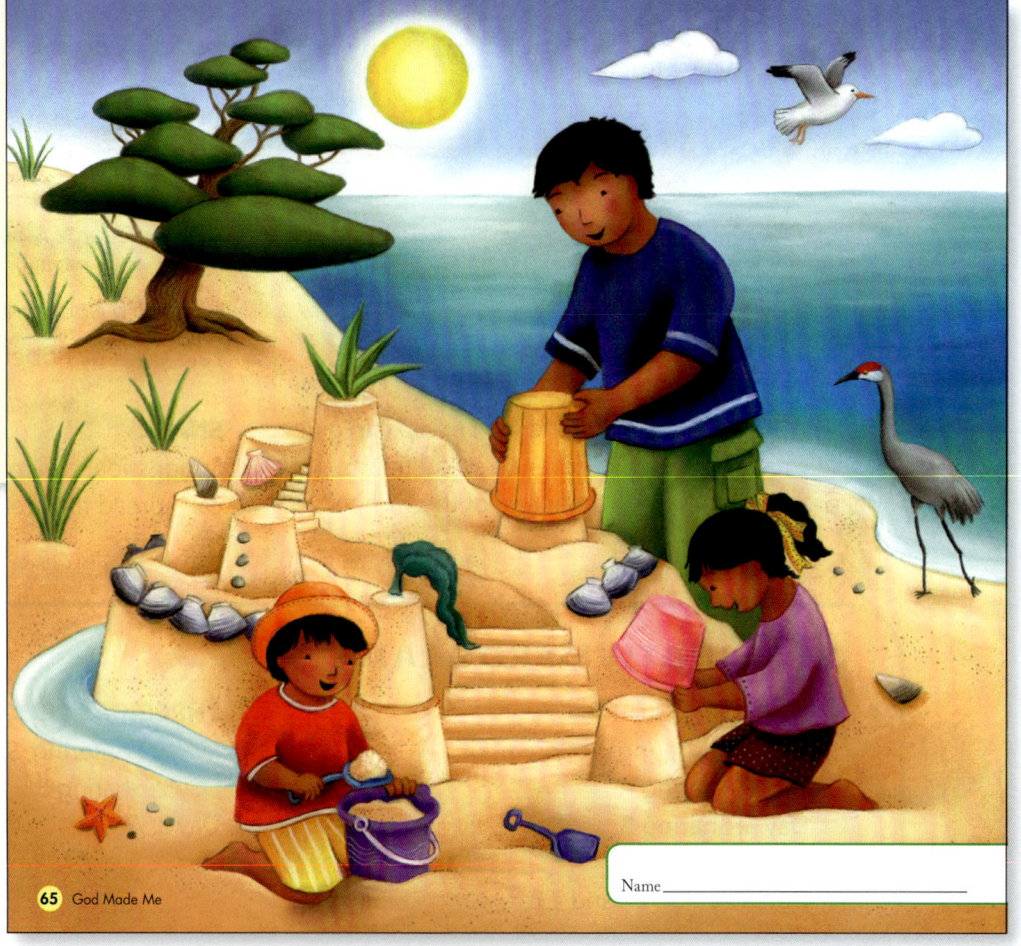

❷ Have the children make necklaces by stringing O-shaped cereal, paper shapes, and tube-shaped pasta on yarn. When the children are finished, tie the ends together for them.

SHARING [A]

❶ **SCRIPTURE** Distribute page 65 and talk about the picture. Read the adaptation of Genesis 1:31 from the Scripture card in the Bible.

- *What are the children doing?* (Making sand castles, digging in the sand)

- *What have you ever made out of sand, mud, or clay?*

- *Did you enjoy making the necklaces?*

- *It's fun to make things. Do you know who makes the best things?* (God)

- *What things in the picture did God make?* (The sun, clouds, water, sand, birds, tree, children)

- [Show the Bible.] ***The Bible tells us that God made everything—all the animals and flowers in the world.*** [Option: Show the flower and talk about how well it is made.]

- *Listen to what the Bible says: "God saw everything he had made and called it very good."*

- *God is very good. God lets us make things too.*

T128 UNIT 4 *God Made Me Active*

❷ Teach the following poem with motions:

What God Made

God made the sun and the great blue sky.
[Make a circle with arms; separate arms and raise hands.]
God made the stars and the moon.
[Open and close fingers.]
God made lakes and birds that fly.
[Flap arms.]
God made the little raccoon.
[Make circles with fingers around eyes.]
God made mountains and green, grassy hills.
[Make a peak with hands.]
God made the fish in the sea.
[Put palms together and wiggle hands forward.]
God made flowers like daffodils.
[Pretend to smell flower.]
But best of all, God made me!
[Point to self.]

Mary Kathleen Glavich, S.N.D.

SHARING [B]

❸ **Talk about our role in** creation.

• *God lets us make things to make the world more beautiful. We can build bridges and buildings. We can plant flowers and trees. We can make beautiful pictures.*

• *God wants us to take good care of what he has made. How can you care for our world?* (Keep it clean. Don't hurt the flowers or trees.)

❹ **Have the children finish** the tree on page 66. Instead of coloring it, they might tear green construction paper into pieces and glue them on.

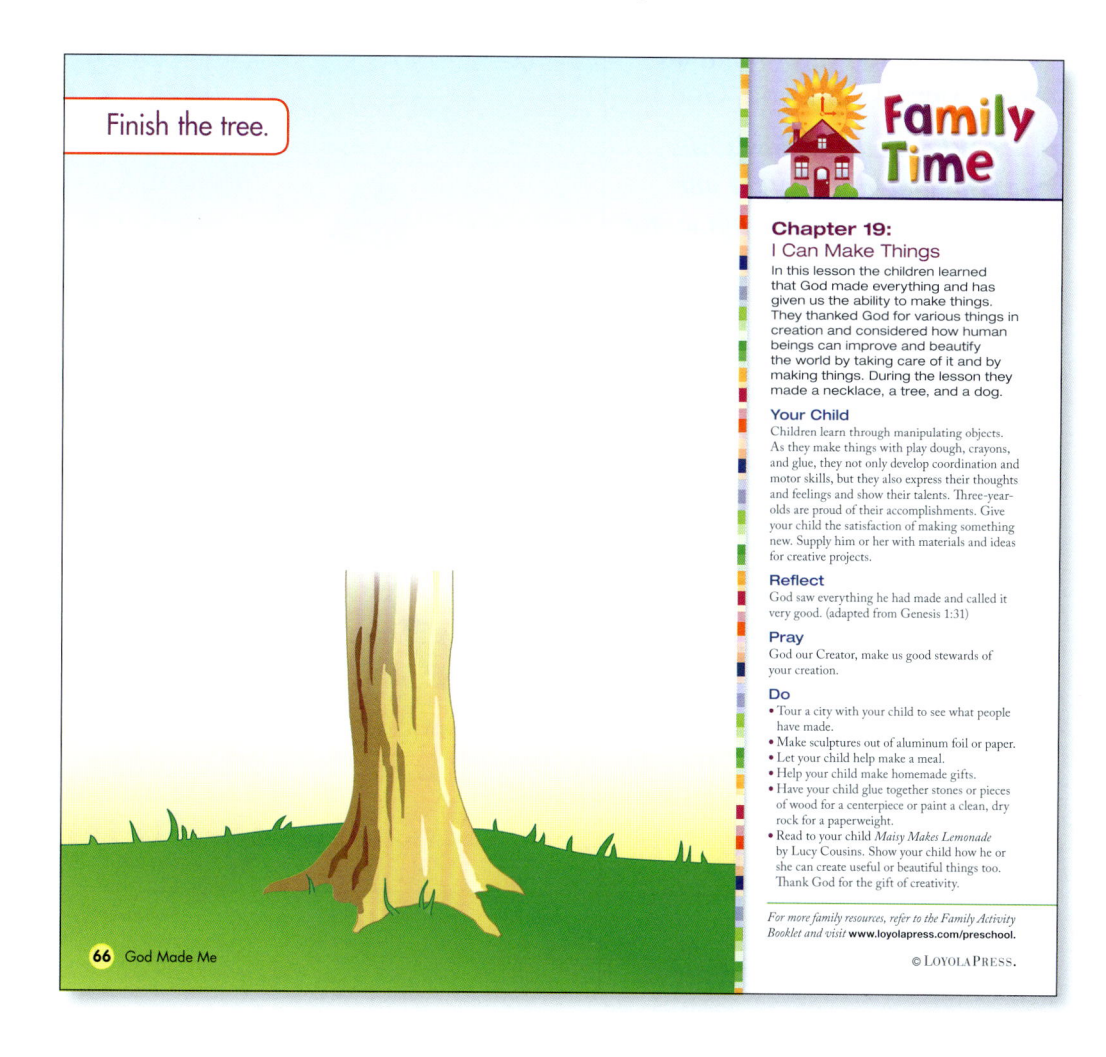

Finish the tree.

66 God Made Me

Family Time

**Chapter 19:
I Can Make Things**
In this lesson the children learned that God made everything and has given us the ability to make things. They thanked God for various things in creation and considered how human beings can improve and beautify the world by taking care of it and by making things. During the lesson they made a necklace, a tree, and a dog.

Your Child
Children learn through manipulating objects. As they make things with play dough, crayons, and glue, they not only develop coordination and motor skills, but they also express their thoughts and feelings and show their talents. Three-year-olds are proud of their accomplishments. Give your child the satisfaction of making something new. Supply him or her with materials and ideas for creative projects.

Reflect
God saw everything he had made and called it very good. (adapted from Genesis 1:31)

Pray
God our Creator, make us good stewards of your creation.

Do
• Tour a city with your child to see what people have made.
• Make sculptures out of aluminum foil or paper.
• Let your child help make a meal.
• Help your child make homemade gifts.
• Have your child glue together stones or pieces of wood for a centerpiece or paint a clean, dry rock for a paperweight.
• Read to your child *Maisy Makes Lemonade* by Lucy Cousins. Show your child how he or she can create useful or beautiful things too. Thank God for the gift of creativity.

For more family resources, refer to the Family Activity Booklet and visit www.loyolapress.com/preschool.

© LOYOLAPRESS.

I Can Make Things CHAPTER 19 T129

ACTING

1 **PRAYER** Lead the children in prayer. As you mention various things in creation, you might draw them or show pictures of them.

• *Let's thank God for some of the things in the world. I'll ask a question in the prayer, and you answer.*

• *Who made the sun?* (God did.) *What do we say?* (Thank you, God.)

• *Who made the moon and the stars?* (God did.) *What do we say?* (Thank you, God.)

• *Who made the mountains and hills?* (God did.) *What do we say?* (Thank you, God.)

• *Who made the oceans and rivers?* (God did.) *What do we say?* (Thank you, God.)

• *Who made the birds, the fish, and all the other animals?* (God did.) *What do we say?* (Thank you, God.)

• *Who made you?* (God did.) *What do we say?* (Thank you, God.)

• *Now let's clap for God for doing such good work.* [Clap.]

2 Help the children make the dog from perforated Card H by following these directions:

- Fold the card so the dog stands.
- Glue on the head by connecting the two blue head circles.
- Glue on the tail by connecting the two orange tail circles.
- Write the name of the dog on the dog tag.

If you plan to teach Chapter 20 next and wish to use the children's baby pictures, call the parents (or send notes home) asking the parents to provide the pictures.

3 Gather the children in a circle for *Music 'n Motion* time. Play the Unit 4 song (Track 4). Invite the children to do motions to the song along with you, using *Music 'n Motion* page T256.

Have the children take home their pages and show their family the Family Time section.

H God Made Me • Ch. 19: I Can Make Things

CHECKPOINT

- Were the learning outcomes achieved?
- Do the children concentrate well on tasks?

ENRICHING THE FAITH EXPERIENCE

Use the following activities to enrich the lesson or to replace an activity with one that better meets the needs of your group.

1 Give the children clay, sand, or play dough to make simple things, such as mountains and snakes.

2 Have the children make a train or a tower out of large cartons or blocks.

3 Hang an old sheet on a wall, with newspapers protecting the floor, or hang the sheet outside. Give the children spray bottles filled with colored water and have them paint the sheet.

4 Teach the children to make a paper chain. Cut one inch by two inch strips of different colors of construction paper. Have the children roll a strip and tape it closed to make a circle. Taking another color, have them insert the strip through the circle they made and tape the new one closed. Have the children continue the process until they have a chain long enough to be a necklace.

5 Have the children make fans. Pass out a sheet of construction paper to each child. Show the children how to make accordion pleats. Staple the ends of the fans closed.

I Can Make Things CHAPTER **19** T131

Chapter 20
I Can Grow

FAITH FOCUS

In God's plan, living things grow.

Luke 2:52

PREPARING THE FAITH EXPERIENCE

LISTENING

And this is my prayer: that your love may increase ever more and more in knowledge and every kind of perception, to discern what is of value, so that you may be pure and blameless for the day of Christ, filled with the fruit of righteousness that comes through Jesus Christ for the glory and praise of God.

Philippians 1:9–11

REFLECTING

Growth is characteristic of life. It is sometimes painful, but necessary and good. A healthy spiritual life allows us to grow in many ways. Our love for God and for others will increase, as will the other virtues: faith, hope, courage, prudence, temperance, and justice. It will become easier for us to do good, and the Fruits of the Holy Spirit will be more obvious in our lives: charity, joy, peace, patience, kindness, goodness, generosity, gentleness, faithfulness, modesty, self-control, and chastity.

Growth in spiritual life preeminently means deepening our relationship with Christ. We come to know and love him more. Christ is not just a historical figure or a distant, unreachable God. He is a close friend who is vitally interested in us and our concerns. He loves us and is ever ready to assist us. Having once saved us by dying and rising, Christ desires that we live life to its fullness and attain heaven, where we will never be separated from him.

Our relationship with Christ is deepened by spending time with him. Aware of Christ's presence, we pay attention to him, devoting part of each day to thinking about him and expressing love for him. When in distress, we turn to Christ for comfort and help. When facing a serious decision or when we do not know what to do, we share our problems with him and count on his light. We read about Jesus and hear him speak to us in Scripture. We celebrate the holy meal that he gave us as a remembrance of him and what he did for us. There at the Eucharist we actually take Christ into ourselves under the signs of bread and wine and are united with him. Gradually we take on his ways and become transformed into his likeness. Once we are united with Christ and Christ speaks and acts through us, we will be credible witnesses for him. People will be drawn to him through us.

Ever since our Baptism, Christ and his Spirit have been within us, calling us to grow to be our best selves. They provide the grace for us to do this. May the prayer of Saint Richard of Chichester be ours:

O most merciful Friend, my Brother, and my Redeemer,
may I know you more clearly,
love you more dearly,
and follow you more nearly,
day by day, day by day. Amen.

RESPONDING

God's Word moves us to respond in word and action. Let God's Spirit work within you as you prayerfully consider how you are being called to respond to God's message to you today. Responding through your journal may help to strengthen your response.

- How deep is my relationship with Christ?

Jesus, may the children's love for you grow stronger each day.

UNIT 4 God Made Me Active

Catechism of the Catholic Church
The themes of this chapter correspond to the following paragraph: 364.

THE FAITH EXPERIENCE
Child's Book pages 67–72

SCRIPTURE IN THIS CHAPTER
- *Luke 2:52*

MATERIALS
- Bible
- Chapter 20 Scripture card
- Option: baby pictures of the children
- Option: your baby picture
- Option: baby clothes or rattle
- Crayons or markers
- Cutouts: #1, Jesus; #46, tree/whale
- Option: tempera paints and paper towels
- Yardstick
- Scale

PREPARATION
- Place the Chapter 20 Scripture card for SHARING #7 in the Bible.
- Write the children's names on pages 67, 69, and 71.
- Accordion-fold Cutout #46.
- Fold pages 69–70 for the children. Write the date of the class on the first line on page 72.

MUSIC 'N MOTION
Use *Music 'n Motion* page T256 and CD Track 4 "Jump Up, Get Down" for this chapter. For a list of additional music, see page T302.

ENRICHING THE FAITH EXPERIENCE
Use the activities at the end of the chapter to enrich the lesson or to replace an activity with one that better meets the needs of your group.

BOOKS TO SHARE
Titch by Pat Hutchins (Aladdin, 1993)

New Shoes for Silvia by Johanna Hurwitz (HarperCollins, 1993)

Leo the Late Bloomer by Robert Kraus (HarperTrophy, 1994)

The Growing Story by Ruth Kraus (HarperCollins, 2007)

SNACK
Suggestion: miniature and regular-sized marshmallows

ALTERNATIVE PROGRAMS

DAILY PROGRAM
Day 1: Centering, Sharing A
Day 2: Sharing B
Day 3: Enriching the Faith Experience choice
Day 4: Enriching the Faith Experience choice
Day 5: Acting

THREE-DAY PROGRAM
Day 1: Centering, Sharing A
Day 2: Sharing B
Day 3: Acting

20 I Can Grow

LEARNING OUTCOMES
The children will
- understand that growth is part of God's plan.
- realize ways in which they are growing.
- plan to eat well, sleep, and exercise in order to grow.

COMMENTS
1. Children are proud of their growth. They will easily be able to talk about how they have grown since they were infants. Three-year-olds experience remarkable growth physically, spiritually, emotionally, socially, and intellectually. Share the children's delight in their growth. If any child is unusually small or large, avoid calling attention to this. Three-year-olds do not like to be different.

2. To foster growth in children, allow them as much free choice as possible in regard to materials or content of projects carried out in the class. Because they educate themselves through discovery, encourage the children to explore and manipulate.

3. If you plan to use baby pictures of the children, plan ahead the week before this lesson to ask the parents to supply them.

CENTERING
❶ Gather the children in a circle for *Music 'n Motion* time. Play the Unit 4 song (Track 4). Invite the children to do motions to the song along with you, using *Music 'n Motion* page T256.

❷ Have the children engage in free play, pretending to take care of a baby. [Option: Display baby pictures that the children have brought in.]

Name_____

T134   UNIT 4   *God Made Me Active*

SHARING [A]

❶ Distribute page 67 and talk about the picture. [Option: Refer to the children's baby pictures and your own.]

• *Which person in the picture is more like you?* (The child)

• *How do you think the child feels about the baby?* (The child loves the baby.) **God loves babies too.** [Option: Show the baby clothes or the rattle.]

• *Look how tiny the baby's fingers are. You were a baby once, but you grew and you are still growing. How do you know you are growing?* (My clothes don't fit after a while. I weigh more.)

• *What can you do now that you couldn't do as a baby?* (Walk, talk, feed myself, go to the bathroom, go to school, color and glue things)

❷ Help the children draw lines to connect the items that babies use to the big-kid versions of those items on page 68.

❸ Talk about growth. Show Cutout #46, tree/whale, folded so the top and bottom quarters show a small tree.

• *God planned that living things grow. What other things grow besides people?* (Plants, trees, animals) [Open Cutout #46 to reveal the tall tree. Fold the card again to show the small whale and open it to reveal the large whale.]

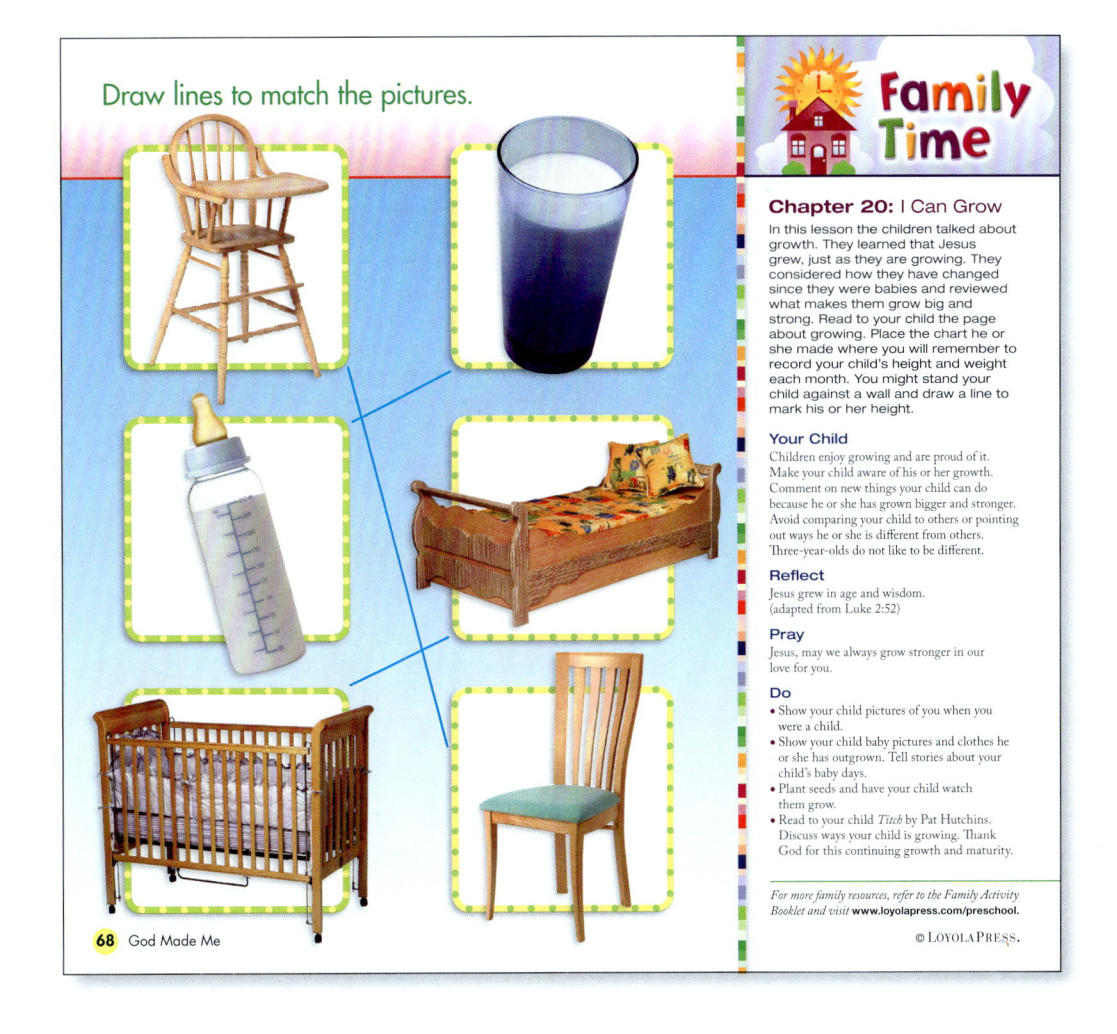

Draw lines to match the pictures.

Family Time

Chapter 20: I Can Grow

In this lesson the children talked about growth. They learned that Jesus grew, just as they are growing. They considered how they have changed since they were babies and reviewed what makes them grow big and strong. Read to your child the page about growing. Place the chart he or she made where you will remember to record your child's height and weight each month. You might stand your child against a wall and draw a line to mark his or her height.

Your Child
Children enjoy growing and are proud of it. Make your child aware of his or her growth. Comment on new things your child can do because he or she has grown bigger and stronger. Avoid comparing your child to others or pointing out ways he or she is different from others. Three-year-olds do not like to be different.

Reflect
Jesus grew in age and wisdom.
(adapted from Luke 2:52)

Pray
Jesus, may we always grow stronger in our love for you.

Do
• Show your child pictures of you when you were a child.
• Show your child baby pictures and clothes he or she has outgrown. Tell stories about your child's baby days.
• Plant seeds and have your child watch them grow.
• Read to your child *Titch* by Pat Hutchins. Discuss ways your child is growing. Thank God for this continuing growth and maturity.

For more family resources, refer to the Family Activity Booklet and visit www.loyolapress.com/preschool.

68 God Made Me

© LOYOLAPRESS.

I Can Grow CHAPTER **20** T135

4 Teach the children this poem with movements:

> When I was a baby
> I was very, very small.
> [Stoop down and be as small as possible.]
> Today I am just this size.
> [Stand and raise hand to top of head.]
> And someday I'll be tall.
> [Stretch hands high.]
> Mary Kathleen Glavich, S.N.D.

SHARING [B]

5 SCRIPTURE Show Cutout #1, Jesus, and talk about Jesus' growth. Read the adaptation of Luke 2:52 from the Scripture card in the Bible.

- *Jesus was a baby once, just as you were. Sometimes he cried and his mother, Mary, had to sing him to sleep. She and Joseph had to carry him. He had to learn to talk and walk.*

- *Listen to what the Bible tells us: "Jesus grew in age and wisdom."*

- *Jesus was your age once too. Then he grew up, just as you will. And as you grow, you become wise, which means you know many things.*

6 Talk about what helps us grow.

- *What makes you grow big and strong?* (Food, rest, play, fresh air)

- *Good food helps you grow. So does a good night's sleep. Your body grows while you are sleeping. Playing also helps you grow. It builds up your muscles. Playing outside is good for you too. It helps you stay healthy and strong.*

I'm Growing

I am growing stronger,
Stronger day by day.
I can help clean up our house
And put things away.

I am growing bigger,
Bigger than my clothes.
At least my skin still stretches
From my fingers to my toes!

I am growing older,
And this is how I know.
Each year upon my birthday cake
Another candle glows.

69 God Made Me

T136 UNIT 4 God Made Me Active

7 PRAYER Lead the children in prayer.

- **Let's thank God for giving us such wonderful bodies. Stand and lift your arms high. Say what I say:**

  O God, you are great.
  [Children repeat.]

  You gave me a body that grows big and strong.
  [Children repeat.]

  I thank you.
  [Children repeat.]

ACTING

1 Distribute pages 69–70 and have the children follow along as you read the poem.

2 Have the children make growth charts from page 71–72. On the cover they may glue their baby pictures, draw their picture, or put a handprint using tempera paint-soaked paper towels. As the children work, measure and weigh each one and fill in the first lines of their charts.

3 Tell the children to ask their parents to fill in the chart from time to time to show how the children are growing.

4 Gather the children in a circle for *Music 'n Motion* time. Play the Unit 4 song (Track 4). Invite the children to do motions to the song along with you, using *Music 'n Motion* page T256.

Have the children take home their pages and show their family the Family Time section.

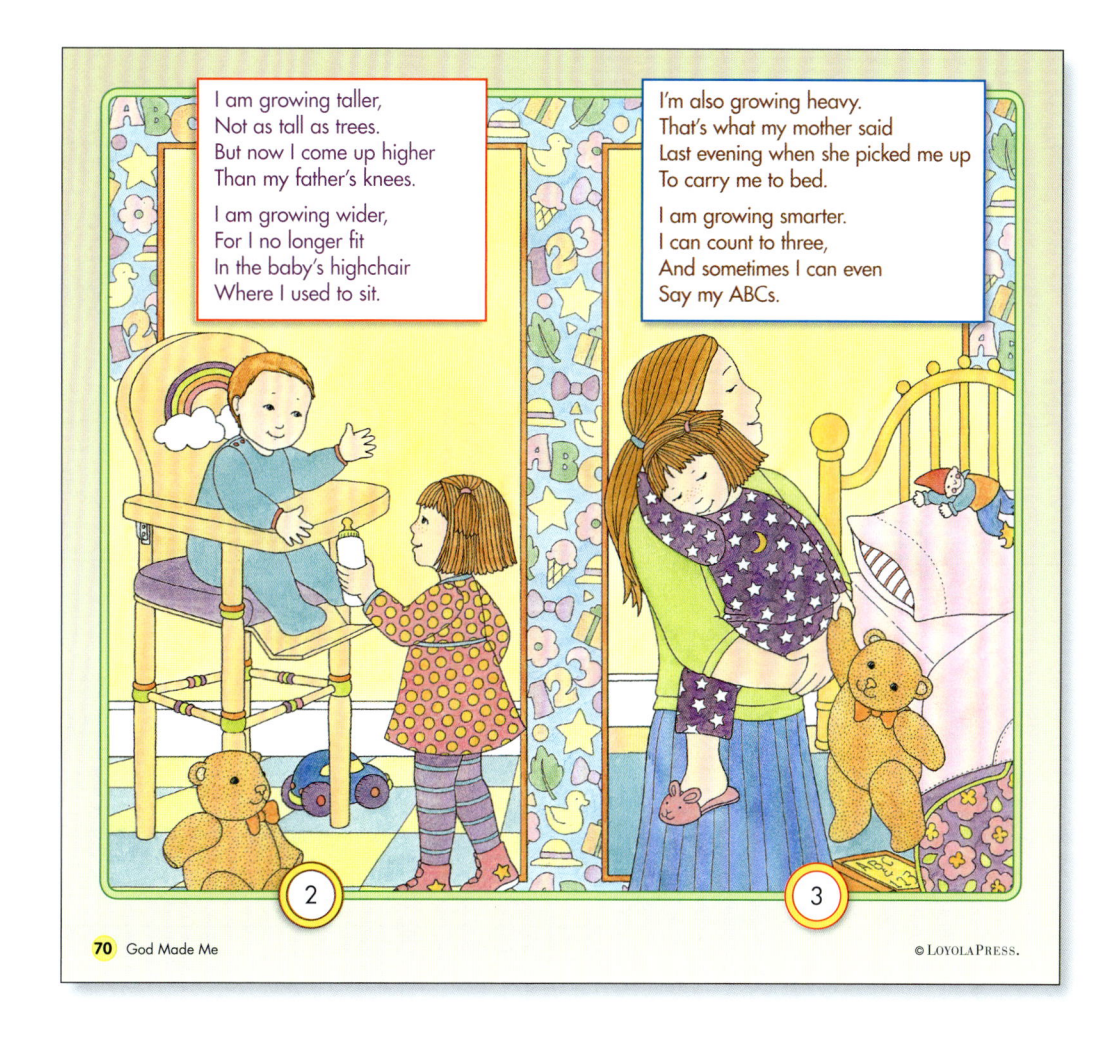

I am growing taller,
Not as tall as trees.
But now I come up higher
Than my father's knees.

I am growing wider,
For I no longer fit
In the baby's highchair
Where I used to sit.

I'm also growing heavy.
That's what my mother said
Last evening when she picked me up
To carry me to bed.

I am growing smarter.
I can count to three,
And sometimes I can even
Say my ABCs.

70 God Made Me   © LOYOLA PRESS.

I Can Grow **CHAPTER 20** **T137**

CHECKPOINT

- Were the learning outcomes achieved?
- Are there any children who seem to be unhealthy? What can you do about it?

ENRICHING THE FAITH EXPERIENCE

Use the following activities to enrich the lesson or to replace an activity with one that better meets the needs of your group.

❶ Make Willie the Worm grow. Cut circles about five inches in diameter for Willie's segments. Make one segment more than the number of children in your group. On one circle, glue or draw eyes, a nose, and a mouth. Give each child a circle with a piece of rolled tape on the back to add, one by one, to Willie.

❷ Show the children seeds. Plant the seeds in class and have the children observe them from time to time as they grow.

❸ Ask the children for the words for baby animals: dog (puppy), cat (kitten), sheep (lamb), deer (fawn), cow (calf), horse (colt, foal).

I Grow

71 God Made Me

T138 UNIT 4 God Made Me Active

4 Do simple exercises with the children, such as stretching or jumping jacks.

5 Try to bring a baby to class for this lesson. Have the children observe the baby. Comment on how small and helpless the baby is. Ask the children what they can do that the baby cannot yet do.

Date	Height	Weight

I Can Grow CHAPTER **20** T139

unit five

God Made Me Special

The children will understand some of their higher-level powers.
They will desire to be the best people they can be.

21 I CAN FEEL

The children experience a surprise and then talk about various feelings. They learn that God loves them no matter how they feel and that Jesus had feelings too. They suggest ways to make people happy. Then they make a lamb's face on each side of a card—one face happy, the other sad.

22 I CAN WISH

The children act out what they want to be when they grow up. Then they talk about wishes and learn the meaning of the phrases "Best wishes" and "God bless you." They hear a story about Benny Bunny who worked to make his wish come true. Then they make a card that expresses best wishes to someone.

23   I CAN LEARN

After learning a new poem, the children are made aware of other things they have learned, such as the letters of the alphabet and numbers. They recall that they are learning more about God. They learn a new song about God and then practice cutting with scissors.

24   I CAN PRETEND

The children pretend to play house and then talk about what fun it is to pretend. They participate in other activities that involve imagining and pretending. Then they make a lion face.

25   I CAN LOVE

The children make a gift for someone they love. They talk about love and the people who love them. After learning that God wants them to love others, they hear that love is shown by words and actions. They make a love pocket to help them show love in three different ways.

God Made Me Special UNIT 5   T141

Chapter 21
I Can Feel

FAITH FOCUS

God has given us different feelings.

John 11:32–36

PREPARING THE FAITH EXPERIENCE

LISTENING

When Mary came to where Jesus was and saw him, she fell at his feet and said to him, "Lord, if you had been here, my brother would not have died." When Jesus saw her weeping and the Jews who had come with her weeping, he became perturbed and deeply troubled, and said, "Where have you laid him?" They said to him, "Sir, come and see." And Jesus wept. So the Jews said, "See how he loved him."

John 11:32–36

REFLECTING

In the popular *Star Trek* TV series, Spock is a character from the planet Vulcan who has no emotions. At times we may wish that we are like Spock—when we are racked with rage, trembling with fear, disappointed in love, or mired in depression. Emotions are part of being human. J. Masai is right to advise, "Feelings are everywhere—be gentle." We must admit that without emotions, life would be rather dull.

Because he was truly human, Jesus experienced emotions. When he saw people who were in need of healing, he was moved with pity. He wept at the news of his friend Lazarus's death and at the destruction of the holy city, Jerusalem. Jesus lashed out in anger at the sellers at the Temple who were desecrating his Father's house. After he foretold that we would eat his body and drink his blood and many of his followers left him, he was sad and disappointed. Jesus was discouraged and frustrated when the apostles failed to understand his message, and he was happy when he found people who had faith. He looked on the rich young man with love and at the widow of Naim with compassion. Jesus was hurt when only one leper out of the ten he cured returned to thank him. At the end of his life, Jesus felt fear and dread as he endured the agony in the garden of Gethsemane.

Because Jesus knows what it is like to be influenced by emotions, he understands us and can sympathize with us when we are experiencing difficult or painful situations. We can share our sorrows with him as well as our joys. We can rely on him for help in coping with our emotions. It is encouraging to know that some of the saints also had strong emotions. Saint Jerome and Saint Francis de Sales, for example, had bad tempers.

Christ in heaven at the right hand of the Father is still man. We can bring joy to his heart by our words and deeds of love.

RESPONDING

Having reflected upon God's Word, take some time now to continue to respond to God in prayer. You might wish to record your responses in your journal.

- What emotions that Jesus experienced do I identify with most?

Loving Father, make the children well-balanced, fully alive people.

UNIT 5 God Made Me Special

Catechism of the Catholic Church

The themes of this chapter correspond to the following paragraphs: 1762–1764, 1769.

THE FAITH EXPERIENCE

Child's Book pages 73–76

SCRIPTURE IN THIS CHAPTER
- *John 15:11-12*

MATERIALS
- Piece of candy or a colorful sticker for each child
- Crayons or markers
- Dance music for SHARING #4
- Bible
- Cutouts: #12, lamb; #47, butterfly
- Hole punch
- 6-inch piece of yarn or ribbon for each child

PREPARATION
- Write the children's names on pages 73 and 75.
- Punch a hole in the top of page 75.

MUSIC 'N MOTION
Use *Music 'n Motion* page T260 and CD Track 5 "You Are the Light" for this chapter. For a list of additional music, see page T302.

ENRICHING THE FAITH EXPERIENCE
Use the activities at the end of the chapter to enrich the lesson or to replace an activity with one that better meets the needs of your group.

BOOKS TO SHARE
When I Feel Angry by Cornelia Maude Spelman
(Albert Whitman & Company, 2000)

The Little Old Lady Who Was Not Afraid of Anything by Linda Williams (HarperTrophy, 1988)

No, David! by David Shannon (Everest Publishing, 1999)

Fun Is A Feeling by Chara M. Curtis
(Illumination Arts Publishing Co., 1998)

SNACK
Suggestion: apple wedges (smiles)

ALTERNATIVE PROGRAMS

DAILY PROGRAM
Day 1: Centering, Sharing A
Day 2: Sharing B
Day 3: Acting #1
Day 4: Enriching the Faith Experience choice
Day 5: Acting #2 and #3

THREE-DAY PROGRAM
Day 1: Centering, Sharing A
Day 2: Sharing B
Day 3: Acting

21 I Can Feel

LEARNING OUTCOMES

The children will
- identify different feelings.
- know that Jesus had feelings.
- desire to cause good feelings in others.

COMMENTS

1. Three-year-old children are just beginning to realize that they have feelings and to discover what events and words evoke these feelings. The children may need help in accepting their feelings as normal and in expressing them appropriately. It is good to have a time-out spot, such as a quiet corner of the room, where children who need to deal with their feelings can be alone for a short time.

2. One characteristic of three-year-olds is that they verbally and physically firmly exclude certain other children from a group. Be alert to this behavior and be creative in helping the outsiders participate, perhaps by assigning them special roles. Remind the children that we do not want anyone to feel left out.

CENTERING

❶ Gather the children in a circle for *Music 'n Motion* time. Play the Unit 5 song (Track 5). Invite the children to do motions to the song along with you, using *Music 'n Motion* page T260.

❷ Announce to the children that you have a surprise for them. Give each child a piece of candy or a sticker and let the children eat the candy or put the sticker on their clothes. Ask:

- *How does my surprise make you feel? Why?*

SHARING [A]

❶ Distribute page 73 and talk about the feelings of the children in the picture.

- *How does the girl feel?* (Happy) *Why do you think so?* (She is smiling. She is holding a kitten.)

- *How does the boy sitting on the chair feel?* (Sad) *How do you know?* (He looks as if he is going to cry.) *Why is he sad?* (His toy is broken.)

- *How does the boy in bed feel?* (Afraid) *Why?* (There is lightning outside. Perhaps it is thundering as well.)

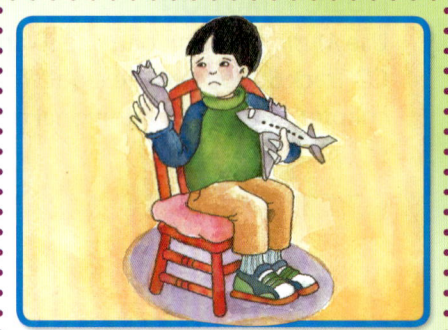

2 Talk about feelings.

- *God made us with feelings. Sometimes we are happy. Sometimes we are sad. Sometimes we are afraid. Sometimes we are angry. No matter how we feel, God loves us. God loves us on days when we are happy. God loves us on days when we are sad or afraid.*

- *What makes you happy? sad? afraid? angry?*

- *Make a face that shows you are happy. How do you look when you are surprised? Now make an angry face. Show us how you look when you are afraid.*

3 Have the children draw a smile on the face next to each child who is happy on page 74.

4 Let the children do a feelings dance. Direct them to show feelings through their dance as you name the feelings. Play music and call out "happy," "sad," "afraid," "angry," and then "happy" again.

SHARING [B]

5 SCRIPTURE Talk about Jesus' feelings and tell the children what Jesus taught about being happy. Show the Bible.

- *Jesus has feelings too. He was happy when he was with his friends. When one of his friends died, Jesus cried. He became angry when people were mean to others or selfish. And sometimes Jesus was afraid.*

- *Jesus wants everyone to be happy. In the Bible, Jesus tells us that we will be completely happy when we show love to others as he did.*
(adapted from John 15:11–12)

- *We can make people happy by being kind.*

6 Ask the children how they can make people they know happy.

7 PRAYER Lead the children in a prayer:

- *Let's talk to God about our feelings. Close your eyes. Say these words in your heart:*

Dear God, thank you for making me happy. [Pause.]

Help me make other people happy. [Pause.]

Keep me from hurting their feelings. [Pause.]

When I am sad or afraid, I know you are with me. [Pause.]

Amen.

Draw a smiling face in the circle next to each happy child.

74 God Made Me

Family Time

Chapter 21: I Can Feel

In this lesson the children learned about various feelings everyone has, including Jesus. They expressed these feelings by making faces and by dancing. The children were led to be sensitive to others' feelings. Have your child hang the lamb made in class on a doorknob and turn it to match his or her feelings.

Your Child
Three-year-olds are usually cheerful. They delight in the world, themselves, and new things. They are becoming aware of feelings. Help your child identify them by making comments such as "I see you are upset" or "You look worried." Remind your child that when he or she has unpleasant feelings, God cares. God loves him or her on good days and bad days.

Reflect
I have told you this so that my joy might be in you and your joy may be complete. This is my commandment: love one another as I love you. (John 15:11–12)

Pray
Jesus, may we know the joy that only you can give.

Do
- Assure your child that it is all right to cry when we are sad or hurt.
- Comment on the feelings of characters in books and shows.
- Point out how your child's actions may make others feel.
- Accept an apology from your child with a hug, saying "I forgive you and I love you." Apologize yourself.
- Read to your child *When I Feel Angry* by Cornelia Maude Spelman. Talk with your child about appropriate ways to express feelings. Thank God for loving us always.

For more family resources, refer to the Family Activity Booklet and visit www.loyolapress.com/preschool.

© LOYOLAPRESS.

I Can Feel CHAPTER 21 T145

ACTING

❶ **Use Cutouts** #12, lamb, and #47, butterfly, to tell the following story. Have the children clap when the lamb is happy, say "Boo hoo" when the lamb is sad, and say "Oh, no" when the lamb is afraid.

Lucy Lamb

Once upon a time there was a lamb named Lucy. One morning she woke up and the sun was shining through the barn windows. Lucy was full of energy, and she felt happy. [Clap.] She ran to the barnyard and ate a good breakfast with her mother and brother. Soon her tummy was full. She felt happy. [Clap.]

A butterfly flew by and Lucy chased it. She ran far away. Suddenly the butterfly flew high up into the air and was gone. Lucy was sad. [Boo hoo.] Then she looked around and didn't know where she was. Lucy was lost. She was afraid. [Oh, no.] Lucy ran until she tripped on a twig and fell. Lucy sat and cried. [Boo hoo.] Suddenly the butterfly came back. "Lucy Lamb," it said, "I know where you live. Follow me." So Lucy ran after the butterfly again until she saw her barn. She was happy. [Clap.]

Lucy ran to her mother. "Baa, baa, where were you?" asked her mother. "I was worried about you. Don't go away like that again." Lucy was sad to be scolded. [Boo hoo.] But she was very glad to be home. [Clap.]

❷ Help the children make lamb faces using pages 75 and 76. Have them color the lamb's eyes on each side of the page. Then tell them to draw a smile on the side without a mouth and to draw tears on the other side. Have them string yarn or ribbon through the hole you have punched. Tie it for them. Suggest that the children hang the lamb at home, perhaps on a doorknob, and turn the card to match their feelings during the day.

❸ Gather the children in a circle for *Music 'n Motion* time. Play the Unit 5 song (Track 5). Invite the children to do motions to the song along with you, using *Music 'n Motion* page T260.

Have the children take home their pages and show their family the Family Time section.

CHECKPOINT

- Were the learning outcomes achieved?
- How accurately did the children express the different feelings as they danced?

75 God Made Me

Name _____

T146 UNIT 5 *God Made Me Special*

ENRICHING THE FAITH EXPERIENCE

Use the following activities to enrich the lesson or to replace an activity with one that better meets the needs of your group.

1 Have the children act out ways to make others happy. Provide suggestions for them.

2 Talk about times when the children may be frightened: during a storm, after having a bad dream, when they are lost. Assure them that God is with them. Teach them to pray: "I fear no harm for you are at my side." (Psalm 23:4)

3 Teach the children this poem with gestures:

My Feelings

When I'm angry, you can tell,
For I stamp my feet and yell. [Stamp feet.]

When I'm sad, I mope about,
Sigh and cry and don't go out. [Put hands under chin and cup face.]

When I'm scared by day or night,
I hide and shake, my eyes closed tight. [Shake.]

When I'm happy, hear me sing.
I laugh at almost anything. [Extend arms to sides.]

Whether I'm feeling good or bad,
God loves me. For this I'm glad! [Clap.]

Mary Kathleen Glavich, S.N.D.

4 Sing or teach the song "If You're Happy and You Know It Clap Your Hands." (See page T69.) Sing the first verse and then sing the verses that substitute "stamp your feet," "nod your head," and "do all three" for the words "clap your hands."

5 Teach the song "Clap, Clap, Clap Your Hands." Add verses with movements such as point your toe, nod your head, and turn around.

I Can Feel CHAPTER **21** T147

Chapter 22
I Can Wish

FAITH FOCUS
God wishes the best for us.
Ephesians 3:14–19

PREPARING THE FAITH EXPERIENCE

LISTENING

Have no anxiety at all, but in everything, by prayer and petition, with thanksgiving, make your requests known to God. Then the peace of God that surpasses all understanding will guard your hearts and minds in Christ Jesus.
                                    Philippians 4:6–7

REFLECTING

We have an innate desire to want what we consider good—in other words, we *wish*. Wishing is akin to hoping. Unable to foresee the future, we are free to hope that our wishes will come true. Sometimes we feel that if we wish for something hard enough, it will come to be. We might even believe in self-fulfilling prophecies. Wishes or dreams are part of the dynamics of progress. They spur us on to action. In order to reach our goals or fulfill our wishes and dreams, we give ourselves wholeheartedly to self-improvement and to working for a better world.

Wishes and dreams are good. Langston Hughes in his poem "Dreams" reminds us that when dreams die, "Life is a broken-winged bird / That cannot fly."

Jesus assures us that God our Father loves us and will always do what is best for us. We do not have to work alone to make our wishes, the desires of our hearts, come true. Jesus said, "Ask and it will be given to you; seek and you will find; knock and the door will be opened to you." (Matthew 7:7) He elaborated that just as you "give good gifts to your children, how much more will your heavenly Father give good things to those who ask him." (Matthew 7:11) Although God reads the secrets of our hearts and knows what we need before we ask, Jesus expressly advises us to verbalize our requests to God.

Sometimes God delays answering our prayers. Then we must remember the persistent Canaanite woman whose daughter was cured by Christ, and Saint Monica, who spent years praying for her wayward son Augustine and eventually was rewarded by his becoming not only a Catholic but also a bishop and a renowned saint.

Sometimes we receive a no to our requests because God has a better idea, which we with our limited vision do not always perceive.

So we go on wishing and hoping. We pray for our personal needs and the needs of the world. We ask God to bless our family and friends. Our prayers spring from our confidence that God will hear and answer them because of a great, unfathomable love for us.

RESPONDING

God's Word calls us to respond in love. Respond to God now in the quiet of your heart, and perhaps through your journal.

- What hopes and wishes do I bring to God in prayer?

God, bless the children with a firm trust in you.

UNIT 5 God Made Me Special

Catechism of the Catholic Church

The themes of this chapter correspond to the following paragraphs: 1046, 1049, 1821.

THE FAITH EXPERIENCE

Child's Book pages 77–82

SCRIPTURE IN THIS CHAPTER
- *Matthew 7:11*

MATERIALS
- Clothes and props for CENTERING #2
- Bible
- Crayons, markers, paint

PREPARATION
- Write the children's names on pages 77, 79, and 82.
- Fold in half pages 79 and 82.

MUSIC 'N MOTION
Use *Music 'n Motion* page T260 and CD Track 5 "You Are the Light" for this chapter. For a list of additional music, see page T302.

ENRICHING THE FAITH EXPERIENCE
Use the activities at the end of the chapter to enrich the lesson or to replace an activity with one that better meets the needs of your group.

BOOKS TO SHARE
The Little Engine That Could by Watty Piper (Grossett & Dunlap, 1978)

I Can Do It Too! by Karen Baicker (Handprint Books, 2003)

Inches and Miles: The Journey to Success by John R. Wooden (Perfection Learning, 2003)

How to Catch a Star by Oliver Jeffers (Philomel, 2004)

SNACK
Suggestion: celery and carrot sticks (You might offer a creamy dip for the children to dip their vegetables in.)

ALTERNATIVE PROGRAMS

DAILY PROGRAM
Day 1: Centering, Sharing A
Day 2: Sharing B
Day 3: Acting
Day 4: Enriching the Faith Experience choice
Day 5: Enriching the Faith Experience choice

THREE-DAY PROGRAM
Day 1: Centering, Sharing A
Day 2: Sharing B
Day 3: Acting

I Can Wish CHAPTER 22 T149

22 I Can Wish

LEARNING OUTCOMES
The children will
- know that they have the power to wish.
- realize that God wishes them well.
- express good wishes.

COMMENTS
1. Three-year-old children like to talk about the future, and they enjoy make-believe. In this lesson they will have fun making wishes. They will soon learn that some wishes—the desires of our hearts—can be realized through prayer, some through hard work, and many by a combination of the two. Our wishes and dreams are the seeds of growth and improvement in our lives, our world, and our Church.

2. Some children have fears about the dark, animals, or loud noises. These fears may be revealed by the kinds of wishes the children verbalize.

3. This lesson introduces the concept of "blessing" as wishing good to someone. According to the *Catechism*, "Every baptized person is called to be a 'blessing,' and to bless." (1669)

CENTERING
❶ Gather the children in a circle for *Music 'n Motion* time. Play the Unit 5 song (Track 5). Invite the children to do motions to the song along with you, using *Music 'n Motion* page T260.

❷ Let the children dress up and act out what they wish to be when they grow up, such as mother, father, police officer, teacher, or veterinarian.

SHARING [A]
❶ Distribute page 77 and talk about wishes.

- *What are the grandfather and granddaughter doing?* (The granddaughter is helping her grandfather blow out the candles and make a wish, celebrating the grandfather's birthday)

- *What do you think the grandfather and granddaughter are wishing for?*

- *Today you acted out what you wish to be when you grow up. We make wishes for things we want for ourselves and for others.*

T150 UNIT 5 *God Made Me Special*

- *Some wishes are silly wishes. We might wish that it would rain lollipops. Some wishes are more serious. We might wish that our sick brother would get better.*

- *Did you ever make a wish? When?* (at birthday parties, on holidays) *What did you wish for?*

2 **SCRIPTURE** Share your wishes and talk about others' wishes. Show the Bible as you talk about God's wishes for us. (adapted from Matthew 7:11)

- *I wish . . .* [Tell your wishes.]

- *What do you think your mother wishes for?*

- *What do you think your father wishes for?*

- *I know what God wishes. In the Bible, Jesus tells us that God wants to give good things to his children. Because God loves you, God wishes that each one of you grows up to be a good, happy person.*

3 Have the children stand up and clap their hands when you name an example of something that God wishes for us.

- *God wishes that we have people who care for us.* [Children stand up and clap.]

- *God wishes that we share our toys with others.* [Children stand up and clap.]

- *God wishes that all elephants can sing and dance.* [Children stay seated.]

- *God wishes that we have healthy food to eat.* [Children stand up and clap.]

- *God wishes that we eat cake five times a day.* [Children stay seated.]

4 Talk about wishing the best for others.

- *When we like people, we wish good things for them. Sometimes we send them best wishes in a card or letter. We can also pray for others. When we pray "God bless you," we mean that we want the best for them.*

SHARING [B]

5 Have the children look at the pictures on page 78 and have them circle the people for whom they will pray. Suggest that the children pray "God bless" as they circle each picture.

Draw a circle around the people you want to pray for.

Family Time

Chapter 22: I Can Wish

In this lesson the children learned about wishes. They recalled times when people make wishes, and they shared some of their own wishes. They learned that God wishes only what is best for them and that we can send best wishes to others. Ask your child to show you the story about Benny Bunny who worked to make his wish come true. Your child made a card expressing best wishes for someone. Help deliver it if necessary.

Your Child
Pay close attention when your child expresses a wish. Help him or her distinguish between wishes that can really come true and those that are impossible. Your child's wishes may reveal his or her fears.

Reflect
"If you then . . . know how to give good gifts to your children, how much more will your heavenly Father give good things to those who ask him." (Matthew 7:11)

Pray
Heavenly Father, we thank you for your goodness and love.

Do
- Share with your child what you wish for him or her.
- Bless your child with the Sign of the Cross on his or her forehead each night.
- At a family gathering have each person complete the statement "I wish . . ."
- Tell your child a story about someone who made wishes.
- Read to your child *The Little Engine That Could* by Watty Piper. Talk about a time your child completed a difficult task. Give thanks to God who always helps us and wants the best for us.

For more family resources, refer to the Family Activity Booklet and visit www.loyolapress.com/preschool.

© LOYOLAPRESS.

I Can Wish **CHAPTER 22** **T151**

6 PRAYER Invite the children to pray for God's blessing. Explain:

• *Let us pray, asking God to bless each person in this class.*

• *I will tap each of you on the shoulder. When I do, you may stand. Then together we will pray "God bless [child's name]."*

Benny Bunny's Wish

Finally Benny Bunny had a beautiful garden in his yard. His wish had come true.

Benny Bunny lived next door to Betty Bunny. She had many pretty flowers in her front yard.

"Mom," said Benny Bunny one morning, "I wish we had pretty flowers like those in Betty Bunny's yard."

"No problem," said Mommy Bunny. "We will have to do some planting."

79 God Made Me

Name _____

T152 UNIT 5 God Made Me Special

7 Distribute pages 79 and 80 and read the story to the children. Ask:

• *What made Benny's wish come true?* (His mother helped him. Benny and his mother worked. The weather helped.)

• *Sometimes the things we do help make our wishes come true.*

Mommy Bunny and Benny Bunny went to the store. They bought some flower seeds.

That afternoon Mommy Bunny and Benny Bunny cleared a patch of ground. They pulled weeds and made the soil soft. Then they planted the flower seeds and watered them well.

Every day the sun shined, and Benny Bunny watered the seeds. Soon green shoots began to peek through the dirt. The shoots grew tall and put out leaves and then buds and then flowers!

80 God Made Me

© LOYOLAPRESS.

I Can Wish CHAPTER **22** **T153**

ACTING

❶ Help the children make someone special a card from pages 81–82. Tell them that the card says "Best Wishes" on the front. Have them think of a person they would like to give best wishes to. Children who can write their names may write them next to the heart on the line inside the card. They may color or paint a design on the front of the card.

❷ Gather the children in a circle for *Music 'n Motion* time. Play the Unit 5 song (Track 5). Invite the children to do motions to the song along with you, using *Music 'n Motion* page T260.

Have the children take home their pages and show their family the Family Time section.

CHECKPOINT

- *Were the learning outcomes achieved?*
- *What did the children's wishes reveal?*

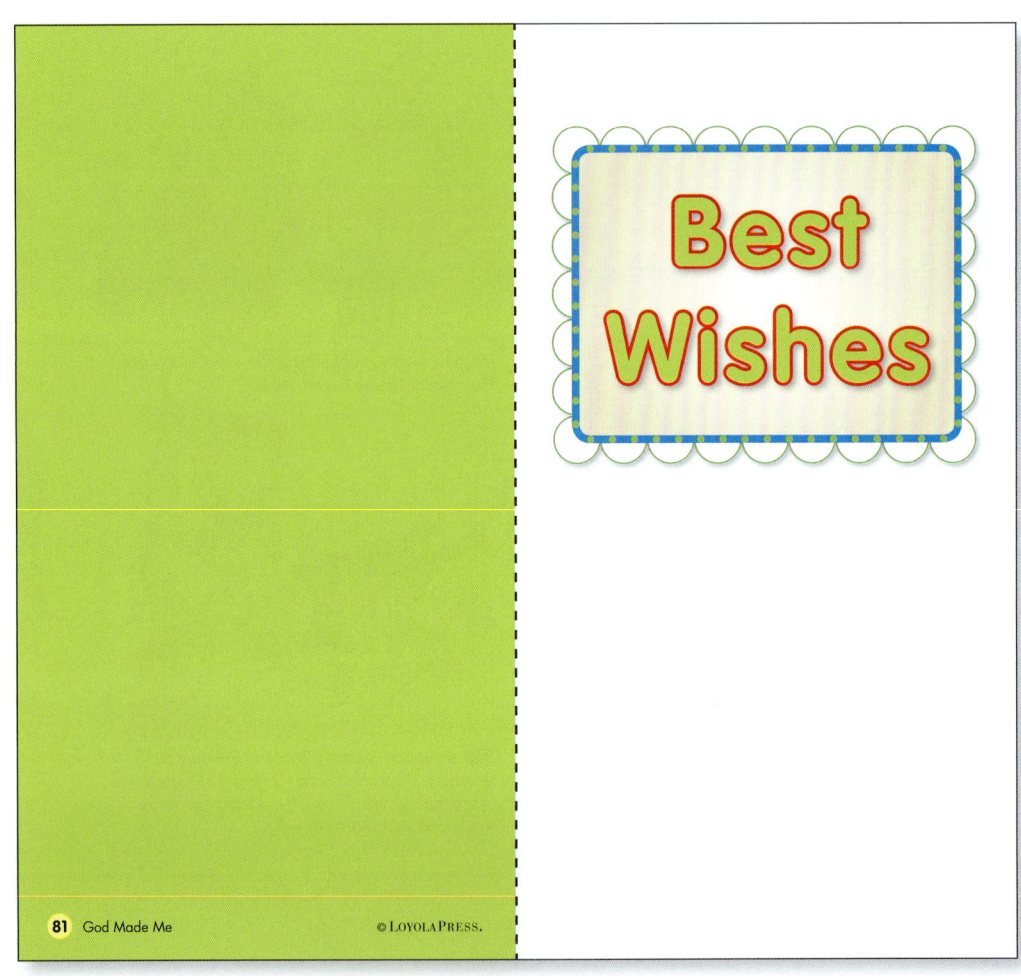

81 God Made Me © LoyolaPress.

T154   UNIT 5 God Made Me Special

ENRICHING THE FAITH EXPERIENCE

Use the following activities to enrich the lesson or to replace an activity with one that better meets the needs of your group.

1 Suggest that the children ask God to bless the people they love in a prayer before they go to bed.

2 Teach the children to say "God bless you" to someone who sneezes.

3 Hide stickers around the room and have the children find them.

4 Play "I Spy." Describe an item or picture in the classroom that represents a good thing that God has given to us until a child guesses what it is.

5 Teach the following poem:

I See the Moon

I see the moon,
And the moon sees me.
God bless the moon,
And God bless me.
Traditional

6 Let the children make silly wishes, such as "I wish I had two more arms" or "I wish I had a pet camel."

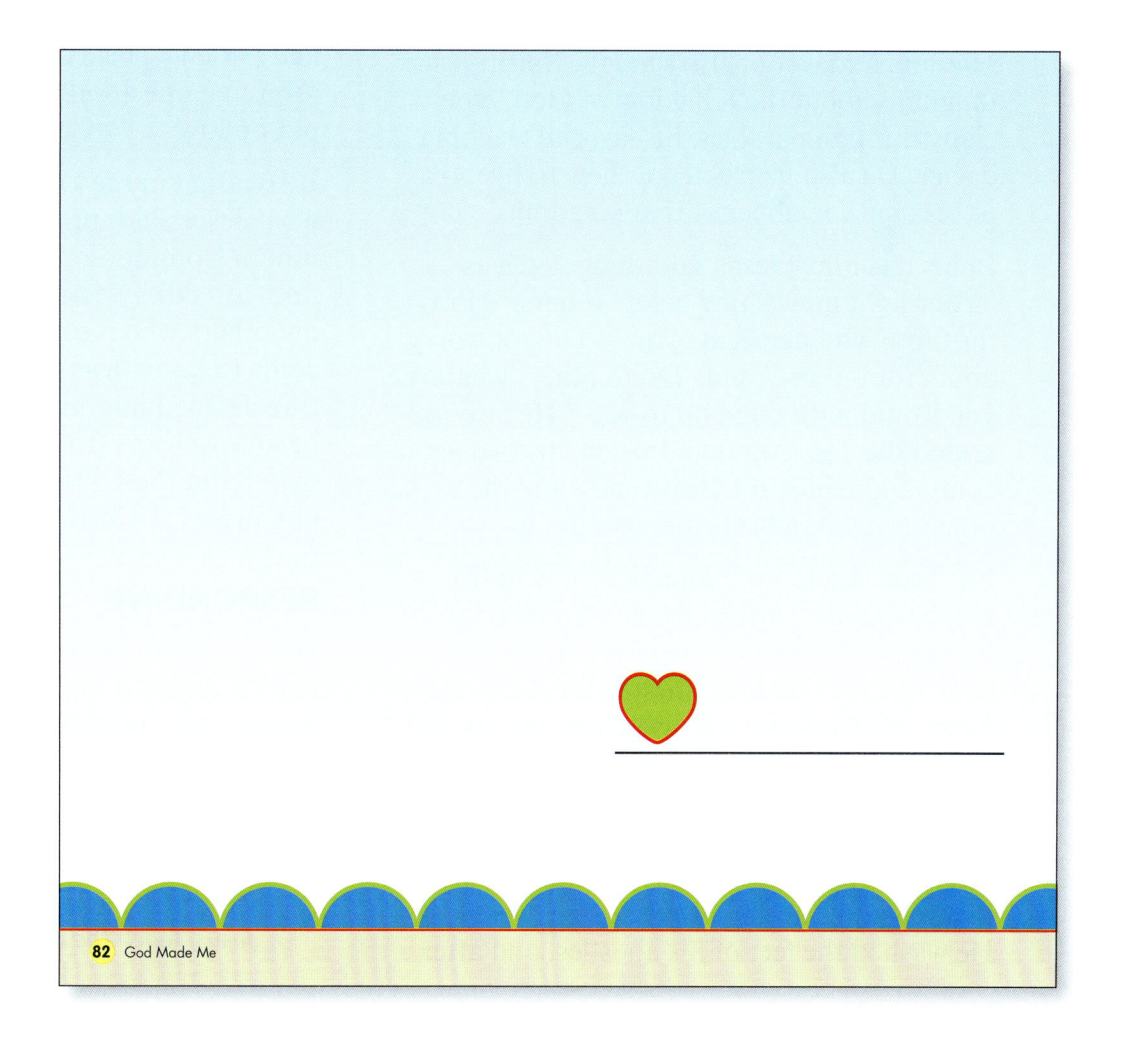

I Can Wish **CHAPTER 22**   **T155**

Chapter 23
I Can Learn

FAITH FOCUS
God gave us the ability to think.
Genesis 1:27

PREPARING THE FAITH EXPERIENCE

LISTENING

"[L]earn from me, for I am meek and humble of heart . . ."

Matthew 11:29

REFLECTING

One reason why God's Son became a human being known as Jesus Christ was to teach us. People called him *rabbi,* which means "teacher." We can learn many important things from Jesus, the Teacher. He taught us about God the Father. He taught that God loves us more than the flowers and the birds and wants us to pray. He revealed that the Father had sent him and would also send the Spirit. Jesus taught us about the Kingdom of God, especially through parables, his favorite teaching device. He also instructed us how to live so as to become a member of that kingdom.

In his teachings Jesus said things such as "Your light must shine before others," "Pray for those who persecute you," "Do not worry about tomorrow," and "Do to others whatever you would have them do to you." He also presented the Ten Commandments, his two great commandments, the Beatitudes, and the works of mercy as standards for right living.

But Jesus did more than tell us how to live. He showed us. Untiringly, he responded to the pleas of those who were sick and those who, like Nicodemus, thirsted for the Good News. He fed those who were hungry through the multiplication of loaves and fish. When a woman caught in adultery was set before him, he treated her with kindness. He searched after others who, like the Samaritan woman at the well and Zacchaeus in the tree, were lost. He washed the feet of his apostles, and after they had deserted and betrayed him, he forgave them. In the end he even gave up his life for us.

We learn from Jesus, our model, how to live perfectly—that is, how to live a life of love. We try to take on Jesus' virtues, his values, and his attitudes. Paul exhorts us, "Put on then, as God's chosen ones, holy and beloved, heartfelt compassion, kindness, humility, gentleness, and patience, bearing with one another and forgiving one another . . . And over all these put on love . . ." (Colossians 3:12–14)

By reading in the Gospels about Jesus and what Jesus said, praying to him, receiving him in Communion, studying books about him, attending lectures about him, and seeing others who resemble him, we gradually come to know Jesus. Little by little we are transformed into his image. Then people will be able to learn from us. We will be able to say with Saint Paul, "Be imitators of me, as I am of Christ." (1 Corinthians 11:1)

RESPONDING

Having been nourished by God's Word, we are able to respond to God's great love for us. In prayer, respond to God's call to you to share his Word with others. You may also wish to respond in your prayer journal.

- What in particular would I like to learn from Jesus?

Jesus, teach the children to find true happiness.

Catechism of the Catholic Church

The themes of this chapter correspond to the following paragraphs: 35, 94.

THE FAITH EXPERIENCE

Child's Book pages 83–86

SCRIPTURE IN THIS CHAPTER
• Matthew 11:29

MATERIALS
• Bible
• Chapter 23 Scripture card
• Option: alphabet blocks
• Crayons or markers
• Cutout #48, "God is so good."
• Scissors with blunt ends, including scissors for left-handed children if needed

PREPARATION
• Place the Chapter 23 Scripture card for SHARING #5 in the Bible.
• Write the children's names on pages 83 and 86.
• Cut out the circle on page 85.

MUSIC 'N MOTION
Use *Music 'n Motion* page T260 and CD Track 5 "You Are the Light" for this chapter. For a list of additional music, see page T302.

ENRICHING THE FAITH EXPERIENCE
Use the activities at the end of the chapter to enrich the lesson or to replace an activity with one that better meets the needs of your group.

BOOKS TO SHARE
Froggy Learns to Swim by Jonathan London (Puffin, 1997)

26 Letters and 99 Cents by Tana Hoban (HarperTrophy, 1995)

Wee Sing & Learn Colors by Pamela Conn Beall and Susan Hagen Nipp (Grosset & Dunlap, 2001)

Wee Sing & Learn ABC by Pamela Conn Beall and Pamela Conn Beall (Price Stern Sloan, 2000)

SNACK
Suggestion: O-shaped cereal or cookies/cupcakes with a letter or number on each

---

ALTERNATIVE PROGRAMS

DAILY PROGRAM
Day 1: Centering, Sharing A
Day 2: Enriching the Faith Experience choice
Day 3: Sharing B
Day 4: Enriching the Faith Experience choice
Day 5: Acting

THREE-DAY PROGRAM
Day 1: Centering, Sharing A
Day 2: Sharing B
Day 3: Acting

23 I Can Learn

LEARNING OUTCOMES
The children will
- enjoy learning something new.
- thank God for their ability to learn.

COMMENTS
1. Human beings are made in the image of God and have the power to think. One of the joys of being human is increasing our knowledge. We constantly learn and discover things about ourselves and our world.

2. Three-year-old children delight in learning new things. By asking the question "why?" they add to their store of knowledge. Each new accomplishment brings satisfaction, builds their self-esteem, and gives them more power and control in a world in which they often feel powerless.

3. Comparing children to their peers can lead to false assumptions. Each child learns at his or her own pace. Parents need not be concerned if their child is not reading yet, even though other children are.

CENTERING

❶ Gather the children in a circle for *Music 'n Motion* time. Play the Unit 5 song (Track 5). Invite the children to do motions to the song along with you, using *Music 'n Motion* page T260.

❷ Teach the children this poem. Have them make fists and, as they say each number, put one fist on top of the other as if building a stack.

> One potato, two potato,
> three potato, four,
> Five potato, six potato, seven potato, more.

SHARING [A]

❶ Talk about learning.

- *You just learned a new poem. And you learned the numbers up to seven, if you didn't know them already. Let's see if we can count to 10 together.* [Lead the group in counting to 10.]

- [Option: Show the alphabet blocks.] *Let's see if we can say the ABCs.* [Lead the group in saying the ABCs.]

- *Can a dog count?* (No.) *Can a dog say the ABCs?* (No.) *God made you special. You can think.*

❷ Challenge the children to think of different ways to make circles in the air with their bodies. Have them stand. After a child suggests a way, have the class do it. The children can move their arms, legs, fingers, or heads and can change the size or direction of the circles.

T158 UNIT 5 God Made Me Special

❸ Distribute page 83 and talk about the picture.

• *What is the girl doing?* (Drawing a picture)

• *Ever since you were born, you have learned many things. You have learned how to walk and how to eat. What else have you learned?*

• *God made you so that you enjoy learning new things all the time. Isn't God good?*

❹ Have the children color the letter *O* on page 84. Comment:

• *You see the letter* **O** *on the page. It is a letter of the alphabet.*

• *Think of a good way to make your letter* **O** *different from everyone else's.*

• *As you get older, you will learn to write the letter* **O** *and all the other letters of the alphabet as well.*

SHARING B

❺ **SCRIPTURE** Tell the children that they are learning more about God. Ask them what they have learned about God. Tell the children that Jesus is God's Son. Read the adaptation of Matthew 11:29 from the Scripture card in the Bible.

• *Jesus teaches us about God. Listen to what Jesus says in the Bible: "Learn from me."*

❻ Teach the children the song "God Is So Good." Show Cutout #48, "God is so good." Read it and have the children count how many times the letter *O* appears. (Four)

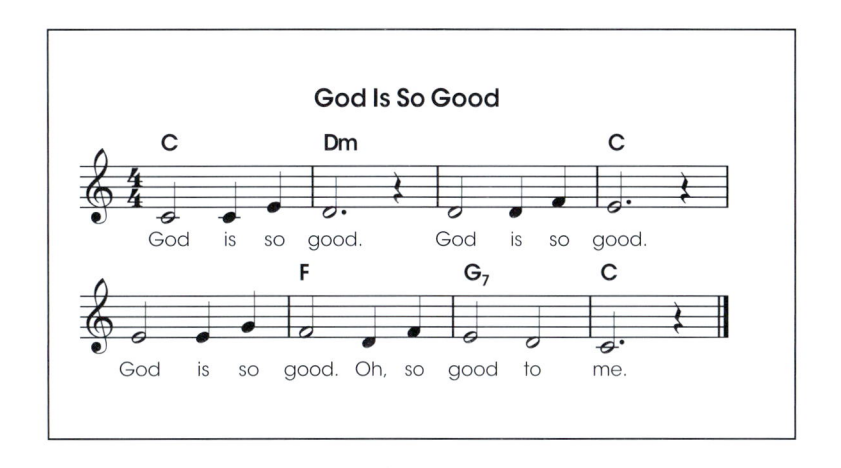

God is so good.

God Is So Good

Color the letter O.

Family Time

Chapter 23: I Can Learn

In this lesson the children heard that they are more special than animals because God gave them the ability to think. They reviewed many of the things they have learned since they were babies. The children were led to realize that they are learning more about God. Ask your child what he or she has learned about God. Admire the spiral design or place mat your child made.

Your Child
Three-year-old children delight in learning things. Help your child acquire new skills and knowledge. As you do so, you are building his or her self-esteem. Be patient in answering when your child asks "Why?" thereby adding to his or her understanding of the world. Teach your child to persevere when things are difficult.

Reflect
Take my yoke upon you and learn from me, for I am meek and humble of heart; and you will find rest for yourselves. (Matthew 11:29)

Pray
Jesus, may we learn to follow your way of love.

Do
• Mention it to your child when you notice that he or she has learned something new.
• Occasionally ask your child what he or she is thinking.
• Give your child choices in clothes, foods, games, or books to be read.
• Teach your child something new this week.
• Ask your child to recite a poem or sing a song he or she knows.
• Read to your child *Froggy Learns to Swim* by Jonathan London. Help your child name some of the many things he or she is learning. Thank God for the ability to think and learn.

For more family resources, refer to the Family Activity Booklet and visit www.loyolapress.com/preschool.

© LOYOLAPRESS.

I Can Learn CHAPTER 23 T159

ACTING

1 **PRAYER** Lead the children in prayer. Have the children tell something they learned and then say "Thank you, God." Begin with the following as a model:

I have learned God is good. Thank you, God.

I have learned to teach. Thank you, God.

2 Distribute page 85 to give the children practice in cutting with scissors. Have the children cut along the line on the front to make a spiral, which can be hung. [Show the front of the card to the children.]

3 Gather the children in a circle for *Music 'n Motion* time. Play the Unit 5 song (Track 5). Invite the children to do motions to the song along with you, using *Music 'n Motion* page T260.

Have the children take home their pages and show their family the Family Time section.

CHECKPOINT

- Were the learning outcomes achieved?
- What do the children's concepts of God reveal?

ENRICHING THE FAITH EXPERIENCE

Use the following activities to enrich the lesson or to replace an activity with one that better meets the needs of your group.

1 Invite a guest speaker to show the children how to do a particular craft, such as painting eggs, making balloon animals, or creating origami.

2 Show a video that gives information about weather, flowers, or a particular animal.

3 Say a word and have the children mention words that are associated with it. Choose words that are related to what is going on in the children's world at the time.

4 Play thinking games with the children. Ask them to think of ways to go from school to home, ways to open a package, or ways to decorate a cake. Ask the children how many uses they can think of for a box, a brick, or a rubber band.

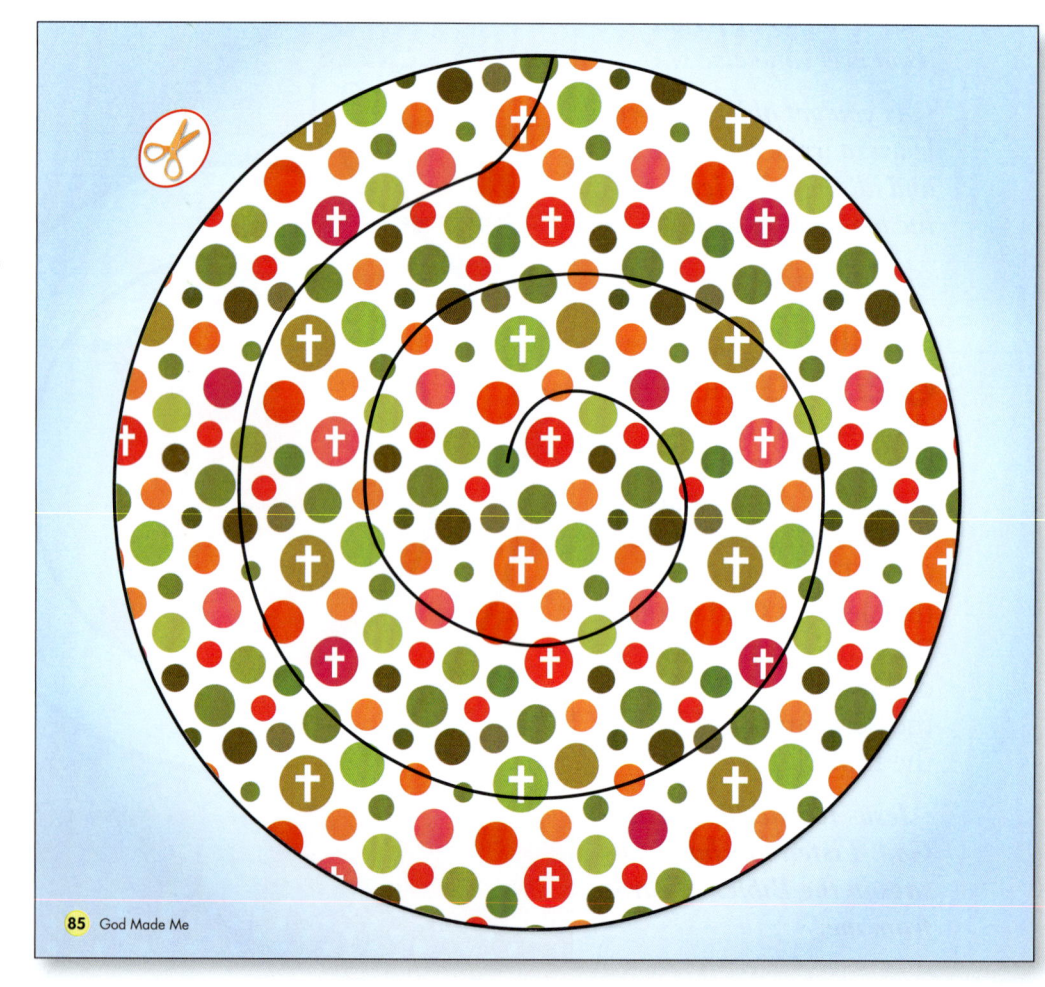

85 God Made Me

T160 UNIT 5 *God Made Me Special*

5 Teach the following song to familiarize the children with numbers. Add these gestures: Put up fingers to match each number. On the second to the last line, hit one fist on the other on *knick*. Hit the other fist on top of the first on *give*. On the last line, roll arms around each other.

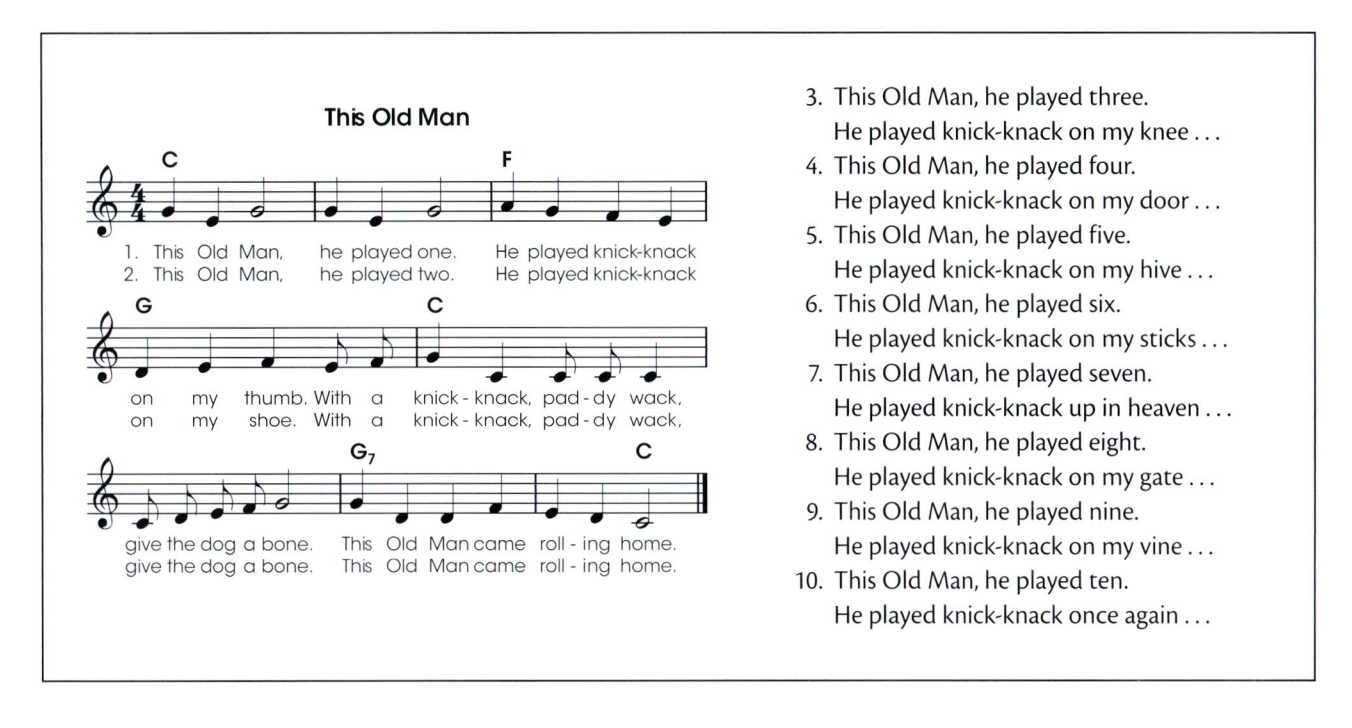

This Old Man

1. This Old Man, he played one.
   He played knick-knack on my thumb. With a knick-knack, paddy wack, give the dog a bone. This Old Man came rolling home.
2. This Old Man, he played two.
   He played knick-knack on my shoe. With a knick-knack, paddy wack, give the dog a bone. This Old Man came rolling home.
3. This Old Man, he played three.
   He played knick-knack on my knee . . .
4. This Old Man, he played four.
   He played knick-knack on my door . . .
5. This Old Man, he played five.
   He played knick-knack on my hive . . .
6. This Old Man, he played six.
   He played knick-knack on my sticks . . .
7. This Old Man, he played seven.
   He played knick-knack up in heaven . . .
8. This Old Man, he played eight.
   He played knick-knack on my gate . . .
9. This Old Man, he played nine.
   He played knick-knack on my vine . . .
10. This Old Man, he played ten.
    He played knick-knack once again . . .

6 Pose situations to the children and have them respond. Ask questions such as the following: What if you forget your raincoat and it rains? What if someone you don't know offers you candy? What if a friend is crying?

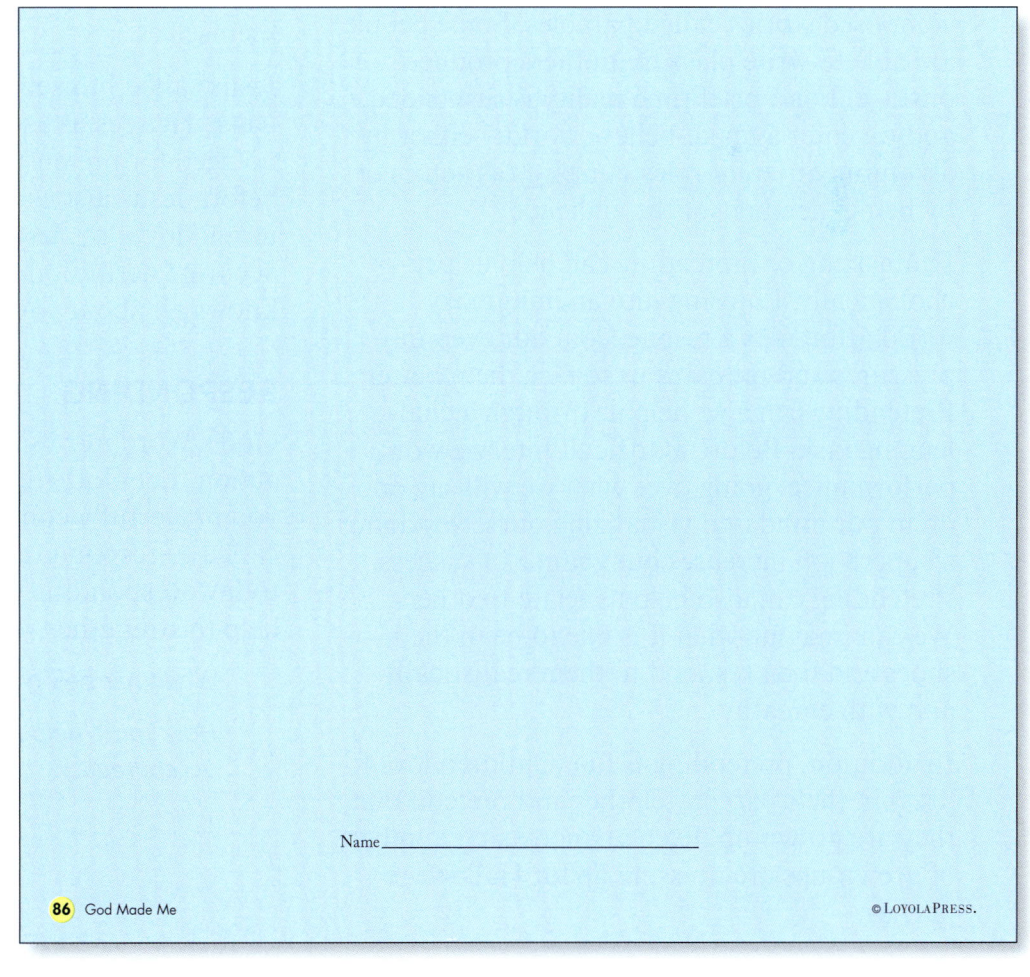

I Can Learn CHAPTER 23 T161

Chapter 24
I Can Pretend

FAITH FOCUS

God gave us the gift of imagination.

Psalm 139:14

PREPARING THE FAITH EXPERIENCE

LISTENING

All these things Jesus spoke to the crowds in parables. He spoke to them only in parables, to fulfill what had been said through the prophet:
  "I will open my mouth in parables,
   I will announce what has lain
     hidden from the foundation
     [of the world]."

Matthew 13:34–35

REFLECTING

The ability to fantasize is a fascinating gift. Our imaginations enable us to weave stories that entertain as well as instruct. Jesus himself composed stories called parables. Some people are able to write plays that others produce onstage. For a brief time reality is suspended, and we enter a make-believe world—either by assuming different roles ourselves as actors or by being members of the audience.

Fantasizing or pretending can help us psychologically. Entering into an imaginary world affords us a respite from our everyday pressures and prepares us to face them better. Pretending can also help us through a challenging task. Before a difficult interview or performance, going over what we will say or do in our mind and visualizing ourselves doing a superb job increases our chance of success. Pretending can also help us relate to others. We can imagine what it is like to be in their shoes and then respond to them realistically and with empathy.

In addition, pretending is fun. Children love to dress in their parents' clothes and pretend that they are grown up. Even an increasing number of grown-ups are dressing up for Halloween parties.

Of course, pretending is not always good. People who pretend that problems do not exist are never able to improve situations. People who pretend that they are immortal and who live recklessly are foolish. People who pretend that they will not be held accountable for their actions in the life to come are in for a surprise. People who pretend that they are greater, smarter, or more wonderful than they really are ultimately hurt themselves.

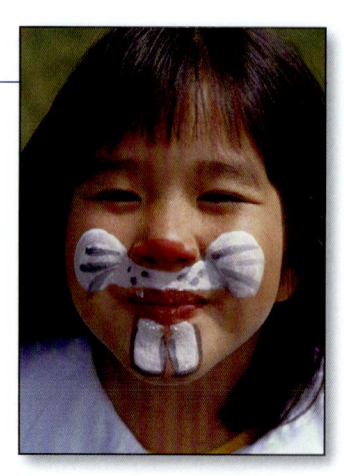

Jesus called himself the Truth. He knows the truth. He sees us as we really are, so there is no need for pretense with him. We can come before Jesus just as we are, and he accepts us and loves us. Jesus fits this humorous but accurate definition of a friend: someone who knows all about you and likes you anyway.

RESPONDING

God's Word moves us to respond in word and action. Let God's Spirit work within you as you prayerfully consider how you are being called to respond to God's message to you today. Responding through your journal may help to strengthen your response.

- When has being able to pretend helped me?

Holy Spirit, help the children enjoy fantasy and accept reality.

UNIT 5 God Made Me Special

Catechism of the Catholic Church

The themes of this chapter correspond to the following paragraphs: 356, 2184.

THE FAITH EXPERIENCE

Child's Book pages 87–88

SCRIPTURE IN THIS CHAPTER
- *Psalm 139:14*

MATERIALS
- Bible
- Chapter 24 Scripture card
- Option: grown-ups' clothes, accessories
- Crayons or markers
- Perforated Card I
- Brown yarn
- White, gray, or black pipe cleaners (two for each child)
- Glue
- Option: hole punch

PREPARATION
- Place the Chapter 24 Scripture card for SHARING #1 in the Bible.
- Write the children's names on page 87 and on perforated Card I
- Punch out the lion heads on perforated Card I.
- Cut the yarn in pieces of different lengths.

MUSIC 'N MOTION
Use *Music 'n Motion* page T260 and CD Track 5 "You Are the Light" for this chapter. For a list of additional music, see page T302.

ENRICHING THE FAITH EXPERIENCE
Use the activities at the end of the chapter to enrich the lesson or to replace an activity with one that better meets the needs of your group.

BOOKS TO SHARE
Where the Wild Things Are by Maurice Sendak (HarperCollins, 1988)

One Day There Was Nothing to Do by Jill Creighton (Annick Press, 1990)

Let's Pretend by Debbie Bailey (Annick Press, 1999)

Grandma Helps Us Pretend by Carol Burns (AuthorHouse, 2005)

SNACK
Suggestion: popcorn

ALTERNATIVE PROGRAMS

DAILY PROGRAM
Day 1: Centering, Sharing A
Day 2: Enriching the Faith Experience choice
Day 3: Enriching the Faith Experience choice
Day 4: Sharing B, Acting #1
Day 5: Acting #2 and #3

THREE-DAY PROGRAM
Day 1: Centering, Sharing A
Day 2: Sharing B, Acting #1
Day 3: Acting #2 and #3

24 I Can Pretend

LEARNING OUTCOMES
The children will
- exercise their imaginations.
- thank God for their ability to pretend.
- enjoy the lesson.

COMMENTS
1. Children love to pretend. Pretending is a means for them to learn about the world and life, experiment with their own ideas, practice language, and relate to others. Their pretending is also the beginning of the creativity and imagination that can blossom into the lasting stories, plays, and paintings of their generation. During free play, the children enjoy the world of pretend and engage in imaginary conversations.

2. Some three-year-olds have imaginary friends, and some imagine that they themselves are animals. It is best to play along with these fantasies rather than dispute them. At this age, children are inclined to tell fantastic stories and fibs. They do not yet perceive the difference between what is true and what is not.

CENTERING
❶ Gather the children in a circle for *Music 'n Motion* time. Play the Unit 5 song (Track 5). Invite the children to do motions to the song along with you, using *Music 'n Motion* page T260.

❷ Invite the children to play house. You might let them wear grown-ups' clothes.

SHARING [A]
❶ **SCRIPTURE** Distribute page 87 and talk about the picture. [Option: Show grown-ups' clothes and accessories, such as a stethoscope, policeman's hat, or jewelry.] Read the adaptation of Psalm 139:14 from the Scripture card in the Bible.

- *What are the children doing?* (Pretending to be doctors and taking care of their patients, the doll and stuffed animals)

- *Do you like to pretend you are a doctor or a teacher or some other grown-up person?*

- *It's fun to pretend. God made us so that we can pretend.*

- *Listen to this psalm prayer from the Bible: "God, I praise you for making me so wonderful."*

- *What do you pretend?*

- *Sometimes for fun, we pretend that there are make-believe things, and we tell stories about them.*

87 God Made Me

T164 UNIT 5 *God Made Me Special*

2 Have the children circle the make-believe things on page 88.

3 Have the children pretend to do the following:
- walk on eggs
- fly like a bird
- drive a car
- have a snowball fight
- try to pull their feet up out of mud

SHARING [B]

4 Pretend to go on a lion hunt. Gather the children around you and have them repeat the words and actions of the following chant, line by line.

I'm going on a lion hunt.
I'm not afraid.
I've got my map
And my camera at my side.

I walk through a field.
 [Tap hands on thighs.]
I walk through the tall grass—
Swish, swish, swish.
I swim across a wide river. [Make swimming motions with arms.]
I go through a swamp.
 [Make slurping sound.]
I walk into a jungle.
 [Tap hands on thighs.]
I climb a tree and look.
 [Make climbing motions and raise hand over eyes to look.]

I go into a cave.
 [Tap hands on thighs.]
I see two eyes.
I hear a roar. [Give a roar.]
I run out of the cave,
 [Tap thighs rapidly to the end of the story.]
Through the jungle,
Back through the swamp,
Across the river,
Through the tall grass,
And through a field
Until I'm safe at home. [Say "Whew!"]
Mom says it was just a little kitty!
 [Say "Meow."]

Circle the make-believe things.

Family Time

Chapter 24: I Can Pretend

In this lesson the children experienced pretending. They played house, made believe they were performing certain actions, and pretended they were on a lion hunt. The children learned that God made them to enjoy pretending. Be creative in making up games to play with the lion your child made. You might pretend that the lion can talk or that he is a guest.

Your Child
Pretending is essential to children's play. It is one way children learn to cope with the world and practice skills. If your child has an imaginary friend, join in the fun instead of fighting it.

Reflect
I praise you that I am wonderfully made. (adapted from Psalm 139:14)

Pray
God our Creator, we praise you for the gifts of imagination and creativity.

Do
- Let your child dress up in grown-ups' clothes.
- Play games, such as store and house, with your child.
- While driving in the car, pretend it is something else, such as a rocket or a submarine.
- Give your child a huge cardboard box or several cartons to play with imaginatively.
- Read or tell your child some fairy tales.
- Play a game of charades with your child.
- Read to your child *Where the Wild Things Are* by Maurice Sendak. Have fun describing imaginary creatures to one another. Thank God for the gift of imagination.

For more family resources, refer to the Family Activity Booklet and visit www.loyolapress.com/preschool.

88 God Made Me

© LOYOLAPRESS.

ACTING

1 **PRAYER** Invite the children to pray. Have the children repeat the words of the prayer after you:

Dear God, thank you for giving me life. Being alive is so much fun.

2 Help the children make a lion face out of perforated Card I following these directions. Have them pretend that the lion is their friend.

- Color the eyes and nose black.
- Fold two pipe cleaners in half and glue them on for whiskers (or draw lines).
- Glue on strands of yarn for a mane.
- Name the lion.

You might punch at least nine holes around the head and give the children an 8-inch piece of yarn for each hole. Teach the children to loop a piece of yarn in each hole: Fold a piece of yarn in half and insert the fold into the hole. Open the folded yarn to make a circle and put the tails from the other side through it. Pull the tails to make a knot.

3 Gather the children in a circle for *Music 'n Motion* time. Play the Unit 5 song (Track 5). Invite the children to do motions to the song along with you, using *Music 'n Motion* page T260.

Have the children take home their pages and show their family the Family Time section.

CHECKPOINT

- *Were the learning outcomes achieved?*
- *How well do the children distinguish between reality and fantasy?*

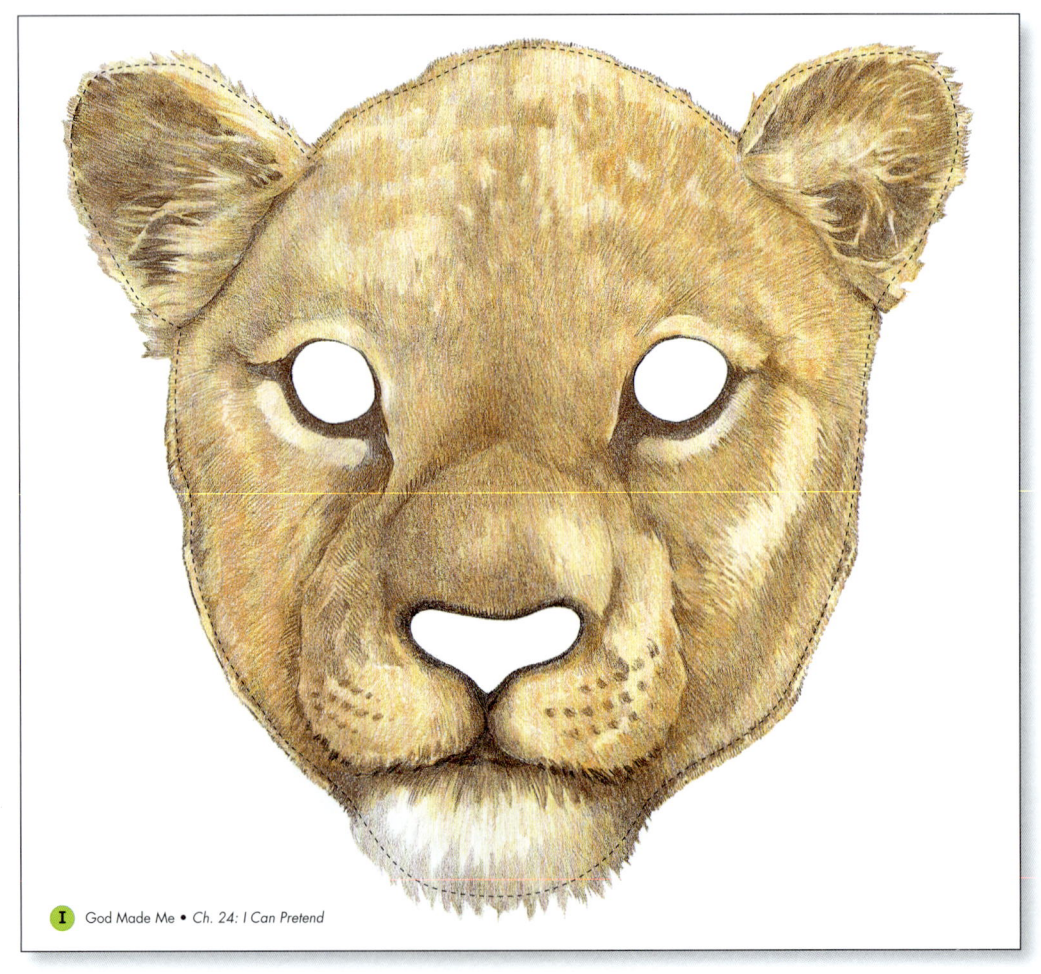

I   God Made Me • Ch. 24: I Can Pretend

T166   UNIT 5   God Made Me Special

ENRICHING THE FAITH EXPERIENCE

Use the following activities to enrich the lesson or to replace an activity with one that better meets the needs of your group.

1 Help the children pretend to be various animals: a frog, a turtle, a snake, a mouse, a rabbit, a dog, an elephant, a monkey, a chick, or a horse. You might have an animal parade.

2 Play store with the children. Provide them with pretend money.

3 Have the children close their eyes and pretend they are at a circus. Ask them to tell you various things that they see there.

4 Play "What If." Ask the children questions, such as the following:

- What if a dragon came to your house?
- What if you woke up and your skin had colored polka dots?
- What if your pet could talk?
- What if all the streets were rivers?

5 Let the children make up simple stories, preferably about something that happened to them. Record their stories on tape and then print them for the children to take home.

My name is:

_____

My lion friend's name is:

_____

© LoyolaPress.

I Can Pretend CHAPTER 24   T167

Chapter 25
I Can Love

FAITH FOCUS

God loves us, and we are to love others.

1 John 4:7–8

PREPARING THE FAITH EXPERIENCE

LISTENING

If I speak in human and angelic tongues, but do not have love, I am a resounding gong or a clashing cymbal. And if I have the gift of prophecy, and comprehend all mysteries and all knowledge; if I have all faith so as to move mountains, but do not have love, I am nothing. If I give away everything I own, and if I hand my body over so that I may boast, but do not have love, I gain nothing.

Love is patient, love is kind. It is not jealous, [love] is not pompous, it is not inflated, it is not rude, it does not seek its own interests, it is not quick-tempered, it does not brood over injury, it does not rejoice over wrongdoing but rejoices with the truth. It bears all things, believes all things, hopes all things, endures all things.

1 Corinthians 13:1–7

REFLECTING

Charity is the heart of moral law. Love is the new commandment that Christ gave us at the Last Supper: "This is my commandment: love one another as I love you." (John 15:12) We are even to embrace our enemies as Christ did. Of all the virtues, love is the most sublime. It motivates us to practice the other virtues. When we love others, we are more like God, who is Love. In the second paragraph from Corinthians above, substitute your name for the word *love* and the pronouns that refer to it. Are the statements true?

The total, unconditional love Christ shows, and which we all strive to imitate, was shown by a small boy in Vietnam. During the war a village orphanage was bombed. One badly injured eight-year-old girl needed a blood transfusion. Two Americans, a doctor and a nurse, asked in halting words and sign language whether anyone would be willing to donate blood. After a long silence, Heng volunteered, and it was found that his blood type was compatible.

As Heng lay on a pallet, a needle in his vein, he began to sob. The nurse asked whether the needle hurt, and Heng replied, "No." He tried to hide his crying. When a Vietnamese nurse arrived and spoke with Heng, she said to the two Americans, "He believed he was dying. He thought you wanted all of his blood so that the little girl would live." When the nurse asked Heng why he had been willing to give up his life, he replied, "She's my friend." We can face anything with love.

We rely on God's grace in our pursuit of perfect love. Pray the Act of Love:

O my God, I love you above all things, with my whole heart and soul, because you are all good and worthy of all my love. I love my neighbor as myself for the love of you. I forgive all who have injured me, and I ask pardon of all whom I have injured. Amen.

RESPOND

Having reflected upon God's Word, take some time now to continue to respond to God in prayer. You might wish to record your responses in your journal.

- How have I shown love for God and for others?

Holy Spirit, inflame the hearts of all the children with love.

T168 UNIT 5 God Made Me Special

Catechism of the Catholic Church

The themes of this chapter correspond to the following paragraphs: 1822–1829.

THE FAITH EXPERIENCE

Child's Book pages 89–92

SCRIPTURE IN THIS CHAPTER
- *John 13:34*

MATERIALS
- Bible
- Chapter 25 Scripture card
- Crayons or markers
- Play dough or finger paint and paper
- Option: object covered with hearts, such as a pillow or a mug
- Cutout #49, heart
- Hole punch
- Yarn or ribbon
- Paper doilies
- Glue

PREPARATION
- Write the children's names on pages 89 and 91.
- Punch two holes in Cutout #49. String yarn or ribbon through the holes and tie it so the heart can be worn around the neck.
- Place the Chapter 25 Scripture card for SHARING #2 in the Bible.
- Cut out the pieces on page 91. Make a sample love pocket to show the children.

MUSIC 'N MOTION
Use *Music 'n Motion* page T260 and CD Track 5 "You Are the Light" for this chapter. For a list of additional music, see page T302.

ENRICHING THE FAITH EXPERIENCE
Use the activities at the end of the chapter to enrich the lesson or to replace an activity with one that better meets the needs of your group.

BOOKS TO SHARE
I Love You More by Laura Duksta
  (Sourcebooks Trade, 2007)

Hug by Jez Alborough (Candlewick, 2001)

Guess How Much I Love You by Sam McBratney
  (Candlewick, 1996)

More More More Said the Baby by Vera B. Williams
  (HarperTrophy, 1996)

SNACK
Suggestion: heart-shaped cookies or crackers

ALTERNATIVE PROGRAMS

DAILY PROGRAM
Day 1: Centering
Day 2: Sharing A
Day 3: Sharing B, Acting #1
Day 4: Enriching the Faith Experience choice
Day 5: Acting #2–4

THREE-DAY PROGRAM
Day 1: Centering, Sharing A
Day 2: Sharing B, Acting #1
Day 3: Acting #2–4

25 I Can Love

LEARNING OUTCOMES
The children will
- realize that God loves them.
- desire to love others.
- discover ways to express love.

COMMENTS
1. Love is the essence of God: "God is love." (1 John 4:8) Love is the chief characteristic of a Christian. At the Last Supper, Jesus said, "This is how all will know that you are my disciples, if you have love for one another." (John 13:35) All the commandments can be summed up in one word: *love*. To love is the most important, most mysterious, and most challenging thing we are called upon to do as human beings.

2. Children are first taught to love in the family circle. They experience the love of God through the love of their family members. Even at age three, children can identify actions that show love. They can differentiate between liking and loving.

3. Your care for the children will show in what you do and say. Convey to them your love and support. Make each child feel special by spending time conversing with him or her.

4. Note that Special Lesson 12, Last Class/Summer, discusses the last day of class.

CENTERING
1 Gather the children in a circle for *Music 'n Motion* time. Play the Unit 5 song (Track 5). Invite the children to do motions to the song along with you, using *Music 'n Motion* page T260.

2 Have the children make a gift for someone they love. They might color a picture, or use finger paint or play dough to make something.

SHARING [A]
1 Distribute page 89 and talk about love.

- *How do you know that the people in the picture love each other?* (They are having fun playing together, and they look happy.)

- *Everyone loves someone. Whom did you make your gift for?*

- *Many people love you. Who are some people who love you?*

- *Do you know who loves you more than anyone else loves you?* (God)

- *How do you feel when someone loves you?*

T170 UNIT 5 God Made Me Special

2 **SCRIPTURE** Read the adaptation of Jesus' command to love in John 13:34 from the Scripture card in the Bible.

• *God wants you to love other people. In the Bible, Jesus says "Love one another as I love you."* [Option: Show the object covered with hearts.]

• *A heart is a sign of love. When we see a heart, we think of love.*

• *Who are some people you love?*

3 Play "Love Bug Tag." Give one child the red heart to wear made from Cutout #49, heart. This child is "It," the love bug. When "It" tags another child, that child puts on the heart and becomes the new love bug. You might have the love bug say "Love Bug!" when he or she tags a child. You might wish to take a turn being the love bug.

4 **PRAYER** Lead the children in prayer.

• *How do you know that your mother loves you?*

• *How do you know that your father loves you?*

• *How do you know that God loves you?*

• *Let's thank God for loving us so much. Close your eyes and thank God for loving you.* [Pause.] *Tell God in your heart that you love him too.*

SHARING [B]

5 Talk about ways to show love.

• *We show love by our words and actions. We can tell people that we love them by saying "I love you." We can show that we love them by being kind and helping them.*

• *How can you show love for your mother? your father? your sisters and brothers? your friends?*

6 Guide the children in coloring the heart near each picture where the children are showing love on page 90.

Color the hearts by the children who are showing love.

90 God Made Me

Family Time

Chapter 25: I Can Love

In this lesson the children talked about the greatest thing that God enables us to do: love. They made a gift for someone they love and talked about God and others who love them. They thought of ways to show their love for people. Help your child deliver his or her gift if necessary. Your child made a love pocket containing three hearts that represent three ways to show love—hugs and kisses, the words "I love you," and loving deeds. Each night you can help your child use these hearts to decide whether he or she has shown love that day.

Your Child
God's love is communicated to your child through the love of your family. Assure your child often of your love. Point out ways that he or she can show love.

Reflect
Love one another as I love you.
(adapted from John 13:34)

Pray
Jesus, help us to love others as you love us.

Do
• Plan with your child a way to show love for a grandparent.
• Tell your child why you love him or her.
• Point out to your child signs of God's love for him or her.
• Take your child on an errand for a neighbor, or when you take a gift to someone who is ill or needs cheering up.
• Read to your child *I Love You More* by Laura Duksta. Talk about ways your family shows love in words and actions. Thank God for helping us show love to others.

For more family resources, refer to the Family Activity Booklet and visit www.loyolapress.com/preschool.

© LOYOLAPRESS.

ACTING

1 Teach the children this poem and the gestures that go with it. You might sing this poem to the tune of "This Old Man."

> God loves me,
> [Clap, clap, point to self.]
> And I love you.
> [Clap, clap, point forwards.]
> We show love
> [Clap, clap, fold hands over heart.]
> By what we do.
> [Clap, clap, hold out hands.]
> Mary Kathleen Glavich, S.N.D.

2 Show a love pocket (pages 91–92) and explain:

- *This love pocket will remind you to love every day. It holds three hearts: one for hugs and kisses, one for the words "I love you," and one for loving acts. Each night take out the hearts and ask yourself whether you showed love that day in these three ways.*

3 Help the children make a love pocket by following these directions.

- Color the hearts on the pocket red. Glue pieces of paper doilies on or around the bigger heart.
- Put glue on the green edges of the pocket and fold up the bottom flap.
- Fold down the top flap.

4 Gather the children in a circle for *Music 'n Motion* time. Play the Unit 5 song (Track 5). Invite the children to do motions to the song along with you, using *Music 'n Motion* page T260.

Have the children take home their pages and show their family the Family Time section.

CHECKPOINT

- Were the learning outcomes achieved?
- How easily did the children suggest ways to show love?

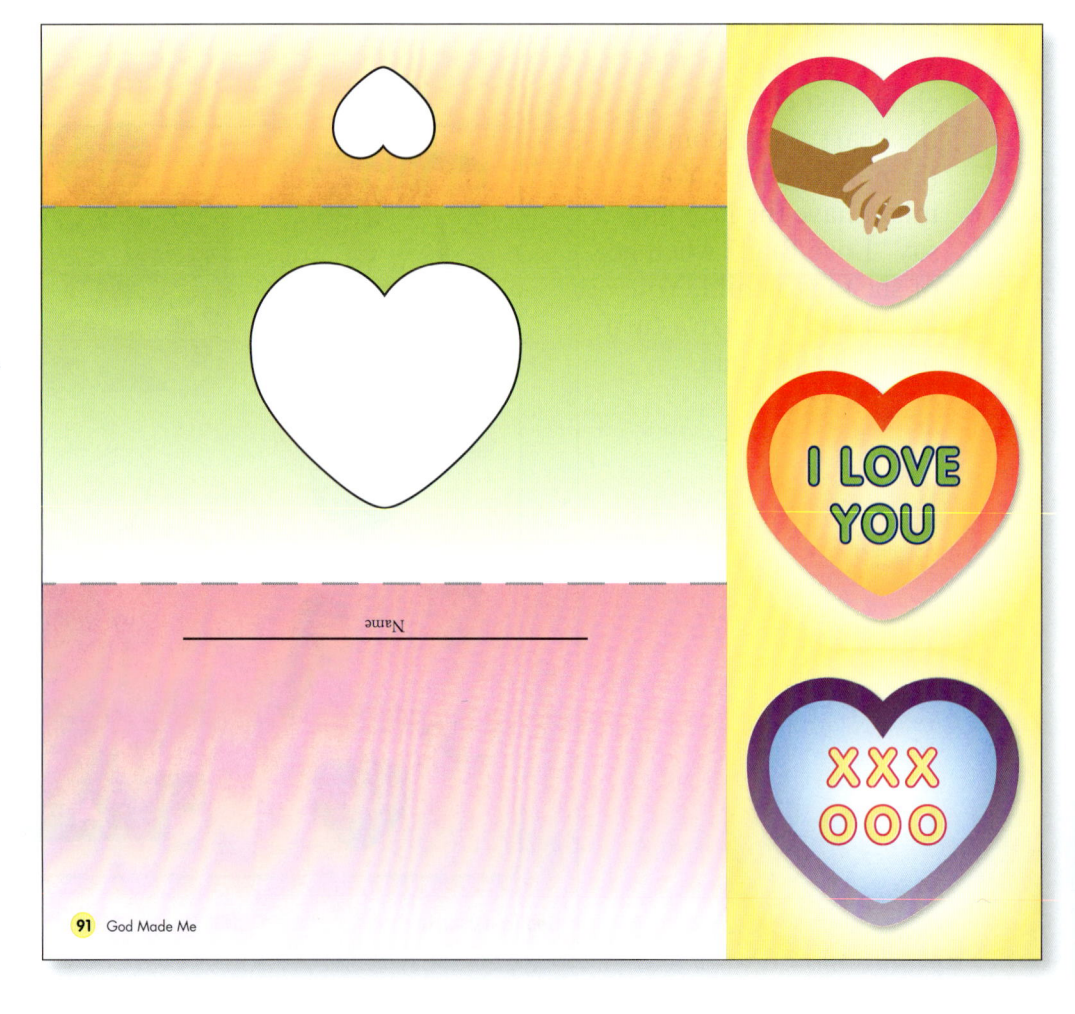

T172 UNIT 5 God Made Me Special

ENRICHING THE FAITH EXPERIENCE

Use the following activities to enrich the lesson or to replace an activity with one that better meets the needs of your group.

1 Ask the children how they could show love in these situations:

- Someone falls down and gets hurt.
- Your father or mother is tired.
- Your mother or father is doing laundry.
- The baby is crying.
- Another child is sad.
- Dad spills something.
- A child needs help getting dressed.
- Toys are all over the floor.
- It is your brother's or sister's birthday.
- Mom is working in the garden.

2 Have the children blow bubbles. Ask them to pretend that each bubble is their love for someone special, which will make him or her happy.

3 Show the children a ring. Ask where it begins and ends. Tell them that the ring is like God's love for them: It has no beginning and no end. God has loved them always. God will love them forever.

4 **PRAYER** Pray a litany of love with the children. Invite them to respond "Jesus, help me love" after each line.

Jesus, you love your Father in heaven.

Jesus, you love Mary and Joseph.

Jesus, you love children.

Jesus, you love those who are sick.

Jesus, you love poor people.

Jesus, you love hungry people.

Jesus, you love me.

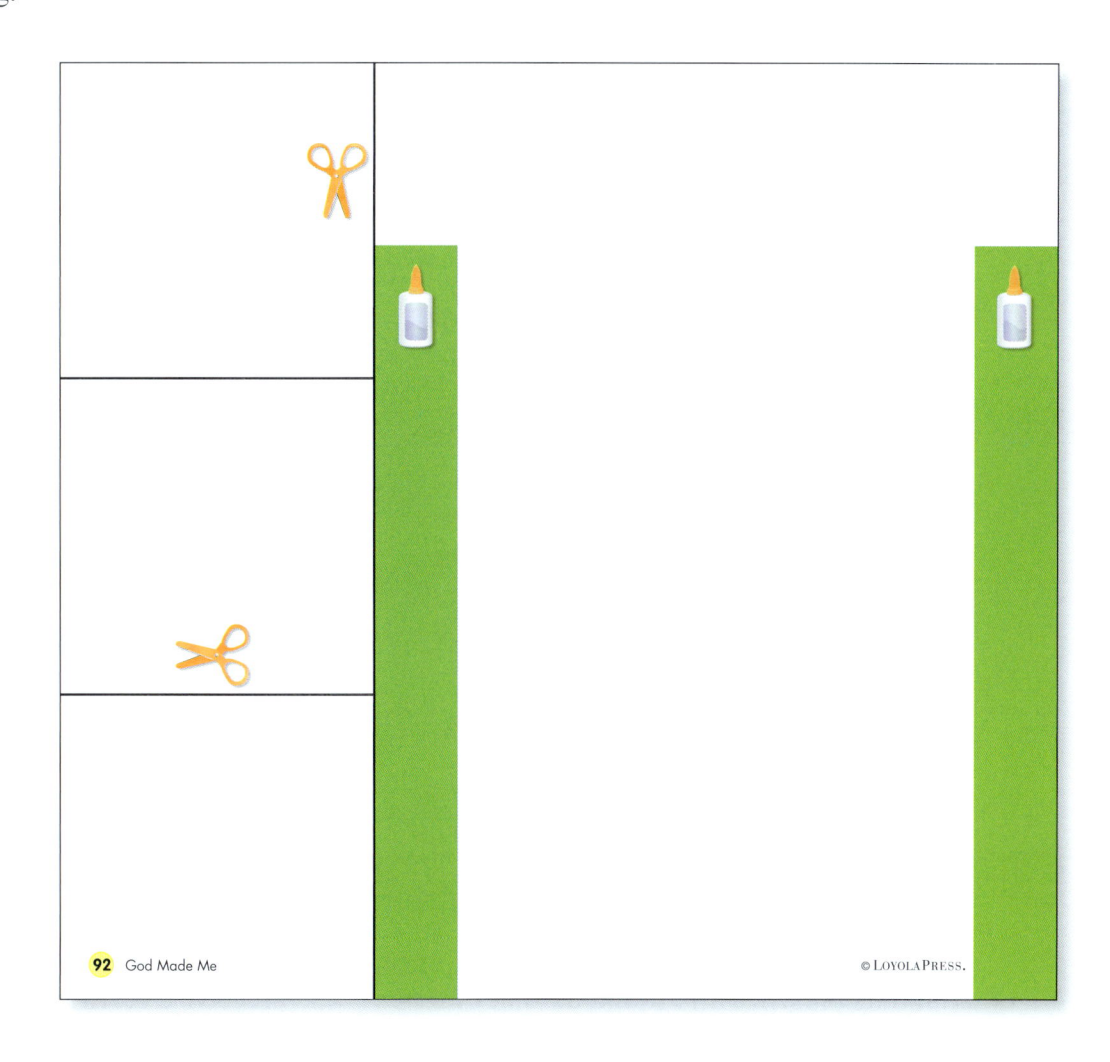

I Can Love CHAPTER 25 T173

Special Seasons and Days

In these lessons the children will learn about seasons and feast days of the Church year, as well as other special days. They will be encouraged to participate more fully in the celebrations that are part of Church and family life.

SPECIAL SEASONS

1. **Halloween/Feast of All Saints**
   The children learn that Halloween is connected to the celebration of saints. They hear about Saint Paul and then participate in a parade of saints. They make a lantern.

2. **Advent**
   The children talk about preparing for Christmas. They learn that wreaths are symbols of God's love. Then they make a wreath.

3. **Christmas**
   The children hear the story of the first Christmas. They talk about celebrating Christmas and participate in a short prayer service in front of the Nativity scene. They make a Christmas card for their families.

4. **Lent**
   The children learn that Lent is a time to grow in God's love as we prepare for Easter. They plant seeds as a reminder to grow always in God's love.

5. **Easter**
   The children talk about baby animals, spring flowers, butterflies, and chicks. They hear that Jesus came to give us life and are introduced to Easter as a day to celebrate life. They make a butterfly.

6. **Pentecost**
   The children talk about air, its importance, and its presence all around us. They learn that God is like air, everywhere and with us always. They make a paper fan.

SPECIAL DAYS

7. **Thanksgiving**
   The children learn that Thanksgiving is a day to thank God and is celebrated by a special dinner. They thank God for everything and then make a paper cornucopia.

8. **Valentine's Day**
   The children are reminded that God loves them and that they are special. They hear that Jesus wants them to love others. They make a giant Valentine for someone.

9. **Mother's Day**
   The children talk about their mothers and then about Mary. After thanking God for their mothers, they make a notepaper holder and card for them.

10. **Father's Day**
    The children make a gift and a scroll for their fathers. They talk about fathers and their own father. They learn that God is the father of Jesus and our father too.

11. **Birthdays**
    The children decorate a birthday cape and then have a celebration of the gift of life. They talk about being a child of God.

12. **Last Class/Summer**
    The children talk about summer activities. They review their favorite games and what they learned in preschool this year. They receive a certificate and join in a prayer service thanking God for everything they are and can do.

The Year in Our Church

Ordinary Time
Lent
Christmas
Holy Week
Advent
Ash Wednesday
Epiphany
Easter Sunday
Christmas
Easter
Winter Spring
Fall Summer
First Sunday of Advent
Feast of All Saints
Pentecost
Ordinary Time

Special Seasons and Days T175

Special Lesson 1
Halloween/Feast of All Saints

FAITH FOCUS

On Halloween/Feast of All Saints, we celebrate friends of God. Revelation 7:9; Revelation 21:22–22:5

PREPARING THE FAITH EXPERIENCE

LISTENING

After this I had a vision of a great multitude, which no one could count, from every nation, race, people, and tongue. They stood before the throne and before the Lamb, wearing white robes and holding palm branches in their hands. They cried out in a loud voice:

*"Salvation comes from our God, who is
  seated on the throne,
  and from the Lamb."*

Revelation 7:9

REFLECTING

Some of the delightful customs of Halloween (trick-or-treating, making jack-o'-lanterns, wearing costumes) originated with the Celts in pre-Christian times. For Christians, however, Halloween marks the beginning of a religious celebration. The word *halloween* is derived from *hallows' eve,* the night before the feast of the hallowed (or holy) ones—the Feast of All Saints.

The canonized saints assure us that sanctity is possible and show us how to acquire it. They are of all ages, of all nationalities, and from all walks of life. The common denominator is that they loved as Christ loved. On the Feast of All Saints, we celebrate all the saints, those who are canonized and the countless others who are not officially recognized. The latter include our family members and friends who are in heaven with God.

Someone once said, "The greatest tragedy in life is not to be a saint." God is calling all of us to be holy. We are redeemed by Christ and given a share in divine life through Baptism. For this reason Saint Paul, in his letters, refers to Church members as "holy ones" or "saints." We are all saints in the making.

When a teacher asked her class, "What is a saint?" one child thought of the stained-glass windows in church and answered, "Someone the light shines through." This answer is true in more ways than one. Saints let the light of Christ shine through them. The joy, love, and goodness that radiated from Jesus radiate from the saints. While on the earth they loved God and others well; in heaven they show love for us by their intercession. The patron saint whose name we bear or favorite saints whom we adopt befriend us in a special way.

We pray to the saints, who are united with us in the Communion of Saints, and we ask them to pray for us. We honor them for their holiness and strive to imitate their outstanding love. At Mass on the Feast of All Saints, we pray,

*God our Father
source of all holiness,
the work of your hands is manifest in your
saints, the beauty of your truth is reflected in
their faith.*

*May we who aspire to have part in their joy
be filled with the Spirit that blessed their lives,
so that having shared their faith on earth we
may also know their peace in your kingdom.*

Alternative Opening Prayer

RESPONDING

God's Word calls us to respond in love. Respond to God now in the quiet of your heart and perhaps through your journal.

- Who are some saints, living and dead, in my life?

Holy Spirit, make the children holy.

T176 Special Seasons and Days

Catechism of the Catholic Church

The themes of this lesson correspond to the following paragraph: 2683.

THE FAITH EXPERIENCE

Child's Book pages 93–94

SCRIPTURE IN THIS LESSON
- *Ephesians 4:32*

MATERIALS
- Bible
- Halloween/Feast of All Saints Scripture card
- Option: pumpkin
- Costumes, props for CENTERING #2
- Crayons or markers
- Perforated Card J
- Glue or stapler

PREPARATION
- Write the children's names on page 93.
- Separate the green strip from perforated Card J. Fold the card in half lengthwise.
- Place the Halloween/Feast of All Saints Scripture card for SHARING #4 in the Bible.

MUSIC 'N MOTION
Use *Music 'n Motion* page T262 and CD Track 11 "When the Saints Go Marching In" for this lesson. For a list of additional music, see page T302.

ENRICHING THE FAITH EXPERIENCE
Use the activities at the end of the lesson to enrich the lesson or to replace an activity with one that better meets the needs of your group.

BOOKS TO SHARE
The Biggest Pumpkin Ever by Steven Kroll (Cartwheel Books, 2007)

On Halloween Night by Harriet Ziefert (Puffin, 2001)

Too Many Pumpkins by Linda White (Holiday House, 1996)

Pumpkin, Pumpkin by Jeanne Titherington (HarperTrophy, 1990)

SNACK
Suggestion: candy corn

ALTERNATIVE PROGRAMS

DAILY PROGRAM
Day 1: Centering, Sharing A
Day 2: Enriching the Faith Experience choice
Day 3: Sharing B, Acting #1
Day 4: Enriching the Faith Experience choice
Day 5: Acting #2 and #3

THREE-DAY PROGRAM
Day 1: Centering, Sharing A
Day 2: Sharing B, Acting #1
Day 3: Enriching the Faith Experience choice, Acting #2 and #3

1 Halloween/Feast of All Saints

LEARNING OUTCOMES

The children will
- know that Halloween is the eve of a celebration in honor of Jesus' friends, the saints.
- enjoy aspects of Halloween.

COMMENTS

1. Three-year-old children are able to learn that Halloween is a holiday related to Jesus and his friends. Making connections between Halloween and All Saints Day prepares the children to understand the Feast of All Saints.

2. Dispel any fright the children may have of Halloween creatures by stressing that ghosts, witches, and other monsters are part of the celebration and for our enjoyment. Halloween is one of the most exciting holidays for children, perhaps because it takes them into the world of fantasy and allows them to pretend.

CENTERING

❶ Gather the children in a circle for *Music 'n Motion* time. Play Track 11. Invite the children to do motions to the song along with you, using *Music 'n Motion* page T262.

❷ Have the children engage in free play in which they use props and dress up in costumes, pretending to be other people or things. Avoid providing masks to wear because many three-year-olds are afraid of them. In addition, masks can limit the children's vision and may lead to accidents.

SHARING [A]

❶ Talk about Halloween.

- *Do you like to dress up and pretend to be someone else?*
- *A special day is coming when people wear costumes. Do you know what it is?* (Halloween)
- *Have you ever dressed up on Halloween? What did you pretend to be? What will you be this Halloween?*
- *What do you do on Halloween night?* (Go trick-or-treating, go to a Halloween party, give treats to children who come to the door)

❷ Distribute page 93 and talk about the picture. [Option: Show a pumpkin.]

- *What is the family doing?* (Making faces on pumpkins)
- *What will they do with the pumpkins?* (Set them on the porch or in a window on Halloween night)
- *What else might you see on Halloween besides pumpkins?* (Black cats, owls, a full moon, witches, ghosts) *We have fun with all these things as we celebrate Halloween.*

T178   Special Seasons and Days

3 Have the children pretend to be one or more of the following creatures:

- Owls flapping their wings and saying "Whoo"
- Cats arching their backs and walking softly
- Ghosts floating and saying "Boo"

4 SCRIPTURE Tell the children about Saint Paul.

• *Halloween night begins our celebration of Jesus' friends, who are with him now in heaven. We call these people saints. The day after Halloween is called All Saints Day.*

• *One special friend of Jesus' is Saint Paul. When Paul was young, he didn't know Jesus. But one day Paul saw a bright flash of light, and then he met Jesus. From that day on he began to tell others about Jesus. Paul traveled from one city to another and told people how wonderful Jesus was. Paul also wrote many letters about Jesus and how to live like Jesus. We say Paul shared the light with others. Some of Paul's letters are in the Bible. I'll read you something Paul wrote.*

• [Read Ephesians 4:32 from the Scripture card in the Bible.] *"Be kind to one another." Paul wrote these words because he knew that Jesus wanted us to love one another.*

• *Paul loved Jesus very much. He gave his whole life to Jesus.*

SHARING [B]

5 Invite the children to color Jesus' friend, Saint Paul, and his walking stick and letter on page 94.

6 Invite the children to join in a parade of Jesus' friends.

• *Are you a friend of Jesus' as Saint Paul was? Then let's have a parade to celebrate.*

7 Hold a parade. Lead the children around the room as you play "Follow the Leader."

Vary your movements: walk, march, tiptoe, skip, and hop. As you do so, sing the words below in a loud voice and then in a soft voice to the tune of "The Farmer in the Dell":

1. We're friends of Jesus Christ.
   We're friends of Jesus Christ.
   Heigh-ho the derry-o.
   We're friends of Jesus Christ.
2. We try to be like him . . .
3. Someday we'll be with him . . .

Mary Kathleen Glavich, S.N.D.

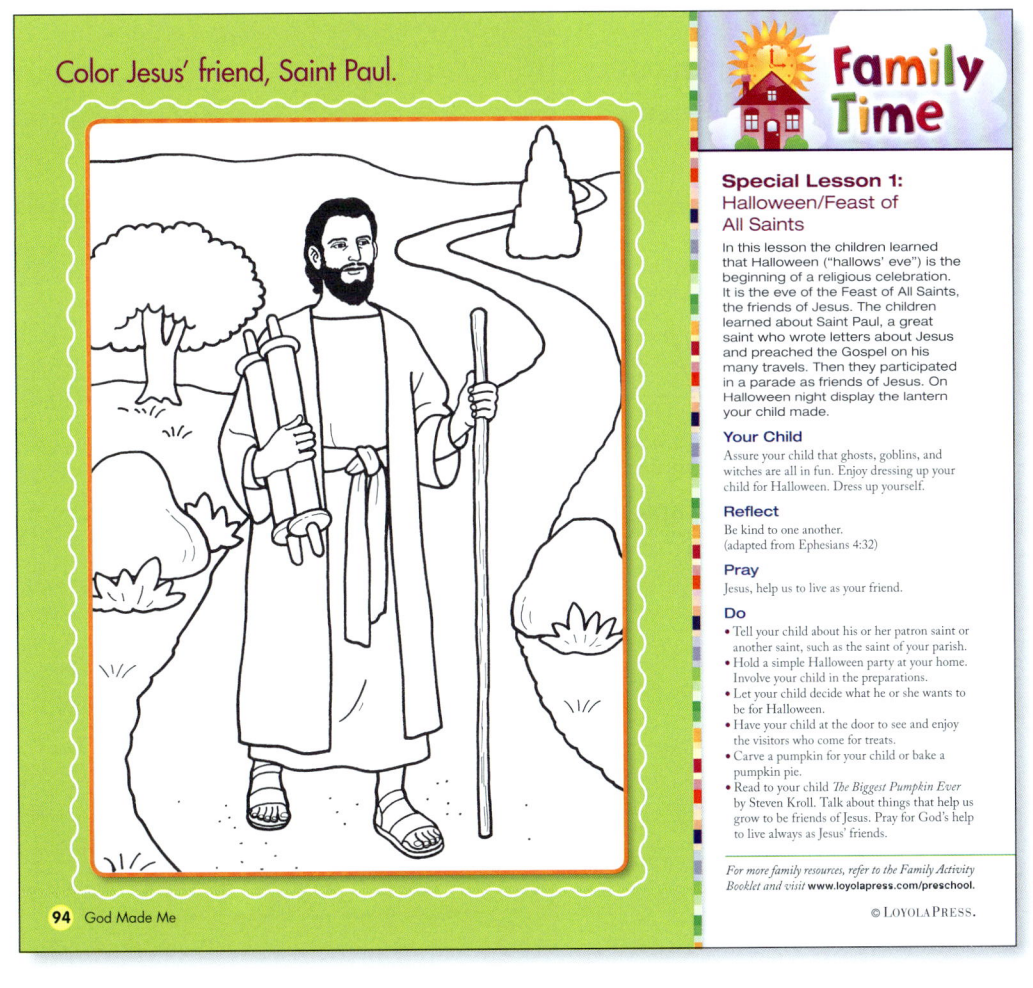

Color Jesus' friend, Saint Paul.

Family Time

Special Lesson 1: Halloween/Feast of All Saints

In this lesson the children learned that Halloween ("hallows' eve") is the beginning of a religious celebration. It is the eve of the Feast of All Saints, the friends of Jesus. The children learned about Saint Paul, a great saint who wrote letters about Jesus and preached the Gospel on his many travels. Then they participated in a parade as friends of Jesus. On Halloween night display the lantern your child made.

Your Child
Assure your child that ghosts, goblins, and witches are all in fun. Enjoy dressing up your child for Halloween. Dress up yourself.

Reflect
Be kind to one another.
(adapted from Ephesians 4:32)

Pray
Jesus, help us to live as your friend.

Do
- Tell your child about his or her patron saint or another saint, such as the saint of your parish.
- Hold a simple Halloween party at your home. Involve your child in the preparations.
- Let your child decide what he or she wants to be for Halloween.
- Have your child at the door to see and enjoy the visitors who come for treats.
- Carve a pumpkin for your child or bake a pumpkin pie.
- Read to your child *The Biggest Pumpkin Ever* by Steven Kroll. Talk about things that help us grow to be friends of Jesus. Pray for God's help to live always as Jesus' friends.

For more family resources, refer to the Family Activity Booklet and visit www.loyolapress.com/preschool.

© LOYOLAPRESS.

ACTING

1 **PRAYER** Have the children sit in a circle and lead them into silent prayer.

• *Let's tell Jesus we love him and want to be his good friend. You may say this to Jesus now in your heart.*

2 Have the children make a lantern from perforated Card J. Help them follow these directions:

- Pull apart the perforated lines to make slits in the middle of the card. (Be careful not to tear the slits to the end of the card.)
- Glue the ends of the lantern together.
- Glue on the green strip as a handle.
- Put out the lantern on Halloween night.

You may prefer to staple the lanterns together for the children.

3 Gather the children in a circle for *Music 'n Motion* time. Play Track 11. Invite the children to do motions to the song along with you, using *Music 'n Motion* page T262.

Have the children take home their pages and show their family the Family Time section.

CHECKPOINT

- Were the learning outcomes achieved?
- Did the children seem eager to celebrate Halloween?

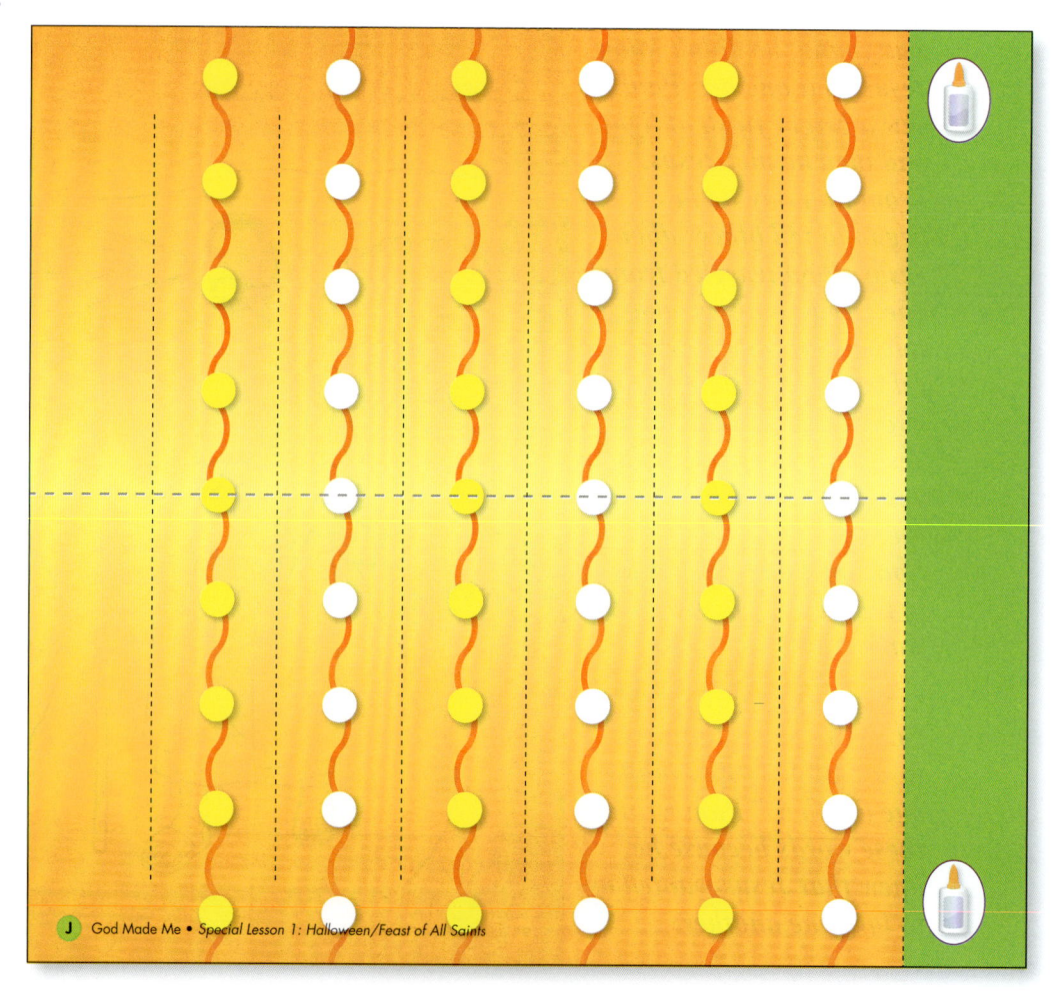

T180 Special Seasons and Days

ENRICHING THE FAITH EXPERIENCE

Use the following activities to enrich the lesson or to replace an activity with one that better meets the needs of your group.

❶ Give the children or have them make ghosts cut of white tissue paper and lollipops. To make a ghost, tie the tissue around a lollipop, which becomes the head. Add eyes, a nose, and a mouth. If you do not wish to use lollipops, roll one tissue into a ball and tie another one around it.

❷ Carve a pumpkin in front of the children.

❸ Have the children finger paint with orange paint.

❹ Tell the children about another saint, perhaps the patron saint of their parish.

❺ Teach the children this finger play:

> Five little pumpkins, sitting on a gate.
> [Show five fingers.]
> The first one said, "It's getting late."
> [Show one finger.]
> The second one said, "There are witches in the air."
> [Show two fingers.]
> The third one said, "We don't care."
> [Show three fingers.]
> The fourth one said, "Let's run, run, run."
> [Show four fingers.]
> The fifth one said, "Halloween is fun."
> [Show five fingers.]
> Then "OOOOOO" went the wind,
> And out went the light.
> [Clap on "out."]
> And the five little pumpkins rolled out of sight.
> [Roll fingers behind you.]

Halloween/Feast of All Saints SPECIAL LESSON 1   T181

Special Lesson 2
Advent

FAITH FOCUS

During Advent we prepare for Christmas, a celebration of love. Isaiah 7:14; Mark 1:2–8; Luke 1:26–38

PREPARING THE FAITH EXPERIENCE

LISTENING

Therefore the Lord himself will give you this sign: the virgin shall be with child, and bear a son, and shall name him Immanuel.

Isaiah 7:14

REFLECTING

Advent is the special season when we often ponder the Incarnation, the mystery of Emmanuel, God among us. The word *advent* means "coming." During the four weeks of Advent, as we wait, preparing to have Christ born in us anew, the Church invites us to let Mary be our model of joyful anticipation.

Mary was humble and trusting enough to let God's Son come into the world through her. Like all mothers, Mary spent much of her life waiting. After the angel's visit, she waited for Joseph to understand what had happened to her. Then in quiet awe she waited for her child's birth. As her Son grew, she waited and wondered what his destiny would be. She waited a long, painful time at the foot of the cross for Jesus' death. Then she waited in hope for his Resurrection. Mary, Mother of the Church, waited for the Holy Spirit to give birth to the Church in wind and flame. Finally, she waited for her own death when she would once again be united with her Son. Through all these periods of waiting, Mary was patient, loving, and faithful.

Mary can help us prepare our hearts for Jesus. Mary's Son comes to us mysteriously in the surprises and routines of daily life. He comes to us in the sacraments, most clearly and wondrously in the Eucharist. He appears in the people we encounter—the familiar face, the occasional visitor, and the stranger. He will come in glory and majesty at the world's end and will call his faithful followers into his kingdom, a kingdom of justice and peace. We wait in joyful hope.

During Advent we pray the seven O Antiphons, singing them in the song "O Come, O Come, Emmanuel." Our cry for the Savior culminates in the final antiphon in a joyful outburst:

> O Emmanuel, God-with-us,
> our King and Lawgiver,
> the awaited of the people
> and their Savior,
> Come to save us, O Lord our God!

RESPONDING

Having been nourished by God's Word, we are able to respond to God's great love for us. In prayer, respond to God's call to you to share his Word with others. You may also wish to respond in your prayer journal.

- Am I open to Christ's coming? Am I ready?

Mary, pray that the children may be prepared to welcome Christ.

T182 Special Seasons and Days

Catechism of the Catholic Church
The themes of this lesson correspond to the following paragraphs: 524, 1171.

THE FAITH EXPERIENCE

Child's Book pages 95–96

SCRIPTURE IN THIS LESSON
- *Luke 1:31–32*

MATERIALS
- Bible
- Advent Scripture card
- Cutout #50, Christmas tree ornament
- Option: bare Christmas tree
- Hole punch
- Wrapping paper
- Box
- Perforated Card K
- Macaroni in various shapes or green paper squares
- Green food coloring, resealable bag, 2 tablespoons of rubbing alcohol
- Glue
- Crayons or markers
- Option: red-ribbon bows, stapler
- 6-inch piece of yarn or ribbon for each child

PREPARATION
- Place the Advent Scripture card for SHARING #3 in the Bible.
- Write the children's names on pages 95 and perforated Card K.
- Punch out the wreath on perforated Card K and punch a hole in the top so it can be hung.
- Cut out the ornament (Cutout #50), put it in a box, and gift wrap it.
- Dye macaroni green by mixing rubbing alcohol, green food coloring, and macaroni in a resealable plastic bag. Shake until colored. Let dry overnight.

ENRICHING THE FAITH EXPERIENCE
Use the activities at the end of the lesson to enrich the lesson or to replace an activity with one that better meets the needs of your group.

BOOKS TO SHARE
Waiting for Christmas: A Story about the Advent Calendar by Kathleen Long Bostrom (Zonderkidz, 2006)

The Christmas Story by Jane Werner Watson (Golden Books, 2000)

My Catholic Advent and Christmas Book by Jennifer Galvin (Paulist Press, 2004)

SNACK
Suggestion: Make wreaths by melting a stick of margarine with 35–40 large marshmallows. Stir in 2 teaspoons of green food coloring and 5 cups corn flakes. Shape into wreaths on waxed paper. Decorate with small red candy pieces or dried cherry bits.

ALTERNATIVE PROGRAMS

DAILY PROGRAM
Day 1: Centering, Sharing A
Day 2: Enriching the Faith Experience choice
Day 3: Sharing B, Acting #1
Day 4: Enriching the Faith Experience choice
Day 5: Acting #2 and #3

THREE-DAY PROGRAM
Day 1: Centering, Sharing A
Day 2: Sharing B, Acting #1
Day 3: Acting #2 and #3

2 Advent

LEARNING OUTCOMES

The children will
- know that Christmas is Jesus' birthday.
- understand that gifts are a sign of love.
- rejoice in God's love for them.

COMMENTS

1. As they listen to this lesson, many children will hear for the first time that Christmas is the celebration of Jesus' birthday. Although the theology of the Incarnation is beyond them, they are quite capable of understanding that Christmas is a feast of love and that God loves them. Through activities, they can be caught up in the Advent spirit of preparation and joy. This is the first year that most will fully enjoy this season.

2. Children who have had the experience of awaiting the birth of a sibling can identify with the waiting and preparation involved in the coming of Jesus.

CENTERING

Show the children a gift-wrapped box. Ask:

- *I have a secret in this box. Guess what it is.*

- *Can some of you help me open the box and show us?* [Have as many children as needed take turns peeling back the wrapping paper.]

- *What is this?* (a Christmas tree ornament)

- *What holiday is coming when we use ornaments?* (Christmas) [Option: Have a bare tree in the room and hang the ornament on it.]

SHARING [A]

❶ Distribute page 95. Ask:

- *What is the family doing?* (Getting ready for Christmas)

- *What do we celebrate on Christmas?* (Jesus' birthday) *Jesus loves us and we love Jesus, so we celebrate his birthday.*

- *How is the family preparing?* (Decorating a tree, wrapping gifts, writing Christmas cards) *Our Church family prepares for Christmas too. We call this time of preparing for Christmas by a special name—Advent.*

- *What is in the window?* (Wreath) *What shape is a wreath?* (Round like a circle or ring)

- *A wreath has no end. It is like God's love for us. God's love for us never ends. God always loves us. At Christmas we celebrate God's love.*

T184 Special Seasons and Days

2 Lead the children in a Circle of Love dance. Have them stand, form a circle, and join hands. Walk around, singing the following song. Then walk in the other direction, singing the song.

Love Is Like a Ring

Love is like a ring. A ring that has no end-ing.

2. God loves you and me.
   God loves us now and always.

SHARING [B]

3 SCRIPTURE Talk about gifts. Read the adaptation of Luke 1:31–32 from the Scripture card in the Bible.

• *Sometimes we show our love by giving gifts. God's gift to us is Jesus. Listen to what the angel said to Mary before Jesus was born: "You will have a son and you shall name him Jesus. He will be great and will be called the Son of God."*

• *On Christmas we give gifts to people we love.*

4 Have the children circle the seven hidden gifts on page 96.

5 Mention our gift for Jesus.

• *Christmas is Jesus' birthday, so we should give him a gift too. Do you know what we can give Jesus? We have to wait for Christmas to come. On the days while we wait, we can be as good as we can be. We can act as Jesus does. That will be our gift for Jesus.*

Find and circle the seven hidden gifts.

Family Time

Special Lesson 2: Advent

In this lesson the children were introduced to Advent as a time of waiting for Christmas, the celebration of God's love and Jesus' birthday. They were encouraged to give Jesus their love. During Advent, display the wreath your child made.

Your Child
Center your celebration of Christmas on its true meaning. Try to avoid the consumerism that marks its secular celebration. Obtain a nativity set if you do not already have one. Have family members try to do one loving thing each day to prepare for Christmas, the feast of love.

Reflect
The angel said to Mary, "You will have a son and you shall name him Jesus. He will be great and will be called the Son of God."
(adapted from Luke 1:30–32)

Pray
God, prepare our hearts to welcome your Son, Jesus.

Do
• Pray a special Advent prayer before dinner, such as "O come, O come, Emmanuel."
• Help your child make gifts for family members and friends.
• Involve your child in Christmas preparations, such as baking cookies, sending Christmas cards, and decorating the house.
• Teach your child two or three Christmas carols.
• Display an empty manger from your nativity set as a reminder that Jesus is coming.
• Mark off each day until Christmas on a calendar.
• Read to your child *Waiting for Christmas: A Story about the Advent Calendar* by Kathleen Long Bostrom. Discuss how your family prepares for Christmas. Ask God to help your family prepare to celebrate Christmas with joy.

For more family resources, refer to the Family Activity Booklet and visit www.loyolapress.com/preschool.

© LOYOLAPRESS.

96 God Made Me

Advent SPECIAL LESSON 2 T185

ACTING

1 PRAYER Lead the children in prayer.

• *Let's give Jesus a gift right now—the gift of our love. Let's tell Jesus we love him. Say after me:*

Jesus, I love you with my whole heart.
[Children repeat.]

I am happy that we're going to celebrate your birthday on Christmas.
[Children repeat.]

2 Have the children make a wreath out of perforated Card K. You might prefer that the children use squares of green paper instead of macaroni. Help them follow these directions:

- Glue green macaroni to the wreath.
- Option: Glue or staple a red-ribbon bow on the wreath.
- String ribbon or yarn through the hole and tie it so that the wreath can be hung.

Have the children take home their pages and show their family the Family Time section.

CHECKPOINT

- Were the learning outcomes achieved?
- What signs are there that the children are looking forward to Christmas?

K God Made Me • *Special Lesson 2: Advent*

T186   Special Seasons and Days

ENRICHING THE FAITH EXPERIENCE

Use the following activities to enrich the lesson or to replace an activity with one that better meets the needs of your group.

1 Have the children make ornaments out of baker's clay and cookie cutters. (See the recipe at the back of this manual.) Before baking, make a hole with a straw in each ornament. After baking, string yarn or ribbon through the holes and tie it so that the ornament can be hung. The ornaments may be sprayed or brushed with paint. For a simpler activity, have the children make ornaments out of aluminum foil.

2 Set up an Advent wreath in the room and explain to the children that each of the four candles stands for a week before Christmas.

3 Provide butter cookies in Christmas shapes, such as trees or ornaments, for the children to decorate. Provide frosting, sprinkles, and colored sugar. Place each child's cookie in its own resealable plastic bag to bring home.

4 Add a few ornaments each day to a classroom Christmas tree to prepare for Christmas.

5 Count down with the children the days until Christmas. Do one of the following:

- Add a sticker to an Advent calendar each day.

- Make a paper chain with a link for each day until Christmas. Have the children remove one link every day. Remove additional links for weekends and other days when the children have no preschool.

- Cut strips of brown construction paper to be straw, one piece for each day until Christmas. Cut an egg carton in half to serve as a manger. Have the children put one piece of straw in the carton each day. When all the straw is in the manger, it's Christmas Day. Put a small paper baby Jesus (Cutout #32) in the manger.

Special Lesson 3
Christmas

FAITH FOCUS

Christmas is Jesus' birthday.

Matthew 2:1–12; Luke 2:1–21

PREPARING THE FAITH EXPERIENCE

LISTENING

"For today in the city of David a savior has been born for you who is Messiah and Lord."

Luke 2:11

"God has visited his people."

Luke 7:16

REFLECTING

God does the most amazing, unexpected things. God sent his Son to save us. Jesus, the Son of God, came as a baby born of a virgin and was laid in a straw-filled manger in a stable. Neither prophets nor priests but poor shepherds were the first outside of the family to hear the Good News and behold the miracle of the Incarnation. Not Jewish kings but foreign Magi from the East were the first to do Jesus homage and bring gifts. The extraordinary thing about Jesus' birth was its ordinariness. Most people who had longed for the Messiah were unaware of his quiet entry into the world. The simplicity of his surroundings hid the splendor of the reality.

The pattern continued. Jesus lived in obscurity for about 30 years, known only as a carpenter's son. After a few years of fame as a preacher and healer, he was condemned as a criminal and sentenced to a brutal, ignominious death. Then Jesus surprised everyone and rose from the dead. It was Jesus' suffering, death, and rising that redeemed us. When he endured death, he vanquished it and brought life for everyone.

Today Jesus still appears in the ordinary and the simple. In the Eucharist, Jesus comes under the forms of bread and wine. In our life he frequently comes in the guise of the poor and weak. Over and over again God's strength is manifested in weakness. And sometimes God still surprises us, breaking into our lives and working in ways we least expect.

Let the Nativity scenes remind us that God's ways are not our ways, that we must be ready for divine surprises and, most of all, that God loves us with a love beyond human understanding.

With awe and gratitude at our eucharistic celebrations, we declare in the Nicene Creed:

*We believe in one Lord, Jesus Christ,
   the only Son of God,
   eternally begotten of the Father,
   God from God, Light from Light,
   true God from true God,
   begotten, not made,
      one in Being with the Father.
   Through him all things were made.
   For us men and for our salvation
      he came down from heaven:
   by the power of the Holy Spirit,
      he was born of the Virgin Mary,
      and became man.*

RESPONDING

God's Word moves us to respond in word and action. Let God's Spirit work within you as you prayerfully consider how you are being called to respond to God's message to you today. Responding through your journal may help to strengthen your response.

- How has God entered my life in an extraordinary way recently?

God, help the children and me become more aware of your presence.

T188 Special Seasons and Days

Catechism of the Catholic Church

The themes of this lesson correspond to the following paragraphs: 437, 525.

THE FAITH EXPERIENCE

Child's Book pages 97–100

SCRIPTURE IN THIS LESSON
- *Luke 2:1–16*

MATERIALS
- Option: Nativity set
- Option: flannel-board figures or puppets
- Crayons and markers
- Option: cotton swabs and tempera paint
- Option: star stickers or glitter and glue

PREPARATION
Write the children's names on page 97.

MUSIC 'N MOTION
Use *Music 'n Motion* page T264 and CD Track 12 "No Place to Stay" for this lesson. For a list of additional music, see page T302.

ENRICHING THE FAITH EXPERIENCE
Use the activities at the end of the lesson to enrich the lesson or to replace an activity with one that better meets the needs of your group.

BOOKS TO SHARE
Saint Francis Celebrates Christmas by Mary Caswell Walsh (Loyola Press, 1998)

Mr. Willowby's Christmas Tree by Robert Barry (Doubleday Books for Young Readers, 2000)

The Sweet Smell of Christmas by Patricia M. Scarry (Golden Books, 2003)

God Gave Us Christmas by Lisa Tawn Bergren (WaterBrook Press, 2006)

SNACK
Suggestion: Christmas cookies

ALTERNATIVE PROGRAMS

DAILY PROGRAM
Day 1: Centering, Sharing A
Day 2: Enriching the Faith Experience choice
Day 3: Sharing B, Acting #1
Day 4: Enriching the Faith Experience choice
Day 5: Acting #2 and #3

THREE-DAY PROGRAM
Day 1: Centering, Sharing A
Day 2: Sharing B, Acting #1
Day 3: Acting #2 and #3

3 Christmas

LEARNING OUTCOMES
The children will
- know that Christmas is Jesus' birthday.
- enjoy celebrating Christmas.

COMMENTS
1. The children are probably very excited because of all the Christmas preparations at home. Try to focus their attention on the real meaning of Christmas and counteract the commercialism of this time of year. The children are not too young to know that Christmas is primarily a religious feast—a celebration of love. Encourage them to express their love for God and others through gift-giving.

2. Three-year-olds are drawn to the image of baby Jesus in the manger. They can easily be led to respond with love for him, the child who is the reason for the season.

CENTERING

❶ Gather the children in a circle for *Music 'n Motion* time. Play Track 12. Invite the children to do motions to the song along with you, using *Music 'n Motion* page T264.

❷ Teach the children a Christmas carol, such as the following one:

Mary Had a Baby

1. Mary had a baby, yes, Lord.
   Mary had a baby, yes, my Lord.
   Mary had a baby, yes, Lord. The
   people keep a-coming and the train is gone.

2. What did Mary name him . . .
3. Mary named him Jesus . . .
4. Where was Jesus born . . .
5. Born in lowly stable . . .
6. Where did Mary lay him . . .
7. Laid him in a manger . . .

97 God Made Me

T190 Special Seasons and Days

SHARING [A]

1 **Talk about the Nativity** scene on page 97.

- *Christmas is a great day. What do we celebrate on Christmas?* (Jesus' birthday)

- *This is a picture of the first Christmas. Who are the people?* (Jesus, Mary, Joseph, shepherd, angel)

- *What do you see in the sky?* (stars)

- *Where are the people?* (In a stable in Bethlehem) [Option: Show a Nativity set.]

- *What do you know about the first Christmas?*

2 **SCRIPTURE** Relate the story of Christmas (based on Luke 2:1–16) simply, pointing to the picture on page 97 or using a Nativity set, flannel-board figures, or puppets.

- *When it was almost time for Mary to have baby Jesus, Joseph had to go to his hometown, Bethlehem. Mary went with him. When they got to Bethlehem, so many people were there that Mary and Joseph couldn't find a room to stay in. Finally a kind man let them use the stable where he kept his animals. That night Jesus was born. Mary laid him in the animals' food box, which was filled with straw. Nearby some shepherds were watching over sheep. Angels came to the shepherds and told them that Jesus was born. The angels sang "Glory to God in the highest." The shepherds ran to the stable to see Jesus.*

3 **Talk about celebrating** Christmas.

- *How do you celebrate Christmas at home?*

- *At Christmas we put up a tree, sing Christmas songs, send cards, and give gifts. Christmas is a time for showing love.*

- *Jesus taught us about God's love. He taught us to love one another.*

4 Have the children add lights and ornaments to the Christmas tree on page 98. They might do this by dipping cotton swabs in tempera paint and then pressing them onto the tree.

SHARING [B]

5 Read the poem on the next page. Ask the children to stand and, as you read, have them pretend to pull a rope to ring a big bell. [Demonstrate the pulling motion, using both hands.]

Put lights and ornaments on the tree.

98 God Made Me

Family Time

Special Lesson 3: Christmas

In this lesson the children heard the story of the first Christmas. They talked about celebrating Christmas at home and then had a short prayer service around a nativity set. Ask your child to tell you the story of Jesus' birth, looking at the picture on page 97.

Your Child
On Christmas Day try to keep your child focused on Jesus, God's gift to us, more than on other gifts he or she receives. Stress that Christmas is a feast of love. Establish family Christmas customs now that will make treasured memories for your child later. Traditions give children a sense of security and teach them values.

Reflect
Mary gave birth to her firstborn son, wrapped him in swaddling clothes, and laid him in a manger. (adapted from Luke 2:7)

Pray
God, help us to celebrate Christmas as a feast of love.

Do
- On Christmas Day sing "Happy Birthday" to Jesus with your child. Have a birthday cake.
- With your child go through the Christmas cards you received. Pray for those who sent them.
- Play religious Christmas songs for your child.
- Read aloud the story of the first Christmas from Luke 2:1–20. Your child will come to understand it gradually.
- Read to your child *Saint Francis Celebrates Christmas* by Mary Caswell Walsh. Have your child tell you the part of the story of Jesus' birth he or she likes best. Pray together by singing a Christmas hymn.

For more family resources, refer to the Family Activity Booklet and visit www.loyolapress.com/preschool.

© LOYOLAPRESS.

Christmas SPECIAL LESSON 3 T191

Christmas Bells

Ring the bells on Christmas morn.
Tell the news that Jesus is born.
Ring them far. Ring them near.
Ring them loud for all to hear:
Over the world let them sing,
Ding, dong, ding, dong, ding, dong, ding.

Mary Kathleen Glavich, S.N.D.

6 PRAYER Lead the children in a Christmas prayer. Have them look at the Nativity scene on page 97, or have them gather around a Nativity set if you have one.

- *Jesus was once a baby, just as you once were. He cried and took naps. His mother Mary loved him and cared for him.*

- *Jesus loves you very much. You may tell Jesus in your heart that you love him too.* [Pause.]

- *Let's show Jesus love by celebrating his birthday. Let's sing "Happy Birthday" to him.* [Sing "Happy Birthday" to Jesus.]

ACTING

1 Invite the children to sing the Christmas carol learned in Centering #2.

2 Have the children make a Christmas card for their families from page 99. Tell them the card says "Jesus is born. Merry Christmas!" Help them do the following:

- Color the picture.
- Put stars in the sky using stickers, crayons, markers, or glitter.
- Fold the card in half.
- Sign the card.

3 Gather the children in a circle for *Music 'n Motion* time. Play Track 12. Invite the children to do motions to the song along with you, using *Music 'n Motion* page T264.

Have the children take home their pages and show their family the Family Time section.

CHECKPOINT

- Were the learning outcomes achieved?
- How devout were the children during the prayer?

ENRICHING THE FAITH EXPERIENCE

Use the following activities to enrich the lesson or to replace an activity with one that better meets the needs of your group.

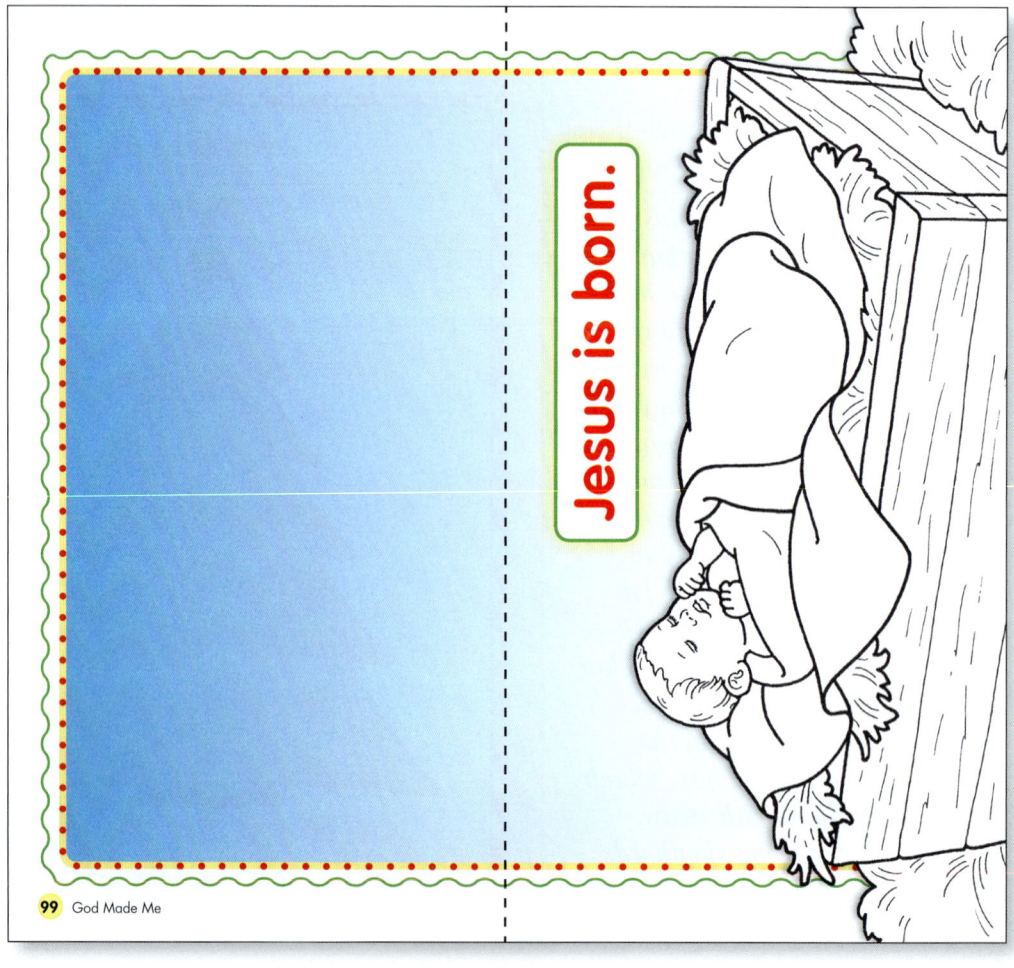

Jesus is born.

99 God Made Me

T192 Special Seasons and Days

1 Teach the children the following song. Tell the children that *Immanuel* means "God with us."

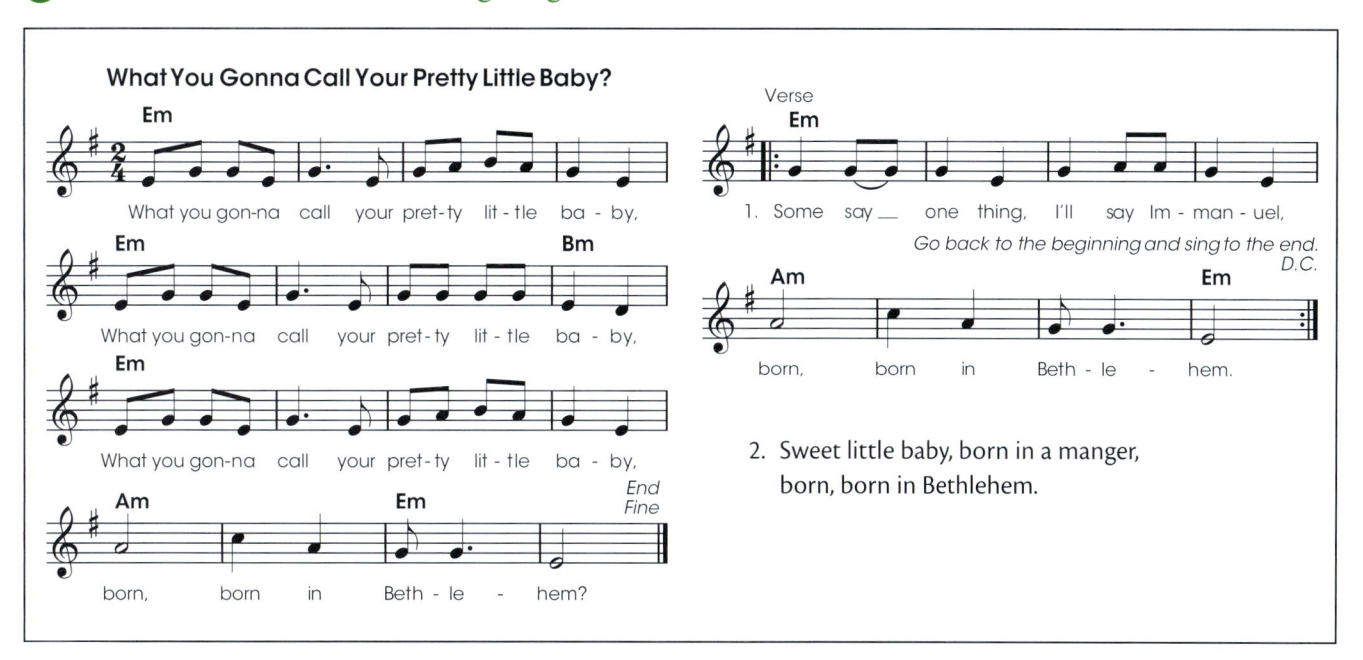

What You Gonna Call Your Pretty Little Baby?

What you gon-na call your pret-ty lit-tle ba-by,
What you gon-na call your pret-ty lit-tle ba-by,
What you gon-na call your pret-ty lit-tle ba-by,
born, born in Beth-le-hem?

Verse
1. Some say one thing, I'll say Im-man-uel, born, born in Beth-le-hem.

Go back to the beginning and sing to the end. D.C.

2. Sweet little baby, born in a manger, born, born in Bethlehem.

2 Have the children make Christmas bells out of egg cartons. Cut the sections apart and poke holes in the bottoms. Help the children paint or add glitter. Then insert a pipe cleaner in the hole and bend it so the bells can be hung.

3 Help the children make a handprint for their family for Christmas. Follow the recipe for salt ceramic in the back of this manual. Have each child flatten a ball of dough and then press in a handprint. Let the dough harden for a few days.

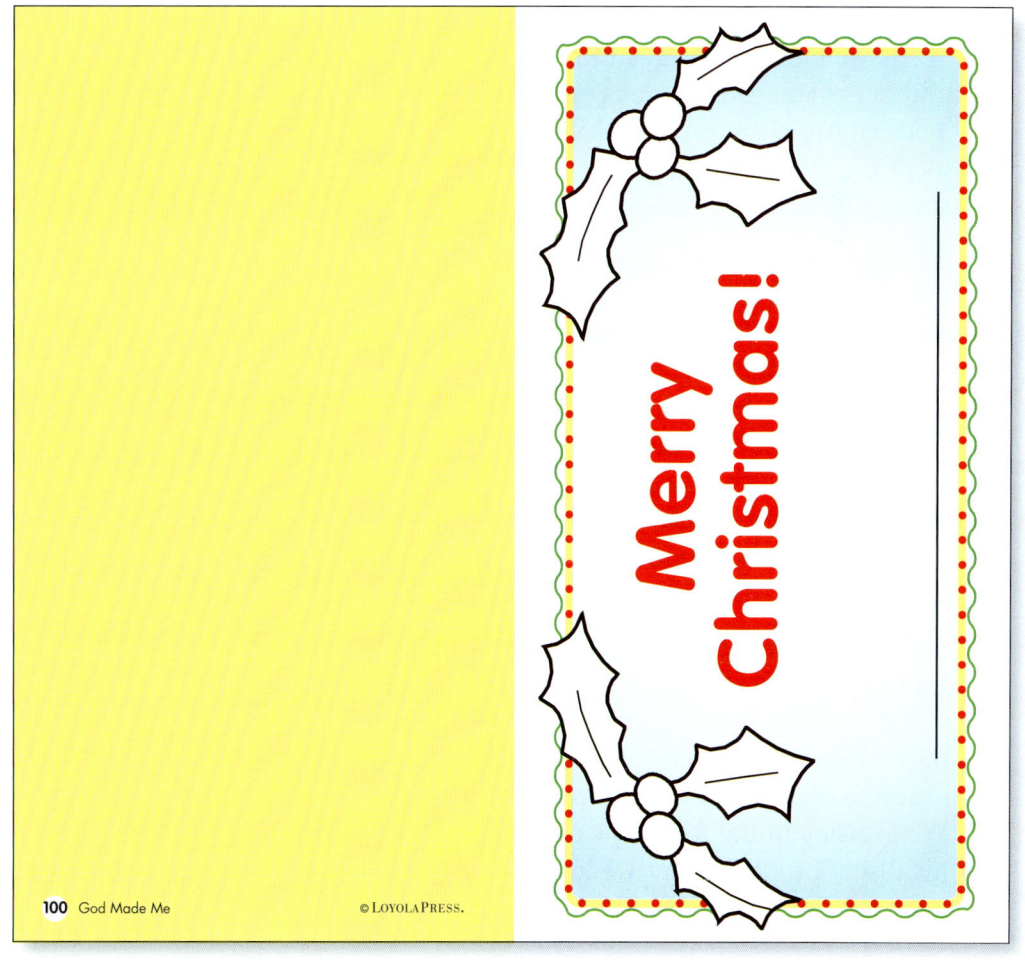

Christmas **SPECIAL LESSON 3** **T193**

Special Lesson 4

Lent

FAITH FOCUS

During Lent, we grow in God's love.

Romans 6:3–11; 1 John 3:16–18

PREPARING THE FAITH EXPERIENCE

LISTENING

"Amen, amen, I say to you, unless a grain of wheat falls to the ground and dies, it remains just a grain of wheat; but if it dies, it produces much fruit. Whoever serves me must follow me, and where I am, there also will my servant be."

John 12:24,26

REFLECTING

Each spring we begin to observe signs of new life awakening around us. Daffodils, tulips, hyacinths, and a myriad of other flowers emerge from bulbs planted in the fall. Caterpillars appear and enter their cocoons to be transformed into beautiful butterflies. Seeds we plant in the ground now will sprout and bear fruit in the weeks and months ahead. These natural signs can serve as reminders to us of the mystery of new life that we receive through Christ.

Through the Paschal Mystery of his Passion, Death, Resurrection, and Ascension, Christ transformed suffering, death, and evil into glorious new life. Strengthened by prayerful union with his Father, Jesus freely accepted the consequences of humanity's sin. He countered hatred with love, arrogant pride with humble docility, death with life. His victory over sin and death gained for us a share of divine life and eternal glory.

In Baptism we died with Christ and rose with him to new life. Through all the sacraments, and especially in the Eucharist, we participate in the Paschal Mystery. We receive God's grace so that we may be more like Christ. We journey in the footsteps of Jesus who told his disciples: "Whoever wishes to come after me must deny himself, take up his cross, and follow me." (Matthew 16:24) We strive to keep the new commandment: love one another as I love you. No one has greater love than this, to lay down one's life for one's friends. You are my friends if you do what I command you." (John 15:12–14) Imitation of Christ—even unto death—is the standard of perfection for the Christian. It is our response to Jesus' words "Do this in remembrance of me." (1 Corinthians 11:24)

During the Lenten season, the Church community as a whole looks at the new life that Jesus offers to all who commit themselves to share in his Paschal Mystery. We devote ourselves to acts of Christian living that increase our participation in Christ's saving Death and Resurrection. The Lenten practices of prayer, fasting, and almsgiving are signs of our repentance and renewed commitment to living as Christ's disciples. Together with the community of faith, we journey with Christ, looking forward to sharing in the joy of the Resurrection.

RESPONDING

Having reflected upon God's Word, take some time now to continue to respond to God in prayer. You might wish to record your responses in your journal.

- What acts of Christian living will I make a priority during this Lenten season?

Holy Spirit, strengthen us to live as Christ's disciples.

Catechism of the Catholic Church

The themes of this lesson correspond to the following paragraphs: 1168, 1438, 2014–2015.

THE FAITH EXPERIENCE

Child's Book pages 101–102

SCRIPTURE IN THIS LESSON
- *John 12:24*

MATERIALS
- Bible
- Lent Scripture card
- Crayons or markers
- Plastic cups
- Potting soil
- Flower seeds

PREPARATION
- Write the children's names on page 101.
- Place the Lent Scripture card for SHARING #2 in the Bible.

ENRICHING THE FAITH EXPERIENCE
Use the activities at the end of the lesson to enrich the lesson or to replace an activity with one that better meets the needs of your group.

BOOKS TO SHARE
The Carrot Seed by Ruth Krauss (HarperCollins, 1989)

The Tiny Seed by Eric Carle (Aladdin, 2001)

The Very Hungry Caterpillar by Eric Carle (Philomel, 1981)

Titch by Pat Hutchins (Aladdin, 1993)

SNACK
Suggestion: pretzels

ALTERNATIVE PROGRAMS

DAILY PROGRAM
Day 1: Centering, Sharing A
Day 2: Enriching the Faith Experience choice
Day 3: Sharing B
Day 4: Acting
Day 5: Enriching the Faith Experience choice

THREE-DAY PROGRAM
Day 1: Centering, Sharing A
Day 2: Sharing B
Day 3: Acting

4 Lent

LEARNING OUTCOMES
The children will
- learn how seeds grow into plants.
- understand Lent as a time to grow in God's love.
- choose to grow in God's love through prayer and action.

COMMENT
The Church season of Lent often corresponds to the change of seasons from winter to spring. The word *Lent* is derived from an Old English word meaning "springtime" and may be a reference to the lengthening of the daylight hours that occurs during this time of year. During the weeks of Lent, we let the warmth of God's love permeate our hearts and transform our lives.

CENTERING
Teach the children this finger play below. You might sing it to the tune of "On Top of Old Smokey."

This is my garden.
[Extend hand, palm up.]
I'll rake it with care.
[Make pulling motion with hands.]
And plant some flower seeds
[Make planting motions with thumb and index finger.]
Right in there.
The sun will shine,
[Make circle with arms above head.]
The rain will fall.
[Flutter fingers downward.]
And my garden will blossom
[Cup hands; raise them slowly.]
And grow straight and tall.

T196 Special Seasons and Days

SHARING [A]

1 Distribute page 101 and talk about seeds and how they grow.

• *In the spring we see many new plants growing. Let's see how a plant grows from a tiny seed.* (Describe the process, using pictures on the page.)

• *What does a plant seed need to grow?* (Water, sun, soil)

2 SCRIPTURE Read the adaptation of John 12:24 from the Scripture card in the Bible.

• *Jesus saw the plants that grew around him. Sometimes he talked about the plants when he was teaching.*

• *Listen to what Jesus says: "Unless a seed falls to the ground and dies, it remains just a seed; but if it dies, it produces much fruit."*

3 Have the children circle the things on page 102 that will help flowers grow.

SHARING [B]

4 Teach this poem. Have the children act it out by curling up on the floor and then rising as flowers.

Buttercup

In the soil, dark and deep,
Lies a seed fast asleep.
Sun and rain wake it up—
It grows up a buttercup.
In this small yellow flower,
We see God's great love and power.

Mary Kathleen Glavich, S.N.D.

5 Tell the children about Lent.

• *We are beginning Lent. Lent is the time of the Church year when we get ready for Easter.*

• *During Lent we grow in God's love. Praying to God helps us grow in God's love. Doing good things for other people helps us grow in God's love.*

Help the children name good things to do to prepare for Easter.

Circle the things that will help flowers to grow.

Family Time

Special Lesson 4: Lent

In this lesson the children were introduced to Lent, a time to grow in God's love as we prepare to celebrate Easter. They talked about how seeds grow into plants. They heard Jesus' words about seeds dying to produce much fruit. Ask your child about the seeds he or she planted. If this was brought home, help your child care for the seedlings as they grow.

Your Child

Lent often corresponds to the change of seasons from winter to spring. Observing signs of new life in the natural world around them prepares children to later comprehend the significance of Jesus' Passion, Death, and Resurrection. Especially during Lent, take time to help your child notice nature's transformation from death to new life.

Reflect

Unless a seed falls to the ground and dies, it remains just a seed; but if it dies, it produces much fruit. (adapted from John 12:24)

Pray

Jesus, help us to grow always in God's love.

Do

• Allow your child to help with springtime gardening activities.
• Tie two twigs to make a cross. Set it in dirt in a flowerpot or cup. Help your child plant grass seeds around the cross.
• Display a cross or crucifix during Lent and include a special Lenten prayer at mealtimes or at bedtime.
• Read to your child *The Carrot Seed* by Ruth Krauss. Talk with your child about seeds and other signs of new life you see in spring. Pray together thanking God for these signs of new life.

For more family resources, refer to the Family Activity Booklet and visit www.loyolapress.com/preschool.

© LOYOLAPRESS.

Lent **SPECIAL LESSON 4** T197

6 Teach the poem "God Loves Me" and the motions that go with it. You might sing the poem to the tune of "This Old Man."

> God loves me. [Clap, clap, point to self.]
> And I love you. [Clap, clap, point forward.]
> We show love [Clap, clap, fold hands over heart.]
> By what we do. [Clap, clap, hold out hands.]
> M. Kathleen Glavich, S.N.D.

ACTING

1 **PRAYER** Lead the children to pray by asking them to repeat each line with you:

Thank you, God, for seeds that grow.

Help us grow always in God's love.

2 Plant seeds in small containers. Have the children fill their cups halfway with potting soil. Give them each a flower seed to plant and water. Keep the containers in the classroom to watch the plants grow or allow the children to take home their containers.

Have the children take home their pages and show their family the Family Time section.

CHECKPOINT

- Were the learning outcomes achieved?
- Were the children familiar with how seeds grow into plants?

ENRICHING THE FAITH EXPERIENCE

Use the following activities to enrich the lesson or to replace an activity with one that better meets the needs of your group.

1 Bring pictures or take a nature walk to observe the variety of plants that grow in your area. Have the children notice the signs of new life in the spring.

2 Teach this finger play:

> Pitter-pat, pitter-pat,
> [Drum fingers on the floor.]
> The rain goes on for hours.
> And though it keeps me in
>   the house,
> It's very good for flowers.
> [Open fists and raise hands.]

3 Give each child a pretzel as a reminder that Lent is a time for special prayer. Explain that the twisted shape of a pretzel looks like arms crossed in prayer.

4 Have the children stand and sing the following verses to the tune of "Here We Go Round the Mulberry Bush" and act out the way we plant seeds.

1. This is the way we dig the soil . . . so early in the morning.
2. This is the way we plant the seeds . . .
3. This is the way we water the seeds . . .
4. This is the way we watch the seeds grow . . .

Special Lesson 5

Easter

FAITH FOCUS

On Easter we celebrate the new life of Jesus.
John 20; Acts of Apostles 2:22–36; 1 Corinthians 15:1–28

PREPARING THE FAITH EXPERIENCE

LISTENING

For his sake I have accepted the loss of all things . . . that I may gain Christ and be found in him, . . . depending on faith to know him and the power of his resurrection . . .

Philippians 3:8–10

REFLECTING

Life in Christ calls us to walk daily in newness of life, a life no longer enslaved to sin. Through his Resurrection, Jesus won for us new life and new hope; we no longer need to fear suffering and death. Belief in the Resurrection moves us from a limited, earthbound outlook to a radically different, eternity-oriented view of life. We can see the suffering that marks segments of our journey as part of the Paschal Mystery:

For this momentary light affliction is producing for us an eternal weight of glory beyond all comparison . . .

2 Corinthians 4:17

The frightened disciples experienced the risen Christ and were radically changed. Christ, raised and glorified, had broken the power of death. The disciples could share his power; through Baptism they would one day share eternal life with him. Jesus fulfills forever the deepest of all desires—the desire of life.

The same risen Jesus is the companion of every Christian, giving each of us courage to accept the Christian mission. Jesus enables Christians to risk their lives, jobs, and reputations for his kingdom of peace and justice. Today some Christians practice their faith where it is forbidden. They bring the Gospel to those who have nothing. Contemplatives embrace a life of prayer and penance that makes no sense to this world but brings strength and hope to many.

Christians everywhere make the risen Christ visible. They endure suffering patiently, give themselves to thankless tasks, and speak the truth in love. They are signs of hope. Through their witness others see how powerful Jesus is and entrust their lives to him.

At each Eucharist we celebrate the dying and rising of Christ. During the Easter season we remember this great mystery in a special way, proclaiming:

This is the night when Jesus Christ
broke the chains of death
and rose triumphant from the grave.

What good would life have been to us
had Christ not come as our Redeemer?

Father, how wonderful your care for us!
How boundless your merciful love!

The power of this holy night
dispels all evil, washes guilt away,
restores lost innocence, brings mourners
    joy;
it casts out hatred, brings us peace,
and humbles earthly pride.

*From the Easter Proclamation
The Easter Vigil*

RESPONDING

God's Word calls us to respond in love. Respond to God now in the quiet of your heart, and perhaps through your journal.

- How do I show my belief in the Resurrection?

Risen Lord, fill the children and me with an abiding hope in you.

T200 Special Seasons and Days

Catechism of the Catholic Church

The themes of this lesson correspond to the following paragraphs: 638, 654–655, 1168, 1171.

THE FAITH EXPERIENCE

Child's Book pages 103–104

SCRIPTURE IN THIS LESSON
- *John 10:10*

MATERIALS
- Bible
- Easter Scripture card
- Cutout #47, butterfly
- Option: spring flowers
- Perforated Card L
- Hole punch
- 30-inch piece of yarn or ribbon for each child
- Glue or tape
- Crayons or markers
- Option: pencils or cardboard tubes from dry-cleaning hangers
- Option: paper towels soaked in tempera paint

PREPARATION
- Write the children's names on page 103.
- Punch out the butterfly on perforated Card L and write the children's names on them. With a hole punch, make holes around the wings.
- Harden the ends of the yarn or ribbon by dipping it in glue or wrapping it with tape.
- Put the Easter Scripture card for SHARING #2 in the Bible.

MUSIC 'N MOTION
Use *Music 'n Motion* page T266 and CD Track 13 "Easter Alleluia" for this lesson. For a list of additional music, see page T302.

ENRICHING THE FAITH EXPERIENCE
Use the activities at the end of the lesson to enrich the lesson or to replace an activity with one that better meets the needs of your group.

BOOKS TO SHARE
Easter by Gail Gibbons (Holiday House, 2005)

The Golden Egg Book by Margaret Wise Brown (Golden Books, 2004)

The Very Hungry Caterpillar by Eric Carle (Philomel, 1981)

Max's Chocolate Chicken by Rosemary Wells (Puffin, 2000)

SNACK
Suggestion: bunny made from half a pear with pretzel ears and marshmallow tail or cookies shaped and decorated like Easter eggs

ALTERNATIVE PROGRAMS

DAILY PROGRAM
Day 1: Centering, Sharing A
Day 2: Enriching the Faith Experience choice
Day 3: Sharing B
Day 4: Enriching the Faith Experience choice
Day 5: Acting

THREE-DAY PROGRAM
Day 1: Centering, Sharing A
Day 2: Sharing B
Day 3: Acting

5 Easter

LEARNING OUTCOMES
The children will
- rejoice in new life.
- be familiar with some Easter symbols.
- be grateful for the gift of life.

COMMENTS
1. The mysteries of Jesus' Death and Resurrection are beyond the scope of the three-year-old mind. Three-year-olds are unable to comprehend the finality of death and think that any dead animal or person can come back to life. You may prepare young children for their introduction to the Easter mystery by having them observe new life. Spring, the season of new life, offers many symbols of the Resurrection: blossoms, flowers, butterflies, and chicks. As the children ponder these natural mysteries of life, they will develop their receptivity for the miracle of the divine life Jesus won for us.

2. The life stages of the butterfly will be presented in greater detail in the program for four-year-olds. Some children might already be familiar with these life stages.

CENTERING

1 Gather the children in a circle for *Music 'n Motion* time. Play Track 13. Invite the children to do motions to the song along with you, using *Music 'n Motion* page T266.

2 Teach the children this finger play:

Baby Chick

A baby chick came out of an egg—
[Make a fist and break through it with the other hand.]
Its beak, its head, a wing, then a leg.
It greeted me with a "peep, peep, peep."
Then nodded its head and went to sleep.
[Fold hands at side of head.]
    Mary Kathleen Glavich, S.N.D.

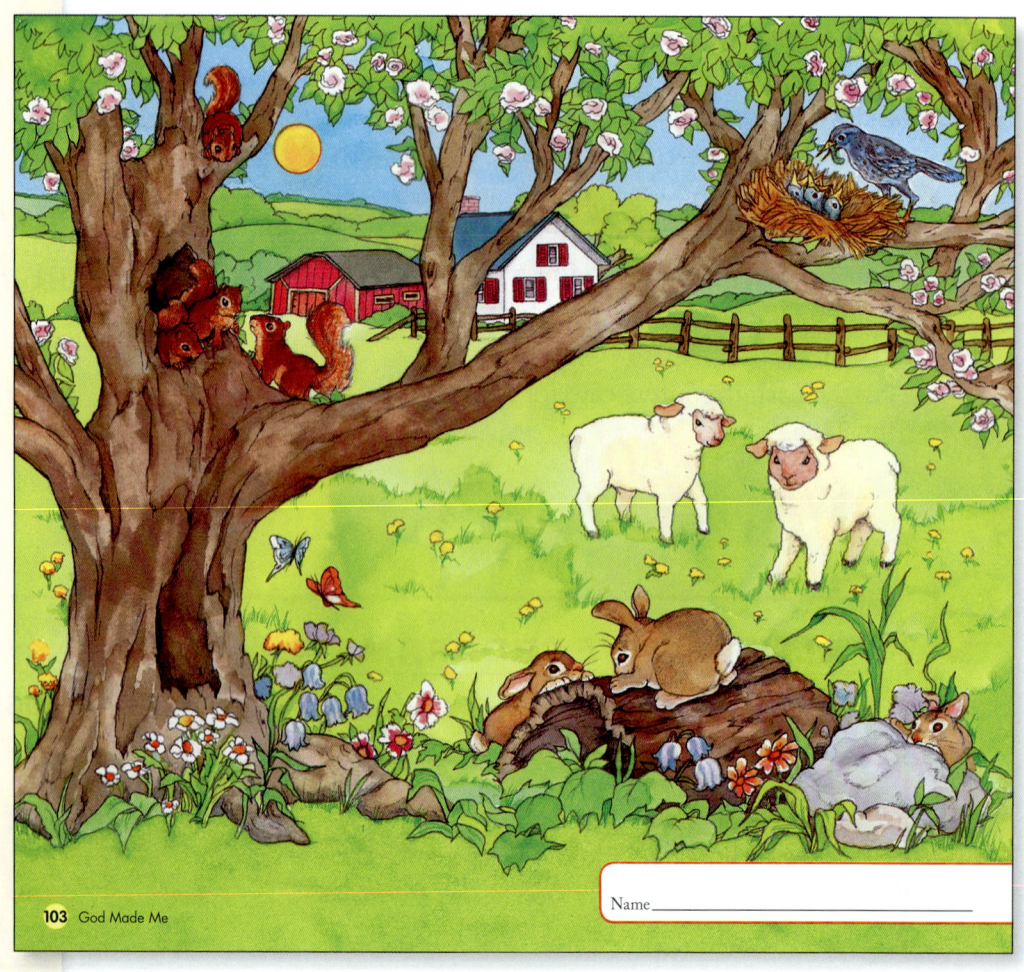

T202 Special Seasons and Days

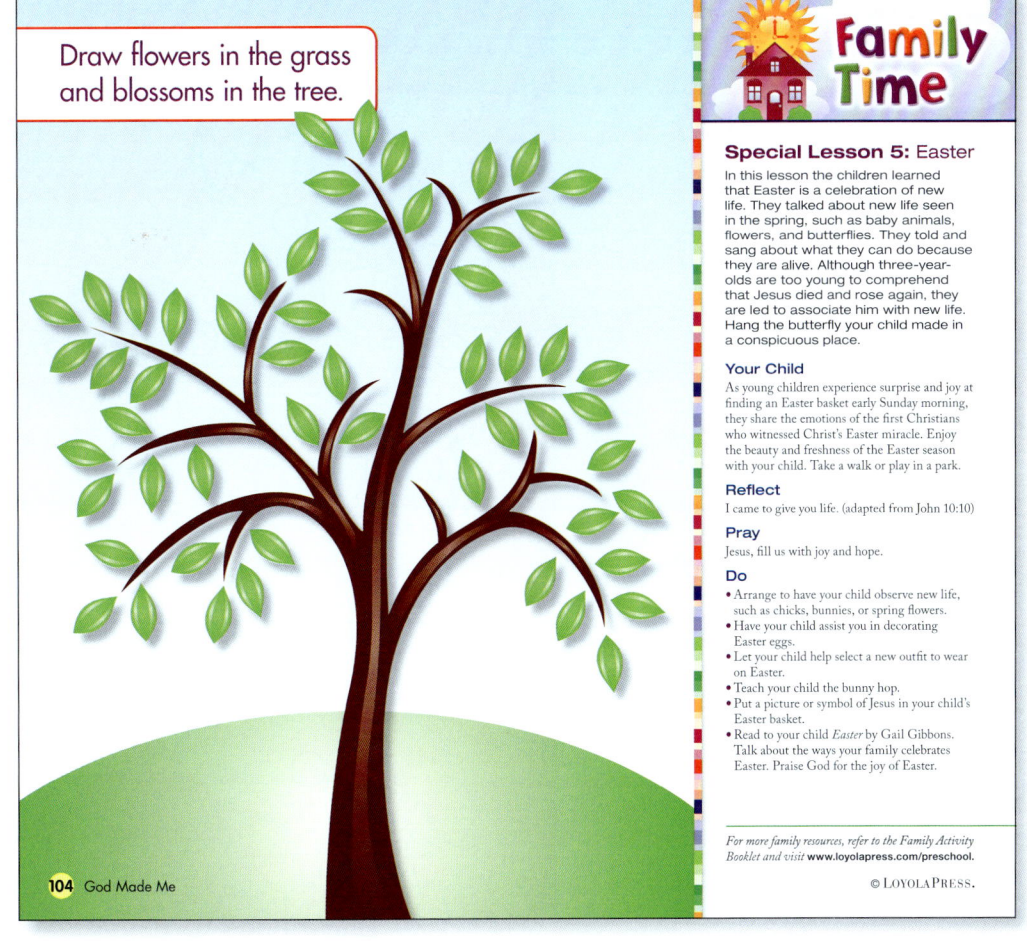

SHARING [A]

1 Distribute page 103 and talk about new life.

• *On Easter we celebrate new life. Spring is a time for new life. What new life do you see in the picture?* (Baby birds, baby animals, spring flowers, blossoms, butterflies) [Option: Show the spring flowers.]

2 SCRIPTURE Read the adaptation of John 10:10 from the Scripture card in the Bible.

• *God gives us life. Listen to what Jesus told us. "I came to give you life."*

3 Have the children draw flowers in the grass and blossoms on the tree on page 104. If you prefer, the children might use pencil ends or cardboard tubes from dry-cleaning hangers and paper towels soaked in different colored tempera paints to print petals on the card.

SHARING [B]

4 Talk about Easter.

• *On Easter we celebrate the life of Jesus, and we celebrate the life that Jesus gives us. How do we celebrate Easter?* (We wear new clothes. We paint eggs that new life comes from. We send Easter cards.)

• *Life makes us happy. What can you do because you have life?*

5 PRAYER Invite the children to pray by singing and acting out the following song of life to the tune of "Mary Had a Little Lamb." The music is on page T9. Let them add verses.

I can run for I have life,
I have life, I have life.
I can run for I have life.
Thank you, God, for life.
I can hop . . .
I can spin . . .
I can wave . . .
I can jump . . .

Draw flowers in the grass and blossoms in the tree.

Family Time

Special Lesson 5: Easter

In this lesson the children learned that Easter is a celebration of new life. They talked about new life seen in the spring, such as baby animals, flowers, and butterflies. They told and sang about what they can do because they are alive. Although three-year-olds are too young to comprehend that Jesus died and rose again, they are led to associate him with new life. Hang the butterfly your child made in a conspicuous place.

Your Child
As young children experience surprise and joy at finding an Easter basket early Sunday morning, they share the emotions of the first Christians who witnessed Christ's Easter miracle. Enjoy the beauty and freshness of the Easter season with your child. Take a walk or play in a park.

Reflect
I came to give you life. (adapted from John 10:10)

Pray
Jesus, fill us with joy and hope.

Do
• Arrange to have your child observe new life, such as chicks, bunnies, or spring flowers.
• Have your child assist you in decorating Easter eggs.
• Let your child help select a new outfit to wear on Easter.
• Teach your child the bunny hop.
• Put a picture or symbol of Jesus in your child's Easter basket.
• Read to your child *Easter* by Gail Gibbons. Talk about the ways your family celebrates Easter. Praise God for the joy of Easter.

For more family resources, refer to the Family Activity Booklet and visit www.loyolapress.com/preschool.

© LOYOLAPRESS.

ACTING

1 Introduce Cutout #47, butterfly, as your friend Flutterby. Ask:

• *Why are butterflies good insects for Easter?* (They come out in the spring. They are full of life. They are pretty.)

• *Did you know that butterflies were once caterpillars? Caterpillars wrap themselves up in a little sac, and while they're inside, they turn into butterflies. Isn't that wonderful?*

2 Help the children make their own Flutterbys from perforated Card L by following these directions:

- Color the butterfly.
- Starting at the top, lace ribbon or yarn through the holes.
- Tie the ribbon or yarn in a bow.

3 Gather the children in a circle for *Music 'n Motion* time. Play Track 13. Invite the children to do motions to the song along with you, using *Music 'n Motion* page T266.

Have the children take home their pages and show their family the Family Time section.

CHECKPOINT

- Were the learning outcomes achieved?
- Did the children enjoy this lesson?

T204   Special Seasons and Days

ENRICHING THE FAITH EXPERIENCE

Use the following activities to enrich the lesson or to replace an activity with one that better meets the needs of your group.

❶ Hide Easter eggs made out of paper—or real Easter eggs—in the room and let the children enjoy participating in an Easter egg hunt.

❷ Make Easter-bonnet cookies. For each cookie, dip a large marshmallow in water and roll it in shredded coconut. Set it on a large, circular cookie and seal it around the bottom with frosting.

❸ Teach the children these songs:

Good News!

Good news! Spring is com-ing! Good news! Spring is com-ing! Good news! Spring is com-ing! Don't leave me be-hind!

Oh! The Pretty Butterflies

Oh! The pret-ty but-ter-flies! How they fly, how they fly! Oh! The pret-ty but-ter-flies! How they cir-cle in the sky!

Easter SPECIAL LESSON 5 T205

Special Lesson 6
Pentecost

FAITH FOCUS

We celebrate the gift of the Holy Spirit. John 15:26–27; John 20:19–23; Galatians 5:22–23

PREPARING THE FAITH EXPERIENCE

LISTENING

When the time for Pentecost was fulfilled, they were all in one place together. And suddenly there came from the sky a noise like a strong driving wind, and it filled the entire house in which they were. Then there appeared to them tongues as of fire, which parted and came to rest on each one of them. And they were all filled with the holy Spirit and began to speak in different tongues, as the Spirit enabled them to proclaim.

Acts of the Apostles 2:1–4

REFLECTING

Wind and air are metaphors often used to describe the action of the Holy Spirit in our lives. We do not see the air that is always around us, yet we feel its effects, especially in its movement as wind, and know its presence. So it is with the life of the Holy Spirit whose effects we can see in our lives. Like wind that can fan a fire's flame, the Holy Spirit can enkindle in us the fire of God's love.

Wind cannot be perceived as any definite shape or form. Rather, it fills out and then is limited only by the size of its container. Similarly, the Holy Spirit has no definite shape or form. The Holy Spirit's presence in our lives, though, is surely discernible as God brings us to completion, limited only by our finite capacity. Our spiritual life is sustained and renewed by the Holy Spirit, who is always working within us to make us holy.

Jesus promised to send his disciples the Holy Spirit, the Advocate who would help them testify on his behalf. This promise was fulfilled on Pentecost. The gift of the Holy Spirit transformed the fearful disciples into a community of believers, making them bold witnesses to the Good News. Jesus, the Crucified One, had been raised from the dead and was revealed as Lord and Savior.

Pentecost is the Greek word for the Jewish Festival of Weeks, celebrated 50 days after Passover. It was originally a celebration of thanksgiving for the grain harvest. It later became a celebration of God's gift of the Law given at Mount Sinai. Pentecost is also the name given to the day Christians celebrate the first outpouring of the Holy Spirit on Jesus' disciples because it occurred on the Jewish feast of Pentecost. The Christian feast of Pentecost is celebrated at the conclusion of the Easter season.

On Pentecost we celebrate the gift of the Holy Spirit and his importance in our lives. We are strengthened and renewed by the Gifts of the Holy Spirit. With the Church we pray that the Holy Spirit will direct our use of every gift and that our lives may bring Christ to others. We seek to know peace and joy and all the Fruits of the Holy Spirit's actions in our lives.

RESPONDING

Having been nourished by God's Word, we are able to respond to God's great love for us. In prayer, respond to God's call to you to share his Word with others. You may also wish to respond in your prayer journal.

- In what ways am I aware of the action of the Holy Spirit in my life?

Holy Spirit, fill the world with your peace and joy.

Special Seasons and Days

Catechism of the Catholic Church

The themes of this lesson correspond to the following paragraphs: 731–732, 733–736, 739, 1287, 2623.

THE FAITH EXPERIENCE

Child's Book pages 105–108

SCRIPTURE IN THIS LESSON
- *Wisdom 1:7*

MATERIALS
- Bible
- Pentecost Scripture card
- Toys that work with air, such as pinwheels, bubbles, sailboats, and flutes
- Crayons or markers

PREPARATION
- Write the children's names on pages 105 and 108.
- Place the Pentecost Scripture card for SHARING #6 in the Bible.

ENRICHING THE FAITH EXPERIENCE
Use the activities at the end of the lesson to enrich the lesson or to replace an activity with one that better meets the needs of your group.

BOOKS TO SHARE
When the Wind Stops by Charlotte Zolotow (HarperTrophy, 1997)

The Swinging Tree by Carol Therese Plum (Our Sunday Visitor, 1989)

The Wind Blew by Pat Hutchins (Aladdin, 1993)

Feel the Wind by Arthur Dorros (HarperTrophy, 1990)

SNACK
Suggestion: popcorn

ALTERNATIVE PROGRAMS

DAILY PROGRAM
Day 1: Centering, Sharing A
Day 2: Enriching the Faith Experience choice
Day 3: Sharing B
Day 4: Enriching the Faith Experience choice
Day 5: Acting

THREE-DAY PROGRAM
Day 1: Centering, Sharing A
Day 2: Sharing B
Day 3: Acting

6 Pentecost

LEARNING OUTCOMES
The children will
- describe the importance of air.
- discuss the effects of wind that can be observed.
- know that God is with us always.

COMMENT
The Holy Spirit is given to us to strengthen our witness to Christ and to make us holy. The Holy Spirit also fills us with peace, joy, and love. Young children find comfort in knowing that God is with us always in the Person of the Holy Spirit.

CENTERING
Have the children engage in free play with toys that are made to work with air, such as pinwheels, bubbles, sailboats, and flutes.

SHARING [A]

❶ Distribute page 105 and talk about the girl in the picture.

- *What is the girl doing in this picture? How do you play with bubbles?*

- *Tell the children that air makes the bubbles work.*

T208 Special Seasons and Days

2 Talk about the importance of air.

- *Air is all around us. Even though we can't see the air, we know it is there. We see the things air can do. When air is moving outside, we call it wind.*

- *We cannot see the wind, but we can see the things that the wind can do. What are some things you have seen the wind do?* (Move the leaves on the trees, make flags move, make waves)

- *Air is important to us. We breathe the air.* [Tell the children to notice that they are breathing air in and out.] *We need air to live.*

3 Direct the children to match the pictures on page 106.

SHARING [B]

4 Have the children stand and make the sounds of air— a gentle breeze, a strong wind, a whistling wind, a howling wind. Encourage them to move their arms and bodies to demonstrate the effects of each kind of wind.

5 Compare the air to God.

- *God is all around us, just like the air is. God is everywhere. God gives us life, just like the air. Even though we cannot see God, we know God is here.*

6 **SCRIPTURE** Read the adaptation of Wisdom 1:7 from the Scripture card in the Bible.

- *Listen to these words from the Bible: "The spirit of the Lord fills the whole world."*

Match the pictures to show how air moves things.

106 God Made Me

Family Time

Special Lesson 6:
Pentecost
We celebrate the gift of the Holy Spirit on Pentecost. This lesson prepared the children to appreciate the work of the Holy Spirit in our lives. They learned about air and its presence all around us. They learned that God's presence with us is like the air: God is everywhere and with us always.

Your Child
As young children grow in their understanding of God, they take comfort in knowing that God is everywhere. Remind your child often that God is always with him or her.

Reflect
The spirit of the Lord fills the whole world. (adapted from Wisdom 1:7)

Pray
Holy Spirit, fill us with your life and love.

Do
- On a breezy day, take a walk with your child and notice the wind's power.
- Enjoy flying a kite or blowing bubbles with your child.
- Hang a decorative flag, windsock, or wind chime outside to help your child observe the effects of the wind.
- Read to your child *The Wind Blew* by Pat Hutchins. Ask your child to name some things the wind can do. Together thank God for being with us always.

For more family resources, refer to the Family Activity Booklet and visit www.loyolapress.com/preschool.

© LOYOLAPRESS.

Pentecost SPECIAL LESSON **6** T209

ACTING

1 PRAYER Lead the children to pray the Scripture with gestures:

"The spirit of the Lord fills the whole world."

[Make large circular motions with your arms, upward, then downward.]

2 Have the children decorate and fold the paper fan made from pages 107–108.

Have the children take home their pages and show their family the Family Time section.

CHECKPOINT

- Were the learning outcomes achieved?
- Were the children able to describe the effects of air and wind?

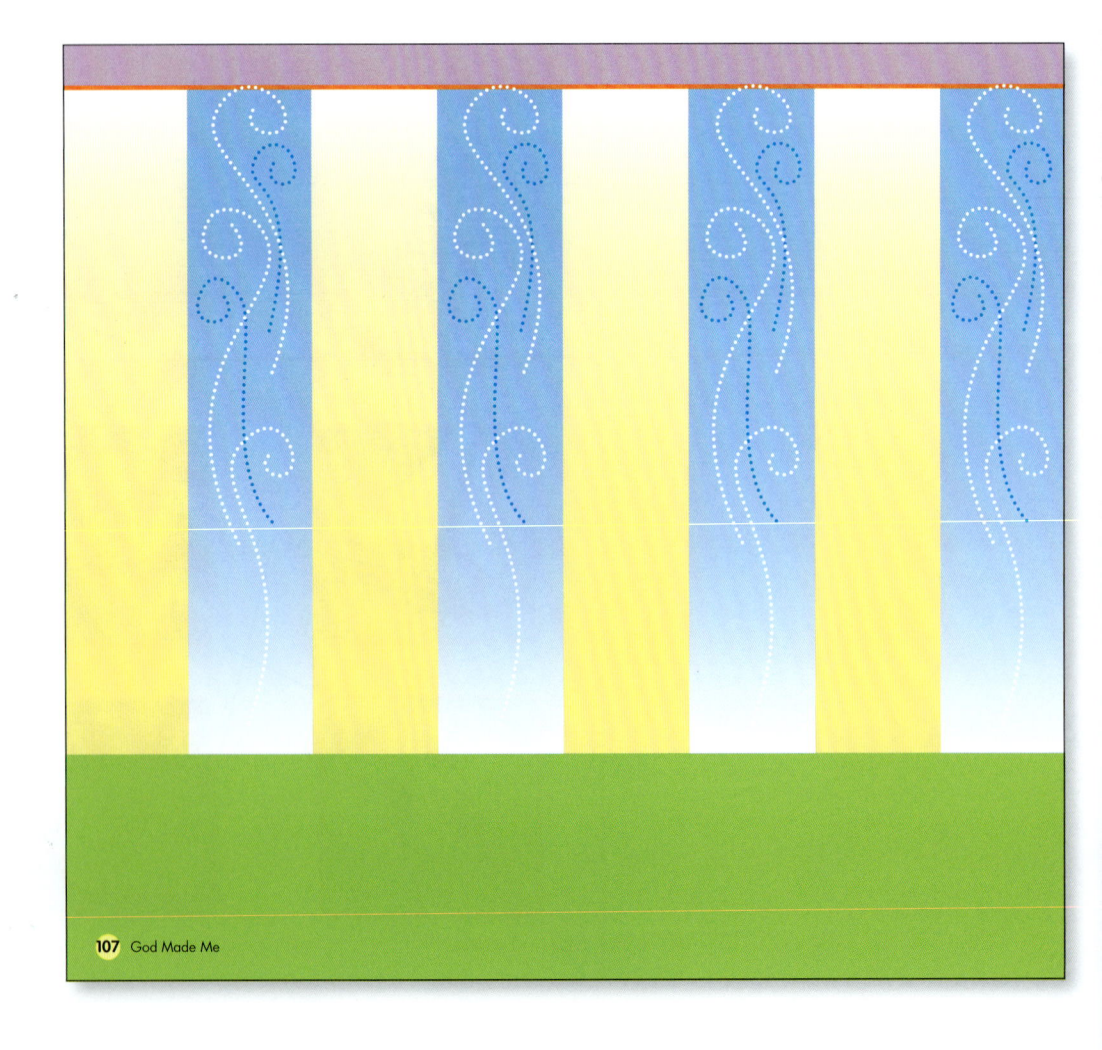

T210 Special Seasons and Days

ENRICHING THE FAITH EXPERIENCE

Use the following activities to enrich the lesson or to replace an activity with one that better meets the needs of your group.

1 Have the children make a wind sock by gluing streamers to a paper plate. Help the children tie yarn to the paper plate so it can hang.

2 Teach the children the poem below. You might sing it to the tune of "Jingle Bells."

> The wind tells me,
> [Sway.]
> The birds tell me,
> [Flap arms.]
> The Bible tells me too,
> [Open hands like a book.]
> How much our Father loves us all,
> [Stretch out arms.]
> And now I'm telling you!
> [Point to self and then point out.]

3 Let the children have a race by blowing cotton balls across a table or boats across a water-filled tub.

4 Take the children for a nature walk on a breezy day and have them observe the effects of the wind.

Special Lesson 7
Thanksgiving

FAITH FOCUS
We thank God for everything on Thanksgiving Day.
Psalm 111; Psalm 145; Luke 17:11–19; Ephesians 5:18–20

PREPARING THE FAITH EXPERIENCE

LISTENING

[b]e filled with the Spirit, addressing one another [in] psalms and hymns and spiritual songs, singing and playing to the Lord in your hearts, giving thanks always and for everything in the name of our Lord Jesus Christ to God the Father.
                                                    Ephesians 5:18–20

REFLECTING

The primary attitudes of human beings toward God are adoration and thanksgiving. We respond to God with adoration because God is infinite and transcendent. We respond with thanksgiving because God is good and loving. Everything we have has been given to us by God—our homes, family, friends, food, our very lives. God has also given us a remarkable gift: the life of Jesus, the Son of God, sacrificed on the cross for our redemption after we showed base ingratitude by sinning. God is probably the only one for whom the expression "Thanks a million" is not an overstatement.

Interestingly, the word *thank* has its origin in the word *think*. To thank is to realize and to acknowledge that someone has bestowed a favor on us. We don't always remember to express gratitude for God's gifts. And yet, God is pleased when we do so, as the story of the ten lepers reveals. (Luke 17:11–19) After Jesus had cured the ten seriously ill people and only one came back to thank him, Jesus asked, "Where are the other nine?" No doubt he was disappointed by their thoughtlessness and lack of manners.

Although every day is really a day for thanksgiving, once a year in the United States a special day—Thanksgiving Day—is set aside to give God thanks and to celebrate. There is no better way to observe this day than to include the Eucharist. The word *eucharist* itself comes from the Greek for "thanksgiving." In the celebration of the Eucharist, we give God thanks in the most effective way possible—through song, prayer, the sacrifice of Jesus, the sacrifice of ourselves, and the sharing of the sacred meal. During the Mass, sometimes we pray:

Father, it is our duty and our salvation, always and everywhere to give thanks through your beloved Son, Jesus Christ.
                                           Eucharistic Prayer II

We also show thanks by using the gifts we have received in ways that show our gratitude for them. As someone put it, "Thanksgiving is thanksliving." If we appreciate life, we respect it. If we are grateful for the earth, we care for it. If we appreciate other people, we show love and concern for them. Above all, we share our gifts, especially with those in need. This is what God, the Giver, intends that we do.

The words of Dag Hammarskjöld offer us a good motto for life: "For all that has been—Thanks! To all that will be—Yes!"

RESPONDING

God's Word moves us to respond in word and action. Let God's Spirit work within you as you prayerfully consider how you are being called to respond to God's message to you today. Responding through your journal may help to strengthen your response.

- What are some things I have never thought to thank God for?

God, give the children thankful hearts.

T212   Special Seasons and Days

Catechism of the Catholic Church

The themes of this lesson correspond to the following paragraphs: 224, 2637–2638.

THE FAITH EXPERIENCE

Child's Book pages 109–112

SCRIPTURE IN THIS LESSON
- *Psalm 138:1*

MATERIALS
- Bible
- Cutouts: #51–60, food pairs; #61, cornucopia
- Option: cornucopia or basketful of fruits and vegetables
- Crayons and markers
- Option: tempera paint
- Stapler

PREPARATION
Write the children's names on pages 109 and 112.

MUSIC 'N MOTION
Use *Music 'n Motion* page T268 and CD Track 14 "Thank You, Jesus" for this lesson. For a list of additional music, see page T302.

ENRICHING THE FAITH EXPERIENCE
Use the activities at the end of the lesson to enrich the lesson or to replace an activity with one that better meets the needs of your group.

BOOKS TO SHARE
Over the River and Through the Woods by Lydia Maria Child (Henry Holt and Co., 1999)

Thanksgiving Is for Giving Thanks by Margaret Sutherland and Sonja Lamut (Grosset & Dunlap, 2000)

The Perfect Thanksgiving by Eileen Spinelli (Square Fish, 2007)

Thanksgiving Is . . . by Gail Gibbons (Holiday House, 2005)

SNACK
Suggestion: graham crackers and cranberry juice

ALTERNATIVE PROGRAMS

DAILY PROGRAM
Day 1: Centering, Sharing A
Day 2: Enriching the Faith Experience choice
Day 3: Sharing B
Day 4: Enriching the Faith Experience choice
Day 5: Acting

THREE-DAY PROGRAM
Day 1: Centering, Sharing A
Day 2: Sharing B
Day 3: Acting

7 Thanksgiving

LEARNING OUTCOMES
The children will
- know that everything comes from God.
- thank God for the gifts of the earth.
- rejoice in God's gifts.

COMMENTS

1. The Pilgrims' first feast in America in 1621 may have been like a harvest festival celebrated in England. Despite a year of hardship and a meager harvest, the Pilgrims held a three-day Thanksgiving. About 90 Native Americans contributed to and shared the banquet and participated in the games that were played. In 1623, when the Pilgrims were threatened by drought and starvation, they held a day of fasting and prayer. The following day brought not only rain but also news of the arrival of a ship with supplies. This led Governor Bradford to proclaim a day of thanksgiving and prayer. Later, in 1863, President Lincoln proclaimed the last Thursday of November as Thanksgiving Day. Now it is a national holiday.

2. Although the story of the first Thanksgiving is not told to the three-year-olds, they certainly can understand the concept of thanksgiving. Make "thank you" part of their working vocabulary by reminding them to say it and by saying thank you to them.

CENTERING

❶ Gather the children in a circle for *Music 'n Motion* time. Play Track 14. Invite the children to do motions to the song along with you, using *Music 'n Motion* page T268.

❷ Have the children play that they are grocery shopping. You might appoint a storekeeper or cashier.

SHARING [A]

❶ Distribute page 109 and talk about the food pictured.

- *What kinds of food do you see in the picture?*

- *What is your favorite vegetable? What is your favorite fruit?*

- *Where do the things we eat come from?*

- *God made the world full of good things for us to eat. One day each year we celebrate all of God's wonderful gifts and give thanks in a very special way. Do you know what day that is?* (Thanksgiving)

- *We celebrate Thanksgiving Day by having a Thanksgiving dinner.*

- *What do we usually eat on Thanksgiving?* (Turkey, sweet potatoes, cranberries, pumpkin pie) [Show Cutouts #51, 53, 55, 57, 59, foods.]

109 God Made Me   Name_____

T214   Special Seasons and Days

- *What else can we thank God for on Thanksgiving?*

2 Have the children trace the "thank-you path" that passes by things for which we thank God on page 110.

3 SCRIPTURE Show the Bible and teach the children this psalm prayer with gestures:

> I thank you, LORD,
> [Raise arms.]
> with all my heart.
> [Cross hands on heart.]
> Psalm 138:1

SHARING [B]

4 Play "Toss the Salad." Have the children stand in a circle and give each child the name of a vegetable, assigning the same vegetable to at least two children. When you call out the vegetable's name, the children with that name exchange places.

5 Show Cutout #61, cornucopia, and explain what a cornucopia is. [Option: You may also wish to show a real cornucopia or a basketful of fruits and vegetables.] Have the children sit in a circle.

- *This is a cornucopia. The word* cornucopia *means "horn of plenty." Say "cornucopia."*
- *A cornucopia is filled with plenty of things God has given us to eat. Some people use cornucopias to decorate their tables on Thanksgiving.*

6 Play "Concentration" with Cutouts #51–60, food pairs. Place three pairs of cards facedown on the floor in the center of a circle. Invite a child to turn over two cards. If they match, the child removes the cards and everyone says "Thank you, God, for [name of pictured food]." If they don't match, the child turns them back over and another child turns over two cards. After two pairs have been matched, add the remaining cards. The game continues until all cards have been matched.

Trace the path past things we thank God for.

Family Time

Special Lesson 7:
Thanksgiving

In this lesson the children were introduced to Thanksgiving as a day to thank God for everything. They heard that we celebrate all God's gifts by a special meal. They learned that a cornucopia filled with food is a Thanksgiving decoration. Use the cornucopia your child made to decorate your home for Thanksgiving. Plan with him or her to say a Thanksgiving prayer before your meal.

Your Child
Help form a thankful heart in your child by pointing out things for which to be thankful. Prompt him or her to give thanks to God and to others. Express thanks yourself, not forgetting to thank your child when it is appropriate.

Reflect
I thank you, LORD, with all my heart[.] (Psalm 138:1)

Pray
God, we thank you for all your wonderful gifts.

Do
- Let your child help with Thanksgiving preparations.
- Have your child draw things he or she is thankful for or glue pictures of them on paper or on a paper plate.
- Take your child to a farm or to a grocery store to see the great variety in our foods.
- Go for a drive and, as you go, pray a litany of Thanksgiving for what you see on the way.
- Read to your child *Thanksgiving Is...* by Gail Gibbons. Talk about how your family celebrates Thanksgiving. Take turns naming things for which you are thankful and pray "We thank you, God" after each is named.

For more family resources, refer to the Family Activity Booklet and visit www.loyolapress.com/preschool.

© LOYOLAPRESS.

Thanksgiving SPECIAL LESSON **7**

ACTING

1 [PRAYER] Invite the children to sing the following words to the tune of "Happy Birthday" as a way of praying to thank God for everything.

> Oh, we thank you we do.
> Oh, we thank you we do.
> Oh, we thank you, dear God.
> Oh, we thank you, we do.

2 Help the children make a cornucopia from pages 111–112. Have them color or paint the fruits and vegetables. Direct the children to bend the card to form a horn and to hold it while you staple it together.

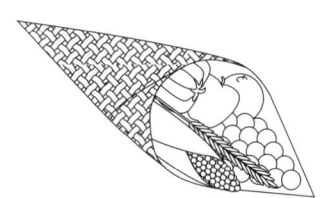

3 Gather the children in a circle for *Music 'n Motion* time. Play Track 14. Invite the children to do motions to the song along with you, using *Music 'n Motion* page T268.

Have the children take home their pages and show their family the Family Time section.

CHECKPOINT

- Were the learning outcomes achieved?
- What indications were there that the children enjoyed this lesson?

ENRICHING THE FAITH EXPERIENCE

Use the following activities to enrich the lesson or to replace an activity with one that better meets the needs of your group.

1 Teach the following song:

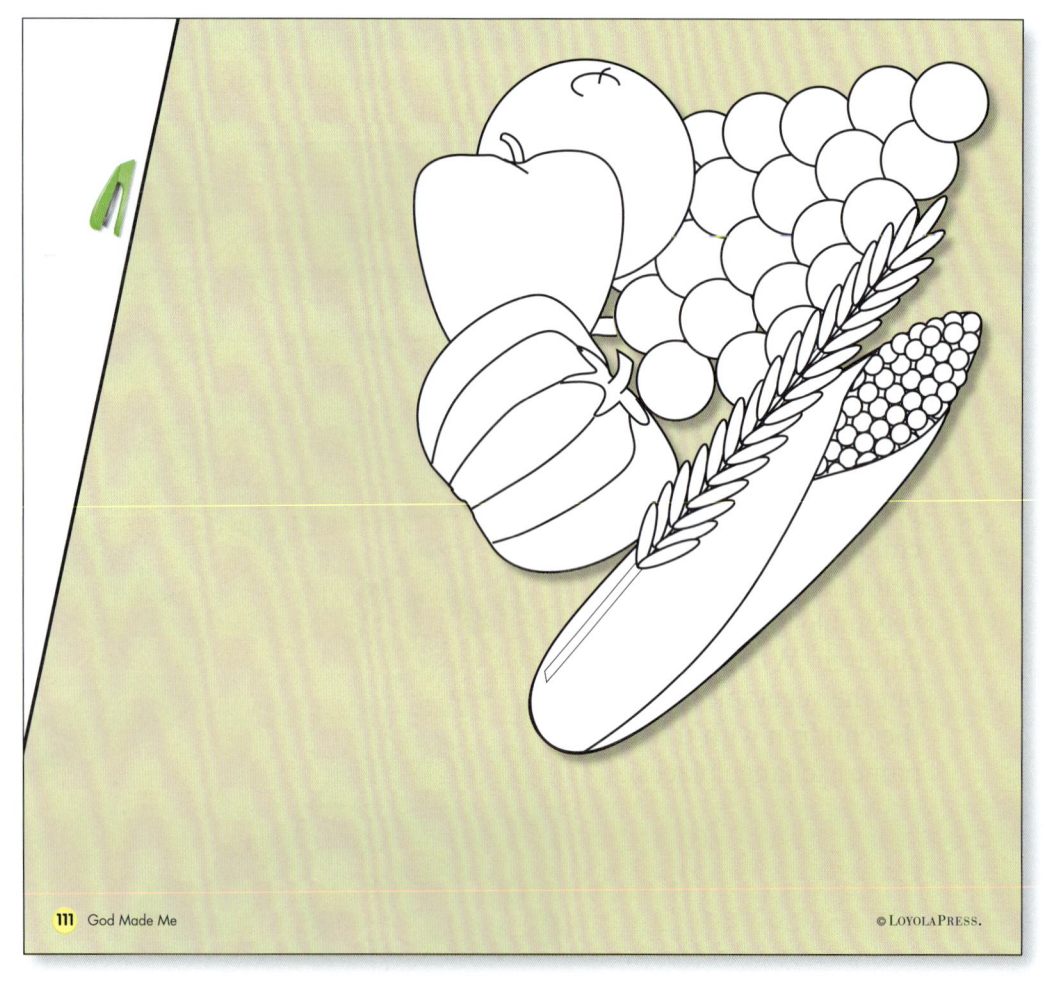

It's Good to Give Thanks to the Lord

It's good to give thanks to the Lord. ___ It's good to give thanks to the Lord. ___ It's good to give thanks. ___ It's good to give thanks. ___ It's good to give thanks to the Lord. ___

T216   Special Seasons and Days

Add verses substituting names of things for which you are thankful, for example, "It's good to give thanks for our food."

❷ **Make fresh orange juice** with the children by squeezing oranges, or make applesauce. For applesauce, have each child bring in an apple. Using these different apples to make applesauce, we teach that when everyone contributes, we can make a delicious treat for all to share. Using a food processor, pulse together until chopped fine the peeled and cored apples (cut into pieces), sugar, and cinnamon.

❸ **Invite the children to sit** in a circle and make one-sentence prayers thanking God for something: "I thank you, God, for _____. Roll a large ball to determine who says a prayer.

❹ **Put into a bag some** pictures of things to be thankful for. Let individual children choose one picture and have everyone pray a prayer of thanks for it.

❺ Teach the children the following song:

Five Fat Turkeys

Five fat tur-keys are we. ___ We slept all night in a tree. ___ When the cook came a-round we could-n't be found, so that's why we're here, you see. ___

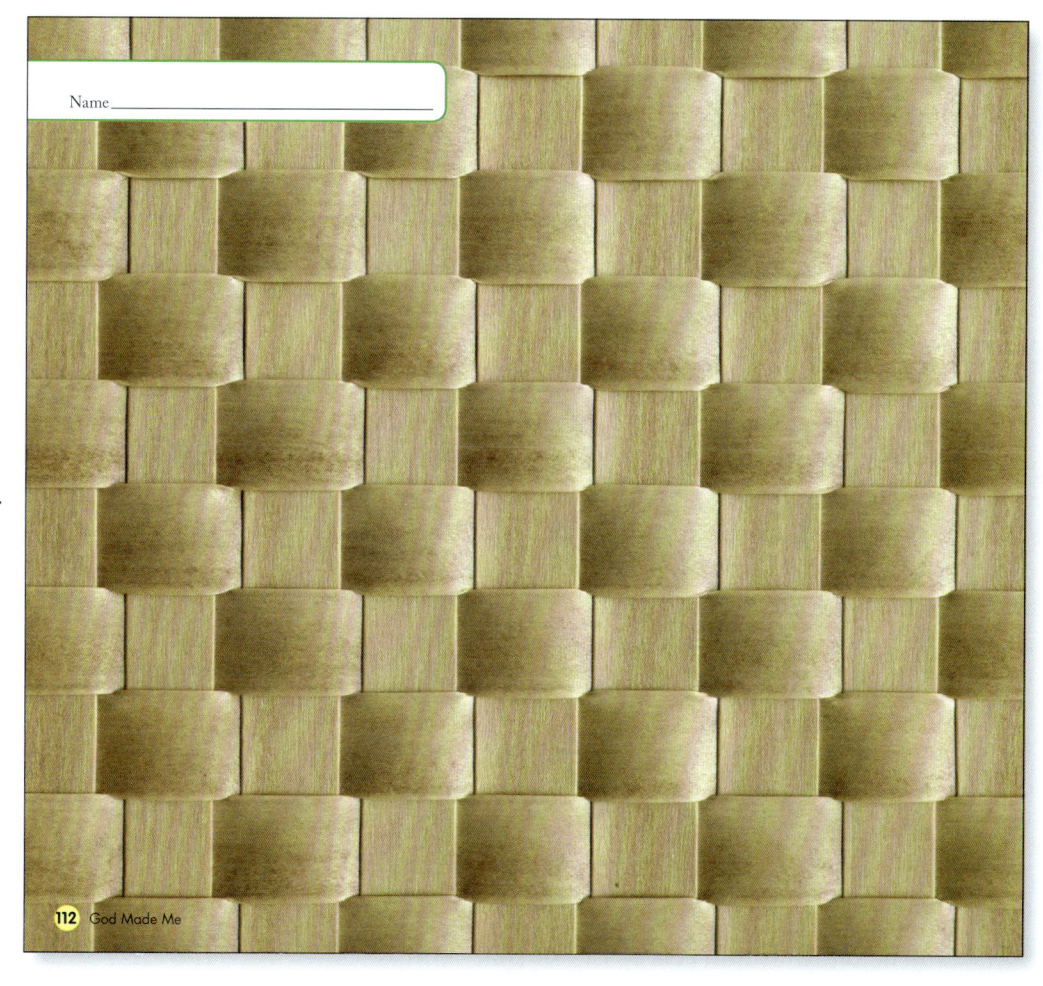

Thanksgiving SPECIAL LESSON 7 **T217**

Special Lesson 8
Valentine's Day

FAITH FOCUS

God loves us.

1 John 4:7–12

PREPARING THE FAITH EXPERIENCE

LISTENING

Beloved, let us love one another, because love is of God; everyone who loves is begotten by God and knows God. Whoever is without love does not know God, for God is love. In this way the love of God was revealed to us: God sent his only Son into the world so that we might have life through him. In this is love: not that we have loved God, but that he loved us and sent his Son as expiation for our sins. Beloved, if God so loved us, we also must love one another.

1 John 4:7–11

REFLECTING

Love is the most wonderful and most important thing in the world. Jesus told us that the greatest commandment is to love. Saint John of the Cross wrote that in the end we will all be judged on love. In Scripture we find that love defines God: "God is love." (1 John 4:8)

Love is ennobling and demanding. Jesus became one of us and showed us how to love. He challenged us to love as he loved—with a love that is universal. Jesus loved the wealthy and the poor, the popular and the outcasts, the educated and the illiterate, the Galileans and the Samaritans. His love encompassed his family and friends as well as his enemies. His heart was large enough to embrace us all. Jesus loved by showing concern for the daughter of Jairus and for the adulterous woman, and compassion for widows and for crowds hungry for truth and bread. He loved by teaching people, by healing lepers and those possessed by evil spirits, and by forgiving his executioners and his fair-weather friend, Peter. He loved us to death—death on a cross. With arms outstretched, Jesus shed his blood for us.

Our heart, that marvelous organ that pumps our lifeblood, is a fitting symbol for love. Saying we love someone with all our heart means that we love with our entire being. When Jesus appeared to Saint Margaret Mary, he used a vision of his heart to express how much he loved us, giving impetus to devotion to the Sacred Heart of Jesus. Someone has called the Bible a book drenched in love. The heartbeat of God can be heard in these verses: Isaiah 42:6, 43:1, 49:15–16, 54:10; Hosea 2:21; Matthew 28:20; John 14:23.

We look to many people and in many places for love. Saint Augustine pointed out the goal of our quest. Addressing God, he wrote, "Our hearts are restless until they rest in you." We pray to be better at loving:

*Father, we honor the heart of your Son
broken by man's cruelty,
yet symbol of love's triumph,
pledge of all that man is called to be.
Teach us to see Christ in the lives we touch,
to offer him living worship
by love-filled service to our brothers and sisters.*

Solemnity of the Sacred Heart
Alternative Opening Prayer

RESPONDING

Having reflected upon God's Word, take some time now to continue to respond to God in prayer. You might wish to record your responses in your journal.

- Who in my life needs to be loved?

Jesus, help the children and me love like you.

T218 Special Seasons and Days

Catechism of the Catholic Church

The themes of this lesson correspond to the following paragraphs: 214, 368, 478, 2055, 2563, 2842–2844.

THE FAITH EXPERIENCE

Child's Book page 113–116

SCRIPTURE IN THIS LESSON
- *Isaiah 49:16*

MATERIALS
- Bible
- Valentine's Day Scripture card
- Cutout #29, heart
- Option: heart-shaped candy box
- Crayons or markers
- Washable red marker or red face paint (See recipe in the back of this manual.)
- Paper scraps, yarn, foil, glitter, sequins, rickrack, ribbon, lace
- Glue

PREPARATION
- Write the children's names on pages 113 and 115.
- Place the Valentine's Day Scripture card for SHARING #5 in the Bible.

MUSIC 'N MOTION
Use *Music 'n Motion* page T270 and CD Track 15 "God Is Love" for this lesson. For a list of additional music, see page T302.

ENRICHING THE FAITH EXPERIENCE
Use the activities at the end of the lesson to enrich the lesson or to replace an activity with one that better meets the needs of your group.

BOOKS TO SHARE
Valentine Surprise by Corinne Demas
 (Walker Books for Young Readers, 2007)

The Story of Valentine's Day by Nancy J. Skarmeas
 (Candy Cane Press, 1999)

Biscuit's Valentine's Day by Alyssa Satin Capucilli
 (HarperFestival, 2000)

Emily's Valentine Party by Claire Masurel (Puffin, 1999)

SNACK
Suggestion: heart-shaped cookies

ALTERNATIVE PROGRAMS

DAILY PROGRAM
Day 1: Centering, Sharing A
Day 2: Sharing B
Day 3: Acting #1
Day 4: Enriching the Faith Experience choice
Day 5: Acting #2 and #3

THREE-DAY PROGRAM
Day 1: Centering, Sharing A
Day 2: Sharing B, Acting #1
Day 3: Acting #2 and #3

8 Valentine's Day

LEARNING OUTCOMES
The children will
- know that God loves them.
- desire to show love to others.

COMMENTS

1. All people, including three-year-olds, need to know that they are loved. Research shows that the emotional and physical health of infants who are hugged, cuddled, and loved is much better than that of infants who do not experience human touch and signs of affection. We all form our self-concepts based on images of ourselves that others reflect to us. It is important that the children in our classes perceive themselves as lovable.

2. Two Saint Valentines are listed in the Roman Martyrology for February 14—one a priest, the other a bishop. No one knows how our Valentine's Day, a day for lovers, is related to these saints, and very little is known about their lives. If, as it is believed, they were martyrs, their lives ended with the supreme sign of love.

CENTERING

❶ Gather the children in a circle for *Music 'n Motion* time. Play Track 15. Invite the children to do motions to the song along with you, using *Music 'n Motion* page T270.

❷ Play "God Loves You," using Cutout #29, heart. Have the children sit in a circle. Explain the game:

- *Valentine's Day is coming, a day on which we celebrate love.*
- *A heart is a sign of love. I will give each of you a heart, one by one. When a child receives the heart, we'll all say "God loves . . ." and say the child's name because he or she is special.*

SHARING [A]

❶ Distribute page 113 and talk about Jesus' love.

- *Who is in the picture?* (Jesus and children)
- *Jesus loves you very much. Jesus loves you with his whole heart. He likes you to be happy.*
- *Jesus told us to love one another.*

113 God Made Me

T220 Special Seasons and Days

2 Talk about showing love.

• *On Valentine's Day we give people we love Valentine cards to let them know we love them. Sometimes we give candy.* [Option: Show the candy box.]

• *How else can we show love?* (Hugging and kissing, doing nice things for other people)

• *Who loves you?*

• *How do people show they love you?*

3 Have the children draw lines to match the hearts that are the same on page 114.

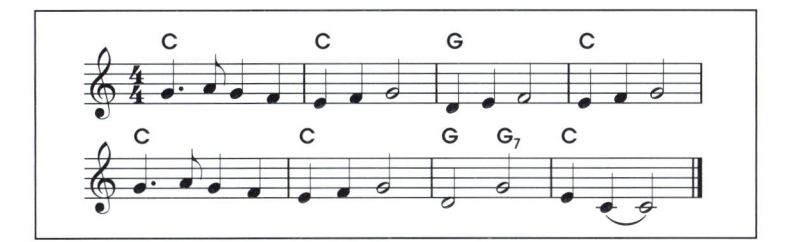

SHARING [B]

4 Have the children play "London Bridge" while singing the words above. Two children hold hands and raise them to form a bridge. The other children walk under the bridge, singing the first verse of the song. On the words "My fair lady," the bridge lowers to capture a child. Everyone claps and sings the second verse. The captured child replaces one child who formed the bridge, and the game continues.

1. Won't you be my valentine, valentine, valentine?
   Won't you be my valentine, my fair lady? (or gentleman)
2. Yes, I'll be your valentine, valentine, valentine.
   Yes, I'll be your valentine, my fair lady (or gentleman).

Draw lines to match the hearts that are the same.

Family Time

Special Lesson 8: Valentine's Day

In this lesson the children learned that Valentine's Day is a day to show love. They recalled God's great love for them. They talked about people who love them and how they can show love for others. Admire the giant valentine your child made. Help deliver it if necessary.

Your Child
Being loved is essential to a child's moral and emotional development. Through your words and actions make sure that your child perceives himself or herself as lovable. Make every day a Valentine's Day at home.

Reflect
See, I have written your name on the palms of my hands. (adapted from Isaiah 49:16)

Pray
God, we praise you for your great love.

Do
• Hold a Valentine's Day party in your home for your child and a few of your child's friends.
• Serve pink or red drinks and dessert on Valentine's Day.
• Give your child a valentine.
• Go with your child to take a valentine to someone who doesn't expect it.
• Make a Valentine's Day phone call with your child to someone special, such as a grandparent.
• Give the gift of yourself to your child on Valentine's Day by doing something together.
• Read to your child *Valentine Surprise* by Corinne Demas. Choose something special to do together to show love to your family for Valentine's Day. Pray in thanks to God who always loves us.

For more family resources, refer to the Family Activity Booklet and visit www.loyolapress.com/preschool.

114 God Made Me

© LOYOLAPRESS.

Valentine's Day SPECIAL LESSON **8** T221

5 **SCRIPTURE** Read an adaptation of Isaiah 49:16 from the Scripture card in the Bible.

• *God loves you every day, not just on Valentine's Day. God gave you the whole world for a valentine. In the Bible, God says "See, I have written your name on the palms of my hands."*

• *That means that God never forgets about you.*

• *We love God too.*

ACTING

1 Write "God" in a red heart on the back of each child's hand who wants you to and tell the children to look at the heart and think about God's love for them. Invite them to pray by saying to God, "I love you."

2 Have the children decorate page 115 as a giant valentine for someone they love, using scraps of paper and other materials. Tell them that the back of the card says the following:

> Because you mean so much to me,
> I made this valentine for you.
> It says I love you with all my heart.
> I hope you love me too.

Have the children sign the cards. Suggest that the children add Xs and Os to represent kisses and hugs.

3 Gather the children in a circle for *Music 'n Motion* time. Play Track 15. Invite the children to do motions to the song along with you, using *Music 'n Motion* page T270.

Have the children take home their pages and show their family the Family Time section.

CHECKPOINT

• Were the learning outcomes achieved?
• How fully did the children participate in the lesson?

115 God Made Me

T222   Special Seasons and Days

ENRICHING THE FAITH EXPERIENCE

Use the following activities to enrich the lesson or to replace an activity with one that better meets the needs of your group.

1 Give each child a valentine from you.

2 Make a love tree in the room. Whenever you notice a child doing something loving, make a remark about it and hang a paper heart on the tree.

3 Have the children finger paint with red paint on heart-shaped paper.

4 Give the children hearts cut from red paper. Have the children take turns putting their hearts in a box. Roll a marble in white tempera paint, put it into the box, and let the children move the box so that the marble decorates the hearts.

5 Teach the children the following song:

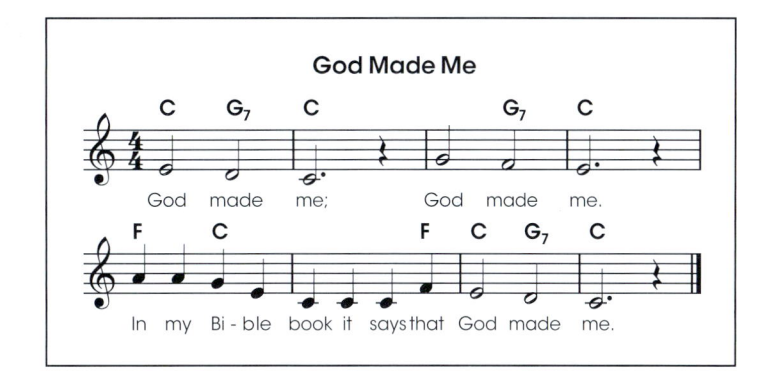

God Made Me

God made me; God made me.
In my Bi-ble book it says that God made me.

2. God loves me . . .
3. God helps me . . .
4. God cares for me . . .
5. God thinks of me . . .

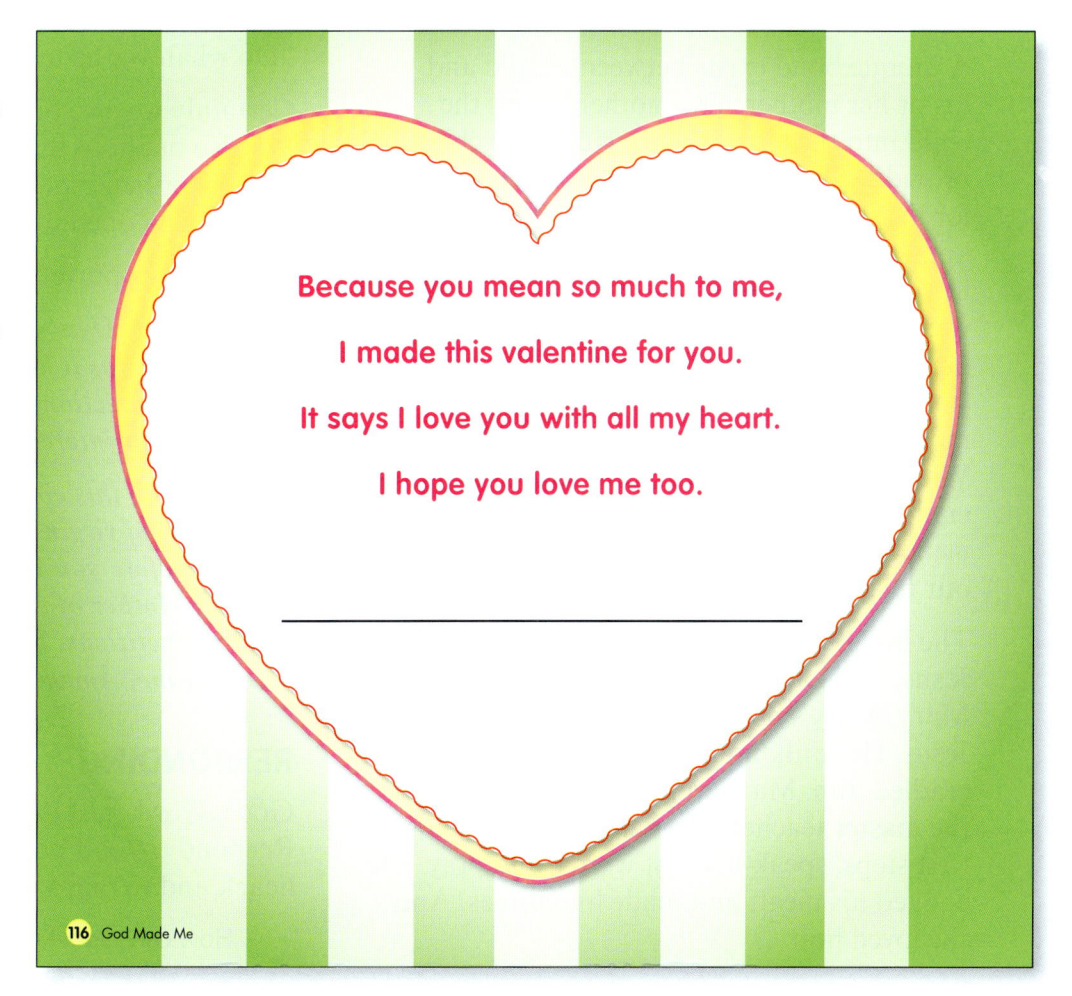

Because you mean so much to me,

I made this valentine for you.

It says I love you with all my heart.

I hope you love me too.

116 God Made Me

Valentine's Day SPECIAL LESSON **8** **T223**

Special Lesson 9
Mother's Day

FAITH FOCUS

God gave us a mother on earth and in heaven.

Isaiah 49:15; John 19:26–27; Ephesians 6:1–3

PREPARING THE FAITH EXPERIENCE

LISTENING

Can a mother forget her infant,
 be without tenderness for the child of her womb?
Even should she forget,
 I will never forget you.

Isaiah 49:15

REFLECTING

The feminist movement has heightened our awareness of the feminine aspects of God, who being pure spirit is really neither male nor female. Even without the benefit of this movement, it is easy to see why the concept of mother is an apt image for God.

A unique bond exists between a child and his or her mother. The mother brings the child into the world and nurtures the child, providing for the child's needs, teaching skills for living, and guiding her child in acquiring knowledge. Most important, a mother loves her child and willingly sacrifices for her child's well-being. The child is dependent on his or her mother and looks to her for help, understanding, and advice. The child trusts in the mother's love and feels secure when she is near. With the passing of years, the love and appreciation the child feels for his or her mother usually grow. These descriptions also apply to our relationship with God.

The bond between mother and child united Jesus, the Son of God, and the Blessed Virgin Mary. Mary's body gave flesh and blood to Jesus. Her milk nourished him, and her arms cradled him. Mary was the first teacher of the master teacher. She helped him take his first steps, speak his first words, and pray. She cooked his meals and made his clothes. And she loved him.

Because Mary gave birth to Christ and because we are the members of his mystical body, it follows that she is also our mother. Tradition holds that from the cross Jesus officially gave us the gift of Mary, his mother, when he said to John, our representative, "Behold your mother" and to Mary, "Behold your son." (John 19:26, 27) Mary loves and cares for us and prays for us. May each of us reflect something of the way she lived. May we heed her advice, her last recorded words in Scripture: "Do whatever he tells you." (John 2:5)

Certainly we owe our mothers on earth thanks. We also ought to thank our heavenly mother and honor her, especially by trying to be as faithful and open to God as she was.

Let us pray a prayer attributed to Saint Bernard:

Remember, O most gracious Virgin Mary, that never was it known that anyone who fled to your protection, implored your help, or sought your intercession was left unaided.

Inspired by this confidence, I fly unto you, O Virgin of virgins, my Mother. To you do I come, before you I stand, sinful and sorrowful. O Mother of the Word incarnate, despise not my petitions, but in your mercy hear and answer me. Amen.

RESPONDING

God's Word calls us to respond in love. Respond to God now in the quiet of your heart, and perhaps through your journal.

- How can I show motherly care for others?

Mary, pray for the children.

T224 Special Seasons and Days

Catechism of the Catholic Church

The themes of this lesson correspond to the following paragraphs: 507, 2215, 2618, 2679.

THE FAITH EXPERIENCE

Child's Book pages 117–120

SCRIPTURE IN THIS LESSON
- *Luke 2:51*

MATERIALS
- Bible
- Mother's Day Scripture card
- **Option:** saucepan, watering can, or other item mothers may use
- Dolls or stuffed animals for free play
- Music for dancing for SHARING #2
- Hole punch
- Tempera paint
- Paper towels
- Kitchen objects for printing: potato masher, cookie cutter, jar lids
- Glue or stapler
- 8-inch pieces of yarn or ribbon, one for each child
- **Option:** small sheets of notepaper

PREPARATION
- Place the Mother's Day Scripture card for SHARING #2 in the Bible.
- Write the children's names on page 117.
- Cut apart the cards and the paper holders on pages 119–120 and put the children's names on the back of the notepaper holders.
- Punch holes at the top of the notepaper holders.
- Make printing pads by soaking paper towels in tempera paint.

ENRICHING THE FAITH EXPERIENCE
Use the activities at the end of the lesson to enrich the lesson or to replace an activity with one that better meets the needs of your group.

BOOKS TO SHARE
On Mother's Lap by Ann Herbert Scott
(Clarion Books, 1992)

The Runaway Bunny by Margaret Wise Brown
(HarperCollins, 2005)

Blueberries for Sal by Robert McCloskey
(Viking Juvenile, 1948)

Five Minutes' Peace by Jill Murphy
(Walker Books Ltd., 2006)

SNACK
Suggestion: graham crackers topped with banana slices

ALTERNATIVE PROGRAMS

DAILY PROGRAM
Day 1: Centering, Sharing A
Day 2: Enriching the Faith Experience choice
Day 3: Sharing B
Day 4: Enriching the Faith Experience choice, Acting #1
Day 5: Acting #2

THREE-DAY PROGRAM
Day 1: Centering, Sharing A
Day 2: Sharing B
Day 3: Acting

Mother's Day SPECIAL LESSON 9 T225

9 Mother's Day

LEARNING OUTCOMES

The children will
- realize what their mothers do for them.
- be grateful for their mothers on earth.
- know that Mary is their mother in heaven.

COMMENTS

1. Mothers are the closest people to three-year-olds and are the most influential in their development. The three-year-old loves being near his or her mother and doing things with her. Although most three-year-olds are dependent on their mothers for almost everything, at the age of three-and-a-half, many of them go through a stage of rebellion. They balk at their mother's orders and advice during routines such as dressing and eating. Nothing seems to please or satisfy them. This stage can be challenging.

2. Be sensitive to those children who have mothers other than their biological mothers or who have recently lost a mother.

3. Knowing that Mary is a mother in heaven who loves and cares about them is comforting to three-year-olds.

CENTERING

Have the children play house in small groups, allowing them to choose their own roles.

SHARING [A]

❶ Talk with the children about their mothers.

- *What does your mother look like?*
- *What did your mother do for you today?*
- *What does your mother do for your family?* [Option: Show an item mothers may use.]
- *What do you like about your mother?*
- *God gave us mothers or people who are like mothers, such as our grandmothers, to help us until we are big enough to take care of ourselves. Mothers and those like them teach us how to live.*

❷ **SCRIPTURE** Distribute page 117 and talk about Mary. Read the adaptation of Luke 2:51 from the Scripture card in the Bible.

- *Who are in the picture?* (Mary and Jesus)

117 God Made Me

T226 Special Seasons and Days

- *Mary did for Jesus what your mother does for you. Mary loved her son, Jesus. Jesus loved his mother, Mary. Listen to what we read about Jesus and Mary in the Bible: Jesus went with Mary and Joseph to Nazareth and obeyed them. Mary remembered all these things in her heart.*

- *What do you think Mary is like from the picture on this page?*

- *Mary is your mother in heaven. She loves you and watches over you. So you have two mothers, one on earth and one in heaven.*

- *You can take home the picture of Mary and Jesus and put it where you will see it every day. When you look at it, remember that Mary is your mother.*

❸ Have the children draw lines to match babies with their mothers on page 118.

SHARING [B]

❹ Play "Mother Wants You." Appoint one child as the "mother." Have the other children move to one end of the room and dance to music. When the "mother" calls "Mother wants you," the children run to her. The first child to tag her becomes the next "mother."

❺ Talk about feeling gratitude to mothers.

- *Mothers and people who are like mothers to us do much for us. What can we do for them?* (Help them, show them love, thank them)

- *On Mother's Day we thank our mothers and show we are grateful for who they are and what they do for us. Today you will make a gift to give your mother or someone like your mother on Mother's Day.*

- *We can thank Mary too for being our mother.*

❻ **PRAYER** Pray a prayer to thank God for mothers.

- *Let's thank God for giving us our mothers. Close your eyes and think about your mother or the person who is like a mother to you.* [Pause.] *Thank God in your heart for her.* [Pause.] *Now think about Mary.* [Pause.] *Thank God for giving you Mary as your mother in heaven.* [Pause.]

Draw lines to match the babies with their mothers.

118 God Made Me

Family Time

Special Lesson 9:
Mother's Day

In this lesson the children talked about their mothers and learned that Mary, the mother of Jesus, is also their mother in heaven. They were encouraged to show love and appreciation for their mothers on earth and for their mother, Mary, in heaven. They thanked God for their mother and for giving them Mary as their mother.

Your Child
Three-year-olds are typically very dependent on their mothers. They love being with their mothers and doing things with them. However, at age three-and-a-half they may experience a period of rebellion. Your child needs your patience and understanding as he or she learns to deal with life and cope with the challenges of being human.

Reflect
Jesus went with Mary and Joseph to Nazareth and obeyed them. Mary remembered all these things in her heart. (adapted from Luke 2:51)

Pray
Generous God, bless all mothers and strengthen them with your love and grace.

Do
- Display in your home a picture or statue of Mary.
- Talk with your child about what Mary must have done for Jesus when he was your child's age.
- Tell your child stories about when you were little and what your mother did for you.
- Visit a zoo or farm at a time when you can see mother animals and their babies.
- Read to your child *On Mother's Lap* by Ann Herbert Scott. Ask your child to describe something a mother does to show love for her child. Ask God to bless all mothers and those who love and care for others.

For more family resources, refer to the Family Activity Booklet and visit www.loyolapress.com/preschool.

© LOYOLAPRESS.

Mother's Day **SPECIAL LESSON 9** T227

ACTING

1 Teach this poem and suggest that the children recite it to their mothers on Mother's Day:

> Mom, you're with me night and day,
> Helping me in every way.
> 'Cause I love you lots I say,
> Have a happy Mother's Day!
> *Mary Kathleen Glavich, S.N.D.*

2 Have the children make a notepaper holder and a Mother's Day card for their mothers from pages 119–120. Help them follow these directions:

- Decorate the yellow sides of the greeting card and the paper holder by making designs with kitchen objects dipped in tempera paint.
- When the paint is dry, fold the card.
- Sign the card.
- Fold the paper holder so that the decoration is on the front.
- Staple or glue the sides of the holder together.
- Punch a hole in the top of the holder and string yarn or ribbon through it.
- Put the card in the holder and, if you wish, add some notepaper.

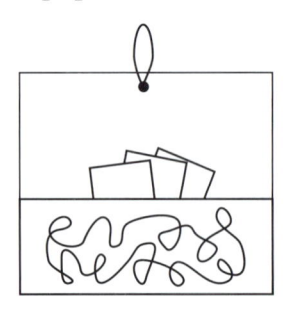

Have the children take home their pages and show their family the Family Time section.

CHECKPOINT

- Were the learning outcomes achieved?
- What signs were there that the children enjoyed the lesson?

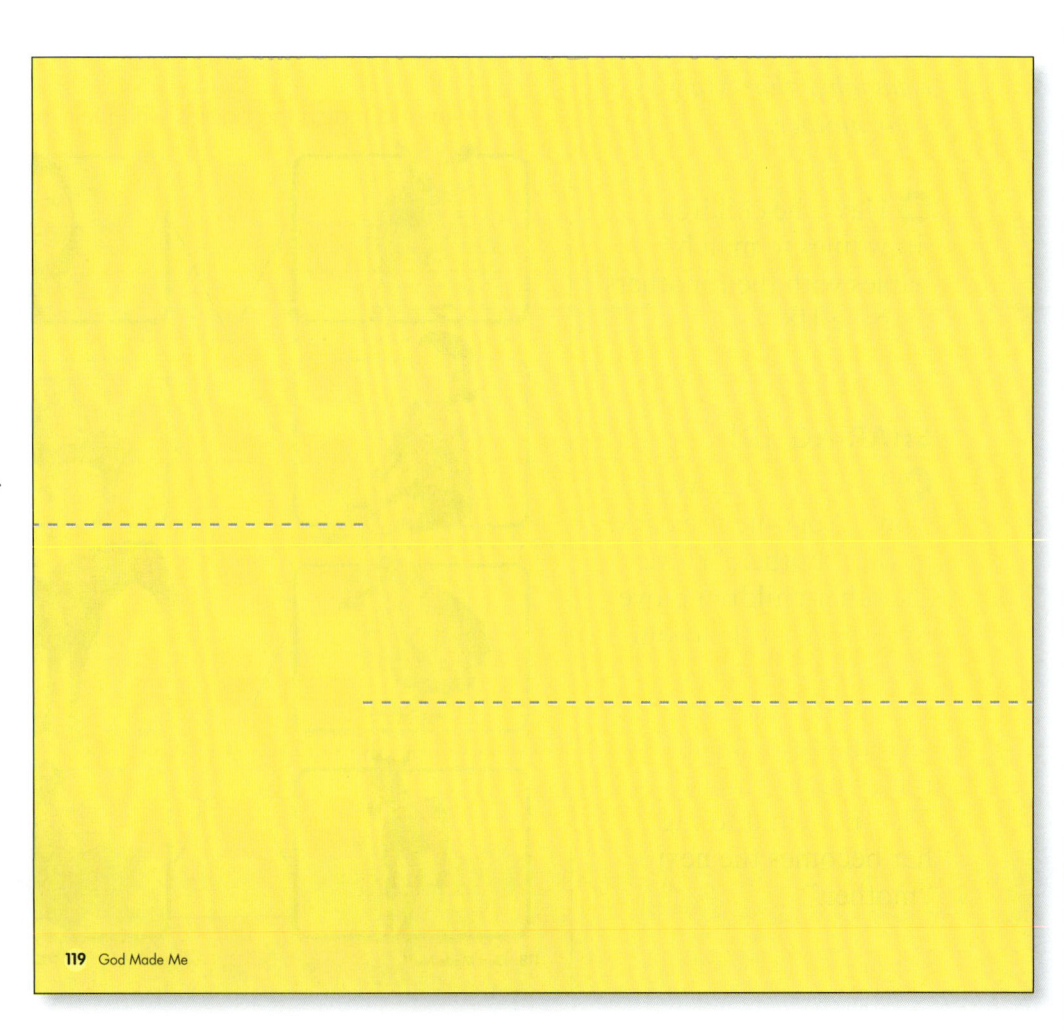

ENRICHING THE FAITH EXPERIENCE

Use the following activities to enrich the lesson or to replace an activity with one that better meets the needs of your group.

❶ Take pictures of the children and have them glue their pictures on their Mother's Day cards.

❷ Have the children draw or paint pictures of their mothers on large sheets of paper.

❸ Hold a May celebration to honor Mary. Have the children put flowers before her picture or statue. Have the children repeat after you:

> Mary, my mother in heaven above,
> This day I thank you and show you my love.
> Help me to grow up to be like your Son,
> Kind and loving to everyone.
> *Mary Kathleen Glavich, S.N.D.*

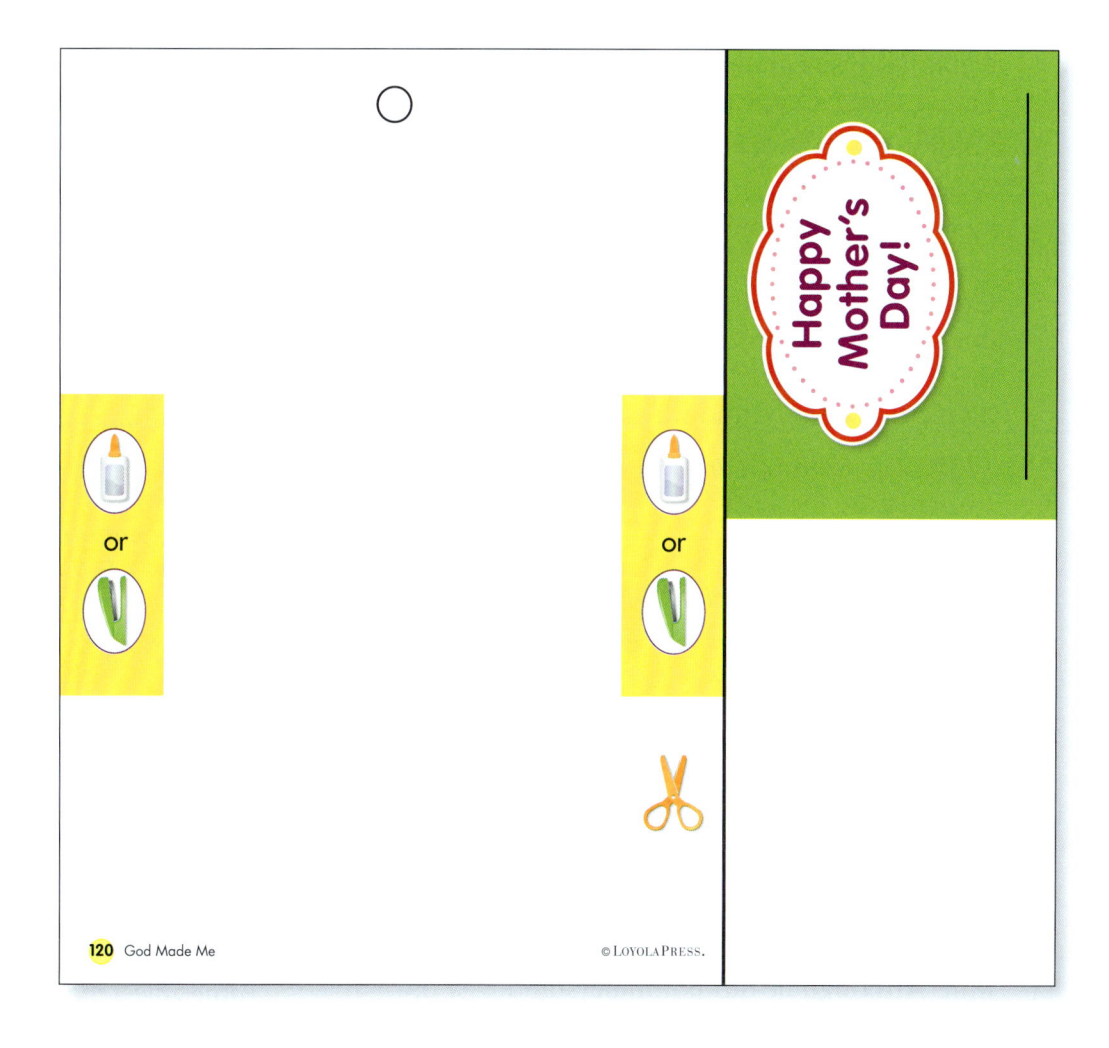

Mother's Day SPECIAL LESSON 9 T229

Special Lesson 10
Father's Day

FAITH FOCUS
God gave us fathers.

Matthew 6:9–13; Ephesians 6:1–3

PREPARING THE FAITH EXPERIENCE

LISTENING

"Righteous Father, the world also does not know you, but I know you, and they know that you sent me. I made known to them your name and I will make it known, that the love with which you loved me may be in them and I in them."

John 17:25–26

REFLECTING

Jesus revealed God to us and showed us that the eternal, infinite and almighty God is also our Father, a Father of love and mercy. Jesus himself addressed God as *Abba*, a term of intimacy similar to *Papa* or *Daddy.* In his teaching, Jesus made it clear that God is our Father too. He repeatedly spoke of "your Father" or "your heavenly Father."

A father loves his children. He cares and provides for them, protects and nurtures them. By calling God our Father, Jesus taught us that God does these things for us. He is not someone far removed from us but someone vitally interested in our well-being. God has shared divine life with us, and we are his children.

[T]hrough faith you are all children of God in Christ Jesus.

Galatians 3:26

As proof that you are children, God sent the spirit of his Son into our hearts, crying out, "Abba, Father!" So you are no longer a slave but a child, and if a child then also an heir, through God.

Galatians 4:6–7

Jesus had a foster father on earth: Saint Joseph, the husband of Mary. Scripture describes Joseph as a just man. He was someone you could trust, a man of integrity. Like his wife, Joseph was open to God's will for him. Although he did not understand why or how Mary was pregnant, at God's command he kept her as his wife. He obeyed the Jewish laws and the mandates of government officials. He provided for his family when they were strangers in Bethlehem and refugees in Egypt. There and in Nazareth, Joseph made a living as a carpenter. He probably taught Jesus his trade.

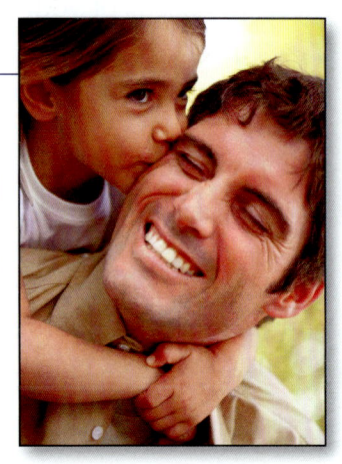

It is not easy being responsible for the lives of others. On Father's Day and on other days, let us pray for the fathers of the world. We might pray to Saint Joseph, who knows what it means to be a father.

In everything, let us turn to our Father, praying as Jesus taught us:

Our Father, who art in heaven,
hallowed be thy name;
thy kingdom come;
thy will be done
on earth as it is in heaven.
Give us this day our daily bread;
and forgive us our trespasses
as we forgive those who trespass against us;
and lead us not into temptation,
but deliver us from evil. Amen.

RESPONDING

Having been nourished by God's Word, we are able to respond to God's great love for us. In prayer, respond to God's call to you to share his Word with others. You may also wish to respond in your prayer journal.

- How has God acted as a loving Father in my life?

Father, bless the children with good homes and loving parents.

T230 Special Seasons and Days

Catechism of the Catholic Church

The themes of this lesson correspond to the following paragraphs: 239, 437, 2781.

THE FAITH EXPERIENCE

Child's Book pages 121–124

SCRIPTURE IN THIS LESSON
- *Matthew 6:9*

MATERIALS
- Bible
- Cutout #1, Jesus
- Option: coffee mug or other small Father's Day present
- Paper for drawing or painting
- Crayons, markers, or paints
- Rubber band or 8-inch piece of yarn or ribbon for each child

PREPARATION
Write the children's names on pages 121 and 123.

ENRICHING THE FAITH EXPERIENCE
Use the activities at the end of the lesson to enrich the lesson or to replace an activity with one that better meets the needs of your group.

BOOKS TO SHARE
Emma's Pet by David McPhail (Puffin, 1993)

We're Very Good Friends, My Father and I by P. K. Hallinan (Ideals Children's Book, 2006)

Daddy, Play with Me! by Shigeo Watanabe (Philomel, 1986)

My Daddy and Me by Amy Sklansky (Cartwheel, 2005)

SNACK
Suggestion: gingerbread people

ALTERNATIVE PROGRAMS

DAILY PROGRAM
Day 1: Centering, Sharing A
Day 2: Enriching the Faith Experience choice
Day 3: Sharing B, Acting #1
Day 4: Enriching the Faith Experience choice
Day 5: Acting #2

THREE-DAY PROGRAM
Day 1: Centering, Sharing A
Day 2: Sharing B, Acting #1
Day 3: Enriching the Faith Experience choice, Acting #2

10 Father's Day

LEARNING OUTCOMES
The children will
- appreciate what their fathers do for them.
- know that God loves them like a good father.
- identify Joseph as the man who was like a father to Jesus.

COMMENTS
1. Fortunate are those children who have good fathers to protect and guide them, to love and care for them. Fathers like this serve as an image of God in the minds of the children. A father plays a particular role in the formation of a son or a daughter that is different from a mother's role. For example, the child's relationship with the father, the first "outside" person, determines to some extent the way the child will relate to others.

2. Be sensitive to children who do not live with their biological fathers or who have recently lost their fathers. Jesus lived in a nontraditional family too. His Father was God, and Jesus lived with Joseph, who is known as his foster father.

CENTERING
Have the children draw or paint a picture as a gift for their father or someone who is like a father to them. (See Enriching the Faith Experience #2 for other gift ideas.) Explain:

- *On Father's Day we show our love for our fathers or people who are like our fathers, such as our grandfathers, and we thank them for all that they do. We like to give them gifts and cards.* [Option: Show a coffee mug.]

SHARING [A]
❶ Distribute page 121 and talk about fathers.

- *Who do you see in the picture?* (A boy and his father)
- *How do you think the boy feels?* (Happy)
- *The father is playing with his son. How does your father or someone who is like a father to you play with you?*
- *What does your father do for you?*
- *What does your father do for your family?*
- *Your father is proud of you. He loves you and wants you to grow up big and strong.*

T232   Special Seasons and Days

❷ Read the children this poem:

My Father

My father is so very good.
He works and keeps our home nice too.
He helps me dress the way I should,
And tells me what I ought to do.
My father is a lot of fun.
He likes to tease and tickle me.
We fly our kite, play ball, and run.
My favorite place is on his knee.
My father is so very smart.
When I ask "Why?" he answers me.
I love my dad with all my heart.
For he's the best. Don't you agree?

Mary Kathleen Glavich, S.N.D.

❸ Have the children draw a line on the path from the girl to her father on page 122.

SHARING [B]

❹ Invite the children to pantomime things they might do with their fathers: swim, cook, hit a ball with a bat, run, fly a kite, do exercises.

❺ **SCRIPTURE** Show Cutout #1, Jesus, and tell the children what Jesus said about our Father in heaven. (adapted from Matthew 6:9) [Show the Bible.]

• *Jesus told us that God is our Father. Jesus taught us to pray to God by saying "Our Father in heaven." God is the Father of Jesus, and God is our Father too. God loves you and cares for you like a good, loving father. God gave you your father on earth, or someone like a father, to love you and take care of you. Isn't God good?*

Trace the path from the girl to her father.

Family Time

Special Lesson 10:
Father's Day

In this lesson the children learned that Father's Day is a day to show love for their fathers and to thank them for all they do. They talked about their fathers and acted out what they do with their fathers. They heard that Jesus called God "our Father in heaven."

Your Child
Tell your child from time to time how much God loves him or her. Whenever something good happens to you and your child see something wonderful, remind your child to thank and praise God, our loving Father, for it. This will help your child live a good moral life not because of the fear of punishment but because of the desire to maintain his or her love relationship with the good God.

Reflect
This is how you are to pray: Our Father in heaven, hallowed be your name. . . (Matthew 6:9)

Pray
God our Father, bless all fathers and encourage them with your steadfast love.

Do
• Plan something special for your child's grandfathers or great-grandfathers.
• Talk about the role of Saint Joseph in the Holy Family.
• Help your child make a gift for his or her father.
• Address family prayers to God our Father.
• Read to your child *Emma's Pet* by David McPhail. Ask your child to describe something a father does to show love for his child. Ask God to bless all fathers and those who love and care for others.

For more family resources, refer to the Family Activity Booklet and visit www.loyolapress.com/preschool.

© LOYOLAPRESS.

ACTING

1 **PRAYER** Invite the children to pray by singing "God Is So Good." (The music is on page T159.)

2 Have the children make the scroll on page 123 for their fathers or for the people who are like fathers to them. You might wish to take a picture of each child to glue on the scroll or the children can draw self-portraits. Read the scroll to the children and then help them follow these directions:

- Write your name on the line.
- Decorate the scroll.
- Roll the scroll.
- Put a rubber band or a piece of ribbon or yarn around the scroll.

Suggest to the children that they give the scroll and gift to their mothers to hold on for them until Father's Day.

Have the children take home their pages and show their family the Family Time section.

CHECKPOINT

- Were the learning outcomes achieved?
- How enthusiastic were the children about preparing for Father's Day?

This is to certify that you are one of the world's greatest dads.

Happy Father's Day!

123 God Made Me

Page 124 is blank.

T234 Special Seasons and Days

ENRICHING THE FAITH EXPERIENCE

Use the following activities to enrich the lesson or to replace an activity with one that better meets the needs of your group.

❶ Teach the children this cheer to say to their fathers on Father's Day:

> My love and thanks to you today.
> For you I say "Hip, hip, hooray!"

❷ Have the children make other Father's Day gifts:

- Glue colorful paper around a can, such as an orange juice container, to make a holder for tools or pencils.

- Wrap a small brick with a piece of wall-paper or other heavy paper to make a doorstop or paperweight.

- Make cookies, put them on a small paper plate, and wrap cellophane around it.

- Decorate the corners of a white handkerchief with permanent markers.

❸ Talk about what God our Father has given us. Have the children draw a picture of a gift from God.

Special Lesson 11

Birthdays

FAITH FOCUS

We thank God for the gift of life.

Psalm 139; Isaiah 43:1; John 10:10

PREPARING THE FAITH EXPERIENCE

LISTENING

You formed my inmost being;
  you knit me in my mother's womb.
I praise you, so wonderfully you made me;
  wonderful are your works!
My very self you knew;
  my bones were not hidden from you,
When I was made in secret,
  fashioned as in the depths of the earth.

Psalm 139:13–15

REFLECTING

Every year on her birthday, a woman gave her mother a present in gratitude for the gift of life. It is fitting on each birthday to thank not only our mothers but also God, who called us into being and sustains us from day to day.

Because of God's gift of life, we are able to know the thrill and satisfaction of running, dancing, watching a sunrise, mastering a new skill, producing a painting or a poem, and loving others. Moreover, God has shown tremendous love in treating us as family and offering us a share in divine life.

Throughout the centuries God has guided the combinations of genes to make us the unique people we are. Irreplaceable creations, we are each special and precious. As a member of the Body of Christ, each of us has definite work to do. When we celebrate someone's birthday, we celebrate the person and the individual's gifts, talents, graces, and contributions to humanity.

God has given us the freedom to live life to the hilt or squander it. We may treasure it or take it for granted. We may live it selflessly or selfishly. In Deuteronomy, God challenges, "I have set before you life and death. . . Choose life, then, that you and your descendants may live, by loving the LORD, your God, heeding his voice, and holding fast to him." (Deuteronomy 30:19–20)

In addition to celebrating the day we were born, we can also celebrate the day we were baptized. On that day we were reborn in the Holy Spirit and became members of God's family. At the end of our lives, we will have a new birthday to celebrate—the day we are born into eternal life. Usually the feast day that the Church assigns to a canonized saint is the day of his or her death. Although we will not all be formally canonized, someday we will all be raised to life to enjoy a celebration that lasts forever.

RESPONDING

God's Word moves us to respond in word and action. Let God's Spirit work within you as you prayerfully consider how you are being called to respond to God's message to you today. Responding through your journal may help to strengthen your response.

- What blessings since my last birthday can I celebrate this year?

Jesus, give the children an appreciation of life.

Special Seasons and Days

Catechism of the Catholic Church

The themes of this lesson correspond to the following paragraphs: 256–257, 2288.

THE FAITH EXPERIENCE

Child's Book pages 125–128

SCRIPTURE IN THIS LESSON
- *Isaiah 43:1*

MATERIALS
- Bible
- Birthday Scripture card
- Hole punch
- Two 8-inch pieces of ribbon for each child
- Wrapping paper
- Small gift for each child, such as a ball, stickers, or a tiny stuffed animal
- Cupcakes, snowballs, or marshmallows (as birthday cakes) for ACTING #2
- Crayons or markers
- Option: crepe-paper streamers

PREPARATION
- Place the Birthday Scripture card for SHARING #3 in the Bible.
- Write the children's names on pages 125 and 127.
- Punch holes in page 127 and tie an 8-inch piece of ribbon through each hole.
- Wrap the small gifts. You might put them all in one box.

MUSIC 'N MOTION
Use *Music 'n Motion* page T271 and CD Track 16 "Happy Birthday! It's Your Day" for this lesson. For a list of additional music, see page T302.

ENRICHING THE FAITH EXPERIENCE
Use the activities at the end of the lesson to enrich the lesson or to replace an activity with one that better meets the needs of your group.

BOOKS TO SHARE
The Birthday Box by Leslie Patricelli (Candlewick, 2007)

Every Year on Your Birthday by Rose Lewis (Little, Brown Young Readers, 2007)

Spot's Birthday Party by Eric Hill (Puffin, 2003)

SNACK
Suggestion: cupcakes topped with yellow, orange, or red gumdrops (to represent lit candles)

ALTERNATIVE PROGRAMS

DAILY PROGRAM
Day 1: Centering, Sharing A
Day 2: Sharing B
Day 3: Enriching the Faith Experience choice
Day 4: Enriching the Faith Experience choice
Day 5: Acting

THREE-DAY PROGRAM
Day 1: Centering, Sharing A
Day 2: Sharing B
Day 3: Acting

Birthdays SPECIAL LESSON 11

11 Birthdays

LEARNING OUTCOMES
The children will
- grow in self-esteem.
- be grateful for the gift of life.
- respect others.

COMMENTS

1. Respect for life can be instilled in children at an early age. This lesson presents a good opportunity for deepening the children's reverence for life—their lives and those of others. Children who love themselves and consider themselves worthy of love will find it easier to reach out to God and others in love. At every meeting with the children, increase their self-acceptance by affirming them whenever possible. By loving the children you will make them more loving.

2. You might hold a more elaborate birthday party that includes decorations, favors, place mats, balloons, and noisemakers.

CENTERING

❶ Gather the children in a circle for *Music 'n Motion* time. Play Track 16. Invite the children to do motions to the song along with you, using *Music 'n Motion* page T271.

❷ Have the children decorate birthday capes from pages 127 and 128 with crayons or markers. (You may prefer to have them decorate their capes by gluing on precut magazine pictures of things they enjoy.) If you wish, staple crepe-paper streamers to the bottom of the capes. Explain:

- *Today we will have a surprise. We will celebrate the gift of life. On your birthday you celebrate your life. Today we will celebrate the life of everyone in this class.*

- *We wear special clothes to a party. Because everyone here is special, everyone will wear a birthday cape. On your cape, draw things you like about your life and about being alive. What might you draw?*

[When the children finish their capes, tie them around their necks with a ribbon.]

T238 Special Seasons and Days

SHARING [A]

1 Distribute page 125 and talk about the picture.

- *What is the girl doing?* (Blowing out candles on a birthday cake) *What do you think she did before she started blowing out the candles?* (Made a wish)

- *How old is the girl?*

- *How many of you are four years old? How many of you will be four years old on your next birthday?*

- *How did your family celebrate your last birthday?* (Gifts, a party, the birthday song)

- *When we celebrate a birthday, we celebrate a person's life. We are happy that God made that person.*

- *Are you happy that God made you? Are you happy that God made the people in this room? Today we will show we are happy by celebrating together.*

- *Let's begin our party by making some birthday balloons.*

2 Have the children trace the dotted lines to make the balloons on page 126. Then have them color the balloons. Tell them they may use their favorite color.

SHARING [B]

3 SCRIPTURE Read the adaptation of Isaiah 43:1 from the Scripture card in the Bible. Talk about being a child of God.

- *Listen to what God says in the Bible: "I have called you by name." Because God made you, you are God's child. [Name] is God's child. [Name] is God's child. I am God's child too. God loves us very much.*

- *God made you so that you can do many wonderful things. Let's do some of these things while we sing a song.*

4 Sing "Did You Ever See a Lassie?" Add the motions or let the children come up with them. (The music is on page T111.)

5 Give each child a small gift.

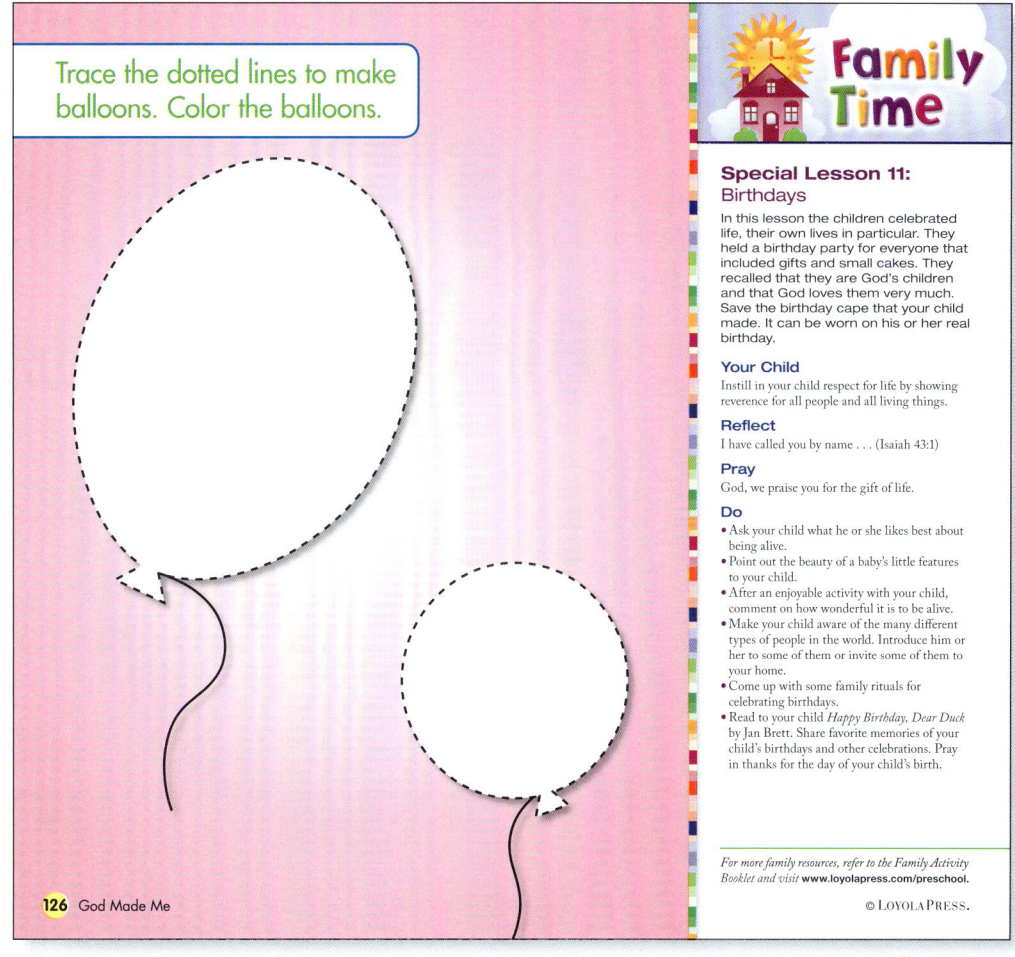

Trace the dotted lines to make balloons. Color the balloons.

126 God Made Me

Family Time

Special Lesson 11: Birthdays

In this lesson the children celebrated life, their own lives in particular. They held a birthday party for everyone that included gifts and small cakes. They recalled that they are God's children and that God loves them very much. Save the birthday cape that your child made. It can be worn on his or her real birthday.

Your Child
Instill in your child respect for life by showing reverence for all people and all living things.

Reflect
I have called you by name . . . (Isaiah 43:1)

Pray
God, we praise you for the gift of life.

Do
- Ask your child what he or she likes best about being alive.
- Point out the beauty of a baby's little features to your child.
- After an enjoyable activity with your child, comment on how wonderful it is to be alive.
- Make your child aware of the many different types of people in the world. Introduce him or her to some of them or invite some of them to your home.
- Come up with some family rituals for celebrating birthdays.
- Read to your child *Happy Birthday, Dear Duck* by Jan Brett. Share favorite memories of your child's birthdays and other celebrations. Pray in thanks for the day of your child's birth.

For more family resources, refer to the Family Activity Booklet and visit www.loyolapress.com/preschool.

© LOYOLAPRESS.

Birthdays SPECIAL LESSON 11 T239

ACTING

1 Direct the children to form a circle and sing "Happy Birthday." Instruct them to point to another child on the word *you* and say "child of God" instead of someone's name.

> Happy birthday to you.
> Happy birthday to you.
> Happy birthday, dear child of God.
> Happy birthday to you.

2 **PRAYER** Enjoy the birthday "cakes." Begin with the following short prayer of thanks for life. Have the children make a wish and pretend to blow out the candles.

O God, you gave me life. I thank you for this great gift.

3 Gather the children in a circle for *Music 'n Motion* time. Play Track 16. Invite the children to do motions to the song along with you, using *Music 'n Motion* page T271.

Have the children take home their pages and show their family the Family Time section.

CHECKPOINT

- Were the learning outcomes achieved?
- Did all the children enjoy this lesson?

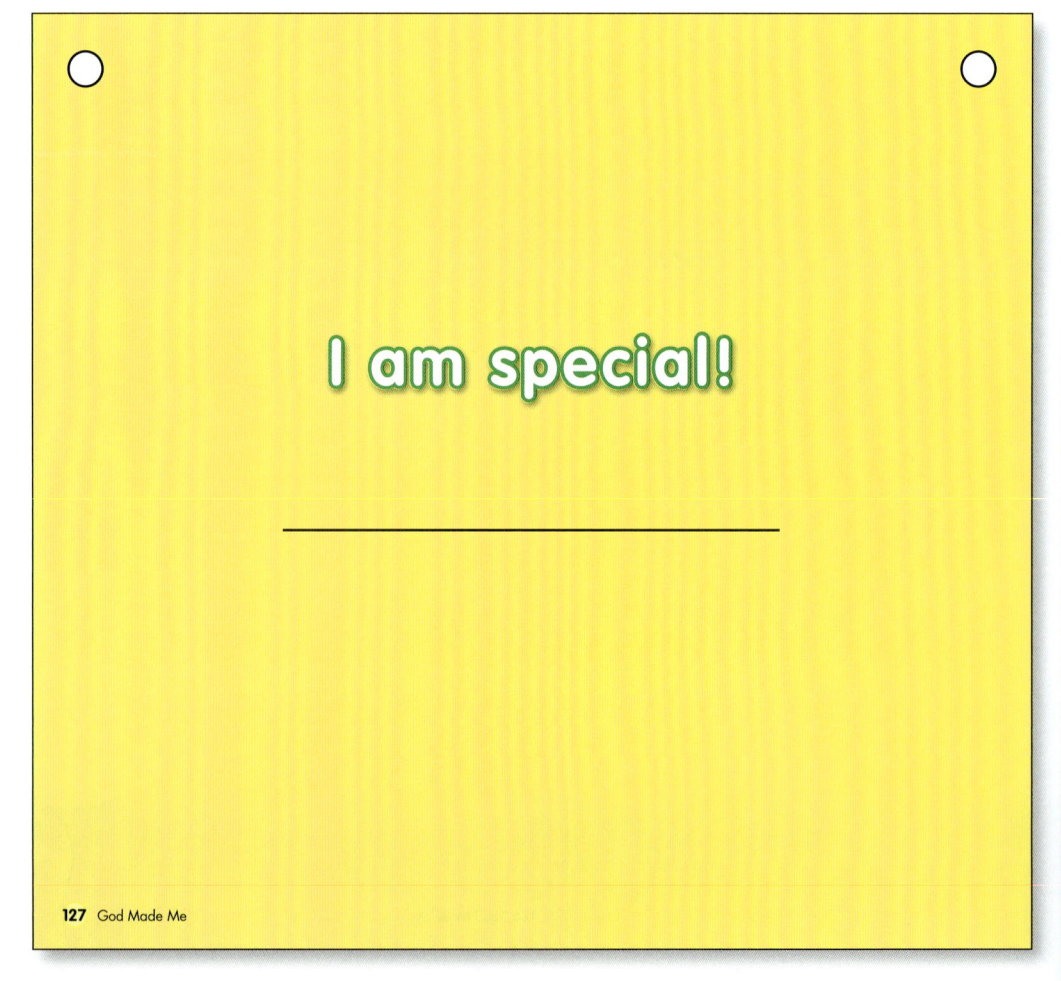

I am special!

127 God Made Me

Special Seasons and Days

ENRICHING THE FAITH EXPERIENCE

Use the following activities to enrich the lesson or to replace an activity with one that better meets the needs of your group.

1 Read the following poem to the children:

Being Special

Being one
Was not much fun.
I wet and wept,
And ate and slept.
Turning two
Was something new.
I learned to walk
And even talk.
Now I'm three.
Just look at me—
Running races,
Drawing faces.
When I'm four,
I'll do much more.
I'll count quite well
And even spell.
But being three
As you can see
Is what makes me
A specialty.

Mary Kathleen Glavich, S.N.D

2 Give each child a birthday card from you on which you have written "I'm glad God made you!"

3 Invite the children to share some of their birthday wishes aloud.

4 Invite a few volunteers to pantomime activities that they particularly enjoy.

Special Lesson 12

Last Class/Summer

FAITH FOCUS

Summer is a time to enjoy being alive.

Genesis 2:1–3

PREPARING THE FAITH EXPERIENCE

LISTENING

So God blessed the seventh day and made it holy, because on it he rested from all the work he had done in creation.

Genesis 2:3

REFLECTING

In these days of concern about stress and burnout, it is good to consider the example that God, the first worker, set for us. According to Scripture, after six days of creating, God "rested." Jesus sometimes invited his disciples to come away from the crowds and rest. He said, "Come away by yourselves to a deserted place and rest a while." (Mark 6:31) As a human being, Jesus needed periods of relaxation too and benefited from the Jewish sabbaths.

Ecclesiastes 3:1 states, "There is an appointed time for everything." One might add, "A time to work and a time to play." We need respites from our labor in order to be refreshed and strengthened. After a break we resume our work with renewed vigor. Collective human wisdom supports the need for recreation in the adage "All work and no play makes Jack a dull boy."

One word for *rest* in the Bible is *menuha*. This word signifies more activity than our word. It involves contemplation, becoming quiet in order to see more deeply into life. *Menuha* conveys the ideas of the good life—inner tranquility, the opportunity for reflection, and the absence of strife. In Psalm 23 the shepherd leads us to green pastures where he gives us rest, *menuha*.

Summer vacation is a time of rest. But it is also a time to think back on what has happened, to enjoy God's world, and to plan for the future. It is a time to be with others and to be with God. Those who are accustomed to real rest will better be able to enjoy life in heaven, also known as eternal rest.

Let us pray this prayer written by Erasmus:

Lord Jesus, the Way,
  the Truth,
  and the Life,
we pray,
do not let us stray from you,
  the Way,
nor distrust you,
  the Truth
nor rest in anything else but you,
  the Life.
Teach us by the Holy Spirit
  what to do,
  what to believe,
  and where to take our rest.

RESPONDING

Having reflected upon God's Word, take some time now to continue to respond to God in prayer. You might wish to record your responses in your journal.

- What plans for this summer will enable me to enjoy a real rest?

God, this summer keep the children and me safe, happy, and close to you.

T242 Special Seasons and Days

Catechism of the Catholic Church

The themes of this lesson correspond to the following paragraphs: 2172, 2184–2185.

THE FAITH EXPERIENCE

Child's Book pages 129–132

SCRIPTURE IN THIS LESSON
- *Psalm 145:8*

MATERIALS
- Bible
- Last Class/Summer Scripture card
- Option: picnic basket
- Crayons or markers

PREPARATION
- Place the Last Class/Summer Scripture card for SHARING #4 in the Bible.
- Write the children's names on page 129.
- Fill out the children's certificates on page 131.

MUSIC 'N MOTION
Use *Music 'n Motion* page T272 and CD Track 18 "God Is Great" for this lesson. For a list of additional music, see page T302.

ENRICHING THE FAITH EXPERIENCE
Use the activities at the end of the lesson to enrich the lesson or to replace an activity with one that better meets the needs of your group.

BOOKS TO SHARE
Summersaults by Douglas Florian (Greenwillow, 2002)

Mouse's First Summer by Lauren Thompson (Greenwillow, 2002)

Summer by Alice Low (Simon & Schuster Children's Publishing, 2004)

Caterpillar Spring, Butterfly Summer by Susan Hood (Reader's Digest; Boardbook Edition, 2003)

SNACK
Suggestion: crispy rice treats or thin pretzel sticks inserted into banana slices

---

ALTERNATIVE PROGRAMS

DAILY PROGRAM
Day 1: Centering, Sharing A
Day 2: Enriching the Faith Experience choice
Day 3: Sharing B
Day 4: Enriching the Faith Experience choice
Day 5: Acting

THREE-DAY PROGRAM
Day 1: Centering, Sharing A
Day 2: Sharing B
Day 3: Acting

12 Last Class/Summer

LEARNING OUTCOMES
The children will
- anticipate summer fun.
- thank God for the experiences of preschool.

COMMENTS

1. This lesson prepares the children for the idea of Sunday as a day of rest. God's Third Commandment (like all the other commandments) is psychologically healthy for us. In our hectic, fast-paced age, it is more necessary than ever to plan "holy pauses" for spiritual celebration and physical and mental rest, times for God and for the family. Leisure time affords us the opportunity to glory in God's gift of creation.

2. You might invite the parents for an end-of-the-year celebration during which the children perform the songs and finger plays that they learned in preschool. Include a display of the children's art and provide refreshments.

CENTERING

❶ Gather the children in a circle for *Music 'n Motion* time. Play Track 18. Invite the children to do motions to the song along with you, using *Music 'n Motion* page T272.

❷ Have the children do a finger play they especially enjoy.

SHARING [A]

❶ Distribute page 129. Talk about the picture.

- *Summer is coming. Your preschool classes are over. During the summer you will do all kinds of exciting things.*
- *Where is the family in the picture?* (On a picnic)
- *What are they doing?* (Resting, eating) [Option: Show a picnic basket.]
- *Do you think you will go to a park this summer?*
- *What other places might you visit during vacation?*
- *What might you do?*
- *God is good to give us times for fun.*

❷ Have the children draw a picture of something they will enjoy this summer on page 130. Ask them about their pictures.

SHARING [B]

❸ Let the children play a game they especially like.

❹ **SCRIPTURE** Remind the children that God will be with them in the summer, loving them and caring for them. Read the adaptation of Psalm 145:8 from the Scripture card in the Bible.

- *Listen to what we read in the Bible: "The Lord is kind and full of love."*

T244 Special Seasons and Days

5 Read the children this poem. Then let them be an echo by repeating certain lines. Point to them when it is their turn.

God Is There

When I run in the sun,
God is there. [Children repeat.]
When I fall playing ball,
God cares. [Children repeat.]
When I'm sad or I'm glad,
God knows. [Children repeat.]
When I mind or I'm kind,
God sees. [Children repeat.]
God is with me day and night,
Helping me to do what's right.
I love you, God!
[Children repeat.]
Mary Kathleen Glavich, S.N.D.

6 Ask the children what they learned during their time at preschool. Show pictures, cutouts, and crafts to jog the children's memories.

ACTING

1 Give each child the certificate from page 131 for completing the preschool course. Congratulate them for their hard work this year.

2 PRAYER Lead the children in a prayer of thanks.

- *Let's thank God for making us special and for all the wonderful things we are able to do. I'll say something. Then you will say "Thank you, God" and raise your arms.* [You may have the children sing a response on one note.]

  For our wonderful bodies . . .

  For being able to see, hear, smell, taste, and feel . . .

  For being able to run, hop, jump, and make things . . .

  For being able to work, play, and celebrate . . .

  For being able to think, learn, and pretend . . .

  For the times we had fun together . . .

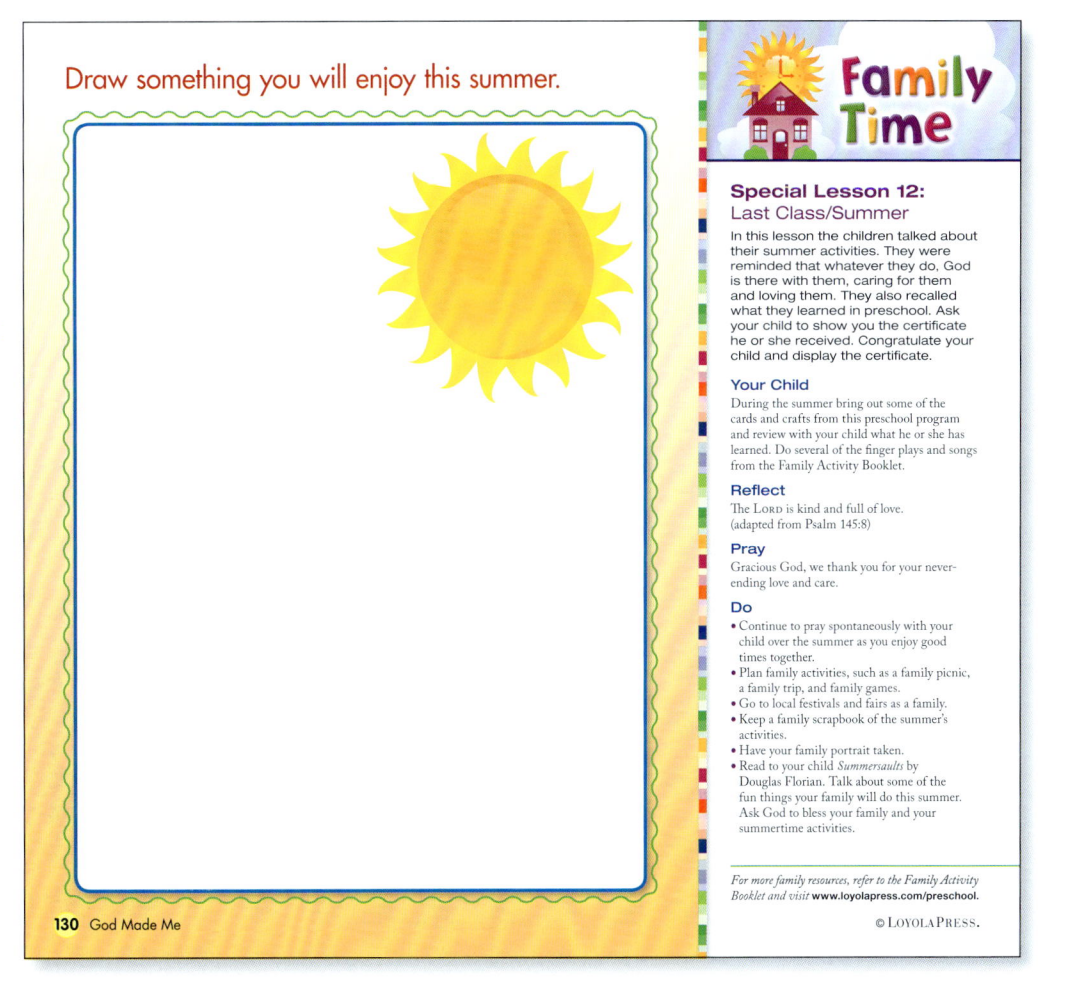

Draw something you will enjoy this summer.

130 God Made Me

Family Time

Special Lesson 12:
Last Class/Summer

In this lesson the children talked about their summer activities. They were reminded that whatever they do, God is there with them, caring for them and loving them. They also recalled what they learned in preschool. Ask your child to show you the certificate he or she received. Congratulate your child and display the certificate.

Your Child
During the summer bring out some of the cards and crafts from this preschool program and review with your child what he or she has learned. Do several of the finger plays and songs from the Family Activity Booklet.

Reflect
The LORD is kind and full of love.
(adapted from Psalm 145:8)

Pray
Gracious God, we thank you for your never-ending love and care.

Do
- Continue to pray spontaneously with your child over the summer as you enjoy good times together.
- Plan family activities, such as a family picnic, a family trip, and family games.
- Go to local festivals and fairs as a family.
- Keep a family scrapbook of the summer's activities.
- Have your family portrait taken.
- Read to your child *Summersaults* by Douglas Florian. Talk about some of the fun things your family will do this summer. Ask God to bless your family and your summertime activities.

For more family resources, refer to the Family Activity Booklet and visit www.loyolapress.com/preschool.

© LOYOLAPRESS.

Last Class/Summer SPECIAL LESSON **12**

❸ Remind the children to thank God when they are having a good time during the summer or when they learn something new. Also remind the children and their families that they can refer to the Family Activity Booklet to recall activities and songs they have learned during the year.

❹ Gather the children in a circle for *Music 'n Motion* time. Play Track 18. Invite the children to do motions to the song along with you, using *Music 'n Motion* page T272.

Have the children take home their pages and show their family the Family Time section.

CHECKPOINT

- Were the learning outcomes achieved?
- Do the children express satisfaction and joy at having completed the preschool year?

ENRICHING THE FAITH EXPERIENCE

Use the following activities to enrich the lesson or to replace an activity with one that better meets the needs of your group.

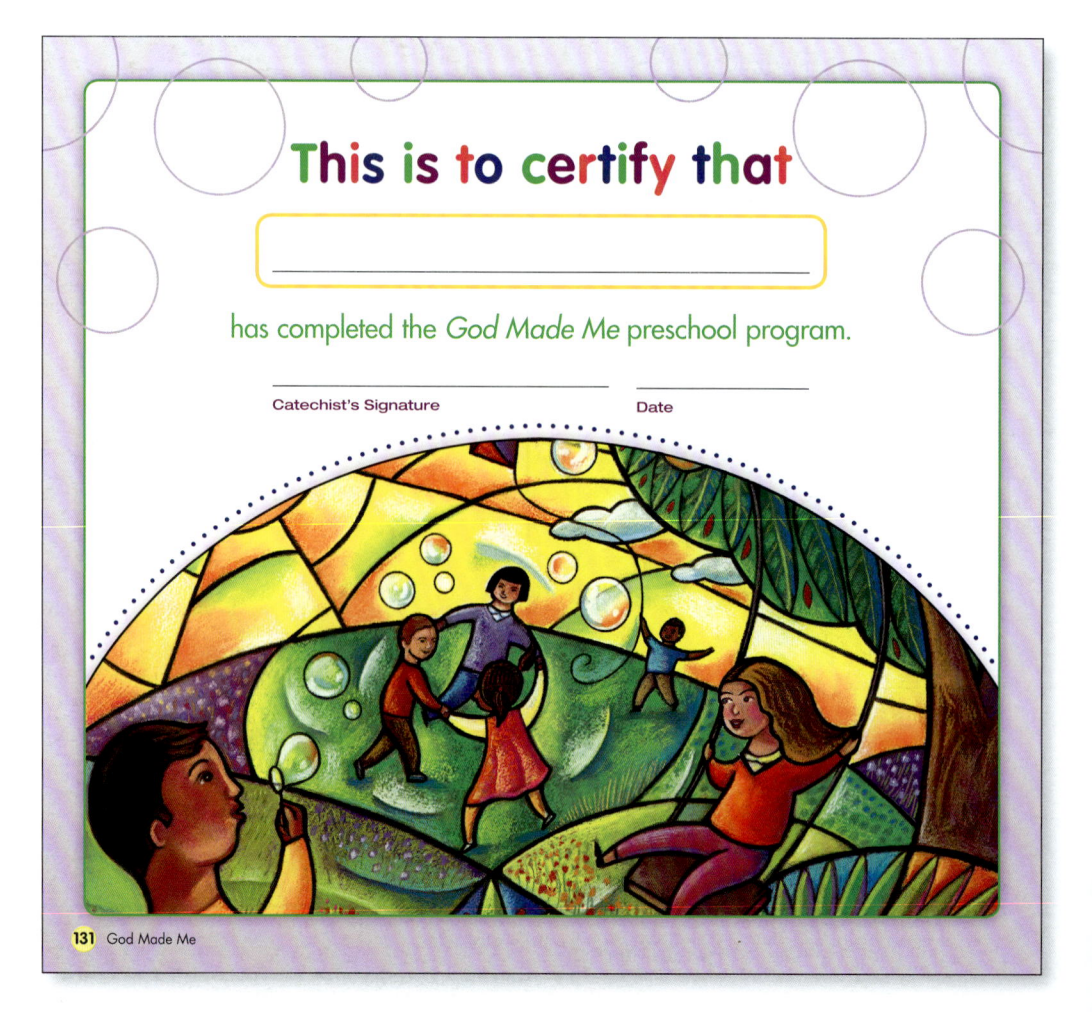

❶ Give each child a small gift, something to use for the summer, such as bubble liquid, a ball, a sand toy, or a holy card to remind him or her of God.

❷ If possible, teach this last lesson or part of it outdoors.

❸ Ask the children what songs or games they liked best in preschool. Then have the children sing or play them together.

This is to certify that

_____

has completed the *God Made Me* preschool program.

_____   _____
Catechist's Signature   Date

131 God Made Me

Page 132 is blank.

T246   Special Seasons and Days

Music 'n Motion

Contents

Songs for Units 1–5

TRACK 1	I Am Wonderfully Made	T250
TRACK 2	Helping	T251
TRACK 3	Peace in My Heart	T252
TRACK 4	Jump Up, Get Down	T256
TRACK 5	You Are the Light	T260

Songs for Special Seasons and Days

TRACK 11	When the Saints Go Marching In	T262
TRACK 12	No Place to Stay	T264
TRACK 13	Easter Alleluia	T266
TRACK 14	Thank You, Jesus	T268
TRACK 15	God Is Love	T270
TRACK 16	Happy Birthday! It's Your Day	T271
TRACK 18	God is Great	T272

Tracks 6–10 and 17 are used with the *God Made the World* (Age 4) program.

MUSIC 'N MOTION

From the earliest days of a child's life, there is music and movement. Even before birth, a child hears the mother's heartbeat varied by tempo and accompanied by a range of sounds. Gently rocking their newborn babe in their arms, parents instinctively sigh, hum, and sing. The infant seems to understand this music, and the music is magic! Toddlers continue to use music to soothe and calm, for fun and play, and for prayer. Gestures accompany favorite melodies as children twirl on tippy toes, bend and leap, responding to the mood and meaning of the music. As preschoolers, children remain rooted in rhythm, movement, and facial expression as the primary means of communication. Preschool children love to imitate, to mime, and to dance hand in hand with a partner. They light up at the sound of music.

Preschool children are eager to learn about God, but are not yet able to grasp the abstract concepts of faith. For them, the gifts of music and dance can help communicate the fullness of faith. By placing their hand over their heart and singing "I've got peace in my heart," children sense that peace finds a home deep within. As they extend their hand and bow toward a classmate, they learn that peace is meant to be shared, joy is to be celebrated, and the love within us is to be given to others. Reaching arms high as they praise God in song, children discover that it takes energy to pray, and they also learn that prayer energizes their spirits. Singing with folded hands and heads bowed, children express reverence. Even if unable to offer a definition, they intuit prayer's meaning through movement and music.

Through movement, children learn that peace is meant to be shared.

Exercise of the creative imagination lays the groundwork for development of the religious imagination. These aesthetic elements—movement, music, and drama—promote empathy, solidarity, courage, and kindness as they enhance prayer. As catechists lead children in prayer, using music and movement, children can see the joy of the Lord on their catechist's face as they hear it in the catechist's voice. Music and movement, dance and drama are precious jewels in the treasure chest of every catechist, providing a means of communication that is deep, spiritual, memorable, and fun.

For the glory of God and the edification of his little ones,

Nancy Seitz Marcheschi

MUSIC 'N MOTION

I Am Wonderfully Made
by Jack Miffleton

TRACK 1 | Use with Unit 1

God gave me hands for clapping,

[Clap four times on beat.]

God gave me toes for tapping,

[Tap right foot, then tap left foot, on beat.]

I am wonderfully made,

[Lean right, stretch arms wide, shake hands.]

I am wonderfully made.

[Lean left, stretch arms wide, shake hands.]

This song is a round and repeats two times. Encourage the children to add their own verses, such as "legs for walking" or "ears for hearing."

T250 God Made Me

I Am Wonderfully Made by Jack Miffleton, copyright © 1978, World Library Publications. www.wlpmusic.com

MUSIC 'N MOTION

Helping
by Jack Miffleton

TRACK 2 | Use with Unit 2

Children act out the typical activities of a particular "helper" in this pantomime song. Teach the motions indicated below for the first verse. For all other verses, quickly call out ideas and model the pantomime while the music plays. Suggestions for each verse are shown below.

All around my neighborhood,

[Reach right hand across body to left and then forward and around back to right.]

I see people* doing good;

[Extend thumb up from closed fist.]

helping, helping

[Scoop up open, cupped right hand, then lower it to right side.]

in my neighborhood.

[Scoop up open, cupped left hand, then lower it to left side.]

*The song repeats as children call out the name of someone who helps.

Firemen: Slide down the pole . . . put on your boots, . . . your coat, . . . your hat. Jump on the truck . . . now jump off . . . grab the hose . . . put out the fire.

Policewomen: Blow your whistle . . . reach out your hand to stop traffic . . . signal the people to cross the street . . . wave to the children crossing.

Farmers: Grab your rake . . . till the ground . . . sprinkle the seeds on the ground . . . cover up the seeds with soil.

Bus Drivers: Grab your wheel and drive the bus . . . put your foot on the brake and stop . . . pull the lever to open up the doors to let people out . . . here come some new passengers . . . take their tokens and start driving again.

Grocers: Scan the groceries on the moving counter . . . type the codes on the keys of the cash register . . . bag the groceries . . . collect the money from the customer . . . put it in the cash register.

As the children become more familiar with the song, add more verses by asking the children to offer the name of someone who helps, such as painter, mail carrier, and babysitter.

Helping by Jack Miffleton, copyright © 1978, World Library Publications. www.wlpmusic.com

MUSIC 'N MOTION

Peace in My Heart
by Mary Ann Renna

TRACK 3 | Use with Unit 3

Verse 1:

I've got peace in my heart.

[Place right hand over heart and tap to beat.]

I've got peace in my heart.

[Place left hand over heart and tap to beat.]

I've got peace in my heart

[Place right hand over heart and tap to beat.]

and I will give peace to you

[Lift right hand up and over to right, palm up, bending to right.]

and I will give peace to you

[Lift left hand up and over to left, palm up, bending to left.]

and I will give peace to you

[Lift right hand up and over to right, palm up, bending to right.]

T252   God Made Me

Peace in My Heart by Mary Ann Renna, copyright © 2004, World Library Publications. www.wlpmusic.com

and I will give peace to you.

Verse 2:
I've got joy in my heart.

I've got joy in my heart.

[Scoop up both hands and reach them forward with palms up, leaning slightly forward.]

[Place right hand over heart and lift, shaking hand to beat.]

[Place left hand over heart and lift, shaking hand to beat.]

I've got joy in my heart

and I will give joy to you

and I will give joy to you

[Place right hand over heart and lift, shaking hand to beat.]

[Lift right hand up and over to right, palm up, bending to right.]

[Lift left hand up and over to left, palm up, bending to left.]

MUSIC 'N MOTION

and I will give joy to you

[Lift right hand up and over to right, palm up, bending to right.]

and I will give joy to you.

[Scoop up both hands and reach them forward with palms up, leaning slightly forward.]

Verse 3:
I've got love in my heart.

[Place left hand over heart.]

I've got love in my heart.

[Place right hand over left hand.]

I've got love in my heart

[Tap crossed hands to beat.]

and I will give love to you

[Lift right hand and extend to right, bending slightly to right.]

T254   God Made Me

MUSIC 'N MOTION

and I will give love to you

[Lift left hand and extend to left, bending slightly to left.]

and I will give love to you

[Scoop up both hands and reach them forward with palms up, bending slightly to right.]

and I will give love to you.

[Scoop up both hands and reach them forward with palms up, bending slightly to left.]

Repeat all three verses a second time.

Music 'n Motion   T255

MUSIC 'N MOTION

Jump Up, Get Down by Mary Ann Renna

TRACK 4 | Use with Unit 4

Jump up, get down,

[Jump in place. Squat down.]

stand up, turn around.

[Straighten up. Walk in a circle.]

Jump up, get down,

[Jump In place. Squat down.]

play it on your knees.

[Tap knees with hands.]

Jump up, get down,

[Jump in place. Squat down.]

stand up, turn around.

[Straighten up. Walk in a circle.]

T256   God Made Me

Jump Up, Get Down by Mary Ann Renna, copyright © 2004, World Library Publications. www.wlpmusic.com

MUSIC 'N MOTION

Jump up,

[Jump in place.]

shout it out,

[Cup hands around mouth.]

"Jesus loves me!"

[Reach arms out to sides, then wrap arms around yourself.]

Jump up,

[Jump in place.]

shout it out,

[Cup hands around mouth.]

"Jesus loves me!"

[Reach arms out to sides, then wrap arms around yourself.]

The final refrain repeats the last line two times.

Music 'n Motion **T257**

MUSIC 'N MOTION

Verse 1

When I was a baby, just a little child,

[Pantomime rocking a baby side to side.]

my mama told me I was her gift from God on high.

[Open hands, raise arms, look up.]

She said God made me special, special as can be.

[Cross arms at wrist and place over heart, then twist from right to left.]

Then she'd shout it out: "Jesus loves me!"

[Cup hands around mouth. Reach arms to side, then wrap arms around yourself.]

Then she'd shout it out: "Jesus loves me!"

[Reach arms to side, then wrap arms around yourself.]

Verse 2

Now that I am older, my brains are growing strong,

[Tap sides of head with hands.]

T258   God Made Me

MUSIC 'N MOTION

my muscles getting bigger, my legs are growing long.

[Make fists, bend elbows, flex muscles. Kick right leg, then kick left leg.]

I see God made me special, special as can be.

[Hug yourself and twist from side to side.]

I will shout it out: "Jesus loves me!"

[Cup hands around mouth. Reach arms to side, then wrap arms around yourself.]

I will shout it out: "Jesus loves me!"

[Reach arms to side, then wrap arms around yourself.]

Music 'n Motion   T259

MUSIC 'N MOTION

You Are the Light
by Michael Mangan

TRACK 5 | Use with Unit 5

You are the light that shows the way.

[Reach hands high and bring down, alternating from right to left.]

You keep me safe. I'm not afraid.

[Give yourself a hug, then push both hands out to sides.]

You are the light that shows the way.

[Reach hands high and bring down, alternating from right to left.]

I have no fear.

[Push both hands out to sides, then bring hands in and down.]

You are the light.

[Reach both hands high and shake.]

Verse 1:
I only ask God one thing: Let me live in your house forever,

[Fold hands in prayer.]

T260 God Made Me

You Are the Light by Michael Mangan, copyright © 2004, Litmus Productions
Exclusive licensing agent in North America: World Library Publications. www.wlpmusic.com

MUSIC 'N MOTION

That I may see your majesty, as I live in your house forever.

[Make a slow, reverent bow, bending down on one knee, then return to standing.]

Verse 2:
I know that I shall live to see the goodness of God.

[Fold hands in prayer, then extend hands to sides with palms up.]

Trust in God, be strong, take heart.

[Slowly look up while raising arms up, making fists on raised hands.]

Put your faith in God.

[Lower and fold hands in prayer. Bow head.]

Music 'n Motion **T261**

MUSIC 'N MOTION

Songs for Special Seasons and Days

When the Saints Go Marching In

TRACK 11 | Use with Halloween/Feast of All Saints

Have the children take turns being the leader of the procession of saints (in Dixieland style). March in place during the instrumental parts of the song.

Verse 1:

Oh, when the saints go marching in.
Oh, when the saints go marching in.

Oh, Lord, I want to be in that number
when the saints go marching in.

[Bend from side to side while you march to the beat. Shake "jazz hands" and reach arms from shoulder height.]

Verse 2:

And when the stars refuse to shine.
And when the stars refuse to shine.

Oh, Lord, I want to be in that number
when the stars refuse to shine.

[Alternate reaching arms straight up high over head while shaking "jazz hands."]

T262   God Made Me

MUSIC 'N MOTION

Verse 3:

Oh, when I hear that trumpet sound.
Oh, when I hear that trumpet sound.

Oh, Lord, I want to be in that number
when I hear that trumpet sound.

[Imagine you are playing a trumpet. Continue to step to the beat while moving the trumpet up and down and from side to side.]

Repeat verse 1:

Choose any instrument you wish to play . . . a clarinet, a saxophone, a flute, a guitar, or a drum. Pantomime playing your instrument while you step to the beat in the procession.

Music 'n Motion T263

MUSIC 'N MOTION

No Place to Stay

TRACK 12 | Use with Christmas

Clop, clop, clop went the donkey's feet.
Clop, clop clop down the stony street.

[Stomp right foot, then left, then right.]

Nod, nod, nod went Mary's head.

[Drop head, lower, then lower again.]

Nod, nod, nod she needed a bed.

[Yawn, then lean head on folded hands.]

Knock, knock, knock went Joseph at the door.

[Pretend to knock on a door.]

Knock, knock, knock is there room for more?

[Pretend to knock on a door, then open hands and reach forward.]

No, no, no the innkeeper said.

[Shake head from side to side.]

T264 God Made Me

No Place to Stay, music by Mary Beth Kunde Anderson
Music copyright © 2008, World Library Publications. www.wlpmusic.com

MUSIC 'N MOTION

No, no, no not even one bed.

[Shake head from side to side, then hold up index finger.]

Wait, wait, wait the innkeeper said.

[Flex both hands, with palms facing out.]

Wait, wait, wait use my stable instead.

[Flex both hands, with palms facing out. Then point or thumb behind you.]

Sh, sh, sh what do I hear?
Sh, sh, sh Baby Jesus so dear!

[Place right index finger over lips.]

Oh, oh, oh what do I see?

[Imagine seeing Baby Jesus in the manger. Kneel down on left knee.]

Oh, oh, oh Jesus born for me!

[Kneel on both knees, fold hands, then bow head and body.]

Music 'n Motion **T265**

MUSIC 'N MOTION

Easter Alleluia by Michael Mangan

TRACK 13 | Use with Easter

Alleluia! He is risen!

[Reach right arm across body, then make an arc up high and bring back to right.]

Alleluia! He's alive!

[Reach left arm across body, then make an arc up high and bring back to left.]

Alleluia! Sing for joy now.

[Reach right arm across body, then make an arc up high and bring back to right.]

Jesus is alive!

[Place hands on heart, then reach arms forward.]

Verse 1:
Open up your hearts. See the empty tomb.

[Place hands over heart.]

Though he died on Calvary,

[Bow head reverently.]

T266 God Made Me

Easter Alleluia by Michael Mangan, copyright © 1993, Litmus Productions
Exclusive licensing agent in North America: World Library Publications. www.wlpmusic.com

MUSIC 'N MOTION

Jesus is alive!

[Raise head, then reach arms forward.]

Verse 2:
Sing your songs of joy. Lift your voices high.

[Tilt head and body side to side on beat.]

His glory fills the earth.

[Reach both hands forward, then smoothly move them to sides.]

Jesus is alive!

[Raise head, then reach arms forward.]

Verse 3:
Go and tell the world. Go and sing Good News.

[Cup hands around mouth. Lean to right, then lean to left.]

Spread this message everywhere,

[Reach both hands forward, then smoothly move them to sides.]

"Jesus is alive!"

[Raise head, then reach arms forward.]

The final refrain repeats two times.

Music 'n Motion   T267

MUSIC 'N MOTION

Thank You, Jesus by Mary Ann Renna

TRACK 14 | Use with Thanksgiving

Thank you, Jesus, thank you, Jesus, thank you, Jesus.
Thank you, Jesus, thank you, Jesus, thank you, Jesus.

[Tilt head from side to side and clap on beat.]

Verse 1:
I thank you, Jesus, for my hands

[Shake "jazz hands."]

'cause I can shake them as fast as I can.

[Shake "jazz hands" twice, then shake as fast as possible.]

And thank you for my fingers, too,

[Wiggle fingers to beat.]

'cause I can wave right back at you.

[Alternate waving hands, right and left, to beat.]

Verse 2:
Thank you, Jesus, for my eyes 'cause I can close them shut or open wide.

[Open eyes wide, close eyes, then open wide again.]

T268   God Made Me

Thank You, Jesus by Mary Ann Renna, copyright © 2004, World Library Publications. www.wlpmusic.com

MUSIC 'N MOTION

And thank you for my elbows, too,

[Lift arms with bent elbows pointing to sides.]

because I like the way they move.

[Alternate lifting elbows, right and left, to beat.]

Verse 3:
Thank you, Jesus, for my hips 'cause I can move from side to side like this.

[Put hands on hips, then wiggle hips from side to side.]

And thank you for my legs so strong

[Lift right leg, then left leg, alternating to beat.]

'cause I can run and jump along.

[Run in place, then jump in place.]

The final refrain repeats two times.

Music 'n Motion T269

MUSIC 'N MOTION

God is Love by James V. Marchionda, O.P.

TRACK 15 | Use with Valentine's Day

God is love. God is love.
The living God is love.
And when we live in love,
we live in God and God lives in us.

Verse 1:
Our God has loved us so.
Now we can love each other.
And in the love we share,
our God will be made known.

[Form a large circle. Join hands with the people next to you. When the song begins, walk slowly counterclockwise in the circle. As the refrain ends, turn to your partner standing next to you.]

Verse 2:
The way we live in God
is through the Holy Spirit.
And we know this is true,
because of Jesus Christ.

Verse 3:
All people who know Christ
have God alive within them.
And we have come to trust
the love God has for us.

[Take your partner's hands and walk slowly in place, making your own little circle. When the refrain begins again, return to the large circle and begin walking counterclockwise.]

God Is Love by James V. Marchionda, O.P., copyright © 1988, World Library Publications. www.wlpmusic.com

MUSIC 'N MOTION

Happy Birthday! It's Your Day

TRACK 16 | Use with Birthdays

Happy Birthday, it's your day.
We're so glad you're four today.

[Join hands and form a large circle around the "birthday child," who is seated in a chair in the middle of the circle. All sing while walking counterclockwise in the circle.]

God made you, so stand up now.

[Children in the circle stop walking and stand still.]

Turn around and take a bow.

[Birthday child stands, turns in place, and then bows.]

MUSIC 'N MOTION

God Is Great by Michael Mangan

TRACK 18 | Use with Last Class/Summer

Verse 1:

Clap your hands.

[Clap hands three times.]

Sing "Jubilee!" ("Jubilee!")

[Reach arms forward.]

This is a time to celebrate.

[Twist hands at wrists.]

Clap your hands.

[Clap hands three times.]

Sing "Jubilee!" ("Jubilee!")

[Reach arms forward.]

God is good and God is great! (God is good and God is great!)

[Raise arms slowly, looking up. Then bring arms down slowly and fold hands in prayer.]

T272 God Made Me

God Is Great by Michael Mangan, copyright © 2004, Litmus Productions
Exclusive licensing agent in North America: World Library Publications. www.wlpmusic.com

MUSIC 'N MOTION

Verse 2:

Stamp your feet.

[Stamp feet three times.]

Sing "Jubilee!" ("Jubilee!")

[Reach arms forward.]

This is a time to celebrate.

[Twist hands at wrists.]

Stamp your feet.

[Stamp feet three times.]

Sing "Jubilee!" ("Jubilee!")

[Reach arms forward.]

God is good and God is great!
(God is good and God is great!)

[Raise arms slowly, looking up. Then bring arms down slowly and fold hands in prayer.]

Music 'n Motion **T273**

MUSIC 'N MOTION

Verse 3:

Pat your knees.

[Pat right knee, then left, then right.]

Sing "Jubilee!" ("Jubilee!")

[Reach arms forward.]

This is a time to celebrate.

[Twist hands at wrists.]

Pat your knees.

[Pat right knee, then left, then right.]

Sing "Jubilee!" ("Jubilee!")

[Reach arms forward.]

God is good and God is great! (God is good and God is great!)

[Raise arms slowly, looking up. Then bring arms down slowly and fold hands in prayer.]

T274   God Made Me

MUSIC 'N MOTION

Verse 4:

Click your tongue.

[Click tongue three times.]

Sing "Jubilee!" ("Jubilee!")

[Reach arms forward.]

This is a time to celebrate.

[Twist hands at wrists.]

Click your tongue.

[Click tongue three times.]

Sing "Jubilee!" ("Jubilee!")

[Reach arms forward.]

God is good and God is great! (God is good and God is great!)

[Raise arms slowly, looking up. Then bring arms down slowly and fold hands in prayer.]

Music 'n Motion   **T275**

MUSIC 'N MOTION

Verse 5:

Shout "Hip hooray!" ("Hip hooray!")

Sing "Jubilee!" ("Jubilee!")

This is a time to celebrate.

[Bend knees, then straighten knees, and raise hands high.]

[Reach arms forward.]

[Twist hands at wrists.]

Shout "Hip hooray!" ("Hip hooray!")

Sing "Jubilee!" ("Jubilee!")

God is good and God is great! (God is good and God is great! Yeah!)

[Bend knees, then straighten, and raise hands high.]

[Reach arms forward.]

[Raise arms slowly, looking up. Then bring arms down slowly, then slowly raise arms. On final beat, reach arms even higher.]

T276   God Made Me

CATECHIST'S HANDBOOK

Sharing the Good News

Effective catechists are people who live their faith and share the Good News of Jesus with others, inviting them to develop and deepen their relationship with Christ. Catechists attend to their own faith and spiritual growth. In addition, catechists seek to increase their knowledge and skills in a variety of areas.

Effective catechists are

- sensitive to the developmental characteristics of those they will teach.
- aware of the process of faith and spiritual growth.
- knowledgeable about the role of the catechist in faith formation.
- grounded in the Church's faith tradition, including the *Catechism of the Catholic Church*.
- familiar with a variety of effective teaching methods, tools, and techniques.

This Catechist's Handbook provides essential information to help catechists craft their lessons with confidence and skill.

PROFILE OF A THREE-YEAR-OLD

Three-year-olds . . .
• are enthusiastic • are egocentric • like to please • are full of wonder

Physical Characteristics
- have developed large-muscle control
- are just developing small-muscle control; cannot manipulate scissors well
- are full of energy
- need to move and stretch often
- love to climb and run
- are developing a sense of rhythm

Socioemotional Characteristics
- do not like to be told what to do
- need freedom to make choices
- are still self-centered but may share with a friend
- need help to handle feelings and relate to others
- like to celebrate
- prefer to play alone
- need frequent encouragement and reassurance from grown-ups
- operate on an emotional level and spontaneously express their feelings
- like to be independent
- are amiable
- are continually growing in sensitivity to other people

Intellectual Characteristics
- are curious
- speak and understand short sentences
- have an attention span of about five minutes
- do not understand symbols
- are imaginative and creative
- like silliness, rhyming, and long words

Religious Characteristics
- begin to understand God's love by experiencing human love
- need to see that God made them and every other child unique and special
- need to experience success
- like to help
- are full of wonder at creation and at their own powers
- delight in simple prayer

God Made Me

AREAS OF GROWTH

Faith

God Made Me was designed for three-year-old children, recognizing that young children possess the gift of faith from Baptism and, therefore, have an innate readiness for things of God. It engages them in experiences that prepare them to hear God's message and helps them respond to it in their lives. Through the *God Made Me* program, three-year-old children develop a sense of self-worth by learning that God made and loves them. As they explore their abilities, they come to realize that they are special. They are also initiated into Catholic traditions and prepared for a life within the Christian community.

God is presented to the children as the good God who made them and the world, who loves and cares for them, and who is always with them. The program helps children see Jesus as a friend who wants them to be happy. They learn a little about his life on earth with Mary, his mother; Joseph, his foster father; and his friends. They are introduced to some stories of faith from the Bible. The children will hear and respond to God and these stories differently from the way they will respond when they are older.

Prayer

An ultimate purpose of catechesis is to enable the children to sense God's loving presence, to encounter him, and to enter into communion with him. In the *God Made Me* program, the focus is on prayers of praise and thanksgiving, which the children easily understand. The children learn to quiet themselves for prayer and are encouraged to pray to God in the morning, in the evening, and during the day. They take part in a variety of prayer experiences to help them respond to God, including

- vocal prayer
- spontaneous prayer
- dance prayer
- psalm responses
- litanies
- silent prayer of the heart
- song
- celebrations

Liturgical Life

The *God Made Me* program initiates children into the liturgy by having them

- experience simple symbols such as water and incense.
- use gestures in prayer.
- sing praise and thanks to God.
- participate in simple rituals.
- be quiet.
- share food with others.
- experience a sense of mystery and awe.
- learn about the special seasons and feasts of the liturgical year. For reference, a calendar showing the seasons of the Church year is found on page T175.

Morality

The preschool years are a crucial time for building attitudes and dispositions upon which a good Christian moral life can develop. The foundation for good decision making is also laid in a child's early years. The *God Made Me* program also fosters the awakening of a Christian conscience in the children by leading them to

- appreciate God's goodness and personal love for them.
- respect all people and all forms of life.
- value God's world and care for it.
- develop self-discipline and form good habits.
- desire to share with those in need.

Social Justice and Service

In the *God Made Me* program, the children engage in activities that nurture kindness, honesty, forgiveness, and concern for others. Three-year-olds are emerging from a stage in which they prefer to play alone and are discovering what it means to work and play with others. Some activities that promote social justice and service are

- talking about kindness, sharing, and love.
- listening to stories of saints who have shown concern for others and for God's world.
- engaging in music and art activities that promote a spirit of sharing and caring for others.

Catechist's Handbook

THE CATECHIST

The effectiveness of religious instruction is closely tied to the personal witness given by the teacher; this witness is what brings the content of the lessons to life. . . . A teacher who has a clear vision of the Christian milieu and lives in accord with it will be able to help young people develop a similar vision, and will give them the inspiration they need to put it into practice.

Congregation for Catholic Education,
The Religious Dimension of Education in a Catholic School, 96 (April 7, 1988)

Spiritual and Professional Growth as a Catechist

The *National Directory for Catechesis* names six tasks in catechesis:

- to promote knowledge of the faith
- to promote knowledge of the meaning of the Liturgy and the sacraments
- to promote moral formation in Christ
- to teach the Christian how to pray with Christ
- to prepare the Christian to live in community and to participate actively in the life and mission of the Church
- to promote a missionary spirit that prepares the faithful to be present as Christians in society (*NDC,* 20)

In accomplishing this sixfold task, catechists are aided by the Holy Spirit. However, to reflect effectively the teaching and the life of Jesus in their words and behavior, catechists need to grow continually in their faith. They should

- know and study further the teaching of the Church's Magisterium through lectures, courses, and Catholic publications.
- become imbued with the thought and spirit of the Bible through prayerful reflection.
- have a profound spirit of prayer and a deep sacramental life, for only union with Christ gives the light and strength needed for authentic catechesis.
- give service to others and encourage the children to serve.
- become more aware of the missionary nature of the Church and educate the children in global problems and needs.
- become better trained for the task of catechizing by always seeking better methods.

Ways to Build a Faith Community as a Catechist

- Communicate with parents and value their primary role in their children's faith formation.
- Share goals, values, projects, and ideas with fellow catechists and parish leaders.
- Be familiar with guidelines for parish and diocesan catechetical programs.
- Cooperate with others in making the parish a focal point of the community, especially in grade-level planning and projects.
- Participate in meetings and prayer services for catechists.
- Seek out opportunities for spiritual enrichment.
- Accept the strengths and weaknesses of the faith community and strive together to witness the Gospel.

God Made Me

A Catechist Is

confident, but dependent on God.

knowledgeable, but open to children's ideas.

efficient, but relaxed.

spiritual, but practical.

professional, but caring.

enthusiastic, but calm.

Professional Ethics for Catechists

- Keep comments about the children and their families on a professional level.
- Use information about the children and their families prudently and discreetly. Observe professional confidentiality.
- Hold conferences with or about the children at appropriate times and places.
- Inform the coordinator, a priest, or other appropriate person when you discern unusual needs or problems of the children.
- Strive to make your daily living reflect your faith.
- Prepare thoroughly for each lesson.

A Guide for Self-Improvement

As a catechist, you are a minister of the Word of God. Every child hopes to see and hear the kindness, the warmth, and the love of Jesus reflected in your facial expressions, your voice, and your very life. If you are receptive to God each day, if you take time to ponder his Word and deepen your relationship with God, if you are convinced of the power of the Gospel message, then the children will hear the Lord reveal the mystery of his love through you. You will discover that as you share your faith, you are personally enriched. Reflect on the following questions periodically to examine your effectiveness as a catechist and to determine areas for improvement:

- Do I present the message with the conviction, joy, love, enthusiasm, and hope that come from a commitment to Christ?
- Do I pray for light to understand what I am teaching and to know how to present God's Word persuasively?
- Do I reflect on Scripture as part of my preparation for each lesson?
- Do I have all materials ready before class time?
- Do I share my heart, my spirit, and my personal faith story as I convey the Christian message?
- Do I lead the children in prayer? Do I use a variety of prayer forms?
- How sensitive am I to the individual needs of the children?
- Have I communicated with the parents?
- Do I make an evaluation after each lesson and use it in future planning?
- Am I willing to spend time to promote my own growth in faith and understanding?

Catechist's Handbook **T281**

WHAT THE CATECHISM SAYS TO CATECHISTS

The *Catechism of the Catholic Church* is a marvelous tool for catechists. It provides information that can be useful in preparing lesson plans, and it also serves as a reference book. Each chapter in *God Made Me* includes references to paragraphs in the *Catechism* that are related to it.

Catechists are cautioned, however, that the *Catechism* is not intended to be used as a student textbook.

In addition to being a source of background material, the *Catechism* contains messages specifically for catechists. Paragraphs 426 through 429 are the centerpiece of what it says to us. They contain our mission statement, our goal, and our job description. The boldface title for this passage says it all—"At the heart of catechesis: Christ." Paragraph 426 states, "'At the heart of catechesis we find, in essence, a Person, the Person of Jesus of Nazareth, the only Son from the Father . . . who suffered and died for us and who now, after rising, is living with us forever.' To catechize is 'to reveal in the Person of Christ the whole of God's eternal design reaching fulfillment in that Person. It is to seek to understand the meaning of Christ's actions and words and of the signs worked by him.'" Only Christ "'can lead us to the love of the Father in the Spirit and make us share in the life of the Holy Trinity.'"

Our call is to bring people to the person of Jesus Christ, who lives and who is with us and who loves us. Religion class is a community of people who are journeying together, sharing faith in Jesus Christ, and growing in it. Religion class is a matter of formation—changing lives to be more Christlike. The room where it is held is sacred space, as holy as the catacombs where the first Christians gathered to deepen their relationship with Christ and their commitment to him.

We cannot give what we do not have. It was only after Paul encountered the risen Lord for himself that he was enflamed with a passion for teaching the world about him. The more we ourselves come to know Jesus Christ, the more zealous and convincing we will be in persuading others to live for him. The more we enter into the mystery of Christ's death and Resurrection in our daily lives, the more we will be able to persuade others to live like him.

We can take heart that when we teach in the name of Jesus, he teaches through us, because we have been mandated and commissioned by him. Through his Spirit, he is our invisible partner.

Seven essential messages from the *Catechism* are listed here, along with with their paragraph numbers for reading and reflection:

131–133	**Teach Scripture.** By reading it, we learn "'the surpassing knowledge of Jesus Christ.'"
282	**Teach Creation.** It is of major importance because it concerns the very foundations of human and Christian life.
426–429	**Teach Christ.** Put people in communion with him.
1072	**Teach Liturgy.** In the sacraments, especially in the Eucharist, Christ Jesus works in fullness for our transformation.
1697	**Teach the Way of Christ.** Reveal the joy and the demands of the way of Christ.
1917	**Teach Hope.** "[T]he future of humanity is in the hands of those who are capable of providing the generations to come with reasons for life and optimism."
2663	**Teach Prayer.** Explain its meaning, always in relation to Jesus Christ.

God Made Me

CATECHIST'S RESOURCES

Recent Church Documents for Catechesis

1979	*Catechesis in Our Time* (Pope John Paul II)
1992	*Catechism of the Catholic Church*
1997	*General Directory for Catechesis*
2005	*National Directory for Catechesis*
2005	*Compendium of the Catechism of the Catholic Church*
2006	*United States Catholic Catechism for Adults*

Other Papal and Vatican Documents

1963	*Peace on Earth* (Pope John XXIII)
1963–1965	*Documents of the Second Vatican Council*
1987	*On Social Concern* (Pope John Paul II)
1991	*The Hundredth Year* (Pope John Paul II)
1991	*Dialogue and Proclamation* (Pontifical Council for Interreligious Dialogue and the Congregation for the Evangelization of Peoples)
1993	*The Splendor of Truth* (John Paul II)
1994	*Letter to Families* (Pope John Paul II)
1998	*Towards a Better Distribution of Land* (Pontifical Council for Justice and Peace)
1998	*The Day of the Lord* (Pope John Paul II)
1998	*The Dignity of Older People and Their Mission in the Church and in the World* (Pontifical Council for the Laity)
1999	*The Family and Human Rights* (Pontifical Council for the Family)
1999	*Memory and Reconciliation: The Church and the Faults of the Past* (International Theological Commission)
2001	*Directory on Popular Piety and the Liturgy* (Congregation for Divine Worship and the Discipline of the Sacraments)
2001	*The Jewish People and Their Sacred Scriptures in the Christian Bible* (Pontifical Biblical Commission)
2003	*The Eucharist in Its Relationship to the Church* (Pope John Paul II)
2006	*God Is Love* (Pope Benedict XVI)
2007	*On Christian Hope* (Pope Benedict XVI)

Other Documents of the United States Bishops

1991	*Putting Children and Families First: A Challenge for Our Church, Nation, and World*
1992	*Go and Make Disciples: A National Plan and Strategy for Catholic Evangelization in the United States*
1995	*Called and Gifted for the Third Millennium*
1998	*Sharing Catholic Social Teaching: Challenges and Directions*
1999	*Our Hearts Were Burning Within Us: A Pastoral Plan for Adult Faith Formation in the United States*
1999	*In All Things Charity: A Pastoral Challenge for the New Millennium*
2000	*Welcoming the Stranger Among Us: Unity in Diversity*
2001	*The Real Presence of Jesus Christ in the Sacrament of the Eucharist: Basic Questions and Answers*
2003	*General Instruction of the Roman Missal*

Most of these documents are available from www.usccb.org.

Catechist's Handbook T283

TIPS FOR GOOD CATECHESIS

Prepare the Learning Space

- Divide the room into several areas.
  1. A free-play area supplied with picture books, wooden blocks, a carton of dress-up clothes, beads to string, toys, housekeeping materials, sand (or large kosher-size salt), cartons and large packing boxes, cereal boxes, shoe boxes, and cardboard cylinders
  2. An area where children may sit in a circle on a rug or carpet squares
  3. A large, clear space to play games and dance
  4. An activity area supplied with low tables and craft supplies, such as glue sticks, paints, scissors, crayons, and markers

Although the classroom setting is important, keep in mind that much can be done with little. The catechist's care, love, and acceptance far outweigh any benefits that the physical surroundings alone might offer.

- Arrange and decorate the room so that it is bright, interesting, and safe as well as aesthetically inviting and attractive.
- Keep the room neat and clean. Avoid a lot of distracting clutter. Reduce the noise level by hanging draperies, carpeting the floor, or using other sound-muffling devices.
- Arrange a prayer center with a cloth-covered table. Place there a Bible, a cross, flowers, and other items that might be suggested in the lesson. For more information about praying with the children, see Prayer on page T279 and T296.
- Provide a special-interest table for displaying objects related to the lesson and for objects the children bring to class.
- Post pictures related to the theme of the day at the eye level of the children.
- Designate a special table or space as a quiet place for children who need to calm down, deal with their emotions, or withdraw from the group for another reason. Never force a child to join the group.
- Display the work of all the children. If there is no bulletin board, string a line across the room and hang up the children's work with clip clothespins.
- Note whether there is adequate light, heat, and ventilation in the room.
- Have recorded music playing as the children enter each day.
- Imagine how the children will move about in the room. Plan where they will carry on activities, keep their belongings, and eat their snacks.

Recruit Helpers

- Arrange for teacher assistants, parents, and grandparents to help with lessons. Young children need individual attention. Two adults or older helpers should be in the room for all classes, not only to help with the activities but also to take charge if there is an emergency and you must leave the room. Send a volunteer chart to parents before the preschool classes begin or ask them to sign up during a parent-catechist meeting.

Gather Supplies

- Use simple containers for supplies and keep them in the same place so that the children know where they belong. You might keep supplies on a cart and wheel it to the work area when needed.
- Make sure that scissors have blunt ends and that they work easily. A drop of oil fixes scissors that are difficult to use. Teach the children to carry scissors with the blunt ends down. Provide left-handed scissors and mark them as such.
- Put petroleum jelly on the threads of paint jars so that the lids come off easily.
- Keep newspapers on hand to protect surfaces during art activities.
- Keep magazines in the room to place under the lesson pages if the children use crayons and pencils on a carpeted floor.
- Have equipment for cleaning up after art activities and snacks: pails or dishpans, paper towels, soap, large sponges, mop, broom, and dustpan.

God Made Me

Plan for the Year

- If you wish, tear out the pages of the Child's Book and sort them for the children according to lesson, keeping together the pages for each chapter, including the lesson page, activity page, story booklet, and perforated cards, if there are any needed. Fold a sheet of paper around the top of each set of pages or insert a divider to separate them. Store the pages in a file, a desk drawer, or a carton until needed.
- Separate the cutouts and the Scripture cards in the back of this manual and store them in an envelope or file.
- Obtain the Spanish translations of Family Time (Tiempo en familia) sections of the Child's Book and have them ready to photocopy for parents who may benefit from them. Visit www.loyolapress.com/preschool.
- Return to this Catechist's Handbook throughout the year, especially as you evaluate your lessons.
- Decide which lessons you will teach and fill in the chart on pages OV-12 and OV-13.

Prepare the Lesson

- Plan and prepare well. Prayerfully read the Faith Focus and the Preparing the Faith Experience sections for the lesson. Consider using a journal to record your responses.
- Arrive for the lesson at least a half hour before the children arrive.
- Have everything set up for the lesson ahead of time, including materials for free play.
- Cut out the items on the activity pages as required to save class time, especially if the children have difficulty using scissors.
- Write the children's names on the appropriate Child's Book pages.
- Hand out name tags as long as you need them.
- Find out whether any child is celebrating a birthday during the week and if so, plan to celebrate in class. Seat the child in a specially decorated birthday chair and have the group sing "Happy Birthday." You may wish to establish additional birthday traditions, such as displaying a birthday banner or having the child wear a birthday crown.

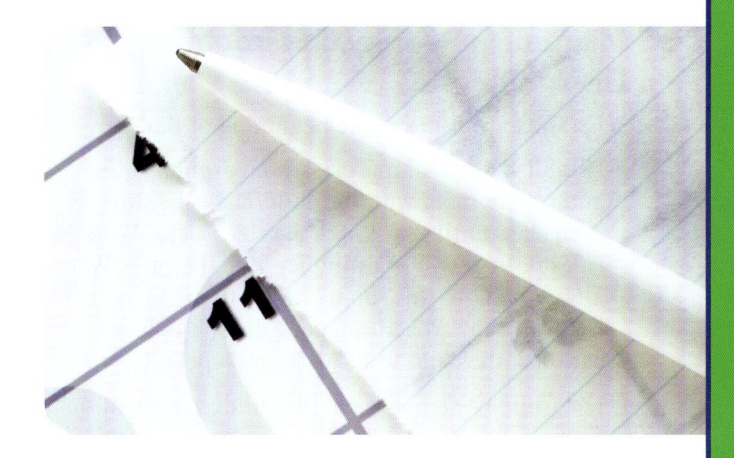

Establish a Climate for Growth

- Address the children by name. Be sure to pronounce and spell their names correctly.
- Make the lesson a joyful experience for the children. Be warm and encouraging. Smile often.
- Be calm in your manner, reverent in your gestures, and joyful in your presentation.
- Demonstrate respectful behavior.
- Speak in a well-modulated voice, loud enough for everyone to hear you but soft enough to convey the wonder of the message you share.
- Be animated. Children will catch your enthusiasm.
- Ask the children about their families and interests.
- Listen to what the children are saying verbally and nonverbally. Be eager to understand their fears, worries, plans, stories—even their complaints.
- Express confidence in the children.
- Give words of encouragement for the children's efforts. Avoid giving too much or insincere praise for the end product. For young children, process is more important than product.
- Seek to provide the children with a sense of security. Reassure them of your care and acceptance with hugs and pats on the head. Avoid favoritism.
- Convey happiness to the children by your words and your tone of voice.
- Use frequent eye contact so each child feels you are speaking personally to him or her.
- Play music as the children work.
- See the children as individuals. Try not to generalize, but see each child as gifted by God. Make allowances for individual circumstances.
- Love your work. Teaching is hard work, but it is also a privilege. Show the children that you like teaching because you like them. Even more importantly, love your work as a person who shares the work of Jesus the Teacher.

TIPS FOR GOOD CATECHESIS

Maintain a Healthy Classroom Discipline

- Establish routines at the beginning of the year.
- Establish a few simple classroom ground rules and review them with the children at the start of each class until they know the rules well. Word the rules positively. For example, state the rule "We always walk in this room" rather than "Don't run in this room." When someone doesn't follow a rule, ask the child to recall it and repeat it.
- Determine a signal to get the children's attention for a change of activity. This can be having a child ring a bell, whispering a phrase, or clapping one's hands to a specific rhythm.
- Do not expect all the children to participate in all group activities. Allow them the freedom to wander in and out of the group at will if necessary.
- Use special techniques if you want only a small number of children in the group to move at one time to form a line or to come to the front of the room. For example, have those who are wearing red clothing go first, those wearing blue go second, and so forth. You might sing or call children's names.
- Stress the positive by commenting on good behavior.
- Be observant while you are teaching.
- Expect good behavior. Don't tolerate misbehavior.
- When a problem arises, use a pleasant but firm tone of voice. In order to win over the child or children involved, keep calm and avoid becoming angry.
- Avoid letting one child prevent others from learning and cooperating. Suggest an alternative activity if a child's behavior is inappropriate.
- Plan for handling and putting away materials.
- Warn the children a few minutes ahead of time when an activity is drawing to a close so that they can finish the task.
- Show the children where the restroom is located. If it is outside the classroom, have a specific time for the group to go together.
- Pray for the children.

Teaching Tips

- Have the children sit in a circle on the floor.
- Include as many of the children as you can in the activities and discussions.
- Allow sufficient thinking time for children when they are responding to a question.
- Some unplanned experiences present opportunities for teaching a lesson. Take advantage of them.
- When the children are restless, adapt your plan.
- Let the children use pencils instead of crayons or markers on the Child's Book pages when appropriate.
- Repetition is important for children. Do not be afraid to repeat activities.
- Remember that young children learn through play and hands-on activities.

God Made Me

Prepare for Arts and Crafts

- Have the children sit at low tables for craft activities. If your room has no tables, children may work on the floor. For water and art activities, cover the carpet with a plastic tablecloth.
- Set rules about splashing paints, dropping clay, and washing hands.
- Encourage creativity and allow for choices.
- Provide smocks, aprons, or old shirts for the children to wear when they are painting. Cover the work area with newspapers.
- For a gluing activity, tell the children to apply glue to the area to be covered and then place the object on that area. Demonstrate that a small amount of glue is sufficient. Glue sticks are easier for the children to control than liquid glue.
- Give concise, simple directions, one step at a time.
- Prepare a model of the craft for the children if it will not hinder their creativity.
- In commenting on a child's work, do not ask "What is it?" Instead say "Tell me about your picture."
- Give children specific directions for cleanup. Make it every child's responsibility.
- Remedy mistakes and accidents as inconspicuously as possible. Use a blow dryer if necessary to dry paint before the children are dismissed.
- Send potentially messy projects home in paper bags or rolled up and fastened with a rubber band.
- Recipes for homemade materials for arts and crafts are provided beginning on page T308.

Plan for Physical Activities and Games

- Balance physical activities with quiet activities. Young children love action poems, finger plays, dancing, games, and physical exercises. Moreover, they cannot sit still longer than five minutes.
- Play games in which no child loses or is out. Young children have difficulty with losing games.
- Join in the children's games.

Prepare for Snacks

- Provide or have parents provide nutritious snacks for the lesson. Be aware of and communicate to others any food restrictions or allergies.
- Set up the snacks on trays ahead of time, with portions for each child.
- Begin the snack period with a prayer of thanks.
- Encourage the children to keep their cups in the center of the table to avoid spills.
- Let the children assist in preparing and distributing snacks and in the cleanup.

Catechist's Handbook

TEACHING EXCEPTIONAL CHILDREN

Each person is created in God's image, yet there are variations in individual abilities. Positive recognition of these differences discourages discrimination and enchances the unity of the Body of Christ.

Statement of the U.S. Bishops: Welcome and Justice
for Persons with Disabilities (1998)

By choosing a variety of teaching techniques, catechists make use of the strengths of children's various learning styles and also attend to the needs of exceptional children. These children can include both those with some form of learning difficulty, as well as those who are considered gifted. Efforts made in this area enhance the learning experience for all children.

Use of Scripture Stories

- Tell some stories as an eyewitness, using direct address. Be dramatic.
- Use the Bible and pictures during storytelling.
- After the story is read, have the children dramatize it, perhaps by using pantomime.

Use of Music and Gesture

- Provide silent, reflective time to draw the children into a sense of the sacred.
- Play peaceful, calming music to help the children quiet themselves for prayer.
- Engage the children with echo-type songs and prayers. Use songs with direct, simple messages about the faith to help the children retain the basic truths. Suggested songs are found on the CD. For a list of additional music, see page T302.
- Use simple gestures for refrains to promote the children's participation. Use *Music 'n Motion* beginning on page T247 to incorporate gestures and music in the lessons.

Questioning Techniques

- State questions in their entirety, and then break them down into basic components.
- Use simple questions to increase group participation, for example, use repeat-after-me questions or statements or use simple completion questions.
- Ask questions immediately following what was taught.
- Use critical-thinking questions for those children who can handle them.

Physical Impairment

- Adapt your teaching to fit the needs of the child with a physical disability, using individualized instruction.
- Use devices or a buddy system to help the child with materials and group activities.
- If a child has symptoms that at times might be disruptive, be prepared to address the situation in a way that will minimize embarrassment to the child.
- Encourage social interaction through verbal activities and other opportunities.

Visual Impairment

- Consider range of vision and lighting needs when seating the child.
- Permit the child to move for closer views of charts or demonstrations.
- Provide large-print books, audio materials, and materials he or she can touch.
- Plan lessons that involve other senses besides sight.
- Assign a partner for visual activities.
- Keep the learning area clear of hazards.

T288   God Made Me

Hearing Impairment

- Face the child when you talk to him or her.
- Seat the child near the front of the room or close to audio equipment.
- Seat a child who has a hearing loss in one ear so that the impaired ear is toward the wall.
- Avoid standing where glare from light inhibits the child's ability to read your lips.
- Speak clearly, using a normal tone and pace.
- Reword directions often. Some sounds are heard better than others.
- Encourage verbal interaction.
- Make arrangements for a sign-language interpreter to work with you as needed.

Speech Impairment

- Speak distinctly and in short phrases.
- Use visual as well as oral instruction.
- Work individually in a separate area with the child whose oral work needs attention.
- Allow extra time for the child to respond to your questions and comments.

Handling Social and Behavioral Problems

- Arrange the room to minimize distractions. Carpeting, sound-absorbing materials, and room dividers can help.
- Structure the schedule to avoid last-minute changes and to allow mastery of content within the child's attention span.
- Help the child develop routines.
- Prepare change-of-pace activities between learning periods and give the child opportunities to move about the room.
- Give specific tasks that are interesting to the child.
- Plan stimulating activities for after—not before—periods of concentration.
- Explain the rationale for what the child is learning.
- Establish a plan of action for completing work.
- Reward the child for demonstrating self-control and responsibility and for completing a task in the appropriate length of time.
- Use strategies that provide immediate feedback, such as hand-raising and flash cards.

TEACHING EXCEPTIONAL CHILDREN

Learning Disabilities

- Provide routine and orderly procedures. Minimize distractions.
- Keep lessons short and varied, introduce skills one at a time, and review often. Allow extra time.
- Use books and materials with large print and a simple setup.
- Reinforce verbalized concepts with visual and kinesthetic cues.
- Set up situations in which the child will experience success. Frequently compliment the child on his or her strengths.
- Review and clarify directions.
- Ask questions often to assess the child's understanding of the lesson.

Mental Impairment

- Adjust class work to the child's attention span and level of coordination and skill.
- Individualize learning and use teacher aides.
- Simplify concepts, overteach in a concrete manner and with a variety of forms, and repeat periodically.
- Allow the children to assist one another as appropriate.

Giftedness

- Suggest independent study, small-group work, enrichment activities, and discovery learning that is related to the child's interests.
- Provide supplementary resources and direct the child to pursue more challenging topics.
- Capture the child's interest with puzzles and games.
- Ask the child to help with preparing materials and demonstrations and with teaching other children.
- Encourage high-level thinking skills and persistence in difficult learning.

T290   God Made Me

MULTICULTURAL AWARENESS

From the beginning, this one Church has been marked by a great diversity which comes from both the variety of God's gifts and the diversity of those who receive them. Within the unity of the People of God, a multiplicity of peoples and cultures is gathered together. Among the Church's members, there are different gifts, offices, conditions, and ways of life.

Catechism of the Catholic Church, 814

Convinced of this truth, the Church urges its catechists to

- incorporate the cultures of the people in their catechesis.
- address the needs of various groups of people.
- respect and cherish the uniqueness of different groups.
- lead others to know and respect cultures different from their own.

The following suggestions can help catechists teach more effectively as they promote multicultural awareness and respect.

Responding to the Needs of Various Cultures

- Understand and be sensitive to both the home and the community of each child.
- Learn about the history, traditions, and values of the ethnic groups to which the children belong.
- Make sure that your teaching takes into account the life experiences of the children.
- Make the effort to have all written communications to parents or guardians translated into the language spoken at home.
- Be aware that there are subgroups within larger groups. For example, Spanish-speaking people come from Mexico, Puerto Rico, Cuba, and other countries. Each has a distinct culture. The same is true for people of Native American, African American, Asian, and other ancestries.
- Consider your group's special needs in relation to justice and peace. Prepare the children to assume responsibility for achievement of their goals.
- Become familiar with popular devotions unique to the ethnic groups that make up your class.
- Read books with positive reflections of multicultural diversity to the children.

Incorporating the Gifts of Various Cultures

- Encourage the children to share their customs and family celebrations with one another.
- Integrate cultural holidays and feasts, special events, and neighborhood celebrations into the life examples you use in your teaching.
- In liturgical and social celebrations, especially on important occasions, incorporate the language and symbols of the groups that make up your learning community.
- Encourage liturgical and social celebrations that express the spirit, history, and traditions of the cultural groups in your learning community.

Educating Children to Know and Respect Various Cultures

- Watch for unjust or stereotypical treatment of sexes, races, and cultures in the materials you use and in your own words as you teach. Raise the consciousness of those around you.
- Do not use racial, ethnic, or cultural nicknames or make jokes that label or stereotype.
- Be alert to ways of acknowledging contributions made by various cultural groups to the rich traditions of the Catholic Church.
- Share stories about saints from a variety of cultures and social conditions.
- Be understanding of the present struggle of various cultural groups in finding their place in U.S. society and in the Church.

Catechist's Handbook **T291**

TECHNIQUES AND TOOLS OF TEACHING

Art

Throughout history, faith has been expressed in painting and sculpture. Art is a concrete expression of a person's thoughts and feelings. When children see their inner religious thoughts and feelings expressed visually, they can grow spiritually. Art helps them become more aware of religious concepts and relates the messages they have heard to their own lives. Young children express their ideas through drawing and painting, using lines and forms that will later develop into writing.

- Give clear directions. Provide a sample.
- Create a quiet, reflective atmosphere by playing appropriate background music as the children work. Encourage them to think about what they have just experienced or learned.
- Give the children who wish to do so an opportunity to talk about their work.
- Display the work at the children's eye level so that it can be appreciated.
- Be aware that coloring books and patterns do not stimulate creativity. For a drawing activity, stimulate ideas and guide the children by making comments such as "I wonder whether you will draw green grass in the background" or "I wonder whether you will make your picture fill the whole sheet."

Audiovisuals

Audiovisuals (movies, videotapes, DVDs, slides, audio CDs, and audiotapes) can lead the children to a deeper appreciation of the message in each chapter.

- Preview the entire audiovisual and read the guide that comes with it. Determine whether it is appropriate for your lesson and your group. Decide how you will use the audiovisual—to introduce a subject or to review it.
- Prepare to introduce audiovisual presentations. Give adequate background information and tell the children what to look for, focusing attention on the main purpose for listening or viewing.
- Plan discussion questions and activities to follow the presentation.
- Introduce new vocabulary and concepts before showing the audiovisual.
- After the presentation, provide time for quiet reflection or written response.

Bulletin Boards

An effective bulletin-board display is simple, timely, and catches people's attention. Its unity, with emphasis on the more important elements, and its balanced arrangement, with movement (or flow), make it educational as well as attractive. It is an easily understood teaching aid.

- Think of a caption that draws attention, such as a question, a three-dimensional device, a current idiom, or "big" or stylized words.
- Create an overall effect to hold interest.
- Plan the movement of the board. Displays are usually viewed left to right, top to bottom. Figures of people and animals draw attention. Repeat shapes, textures, and colors—or related variations—for unity.
- Achieve balance, which can be symmetrical or asymmetrical. For informal balance, use two or more small shapes with a larger one, a small colorful shape with a larger dull one, a small shape near the bottom with a larger shape near the top, or a small eye-catching shape with a larger common shape.
- Make objects touch one another, or connect them with yarn, paper, or colored lines. An odd number of items is better than an even number.
- Use wallpaper, wrapping paper, construction paper, shelf paper, velour, felt, or burlap as a background for letters and pictures.
- Arrange the children's papers so that they can be easily seen; never place one on top of another.

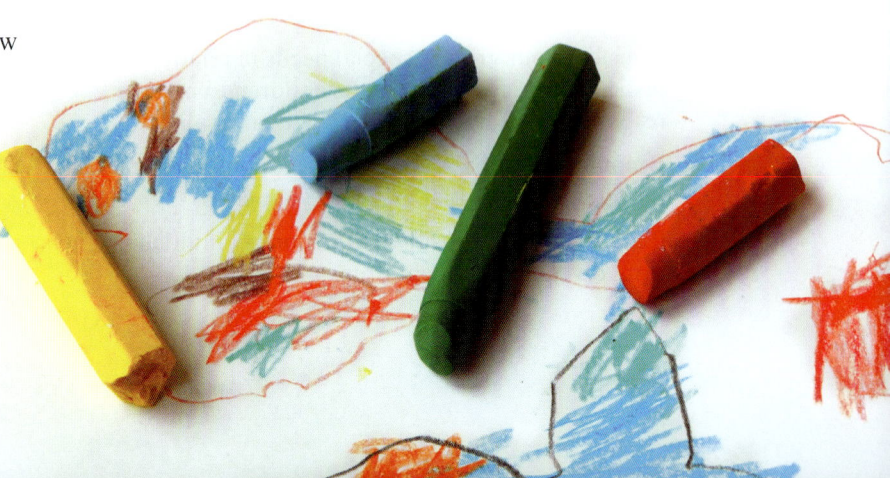

God Made Me

Celebrations

Celebrations, including song, prayer, Scripture, ritual, and symbol, draw the children more deeply into the message of the lesson. Through communal prayers and private reflections in the celebrations, the children are imbued with the mystery of faith celebrated and come to appreciate liturgical elements. The impressions that celebrations make on the children justify the time, preparation, and practice they entail.

- Create an atmosphere of beauty, peace, and prayer through the use of candles, flowers or plants, cloth, religious art, music, and symbols. (Check with the proper authority regarding local regulations for using candles in a classroom setting.)
- Make sure all the children know what to do and say. Practice the songs used.
- Remind the children that they are praising and thanking God through their celebration.

Children's Literature

Books are highly effective tools for shaping attitudes and imparting values. Through stories, the children come to understand themselves and others, and they learn to relate to others and to their world in a better way. Good literature confronts readers with basic human problems and helps them deal with these problems. Stories can reinforce the Christian message presented in class and help children apply Christian principles to their lives. Jesus was conscious of the power of stories and used them in his teaching. Recommended books are listed for each chapter under the feature title "Books to Share."

- As you read a story, make your voice and face full of expression.
- Show the pictures and call attention to certain features in them. Give the children the opportunity to respond to the story and pictures.
- Involve the children in the story by asking questions or having them add sounds, words, or gestures. Prepare props ahead of time.

Dramatization

Dramatization effectively reinforces the Christian message and helps children internalize it. Role-playing enables children to apply religious truths to their daily life.

- Maintain an atmosphere of security and seriousness needed to give the children self-confidence. Use role-playing only when the children are comfortable with one another.
- Ignore giggles and awkwardness.
- Allow the children to choose their roles. Have them take turns.
- Use simple props and costumes.
- Prepare the performers sufficiently.
- Put signs on the participants for identification if necessary. Children like to wear sandwich boards to identify who they are.
- Accept the children's interpretations and praise their efforts. However, if their interpretations lack insight, guide them to understand the feelings of the people in the situations.
- Discuss the activity with the children in the light of Christian values.

Visit www.loyolapress.com/preschool for suggestions about using storybooks in prayer and catechesis.

TECHNIQUES AND TOOLS OF TEACHING

Flannel Board

Flannel-board figures add another dimension to storytelling. Sets of flannel figures can be purchased, or you can make your own. Glue small pieces of flannel or felt to the back of paper figures, or use flannel or felt to make the figures.

- Arrange the figures in order of use.
- Practice telling your story until you feel at ease with the story and the movement of the figures.
- Use the figures for review. For example, distribute them to the children and have them tell the story, or have them give a clue about their figure and ask the group to guess which one they have.

Group Projects

As the children work together to reach a common goal, qualities needed in community are fostered: consideration, understanding, cooperation, patience, initiative, and responsibility. Small-group activities afford the children an experience of interdependence and provide a welcome change from the classroom routine.

- Explain the directions clearly and demonstrate when appropriate.
- Show interest in the groups' work by encouraging them, offering suggestions, and asking questions.
- Make sure that all the children are participating.

Games

Playing games is fun for children and also contributes to their development. Games provide practice in mental, physical, and social skills; offer opportunities for problem solving and creativity; stimulate imagination; and increase attention spans.

- Remove potential hazards from the play area.
- Explain the game clearly and simply. Establish ground rules. Demonstrate when necessary.
- Let the children take turns being the leader. Assist children who need help.
- Have several groups play a game to allow the children to have more turns. Avoid games that eliminate children, or plan something to occupy those who are out of the game.
- Replay the children's favorite games.

Memorization

Knowledge of certain elements of Catholic belief is best acquired by memorizing them. Pope John Paul II pointed out that "the blossoms . . . of faith and piety do not grow in the desert places of a memoryless catechesis. What is essential is that the texts that are memorized must at the same time be taken in and gradually understood in depth, in order to become a source of Christian life on the personal level and the community level." (*On Catechesis in Our Time,* 55)

- Lead the way by memorizing the material first. Children memorize easily and will naturally repeat psalm verses prayed as a group.
- Integrate memorized material into the lesson in a meaningful way. The children should understand the material they are memorizing.

T294 God Made Me

Music

Music can set the mood for the lesson and predispose the children to receive God's message. Besides introducing the lesson, music can be used to review and reinforce the message. It can serve as a prayer before or after class. Music unites the group, provides an enjoyable opportunity for self-expression, and stirs up feelings of love and loyalty to Christ and his Church. Both singing and listening to music have the power to open hearts to the Lord.

- As you teach a song, consider the following steps:
  1. Give a general introduction and ask the children to listen to the song.
  2. Have them listen again for specific ideas. Discuss difficult lyrics.
  3. Have them sing the song softly or hum along as you sing or play it.
- Ask the children to sing with enthusiasm and make the song a prayer. Suggest that they think about the meaning of the song and sing with all their hearts.
- Invite the children to add gestures or interpretive dance steps. See *Music 'n Motion,* beginning on page T247.
- If you lack musical talent, find ways to compensate. For example, use recorded music or invite assistance from other members of the community.
- Encourage the children to sing spontaneous original songs and create your own.

Pictures and Visuals

The icons of the Eastern Churches are treasured because of their power to sweep us up to God. Stained-glass windows have been a medium of religious instruction for centuries. Similarly, pictures such as art masterpieces and the photos and illustrations in the Child's Book can influence the children's response to the catechesis. They can stimulate learning, awaken an appreciation of the message, and lead to prayer.

- Use visuals to arouse interest, to raise questions, and to clarify concepts.
- Choose visuals that are artistically good, convey an accurate religious message, and are large enough to be seen by all.
- Use questions or comments to lead the children to share insights. Ask them how the picture makes them feel and how it relates to the lesson. Have them create a story based on the picture or role-play the situation depicted.

Catechist's Handbook **T295**

TECHNIQUES AND TOOLS OF TEACHING

Play

Children learn through play as they investigate the world, master themselves, and build interpersonal relationships. Children's toys should encourage thinking, exploration, creativity, and communication. Provide a variety of toys for the children. Share play experiences with the children to understand their world better.

- Provide toys that allow children to engage in free-form, open-ended play: wooden blocks, playhouses, puppets, dolls, and trucks. Allow freedom for the children in their play.
- Select toys that encourage the children's creativity. A nonspeaking doll engages the children's imaginations better than a doll that talks. A toy that the children move is better than a battery-run toy. Rotate toys to maintain the children's interest.
- Make sure that the toys are safe. Do not give the children toys with sharp edges, small parts, or projectiles, or toys that may present potential danger if they are broken. Check to make sure that fabric is labeled "flame-retardant" or "flame resistant." Painted toys should have nontoxic paint.
- Create toys with the children.

Prayer

Prayer opens children's hearts to God's message. It gives them the time and space they need to reflect on God's words and the meaning the words have for their lives. Most important, it provides an avenue for God to touch the children and to change them by his love.

- Be a person of prayer yourself, and share your own prayer life with the children as appropriate.
- Respect each child's needs. Some will feel comfortable praying aloud and spontaneously. Others will prefer to pray silently. Show respect and appreciation for the various types of prayer.
- Prepare the children for prayer. Provide time for them to settle down and focus on God. Teach them to adopt a posture that is conducive to prayer.
- Create an attractive prayer center. Place there a Bible, a crucifix, a banner, a candle, religious statues, or pictures related to the feast, season, or topic of study. Regularly gather the group in the prayer center for prayer experiences. Encourage the children to use the area for personal prayer. Suggest that they have their families arrange similar prayer centers at home.

God Made Me

Puppets

Puppets are a valuable teaching aid, especially for young or shy children. Since puppets are merely toys, they should not pray or speak the religious message. The faith message should be grounded in reality.

Puppets can be made in the following ways:

- Lunch bags—Draw, paint, or glue on features. The bags may be stuffed and tied or left open so that a hand can be inserted.
- Paper—Mount paper cutouts on pencils, rulers, craft sticks, kitchen utensils (such as spoons or spatulas), or even brooms. Paper plates make good puppet faces.
- Socks and mittens—Fabric scraps and other decorations can be sewed or glued to them to make faces and clothing.
- Finger puppets—These can be cut from paper and taped together to fit a finger, or they can be made from felt or old gloves.
- Puppets with arms—Use a paper cup or a cardboard tube, cutting holes on the sides for a thumb or finger.
- Wooden clothespins—Decorate them with felt-tipped pens, yarn, and fabric.

Questions

Posing questions is a time-honored technique for leading children to the truth. Both Socrates and Jesus relied heavily on questions when they taught. Asking questions keeps the children's attention.

- Vary the types of questions you ask, from simple recall questions to those that require some explanation. Address questions to the entire group before calling on a child to answer.
- Be comfortable with the silence as the children reflect on the question. To encourage children to give more thoughtful responses, avoid calling on the first child who raises his or her hand.
- Implement strategies that allow all children to participate. For example, give a child an object such as a beanbag to hold while answering. Then have the child pass the object to the next speaker.

Storytelling

Through Bible stories and stories from the lives of Christians past and present, we share the heritage of our faith. Storytelling can also be used to share one's personal faith. Sharing one's faith journey gives witness to the faith. Both forms of storytelling deepen the children's understanding of Jesus and their relationship with him.

- Make a story your own by adapting it to the children and to your message.
- Practice telling the story by using facial expressions, animated gestures, and expression in your voice for effect and emphasis.
- Use visuals to enhance the telling: pictures, puppets, chalkboard, flannel board, and so forth.
- Relate personally to each child as you tell the story. Establish eye contact with individuals and be sensitive to how each is responding to the story.
- Let the story speak for itself. Its message may be less effective if you moralize.

Catechist's Handbook **T297**

PARENT-CATECHIST MEETING

GUIDELINES FOR MEETING WITH PARENTS

REASONS FOR THE MEETING
1. To help parents realize their important role in shaping their children's religious lives

2. To suggest ways parents can make the most of ordinary opportunities to nurture family faith and celebrate God's presence in their lives

3. To help parents understand their children's development and become aware of factors that contribute to their religious development

4. To explain the *God Made Me* program for three-year-old children and to describe how parents can be involved

NUMBER OF MEETINGS
Opportunities for parent education can be an important component of a preschool program. The number of meetings will vary according to the parents' needs and interests. The following suggestions are for one meeting, which you might schedule for two different times to provide an added opportunity for parents to attend.

PRACTICAL POINTS TO CONSIDER
1. Schedule a meeting near the beginning of the year. Select a convenient time (or times) for the parents. Invite a parish priest to participate.

2. Create a comfortable atmosphere for the meeting.
- Select a suitable meeting place.
- Plan to welcome each person individually while volunteers take care of registration, name tags, and so forth.
- Plan refreshments.

3. Decide how to publicize your meeting. Announce the meeting in letters to parents and in parish bulletins. Visit www.loyolapress.com/preschool for sample meeting publicity. Highlight its benefits to parents and clearly state the following details:
- Why the meeting is being held
- Who is involved
- What will be included
- When and where the meeting will take place
- How long it will last
- Whom to contact for further information

Follow written announcements with personal invitations.

4. Create an environment for prayer by arranging a prayer center in your meeting space. Include a Bible, a cross, a copy of the *God Made Me* Child's Book, flowers, and a candle. (Confirm with the proper authority regarding use of candles in your meeting space.) Use lighting and music to set apart the prayer time.

5. Allow time for an adequate exchange of thoughts and feelings.

6. Make available a chart for volunteers to sign to be parent helpers during lessons and, if you wish, a chart for volunteers who offer to supply snacks for the lessons. Visit www.loyolapress.com/preschool for volunteer chart templates.

7. Include parents in an evaluation of the meeting. You may wish to distribute a form for written comments. Visit www.loyolapress.com/preschool for a sample evaluation form.

T298 *God Made Me*

PARENT MEETING
YOUR THREE-YEAR-OLD COMES TO KNOW GOD

PROPOSED MEETING OUTLINE

I. Introduction
   A. Welcome
   B. Affirm the parents' role in shaping children's religious life.
   C. Overview of the meeting
   D. Prayer
II. Presentation: "Your Child and the Preschool Program"
III. Refreshment Break
IV. Presentation: "Nurturing Your Child's Spirituality"
V. Discussion
VI. Closing prayer

CONSIDERATIONS WHEN PLANNING THE PRESENTATIONS

1. Families come in many forms and styles. One thing all participants will have in common is a strong love for their children.
2. Respect the parents' time by preparing well and starting and ending as scheduled.
3. Parents typically value gaining insight into how families function and the developmental stages their children are going through.
4. Raising children in the faith often demands a willingness to make choices as a family that go against the culture.
5. Many parents seek support and authorization to step into their role as spiritual leaders in their families.
6. Some adults in attendance will not have had a thorough catechetical formation, and some may be indifferent to religion.
7. Parents want what's best for their children, but they may need help to see how good moral and spiritual development are essential elements in providing what's best.
8. Families will benefit from understanding their noble mission to bring Christ to their homes, workplaces, neighborhoods, and the world.

SAMPLE MEETING

Part I: Introduction (15 minutes)

A Welcome the parents.

- Introduce yourself and any other catechists in the preschool program. Tell why you are happy to be a preschool catechist.
- Thank the parents for coming; acknowledge the difficulties they may have met in arranging to be present. Invite them to settle quietly in their seats, take a few deep breaths, and let go of the cares of the day.
- Have the parents introduce themselves.

B Affirm the parents' role in shaping their children's religious life.

- Express your awareness of the parents' deep concern for their children. Give specific examples of ways parents show this, by providing for a child's needs and guiding and teaching every day.
- Remind the parents that their children received the gift of faith in Baptism and are open to God and capable of perceiving his presence.
- Discuss the parents' role as their children's first teachers of the faith and their importance to their children's religious development. Describe ways they have helped shape their children's faith through actions of love, acceptance, respect, as well as by praying and worshiping together. Remind them of the help they receive from God in the grace offered throughout each day, and especially in the sacraments—Baptism first of all, the Eucharist, Reconciliation, Confirmation, and Matrimony.
- Explain that parents teach the faith in many ways, most powerfully through their example. When they respond to Christ's call in their daily lives, their children learn to love and follow Christ.

C Briefly outline the meeting and the expectations you have for it.

D Pray together.

- Call attention to the prayer center and invite all to join in a time of prayer.
- Light the candle, then pause to allow everyone to enter into the spirit of prayer.
- Begin with the Sign of the Cross and lead prayer, using this prayer or your own:

  Loving God, we praise you for your many blessings, and especially for the gift of our children. As we guide them to know of your great love for them, may we also experience the grace of your presence in our lives. Bless us as we journey together and seek to grow in your love. We ask this through Christ, our Lord. Amen.

Parent-Catechist Meeting   T299

PARENT-CATECHIST MEETING

Part II: Your Child and the Preschool Program (20 minutes)

A Ask the parents to think about some characteristics that describe their preschool child. Invite a few volunteers to name one of the characteristics. Encourage the parents to keep these in mind as you share with them the characteristics of a three-year-old child as given on page T278. Visit www.loyolapress.com/preschool to offer this as a parent handout.

B Discuss a child's spirituality. You might include the following ideas:

- Three-year-olds build their concepts of God on how they perceive their parents. As parents provide love, care, and security for their children, they are forming in them good attitudes toward God.
- Avoid casting God in the role of judge for three-year-olds.
- Three-year-olds have no concept of sin. They know only that their behavior makes their parents happy or unhappy.
- Children's self-esteem influences faith and how they interact with others. Parents have the power to build a healthy self-concept in their child.
- Through experience, children absorb faith and are guided to live the Christian life. Seeing their parents kneel in church or hearing them spontaneously thank God for a beautiful day makes a lasting impression. Children will imitate family members who do good for others.

C Present the preschool program:

- Examples of different types of activities (See examples in the Family Activity Booklet in the Child's Book.)
- Allow parents to review lesson materials, including the Child's Book and resources found in the Catechist's Guide.

D Show resources available to parents, such as those listed here. Let the parents look through them during the refreshment break. Visit www.loyolapress.com/preschool for a handout listing these resources and for order information.

Raising Faith-Filled Kids: Ordinary Opportunities to Nurture Spirituality at Home. Tips and tools for nurturing family spirituality by Tom McGrath. Published by Loyola Press (also available in Spanish).

52 Simple Ways to Talk with Your Kids about Faith. A guide for family conversations about faith by Jim Campbell. Published by Loyola Press.

A Prayer Book for Catholic Families. Introduces traditional prayers and family prayer traditions. Published by Loyola Press.

Catholic Household Blessings & Prayers. A resource for family prayer. Published by the United States Conference of Catholic Bishops.

The Spiritual Life of Children. A popular book by Robert Coles. Published by Houghton Mifflin.

Your Three-Year-Old: Friend or Enemy. A very helpful book by Louise Bates Ames and Frances L. Ilg. Published by Dell Publishing.

Various children's Bibles and Bible storybooks, such as the following:

All About Jesus. Bible stories selected and illustrated by Martine Blanc-Rerat. Published by Loyola Press.

The Greatest Story Ever Told. A pop-up activity book of stories of Jesus by Linda and Alan Parry. Published by Loyola Press.

Part III: Refreshment Break (10 minutes)

Part IV: Nurturing Your Child's Spirituality (20 minutes)

A Describe resources for families in the preschool program.

- Show the Family Time section of a lesson page from the Child's Book. Mention that this section contains the message of the lesson, tells what the children were taught and how, and suggests Scripture, prayer, and home activities to reinforce and extend the concepts and experiences of the lesson. Indicate if Spanish translations of Family Time (Tiempo en familia) will be made available for parents who may benefit from them. Note that these can be found at www.loyolapress.com/preschool.
- Explain that each Family Time concludes with a storybook suggestion, a discussion prompt, and a prayer suggestion related to the theme of the lesson. Propose to parents that this could be incorporated into their child's bedtime routine or another part of the day. Visit www.loyolapress.com/preschool for additional information about using this feature, including a handout for parents.
- Distribute and explain the Family Activity Booklet. Encourage the parents to use this resource to repeat a newly learned poem, finger play, or song at home with the children after each appropriate lesson. They can also use the directions provided for completing crafts at home as needed. Visit www.loyolapress.com/preschool to download additional copies of this resource.

B Suggest ways to foster faith in the home.

- Worship together as a family at Sunday Mass.
- Establish time each day for family prayers and blessings.
- Share meals together and pray Grace Before Meals. Consider meal prayer traditions, such as holding hands around the table while praying meal prayers.

T300 God Made Me

Look for additional suggestions for making the most of family meals in the pamphlet *Mealtime Matters,* published by Loyola Press.

- Display sacred objects in the home, such as a Bible, a crucifix, or an image of Mary with her Son.
- Celebrate Catholic holy days and feasts, as well as family members' birthdays and name days and anniversaries of Baptisms and First Holy Communions.
- Tell adapted Bible stories and pray psalm verses.
- Maintain open channels of communication.
- Look for opportunities for teaching in everyday experiences.

Part V: Discussion (15 minutes)

Divide the parents into groups and suggest one or more of the following questions for discussion:

- What are some of your memories of your earliest religious experiences?
- What are some teachable moments in everyday life when faith can be introduced?
- How does your family pray?
- What opportunities do you foresee for developing your child's faith?
- In what practical ways can your child see faith lived in your family?
- What religious traditions do you have at home? What ideas do you have for starting some?
- What difficulties might you meet in fostering faith in your child?

Conclude the discussion time by asking volunteers to describe their hopes for their child as they participate in this year's preschool program.

Part VI: Closing (10 minutes)

A Evaluation

- Ask the parents which part of the meeting they found most valuable. Provide an evaluation form with a checklist showing the various parts of the meeting and ask for feedback. Encourage additional comments and use the responses to improve future meetings. Visit www.loyolapress.com/preschool for a sample evaluation form.

B Closing prayer

Give parents a copy of the following prayer (available at www.loyolapress.com/preschool). Invite them to join you in a closing prayer.

- Leader: Let us pray for God's help as we seek to nurture the faith of our children and our families. Let us begin our prayer in the name of the Father, and of the Son, and of the Holy Spirit.
- All: Amen.
- Leader: Lord, you have given us the welcome responsibility of helping form our children into the wonderful persons you made them to be. Let your love flow through us to our children. Give us the courage and faith we need to be good parents. Enlighten us to know how to help our children be faithful Christians. Be with us as we guide them to know, love, and praise you. Amen.
- Reader: A reading from the Letter of Saint Paul to the Ephesians. (Ephesians 3:14–21)
- Leader: In a few moments of silence, let us reflect on our hopes for the children as they continue to grow in God's love. [*Pause.*] Let us pray for ourselves, our families and our children. Our response is "Lord, hear our prayer."
- May the children continue to grow in their awareness of God's love for them, we pray . . .
- May all parents and catechists be strengthened by God's grace, we pray . . .
- May each of us grow in faith to know the fullness of God's love, we pray . . .
- Leader: Let us pray together in the words that Jesus taught us: Our Father . . .
- Leader: God, bless us and keep us faithful to you. Bless the children you have given to our care and guide them in the ways of your love. Send your blessing on all parents and catechists and make us signs of your love. We pray this in Jesus' name.
- All: Amen.

MUSIC LIST

Song	Collection	Publisher
Chapter 1: I Can Hear		
Come, Meet Jesus	*Come, Meet Jesus*	Big Steps 4 U Publishing
Hip Hip Hooray Hippopotamus	*Fingerprints*	Big Steps 4 U Publishing
Jesus Loves the Little Children	*Wee Sing Bible Songs*	Price Stern Sloan
Jesus Loves Me	*Wee Sing Bible Songs*	Price Stern Sloan
God Made Me	*Wee Sing Bible Songs*	Price Stern Sloan
How Much God Loves Us	*Stories and Songs of Jesus*	OCP
Listen, Listen	*Hi God!*	OCP
Every Person Is a Gift of God	*Hi God 3*	OCP
What Is Your Name?	*Learning Basic Skills through Music Vol. 1*	Educational Activities
Chapter 2: I Can See		
God Is So Good	*Wee Sing Bible Songs*	Price Stern Sloan
And It Was Good	*Young People's Glory and Praise Vol. 2*	OCP
Beautiful	*Kid's Praise 4*	Maranatha
Colors	*Learning Basic Skills Through Music Vol. 1*	Educational Activities
Chapter 3: I Can Smell		
Oh, How I Love Jesus	*Hi God!*	OCP
Say to the Lord, I Love You	*Kid's Praise 2*	Maranatha
Chapter 4: I Can Touch		
Touch	*Getting to Know Myself*	Educational Activities
Celebrate God	*Hi God!*	OCP
Chapter 5: I Can Taste		
Love the Lord Your God	*Come, Meet Jesus*	Big Steps 4 U Publishing
It Is Good	*Big Steps for Little Feet*	Big Steps 4 U Publishing
God Made Me	*Wee Sing Bible Songs*	Price Stern Sloan
Anatome	*Music for Kids Vol. 1: Best of Joe Wise*	GIA
The Epic of Peanut Butter and Jelly	*Music for Kids Vol. 1: Best of Joe Wise*	GIA
I Am Wonderfully Made	*Sing a Song of Joy*	WLP
Chapter 6: I Can Help		
Helping	*Sing a Song of Joy*	WLP
God Has Made Us a Family	*Hi God 3*	OCP
Yes, We Will Do What Jesus Says	*Stories and Songs of Jesus*	OCP
God's Love	*Big Steps for Little Feet*	Big Steps 4 U Publishing
Chapter 7: I Can Care		
Water	*Sing a Song of Joy*	WLP

MUSIC LIST

Song	Collection	Publisher
Chapter 8: I Can Clean		
Brush Your Teeth	Singable Songs for the Very Young	Rounder
Chapter 9: I Can Share		
Sharing Comes 'Round Again	Fingerprints	Big Steps 4 U Publishing
Sharing Song	Singable Songs for the Very Young	Rounder
Sharing	Mugwumps & Important Things	Jennie Flack
Chapter 10: I Can Smile		
Count It All Joy	Big Steps for Little Feet	Big Steps 4 U Publishing
Everywhere	Big Steps for Little Feet	Big Steps 4 U Publishing
My Pout Can't Come Out	Fingerprints	Big Steps 4 U Publishing
Down in My Heart	Wee Sing Bible Songs	Price Stern Sloan
Joy, Joy, Joy	Hi God!	OCP
The Joy of the Lord	Hi God!	OCP
Jesus Loves the Little Children	Stories and Songs of Jesus	OCP
Show Me Your Smile	Music for Kids Vol. 1: Best of Joe Wise	GIA
Chapter 11: I Can Talk		
How Much God Loves Us	Stories and Songs of Jesus	OCP
Talk to You	Come, Meet Jesus	Big Steps 4 U Publishing
Chapter 12: I Can Pray		
Praise Him, Praise Him	Wee Sing Bible Songs	Price Stern Sloan
Jesus, I Will Stay with You	Stories and Songs of Jesus	OCP
Thank You, Lord	Hi God!	OCP
Talk to You	Come, Meet Jesus	Big Steps 4 U Publishing
It Is Good	Big Steps for Little Feet	Big Steps 4 U Publishing
Chapter 13: I Can Sing		
Giant Love Ball Song	Hi God!	OCP
Old MacDonald Had a Band	Singable Songs for the Very Young	Rounder
Say to the Lord, I Love You	Kid's Praise 2	Maranatha
Chapter 14: I Can Laugh		
My Pout Can't Come Out	Fingerprints	Big Steps 4 U Publishing
Joy, Joy, Joy	Hi God!	OCP
The Joy of the Lord	Hi God!	OCP
Down by the Bay	Singable Songs for the Very Young	Rounder
Aikendrum	Singable Songs for the Very Young	Rounder
Down in My Heart	Wee Sing Bible Songs	Price Stern Sloan

Music List **T303**

MUSIC LIST

Song	Collection	Publisher
Chapter 15: I Can Celebrate		
What a Miracle	*Walter the Waltzing Worm*	Educational Activities
Love the Lord Your God	*Come, Meet Jesus*	Big Steps 4 U Publishing
Celebration Song	*Big Steps for Little Feet*	Big Steps 4 U Publishing
Let's All Have a Party	*Take Out Your Crayons*	WLP
Celebrate God	*Hi God!*	OCP
Chapter 16: I Can Move		
Walk Like Jesus	*Fingerprints*	Big Steps 4 U Publishing
I Love to Take a Walk	*Wee Sing Bible Songs*	Price Stern Sloan
Sammy	*Getting to Know Myself*	Educational Activities
Chapter 17: I Can Play		
God Made Mud	*Take Out Your Crayons*	WLP
God Likes to Play	*Take Out Your Crayons*	WLP
Thank You, Lord	*Stories and Songs of Jesus*	OCP
Mr. Sun	*Singable Songs for the Very Young*	Rounder
Chapter 18: I Can Work		
Thank You, Lord	*Stories and Songs of Jesus*	OCP
All Your Gifts of Life	*Hi God 2*	OCP
Chapter 19: I Can Make Things		
God Did	*Come, Meet Jesus*	Big Steps 4 U Publishing
All Your Gifts of Life	*Hi God 2*	OCP
Hip Hip Hooray Hippopotamus	*Fingerprints*	Big Steps 4 U Publishing
Chapter 20: I Can Grow		
Giant Love Ball Song	*Hi God!*	OCP
I Wonder If I'm Growing	*Singable Songs for the Very Young*	Rounder
Growing	*Learning Basic Skills Through Music Vol. 1*	Educational Activities
Chapter 21: I Can Feel		
Goobers	*Big Steps for Little Feet*	Big Steps 4 U Publishing
Everywhere	*Big Steps for Little Feet*	Big Steps 4 U Publishing
My Pout Can't Come Out	*Fingerprints*	Big Steps 4 U Publishing
Take Out Your Crayons	*Take Out Your Crayons*	WLP
Jesus Always Helps Us	*Stories and Songs of Jesus*	OCP
Feelings	*Getting to Know Myself*	Educational Activities
You Are Always with Me	*Rise Up and Sing 2d edition*	OCP
Wherever I Am, God Is	*Hi God 3*	OCP
Show Me Your Smile	*Music for Kids Vol. 1: Best of Joe Wise*	GIA

God Made Me

MUSIC LIST

Song	Collection	Publisher
Chapter 22: I Can Wish		
New Hope	*Hi God 2*	OCP
Jesus Loves the Little Children	*Stories and Songs of Jesus*	OCP
People Worry	*Stories and Songs of Jesus*	OCP
Chapter 23: I Can Learn		
I Am Marvelous	*Take Out Your Crayons*	WLP
What God Is Like	*Hi God 2*	OCP
Chapter 24: I Can Pretend		
Come Along with Me to Jesus	*Hi God 2*	OCP
If I Were a Butterfly	*Hi God 2*	OCP
Giant Love Ball Song	*Hi God!*	OCP
Chapter 25: I Can Love		
Jesus Cares for Everyone	*Come, Meet Jesus*	Big Steps 4 U Publishing
Love the Lord Your God	*Come, Meet Jesus*	Big Steps 4 U Publishing
God's Love	*Big Steps for Little Feet*	Big Steps 4 U Publishing
Don't Look for Jesus in the Sky	*I See a New World*	WLP
I'll Need a Friend Like You	*Take Out Your Crayons*	WLP
Yes, We Will Do What Jesus Says	*Stories and Songs of Jesus*	OCP
The Greatest Gift	*Young People's Glory and Praise Vol. 2*	OCP
I Am Wonderfully Made	*Sing a Song of Joy*	WLP

MUSIC LIST

Special Seasons and Days

Song	Collection	Publisher
Halloween/Feast of All Saints		
Halloween Is Coming	My Toes Are Starting to Wiggle	Miss Jackie Music Company
What Do You Like about Halloween?	My Toes Are Starting to Wiggle	Miss Jackie Music Company
Advent		
An Angel Came from Heaven	Stories and Songs of Jesus	OCP
Alleluia! Hurry, the Lord Is Near	Rise Up and Sing 2d edition	OCP
Christmas		
The Little Baby	Big Steps for Little Feet	Big Steps 4 U Publishing
Glory to God	Stories and Songs of Jesus	OCP
Silent Night	Rise Up and Sing 2d edition	OCP
O Come, Little Children	Rise Up and Sing 2d edition	OCP
Children, Run Joyfully	Rise Up and Sing 2d edition	OCP
Lent		
God's Love	Sing a Song of Joy!	WLP
Easter		
Easter Rise Up	Come, Meet Jesus	Big Steps 4 U Publishing
Jesus Lives!	Stories and Songs of Jesus	OCP
We Believe	Stories and Songs of Jesus	OCP
Pentecost		
Go Now in Peace	Singing Our Faith	GIA
Prayer of Peace	Singing Our Faith	GIA
Peace Is Flowing Like a River	Hi God 2	OCP
Thanksgiving		
It Is Good	Big Steps for Little Feet	Big Steps 4 U Publishing
Thank You, Lord	Hi God!	OCP
Things I'm Thankful For	Holiday Magic	Hap Palmer Music
Valentine's Day		
Give It Away	Fingerprints	Big Steps 4 U Publishing
What Makes Love Grow?	Hi God!	OCP
Be My Friend	Getting to Know Myself	Educational Activities

God Made Me

MUSIC LIST

Song	Collection	Publisher
Mother's Day		
Yes, We Will Do What Jesus Says	*Stories and Songs of Jesus*	OCP
Immaculate Mary	*Rise Up and Sing 2d edition*	OCP
Father's Day		
Father, We Thank Thee	*Wee Sing Bible Songs*	Price Stern Sloan
God Is Our Father	*Hi God!*	OCP
What God Is Like	*Hi God 2*	OCP
Going to the Zoo	*Folk Song Carnival*	Hap Palmer Music
Hush, Little Baby	*A Child's World of Lullabies*	Hap Palmer Music
Birthdays		
How Much God Loves Us	*Stories and Songs of Jesus*	OCP
Every Person Is a Gift of God	*Hi God 3*	OCP
I Am Wonderfully Made	*Sing a Song of Joy*	WLP
I Am Marvelous	*Take Out Your Crayons*	WLP
Last Class/Summer		
Take My Hand	*Stories and Songs of Jesus*	OCP
You Are Always with Me	*Rise Up and Sing 2d edition*	OCP
Wherever I Am, God Is	*Hi God 3*	OCP

HOMEMADE MATERIALS

Flannel Board

Cover a sheet of cardboard with flannel. Attach sandpaper or felt strips to the back of pictures.

PAINT

Simple Finger Paint

Add tempera paint to liquid starch.

Finger Paint

- 2 cups flour
- 2 teaspoons salt
- 3 cups cold water
- 2 cups hot water
- food coloring or powdered tempera

Combine flour, salt, and cold water and beat until smooth. Add hot water and boil mixture, stirring constantly until clear. Beat until smooth. Mix in color.

Cornstarch Finger Paint

- 3 tablespoons sugar
- ½ cup cornstarch
- 2 cups cold water
- food coloring or powdered tempera

Combine sugar, cornstarch, and water. Cook over low heat, stirring constantly until mixture thickens. Let cool. Add coloring.

Soap Flake Finger Paint

- 1 cup cornstarch
- 2 cups cold water
- 2 envelopes unflavored gelatin
- 1 cup soap flakes
- food coloring or powdered tempera

Dissolve the cornstarch in 1½ cups cold water. Soften gelatin in remaining cold water and add to cornstarch mixture. Cook over medium heat, stirring occasionally until mixture is thick. Stir in soap flakes. Add coloring. Store in an airtight container.

Easy Soap Flake Finger Paint

- ½ cup soap chips
- 6 cups water
- 1 cup liquid starch
- powdered tempera

Dissolve soap chips in water. Mix water with starch. Add tempera.

Easiest Soap Flake Finger Paint

Mix soap flakes with a little water. Beat with an eggbeater. Add color.

Face Paint

- 1 cup solid vegetable shortening
- 1 cup cornstarch
- water (if necessary)
- food coloring

Mix shortening and cornstarch until smooth. If thick, add water; if thin, add shortening. Add food coloring. Sealed in plastic and refrigerated, this paint will keep for three days.

God Made Me

HOMEMADE MATERIALS

CLAY AND DOUGH

Uncooked Modeling Dough

- 3 cups flour
- 1 cup salt
- 1 cup water with coloring
- 1 tablespoon oil
- 1 tablespoon alum (as a preservative)

Mix dry ingredients. Add water and oil gradually.

Reusable Clay

- 2 tablespoons oil
- 1 cup water
- food coloring
- 1½ cups salt
- 4 cups flour

Mix oil, water, coloring. Mix salt and flour. Add water mixture to salt and flour. Knead. Store in plastic bags or sealed container.

Cooked Modeling Dough

- 1 cup cornstarch
- 2 cups baking soda
- 1¼ cups water
- food coloring or powdered tempera

Combine cornstarch, baking soda, water, and coloring. Cook over medium heat until thick. Cool and knead.

Baker's Clay

- 1 cup salt
- 4 cups flour
- 1½ cups water
- liquid tempera

Mix salt and flour with hands, adding water. Knead five minutes. Add liquid tempera. Bake finished products on foil-covered sheets at 350°F until hard and brown.

Salt Ceramic

- 1 cup salt
- ½ cup cornstarch
- ⅔ cup water
- food coloring

Combine ingredients. Cook over medium heat and stir until thick. Remove from heat. Knead in coloring. Refrigerate.

Cooked Play Dough

- 1 cup flour
- ½ cup salt
- 1 cup water
- 1 tablespoon cooking oil
- 1 teaspoon cream of tartar
- food coloring

Mix ingredients except for food coloring. Cook the mixture over medium heat until it forms a ball. Knead it on waxed paper. Store dough in an airtight container or plastic bag. Shape the dough into balls. Poke a deep hole in each and add a drop or two of food coloring. The children will be surprised to see the dough change color as they work with it.

Uncooked Play Dough

- 2 cups flour
- 1 cup salt
- 6 teaspoons alum
- 2 tablespoons salad oil
- 1 cup water
- food coloring or tempera paint

Mix all ingredients.

Homemade Materials   **T309**

HOMEMADE MATERIALS

Finger Gelatin
- 4 envelopes unflavored gelatin
- 3 packages (3-ounce size) flavored gelatin
- 4 cups boiling water

Combine gelatins. Add water and stir until dissolved. Pour into 9-inch by 13-inch baking pans. Chill. Cut with a cookie cutter. Eat with fingers.

BUBBLES

Bubbles
- ¼ cup dishwashing liquid
- ½ cup water
- 2 drops glycerin
- 1 drop food coloring

Stir the ingredients. Store the mixture in a tightly closed container.

Giant Bubbles
- 6 cups water
- 2 cups dishwashing liquid
- 1 cup corn syrup

Mix the ingredients about four hours ahead of time. Pour the solution into shallow pans. Make a wand with about a 6-inch diameter out of pipe cleaners or wire coat hangers with the sharp ends covered. Dip the wand in the solution and wave it once with a long, sweeping motion. Let the children chase the bubbles.

Alternative Recipe
- 1 gallon water
- ¼ cup dishwashing liquid
- 1 tablespoon corn syrup

Mix the ingredients. Cut off the bottom of a plastic water bottle. Dip the large open end into the solution and blow into the mouth of the water bottle.

Warning: The solution may damage carpeting, floors, and grass.

DIRECTORY OF SUPPLIERS

Ave Maria Press
P.O. Box 428
Notre Dame, IN 46556
(800) 282-1865
www.avemariapress.com

The Center for Learning
P.O. Box 910
2105 Evergreen Road
Villa Maria, PA 16155
(800) 767-9090
www.centerforlearning.org

Coronet, the Multimedia Company
A Division of Phoenix Learning
2349 Chaffee Dr.
St. Louis, MO 63146-3306
(800) 221-1274
www.phoenixlearninggroup.com

The Crossroad Publishing Company
16 Penn Plaza, Suite 1550
New York, NY 10001
(212) 868-1801
www.cpcbooks.com

Daughters of St. Paul
See Pauline Books & Media

Educational Activities, Inc.
P.O. Box 87
Baldwin, NY 11510
(800) 797-3223
www.edact.com

Franciscan Communications
See St. Anthony Messenger Press

Liguori Publications
One Liguori Drive
Liguori, MO 63057-9999
(800) 325-9521
www.liguori.org

Liturgical Press
Saint John's Abbey
P.O. Box 7500
Collegeville, MN 56321-7500
(800) 858-5450
www.litpress.org

Liturgy Training Publications
1800 N. Hermitage Avenue
Chicago, IL 60622-1101
(800) 933-1800
www.ltp.org

Live Oak Media
P.O. Box 652
Pine Plains, NY 12567-0652
(800) 788-1121
www.liveoakmedia.com

Loyola Press
3441 N. Ashland Avenue
Chicago, IL 60657
(800) 621-1008
www.loyolapress.org

National Catholic Educational Association
1077 30th Street, NW, Suite 100
Washington, DC 20007-3852
(800) 711-6232
www.ncea.org

National Conference for Catechetical Leadership
125 Michigan Ave., NE
Washington, DC 20017
(202) 884-9753
www.nccl.org

New City Press
202 Cardinal Rd.
Hyde Park, NY 12538
(800) 462-5980
www.newcitypress.com

Oblate Media and Communication
4126 Seven Hills Dr.
St. Louis, MO 63033
(800) 233-4629
www.videoswithvalues.org

Orbis Books
Price Building
Box 302
Maryknoll, NY 10545-0302
(800) 258-5838
www.maryknollmall.org

Pauline Books & Media
50 Saint Paul's Ave.
Boston, MA 02130
(800) 876-4463
www.pauline.org

Paulist Press
997 Macarthur Boulevard
Mahwah, NJ 07430-9990
(800) 218-1903
www.paulistpress.com

Paulist Productions
Box 1057
17575 Pacific Coast Highway
Pacific Palisades, CA 90272
(310) 454-0688
www.paulistproductions.org

DIRECTORY OF SUPPLIERS

Resource Publications, Inc.
160 E. Virginia St. #290
San Jose, CA 95112
(888) 273-7782
www.rpinet.com

Sacred Heart Kids' Club
869 South Rimpau Blvd.
Los Angeles, CA 90005
(323) 935-2372
www.sacredheartsisters.com/
sacredheartkidsclub

St. Anthony Messenger Press
Franciscan Communications
28 W. Liberty Street
Cincinnati, OH 45202-6498
(800) 488-0488
www.catalog.americancatholic.org

Sheed & Ward
Rowman & Littlefield Publishers, Inc.
4501 Forbes Blvd., Suite 200
Lanham, MD 20706
(800) 462-6420
www.rowmanlittlefield.com/Sheed

Sophia Institute Press
P.O. Box 5284
Manchester, NH 03108
(800) 888-9344
www.sophiainstitute.com

Spoken Arts, Inc.
195 South White Rock Road
Holmes, NY 12531
(800) 326-4090
www.spokenartsmedia.com

Treehaus Communications, Inc.
P.O. Box 249
906 West Loveland Ave.
Loveland, OH 45140
(800) 638-4287
www.treehaus1.com

Twenty-Third Publications
1 Montauk Ave., Suite 200
New London, CT 06320
(800) 572-0788
www.twentythirdpublications.com

United States Conference of Catholic Bishops
3211 Fourth Street, NE
Washington, DC 20017
(800) 235-8722
www.usccbpublishing.org

Vision Video
P.O. Box 540
Worcester, PA 19490
(800) 523-0226
www.visionvideo.com

Weston Woods Studios
143 Main Street
Norwalk, CT 06851
(800) 243-5020
www.teacher.scholastic.com/products/
westonwoods

MUSIC SOURCES

G.I.A. Publications, Inc.
7404 South Mason Avenue
Chicago, IL 60638
(800) 442-1358
www.giamusic.com

Mary Lu Walker Albums & Songbooks (MLW)
http://home.stny.rr.com/maryluwalker

Oregon Catholic Press Publications (OCP)
P.O. Box 18030
Portland, OR 97218-0030
(800) 548-8749
www.ocp.org

Pauline Books & Media
50 Saint Paul's Ave.
Boston, MA 02130
(800) 876-4463
www.pauline.org

World Library Publications (WLP)
J.S. Paluch Company, Inc.
3708 River Rd., Suite 400
Franklin Park, IL 60131
(800) 566-6150
www.wlp.jspaluch.com

INDEX

SCRIPTURE

A

Acts of the Apostles 2:1–4, T206
Acts of the Apostles 2:22–36, T200
Acts of the Apostles 3:1–8, T106
Acts of the Apostles 3:2–8, T106
Acts of the Apostles 17:28, T106

C

Colossians 3:12–14, T156
1 Corinthians 11:1, T156
1 Corinthians 11:24, T194
1 Corinthians 12:24–27, T38
1 Corinthians 13:1–7, T168
1 Corinthians 15:1–28, T200
2 Corinthians 2:15, T18
2 Corinthians 4:17, T200

D

Deuteronomy 30:19–20, T236

E

Ecclesiastes 3:1, T242
Ecclesiastes 3:7, T72
Ephesians 3:14–19, T148
Ephesians 4:25–32, T72
Ephesians 4:32, T179
Ephesians 5:18–19, T84
Ephesians 5:18–20, T84, T212
Ephesians 5:25–27, T52
Ephesians 6:1–3, T224, T230
Exodus 15:19–21, T109
Ezekiel 36:25, T55

G

Galatians 3:26, T230
Galatians 4:6–7, T230
Galatians 5:22–23, T206
Genesis 1:1–31, T126
Genesis 1:27, T156
Genesis 1:28–31, T58
Genesis 1:29–31, T32
Genesis 1:31, T128
Genesis 2:1–3, T242
Genesis 2:3, T242
Genesis 2:15, T46
Genesis 17:15–19, T93
Genesis 18:1–15, T93
Genesis 21:1–7, T93

H

Hosea 2:21, T218

I

Isaiah 7:14, T182
Isaiah 11:8, T112
Isaiah 42:6, T218
Isaiah 43:1, T218, T236, T239
Isaiah 49:15, T224
Isaiah 49:15–16, T218
Isaiah 49:16, T222
Isaiah 54:10, T218

J

James 3:1–10, T72
James 3:2–5, T72
John 2:5, T4, T224
John 6:53–57, T30
John 9:1–11, T52
John 10:10, T203, T236
John 11:32–36, T142
John 12:24, T197
John 12:24,26 T194
John 13:34, T171
John 14:23, T218
John 15:11–12, T145
John 15:12, T168
John 15:12–14, T194
John 15:26–27, T206
John 16:22, T64
John 17:25–26, T230
John 19:26–27, T224
John 20, T200
John 20:19–23, T206
1 John 3:16–18, T194
1 John 4:7–8, T168
1 John 4:7–11, T218
1 John 4:7–12, T218
1 John 4:8, T218

K

1 Kings 17:7–16, T58, T63

L

Luke 1:26–31, T84
Luke 1:26–38, T182
Luke 1:31–32, T185
Luke 1:46–47, T87
Luke 2:1–16, T191
Luke 2:1–21, T188
Luke 2:8–14, T84
Luke 2:11, T188
Luke 2:14, T88
Luke 2:51, T226
Luke 2:52, T132, T136
Luke 5:12–13, T28
Luke 7:16, T188
Luke 9:35, T4
Luke 10:29–37, T38
Luke 10:30,33–34,37, T38
Luke 11:28, T4
Luke 15:8–10, T15
Luke 17:11–19, T212
Luke 18:35–42, T12
Luke 2:52, T132

M

Mark 1:2–8, T182
Mark 3:1–6, T64, T67
Mark 6:31, T112, T242
Mark 6:34–44, T100
Mark 10:13–16, T24
Mark 14:3–9, T22
Matthew 2:1–12, T188
Matthew 6:5–6, T78
Matthew 6:6, T81
Matthew 6:9, T233
Matthew 6:9–13, T78, T230
Matthew 7:7, T148
Matthew 7:11, T148, T151
Matthew 11:29, T156, T159
Matthew 13:3–9, T4
Matthew 13:34–35, T162
Matthew 16:24, T194
Matthew 17:5, T9
Matthew 19:13–15, T24
Matthew 20: 30–34, T41
Matthew 22:1–14, T96
Matthew 25:31–46, T38, T58
Matthew 25:35–36, T61
Matthew 28:20, T218

P

Philippians 1:9–11, T132
Philippians 3:8–10, T200
Philippians 4:6–7, T148
Proverbs 6:6–11, T118
Proverbs 8:12,22,30–31, T112
Proverbs 10:5, T118
Proverbs 17:22, T90
Psalm 5:2, T84
Psalm 8:2, T84
Psalm 8:4–7, T126
Psalm 18:2–3, T84
Psalm 22:12, T84
Psalm 23, T242
Psalm 23:2, T96
Psalm 23:4, T147
Psalm 23:5, T30
Psalm 25:5, T84
Psalm 34:9, T30
Psalm 34:18, T4
Psalm 37:3, T58
Psalm 51:3, T84
Psalm 51:4,9, T52
Psalm 51:9, T52
Psalm 51:17, T75
Psalm 89:2, T89
Psalm 90:17, T118, T120

Index **T313**

INDEX

Psalm 92:2, T89
Psalm 95:1–2, T84
Psalm 100:1–2, T64, T68
Psalm 104:13–14, T49
Psalm 111, T212
Psalm 111:1, T115, T116
Psalm 116:1–2, T84
Psalm 127:1, T126
Psalm 138:1, T215
Psalm 139, T236
Psalm 139:13–15, T236
Psalm 139:14, T162, T164
Psalm 145, T212
Psalm 145:8, T244
Psalm 150:4, T106

R
Revelation 4:8, T96
Revelation 4:11, T96
Revelation 5:12, T96
Revelation 7:11, T176
Revelation 21:22–22:5, T176
Romans 6:3–11, T194
Romans 8:19,22, T46

S
Sirach 30:22, T90

W
Wisdom 1:7, T209

GAMES

B
"Belly Laughs," T92

C
"Concentration," T215

D
"Drop the Clothespin," T117

F
"52 Pickup," T55
"Find the Coins," T15
"Follow the Leader" (to the tune of "The Farmer in the Dell"), T179
"Follow Your Nose," T21
"Frog Hop," T99

G
"God Loves You," T220

H
"Hot Potato," T29

I
"I Spy," T17, T155

J
"Jack-in-the-Box," T49

L
"Love Bug Tag," T171

M
"Mother Wants You," T227

N
"Name Game," T8

P
"Partners," T61
"Photographer," T67

S
"Silly Race," T93
"Squirrel in a Tree," T115

T
"Toss the Salad," T215
"Train, T109," T111

W
What If," T167
"What's Different?", T17

FINGER PLAYS

A
"Away Up High in the Apple Tree," T35

B
"Baby Chick," T202

F
Five Little Pumpkins, Sitting on a Gate, T181

G
"God Loves Me" (to the tune of "This Old Man"), T172, T198

I
"I Have Eyes So I Can See" (to the tune of "Mary Had a Little Lamb"), T16
"I'm Going on a Lion Hunt," T165
"I've a Mouth So I Can Taste" (to the tune of "Mary Had a Little Lamb"), T33
"I've a Nose So I Can Smell" (to the tune of "Mary Had a Little Lamb"), T22
"I've Two Hands So I Can Feel" (to the tune of "Mary Had a Little Lamb"), T28
"I Wiggle My Fingers," T83

J
"Johnny Pounds with One Hammer, One Hammer, One Hammer," T125

P
"Pitter–pat, Pitter–pat," T199
"Playful Kittens," T116

T
"This Is My Garden" (to the tune of "On Top of Old Smokey"), T196

W
"When I Was a Baby," T136

T314   God Made Me

INDEX

POEMS

B
"Being Special," T241
"Buttercup," T197

C
"Christmas Bells," T192

F
"Family Laughs," T95
"Fuzzy Wuzzy Was a Bear," T29

G
"God Is There," T245
"God Who's Near, You Gave Me Ears," T11

I
"I'm Glad the Sky Is Painted Blue," T50
"I See the Moon," T155

M
"Mary, My Mother in Heaven Above," T229
"Mom, You're with Me Night and Day," T228
"My Father," T233
"My Feelings," T147
"My Nose," T23

O
"One Potato, Two Potato", T158

R
"Rain, Rain, Go Away," T117

S
"Sharing Poem," T63

W
"What God Made," T129
"The Wind Tells Me," T211

SONGS

A
"Amen," T89
"Animal Fair," T95

B
"The Bear Went Over the Mountain," T17
"The Bus," T111

C
"Clap, Clap, Clap Your Hands," T147

D
"Did You Ever See a Carpenter, Carpenter, Carpenter?", T121
"Did You Ever See a Lassie?" T111
"Do Your Ears Hang Low?", T10

F
"Five Fat Turkeys," T217
"For Health and Strength," T82

G
"God Is So Good," T159
"God Loves Me" (to the tune of "This Old Man"), T172, T198
"God Made Me," T223
"Good News!" T205

H
"Happy Birthday," T240
"Head, Shoulders, Knees and Toes," T43

I
"I Can Run for I Have Life" (to the tune of "Mary Had a Little Lamb"), T203
"If You're Happy and You Know It," T69
"I Have Ears so I Can Hear" (to the tune of "Mary Had a Little Lamb"), T9
"I Have Eyes So I Can See" (to the tune of "Mary Had a Little Lamb"), T16
"I'm Gonna Sing When the Spirit Says Sing," T89
"It's Good to Give Thanks to the Lord," T216
"I've a Mouth so I Can Taste" (to the tune of "Mary Had a Little Lamb"), T33
"I've a Nose so I Can Smell" (to the tune of "Mary Had a Little Lamb"), T22
"I've Two Hands so I Can Feel" (to the tune of "Mary Had a Little Lamb"), T28

J
"The Jack-in-the-Box," T51

L
"Love Is Like a Ring," T185

M
"Mary Had a Baby," T190
Music List, T302
Music 'n Motion, T7, T10, T14, T16, T21, T23, T27, T29, T32, T34, T40, T44, T48, T50, T54, T56, T60, T62, T66, T68, T74, T76, T80, T83, T86, T88, T92, T94, T98, T102, T108, T110, T114, T116, T120, T123, T128, T130, T134, T137, T144, T146, T150, T154, T158, T160, T164, T166, T170, T172, T178, T180, T190, T192, T202, T204, T214, T216, T220, T222, T238, T240, T244, T246, T247–276

O
"Oh! The Pretty Butterflies," T205
"Oh We Thank You We Do" (to the tune of "Happy Birthday"), T216

T
"Ten in a Bed," T117
"This Is the Way We Dig the Soil" (to the tune of "Here We Go 'Round the Mulberry Bush"), T199
"This Is the Way We Pick Up Our Toys" (to the tune of "Here We Go 'Round the Mulberry Bush"), T41
"This Is the Way We Sweep the Floor" (to the tune of "Here We Go 'Round the Mulberry Bush"), T57
"This Old Man," T161

W
"What You Gonna Call Your Pretty Little Baby?", T193

ACKNOWLEDGMENTS

Photography OV-5 ©iStockphoto.com/Vladimir Melnikov, OV-7 ©iStockphoto.com/Craig Veltri, OV-8 ©iStockphoto.com/Monika Adamczyk, OV-12–OV-13 ©iStockphoto.com/René Mansi, OV-14 Jose Luis Pelaez/Iconica/Getty Images, OV-16 ©iStockphoto.com/Ekaterina Monakhova, T1 ©iStockphoto.com/Ekaterina Monakhova, T36(b) ©iStockphoto.com/lijlexmom, T37(t) ©iStockphoto.com/Jeffrey Zavitski, T70(t) ©iStockphoto.com/Yarinca, T70(b) ©iStockphoto.com/Kativ, T71(t) ©iStockphoto.com/Bulent Ince, T105(t) ©iStockphoto.com/Jason Reekie, T140(t) ©iStockphoto.com/Jan Tyler, T140(b) ©iStockphoto.com/xabicasa, T277 ©iStockphoto.com/René Mansi, T278 ©iStockphoto.com/Paul Tessier, T287(br) ©iStockphoto.com/KMITU, T308 ©iStockphoto.com/Ekaterina Monakhova, T309 ©iStockphoto.com/Dieter Hawlan, T327 ©iStockphoto.com/Nicole S. Young

Tapestry OV-176 ©2003 John Nava/Cathedral of Our Lady of the Angels, Los Angeles California

CHILD'S BOOK ART CREDITS

The stapler, glue bottle, and scissors icons throughout this book were illustrated by Kathryn Seckman Kirsch.

Unit 1 3 Phyllis Pollema–Cahill, 4(tl) iStockphoto.com/Emrah Turudu, 4(br) Anika Salsera, 4(ears) William Wise, 5 Claudine Gévry, 6 Dennis Hockerman, 8 Ginna Hirtenstein, 9 William Wise, 11 Claudine Gévry, 12(tl) Jupiter Images

Unit 2 21–22 Ginna Hirtenstein, 23 iStockphoto.com/Guillermo Lobo, 24 Phyllis Pollema–Cahill, 25 Nan Brooks, 26 (book stack) iStockphoto.com/Julie Deshaies, 26 (blue thongs) iStockphoto.com/Anne Clark, 28 (green towels) iStockphoto.com/Dawn Liljenquist, 29 Nan Brooks, 30 Nan Brooks

Unit 3 37 iStockphoto.com/Ekaterina Monakhova, 38 Phil Martin Photography, 40 Len Ebert, 41 Ginna Hirtenstein, 42 Ginna Hirtenstein, 43 Len Ebert, 45 Nan Brooks, 46(photo) iStockphoto.com/Justin Horrocks, 46(illustrations) Dora Leder, 47 Kathryn Seckman Kirsch, 49 Claudine Gévry, 50 iStockphoto.com/Anant Dummai, 51–52 Ethel Gold

Unit 4 54 William Wise, 55 Claudine Gévry, 56 Len Ebert, 57–58 Kristin Goeters, 60 Yoshi Miyake, 61–62 Dennis Hockerman, 65 Claudine Gévry, 66 William Wise, 67 iStockphoto.com/Karen Roach, 68(bottle) iStockphoto.com/Christine Balderas, 68(bed) iStockphoto.com/Mykola Velychko, 68(chair) iStockphoto.com/Simon Krzic, 69–70 Ginna Hirtenstein, 72 Kristin Goeters

Unit 5 73 Nan Brooks, 74 Nan Brooks, 75–76 Kristin Goeters, 78(illustrations) Nan Brooks, 79–80 Dennis Hockerman, 83 iStockphoto.com/Rosemarie Gearhart, 84 Meg Elliott Smith, 87 iStockphoto.com/Marzanna Syncerz, 88 Ethel Gold, 90(tl) iStockphoto.com/Nicole S. Young, 90(bl) Jupiter Images, 90(br) iStockphoto.com/Franky De Meyer

Special Lessons 93 Peter Dazeley/Getty Images, 94 Yoshi Miyake, 95 Ginna Hirtenstein, 96 Ginna Hirtenstein, 97 Phil Martin Photography, 99 Yoshi Miyake, 101(hands) Phil Martin Photography, 101(grass) iStockphoto.com/Helle Bro, 102(tl) Jupiter Images, 103 Dora Leder, 104 iStockphoto.com/Yiying Lu, 105 iStockphoto.com/Debi Bishop, 106(tr) iStockphoto.com/John Said, 106(bl) Jupiter Images, 106(br) iStockphoto.com/Slawomir Jastrzebski, 109(tl) iStockphoto.com/Nikolay Suslov, 109(tr) iStockphoto.com/Mikael Damkier, 110 Len Ebert, 111 Meg Elliott Smith, 112 iStockphoto.com/Bill Noll, 113 Phyllis Pollema–Cahill, 114 Meg Elliott Smith, 117 Phyllis Pollema–Cahill, 118(mother) iStockphoto.com/Justin Horrocks, 118(horses) iStockphoto.com/Eric Isselée, 121 iStockphoto.com/Marzanna Syncerz, 122 Claudine Gévry, 126 Meg Elliott Smith, 129 iStockphoto.com/Ron Chapple, 130(sun) iStockphoto.com/Luciade Salterain, 131 Susan Tolonen

Family Activity Booklet 133(tc,tr) Jupiter Images, 133(bl) iStockphoto.com/Achim Prill, 133(br) iStockphoto.com/Katuya Shima, 134(l) iStockphoto.com/Alexander Hafemann, 134(tr) iStockphoto.com/Danny Hooks, 134(br) Jupiter Images, 135(tl,bl) Meg Elliott Smith, 135(tr) iStockphoto.com/Sean Locke, 135(br) iStockphoto.com/David Hernandez, 136(bl) Meg Elliott Smith, 136(tr) iStockphoto.com/Nicole S. Young, 136(br) iStockphoto.com/Wojtek Kryczka, 137(bl) iStockphoto.com/Ivan Mateev, 137(br) Meg Elliott Smith, 138(tl) iStockphoto.com/Derek Thomas, 138(tr,br) Meg Elliott Smith, 139(bl,br) Meg Elliott Smith, 140(br) Jupiter Images

Art Credits 141–142(paint drips) iStockphoto.com/Slavoljub Pantelic

Perforated Cards A(window, curtains) iStockphoto.com/Jolande Gerritsen, B Juan Castillo, C Juan Castillo, E(sun, moon, stars) iStockphoto.com/Prohor Gabrusenoc, G(bells) Jupiter Images, G(musical notes) iStockphoto.com/Maria Ahlfors, H(dog tag) Jupiter Images, H(illustration) Kristin Goeters, I Kristin Goeters, L (butterfly) William Wise

Photos and illustrations not acknowledged above are either owned by Loyola Press or from royalty-free sources including but not limited to Agnus, Alamy, Comstock, Corbis, Creatas, Fotosearch, Getty Images, Imagestate, iStock, Jupiter Images, Punchstock, Rubberball, and Veer. Loyola Press has made every effort to locate the copyright holders for the cited works used in this publication and to make full acknowledgment for their use. In the case of any omissions, the Publisher will be pleased to make suitable acknowledgments in future editions.

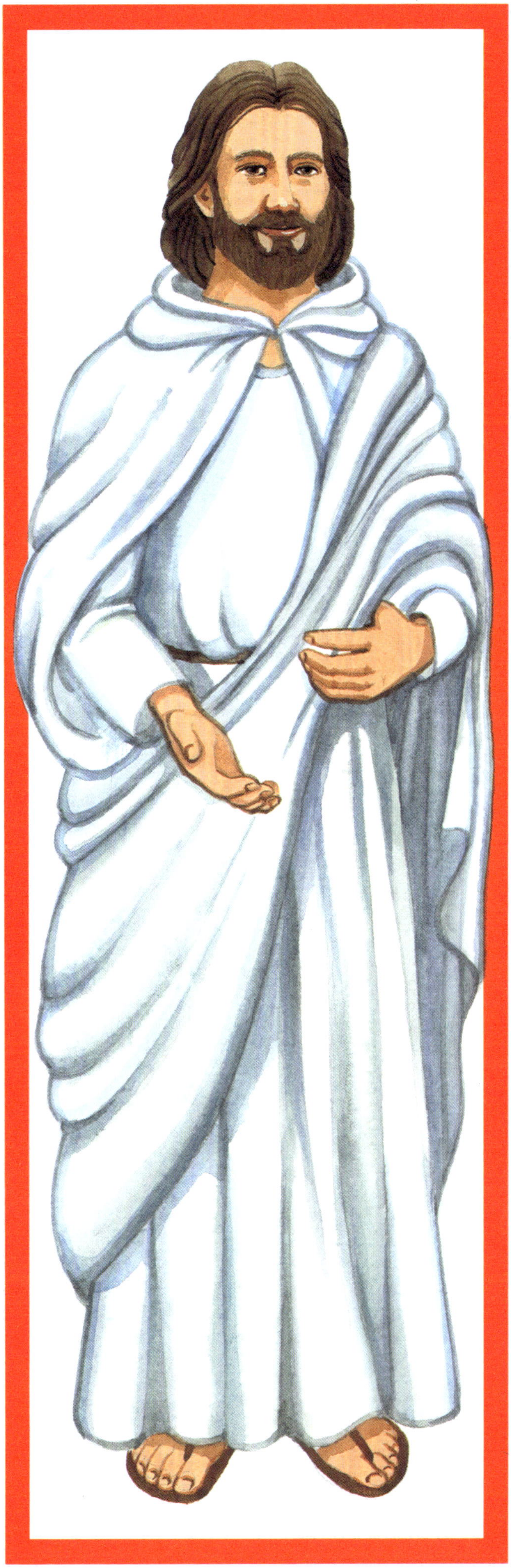

#1 Jesus
© LoyolaPress.

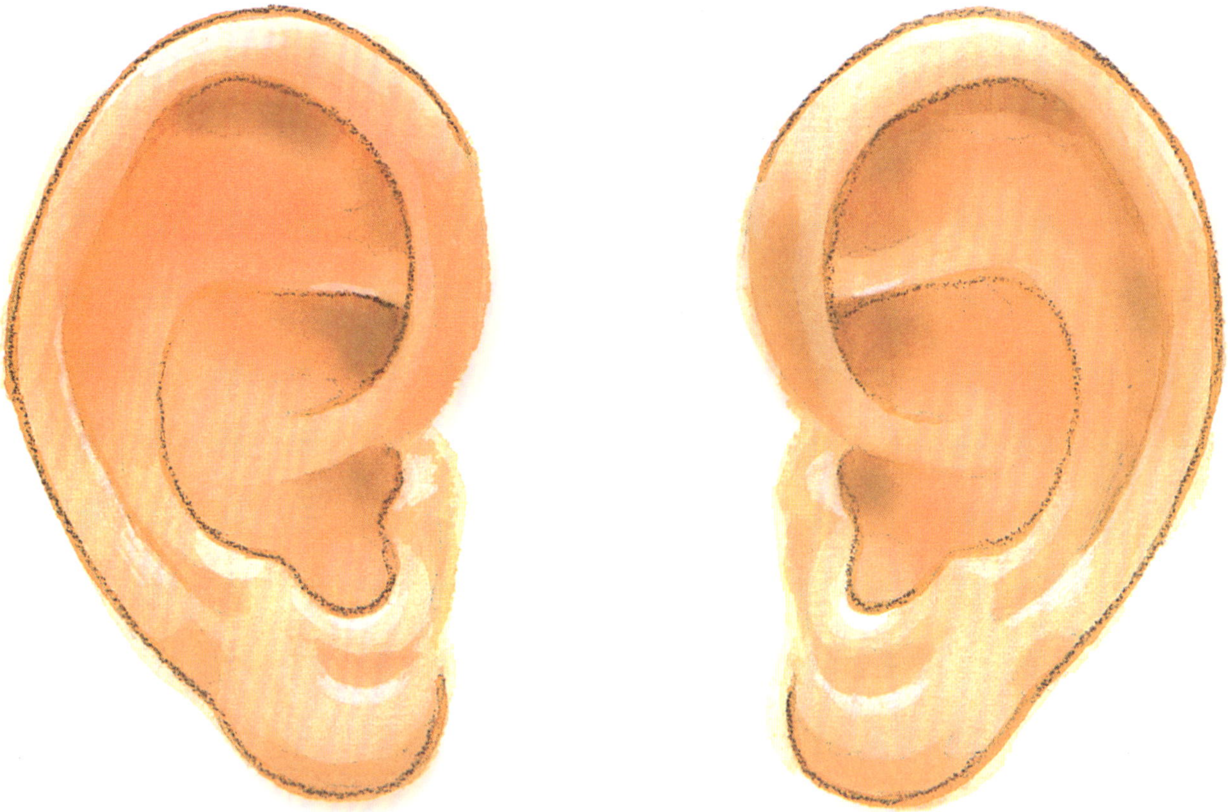

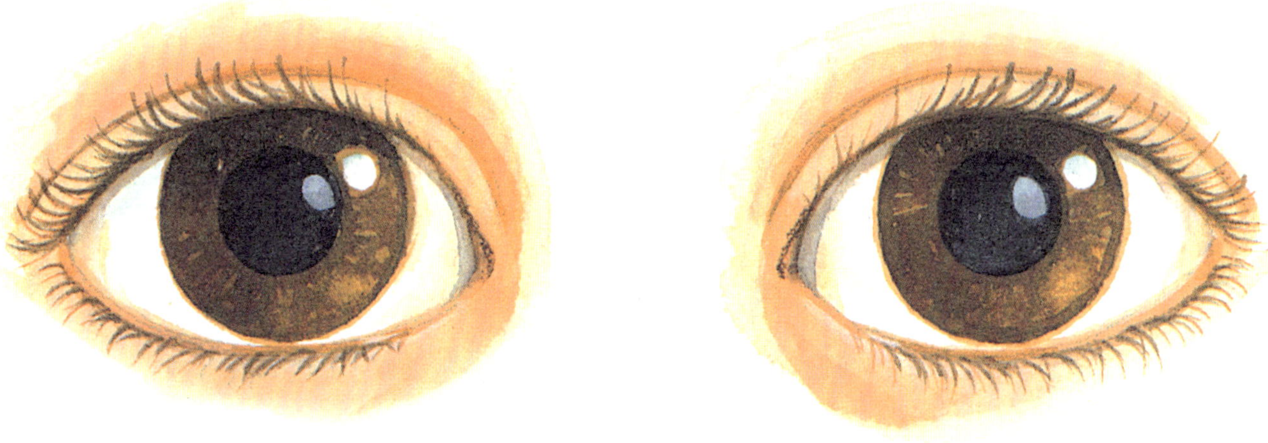

#2 ears
© LOYOLA PRESS.

#3 eyes
© LOYOLA PRESS.

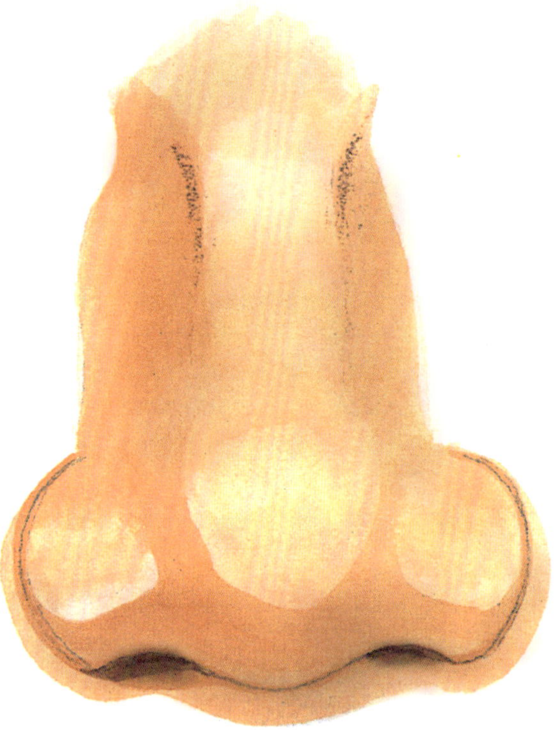
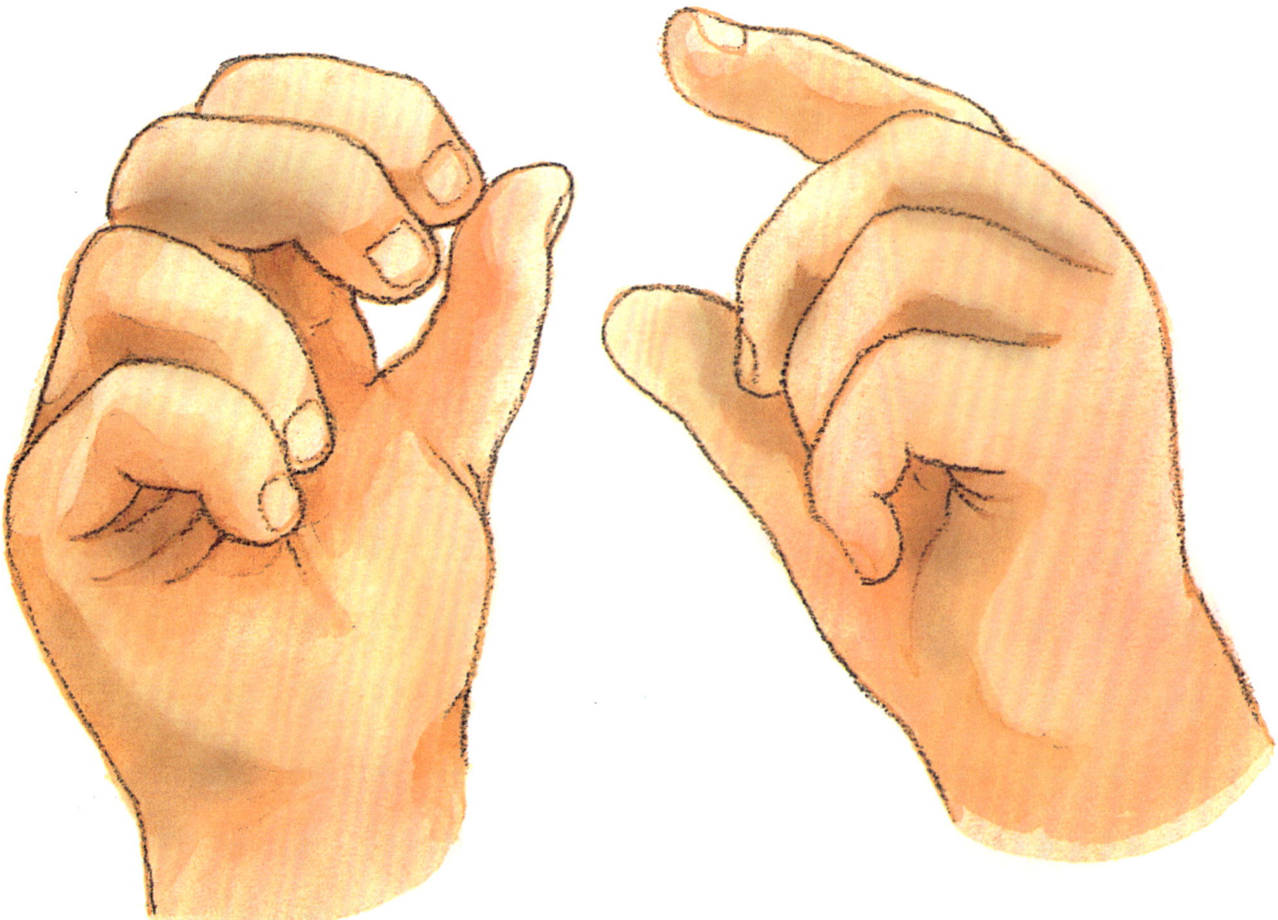

#4 nose
©LoyolaPress.

#5 hands
©LoyolaPress.

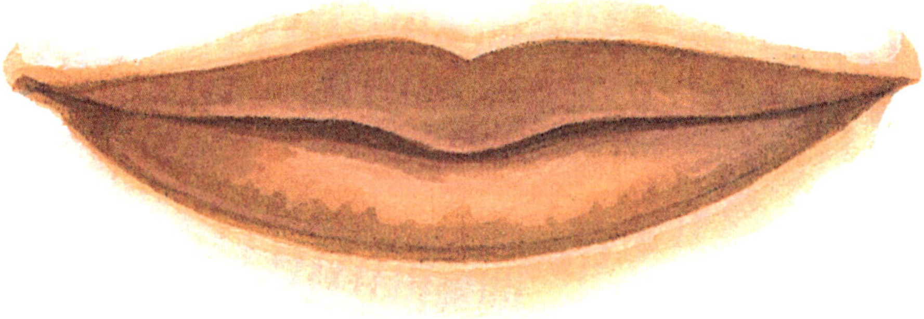

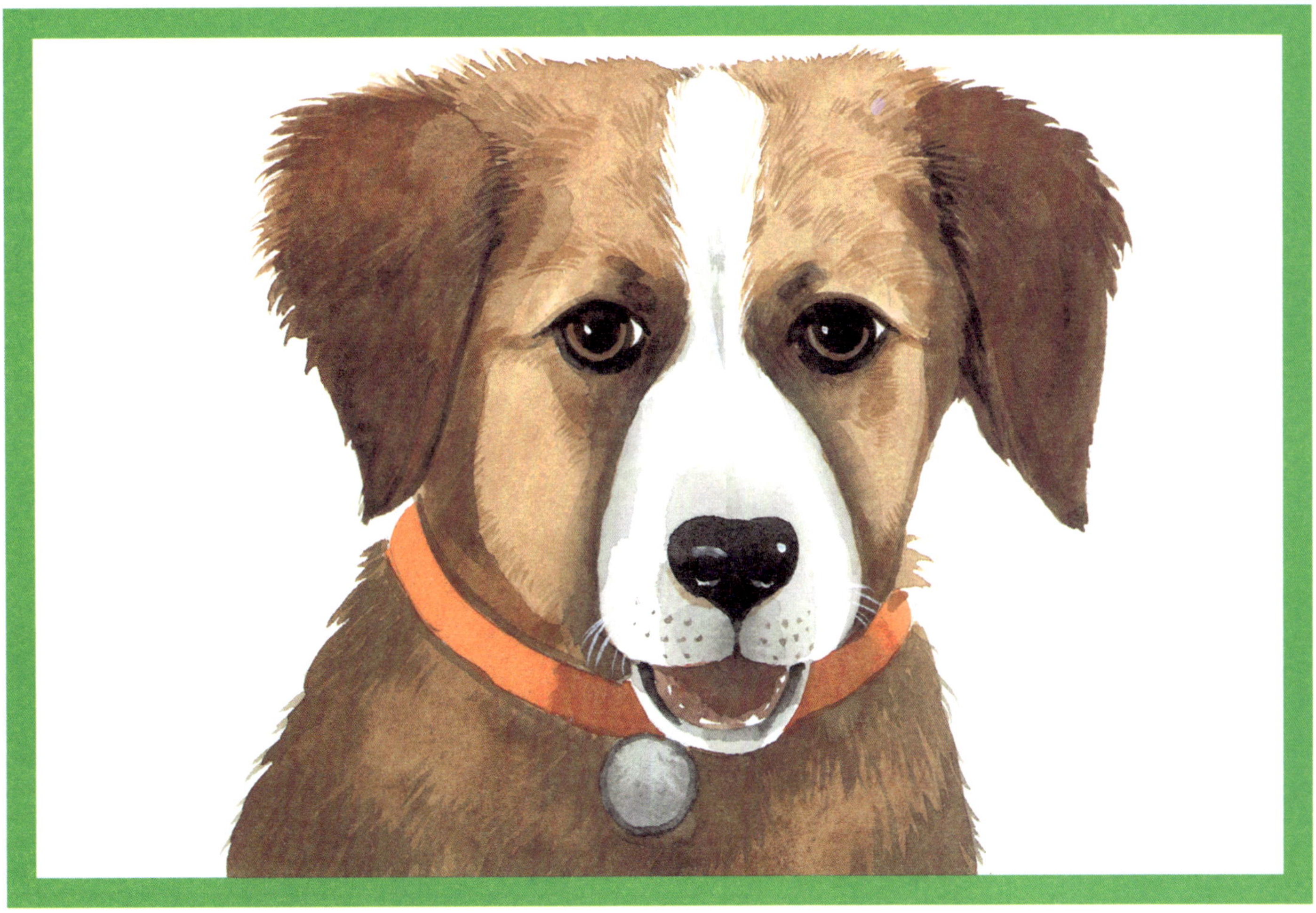

#6 mouth
© LOYOLA PRESS.

#7 dog
© LOYOLA PRESS.

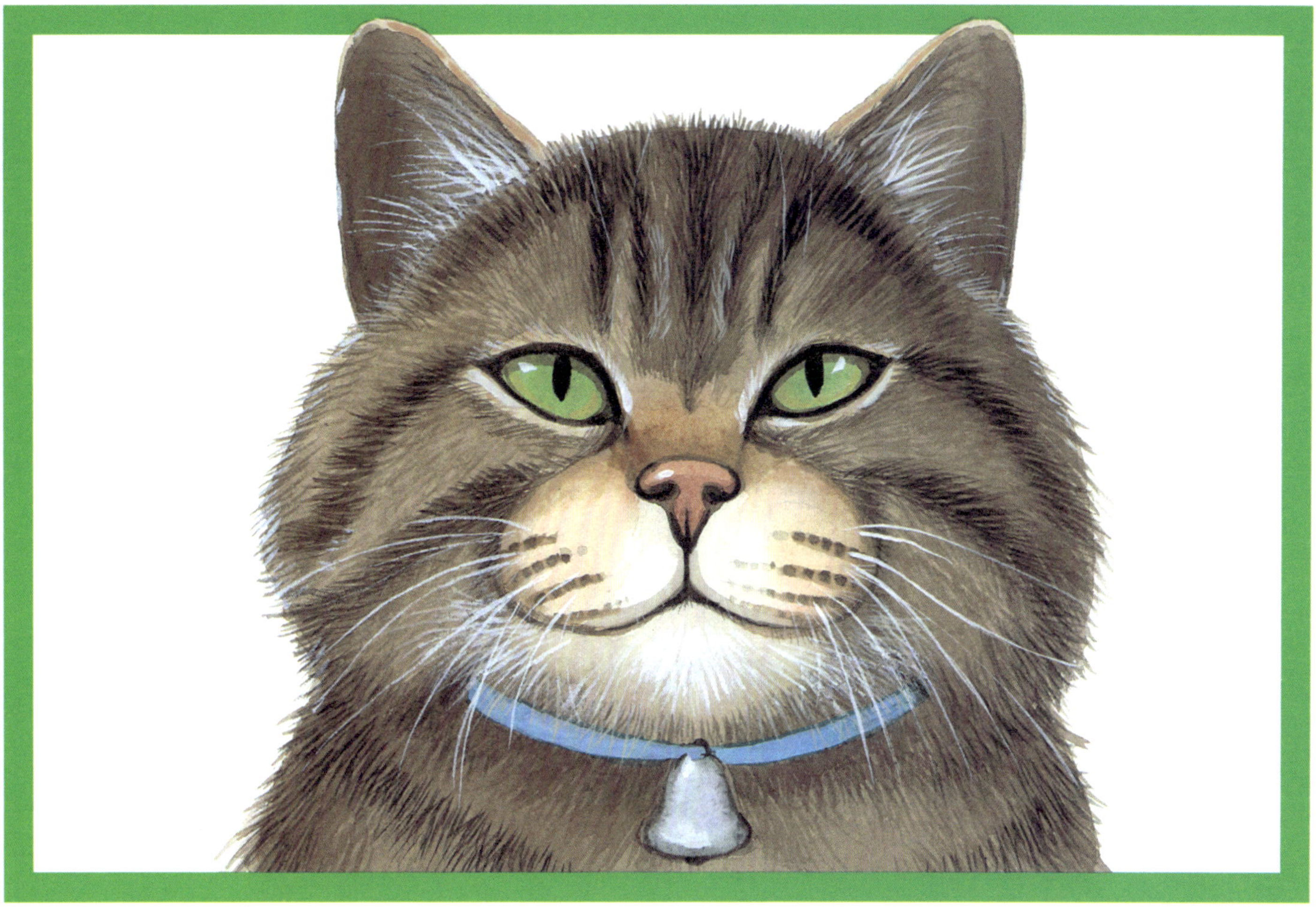

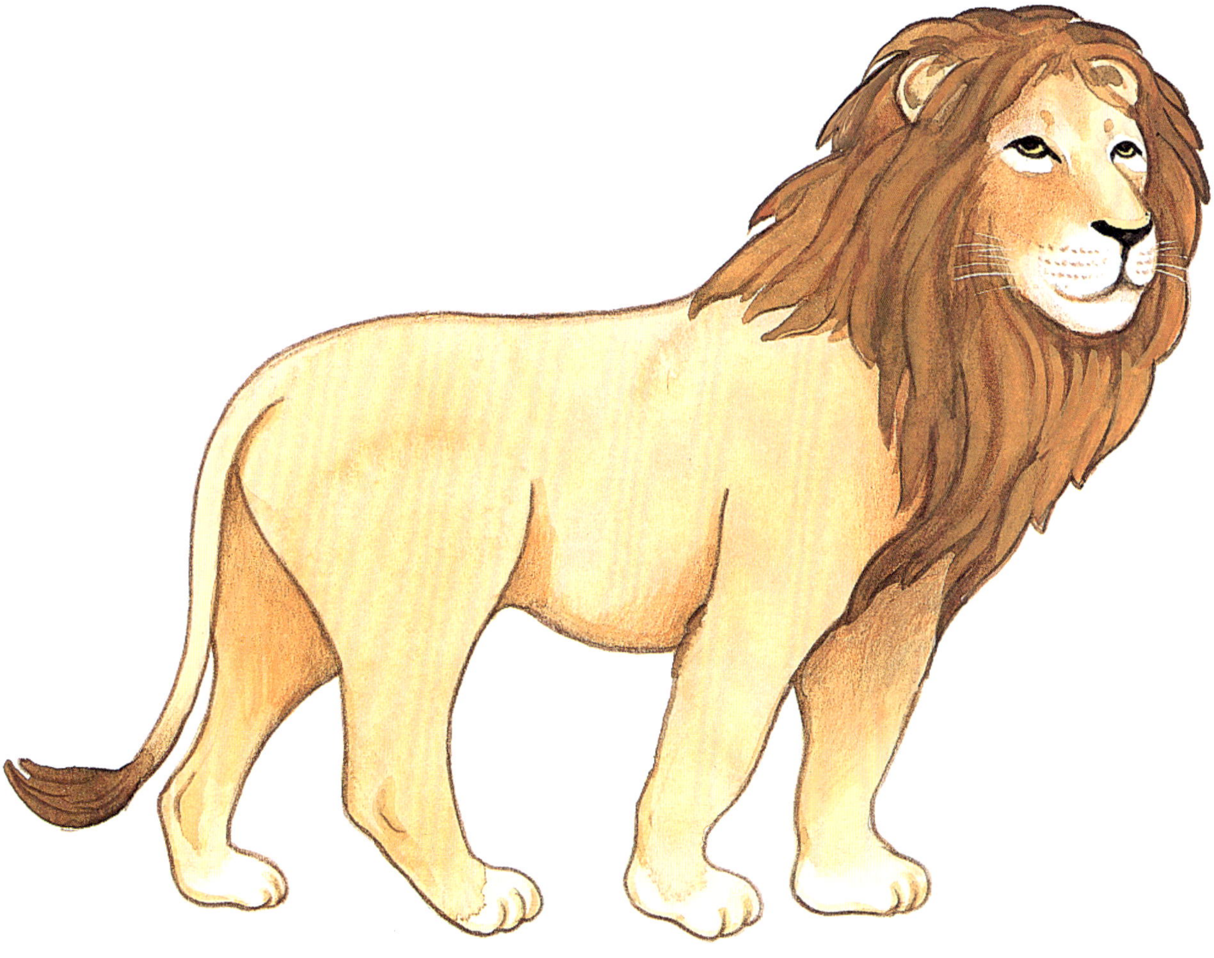

#8 cat

©LoyolaPress.

#9 lion

©LoyolaPress.

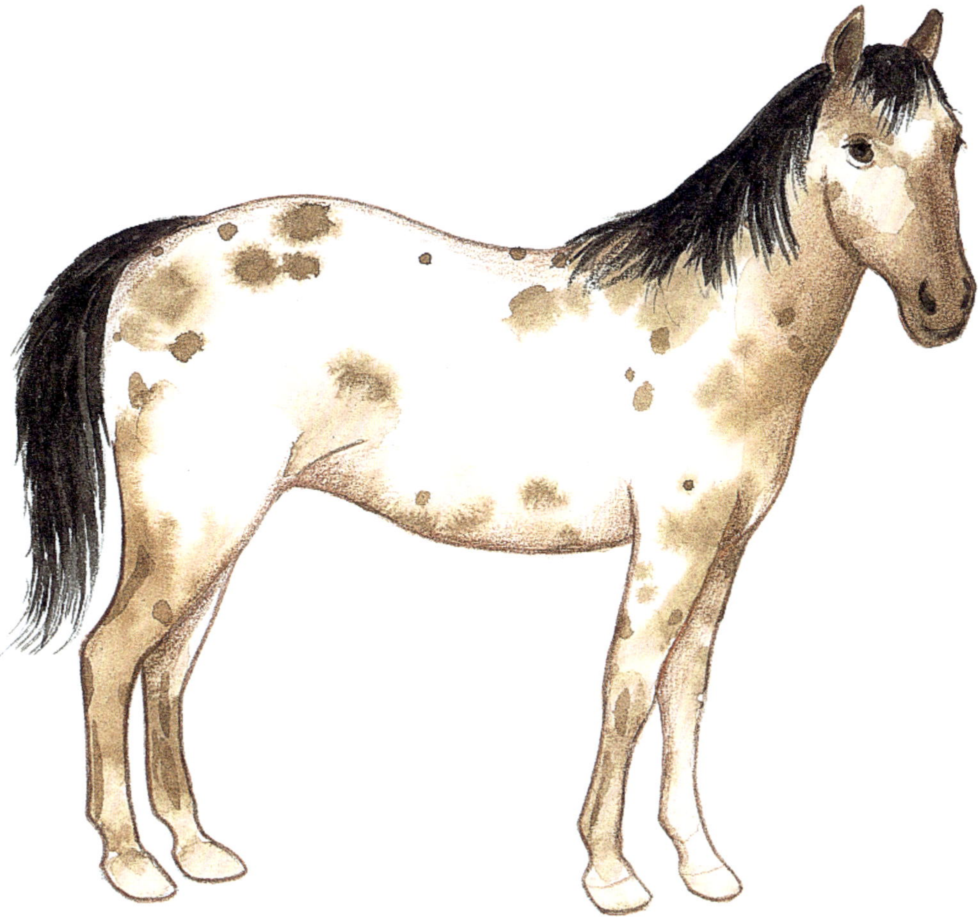

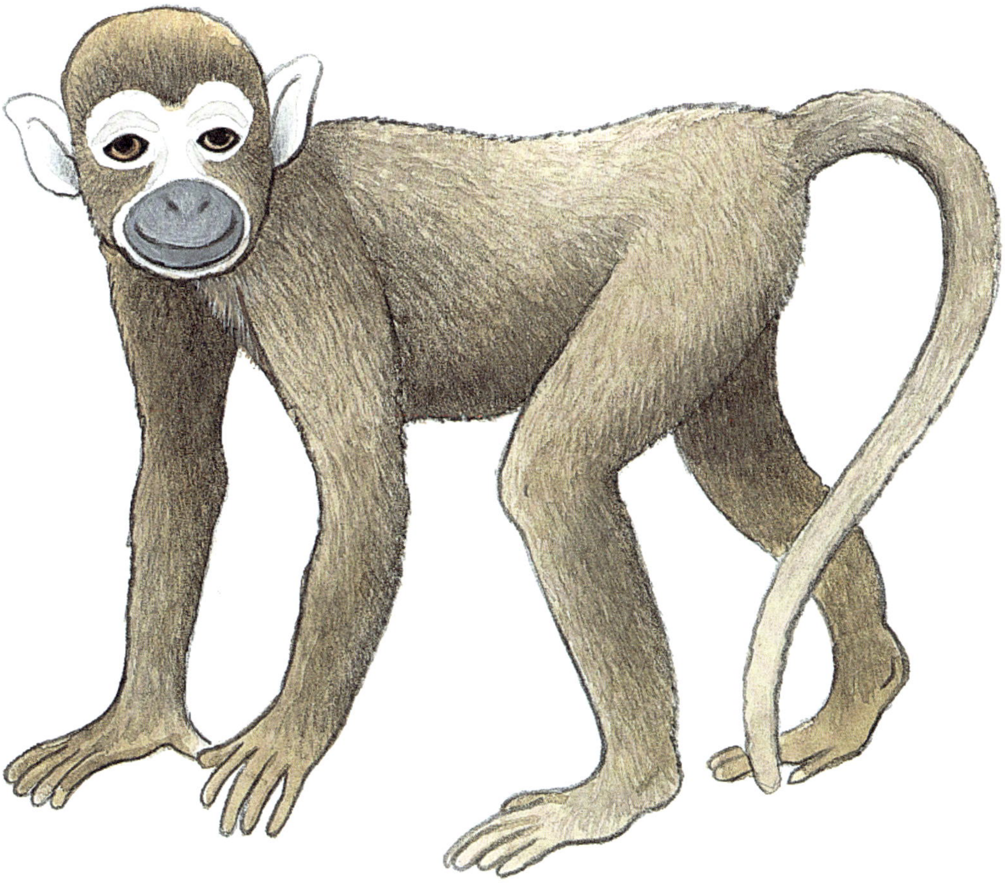

#10 horse
© LOYOLA PRESS.

#11 monkey
© LOYOLA PRESS.

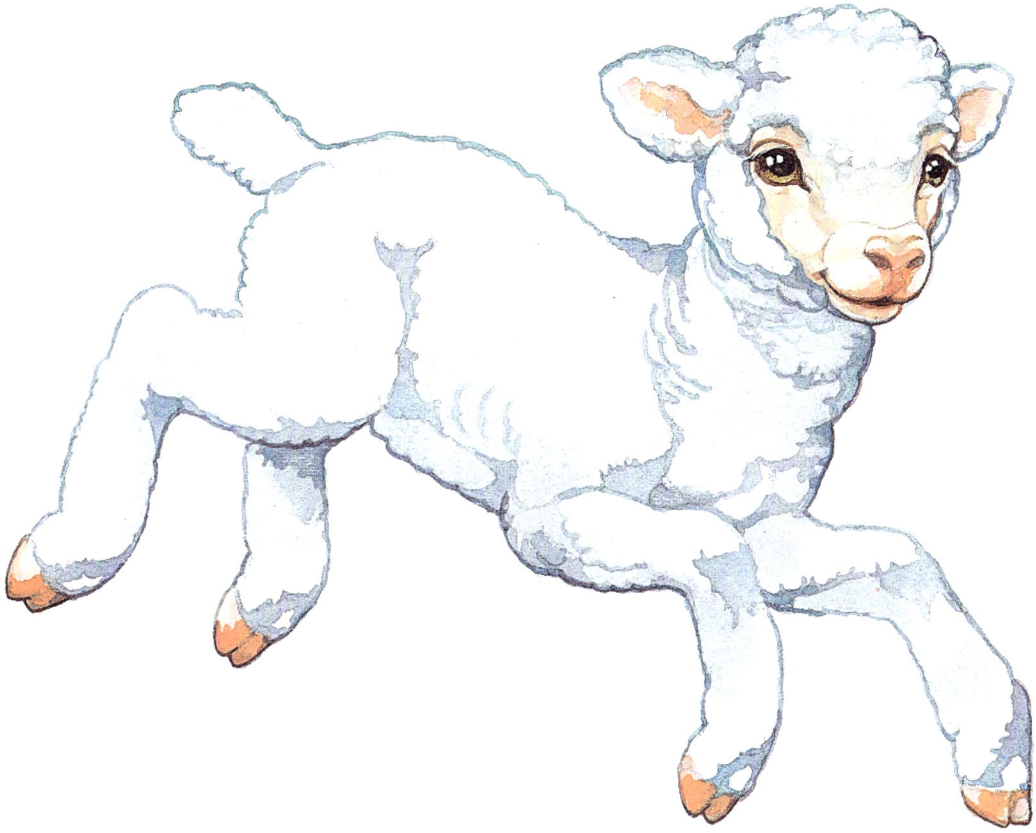

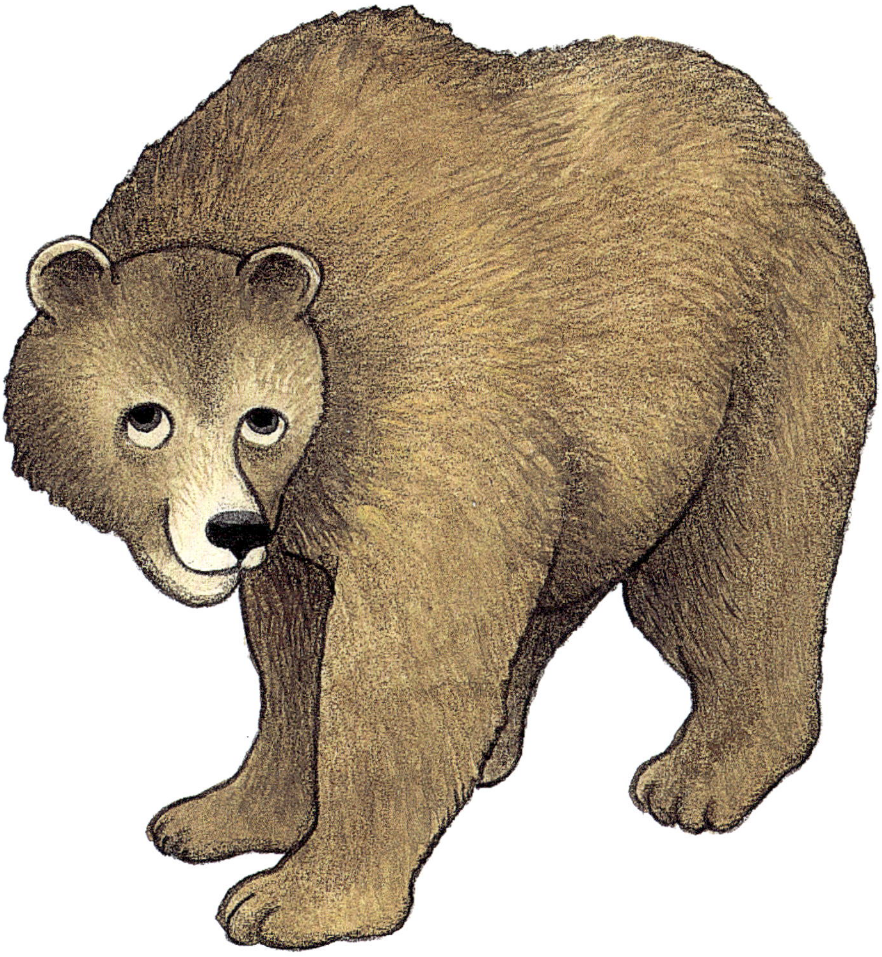

#12 lamb

©Loyola Press.

#13 bear

©Loyola Press.

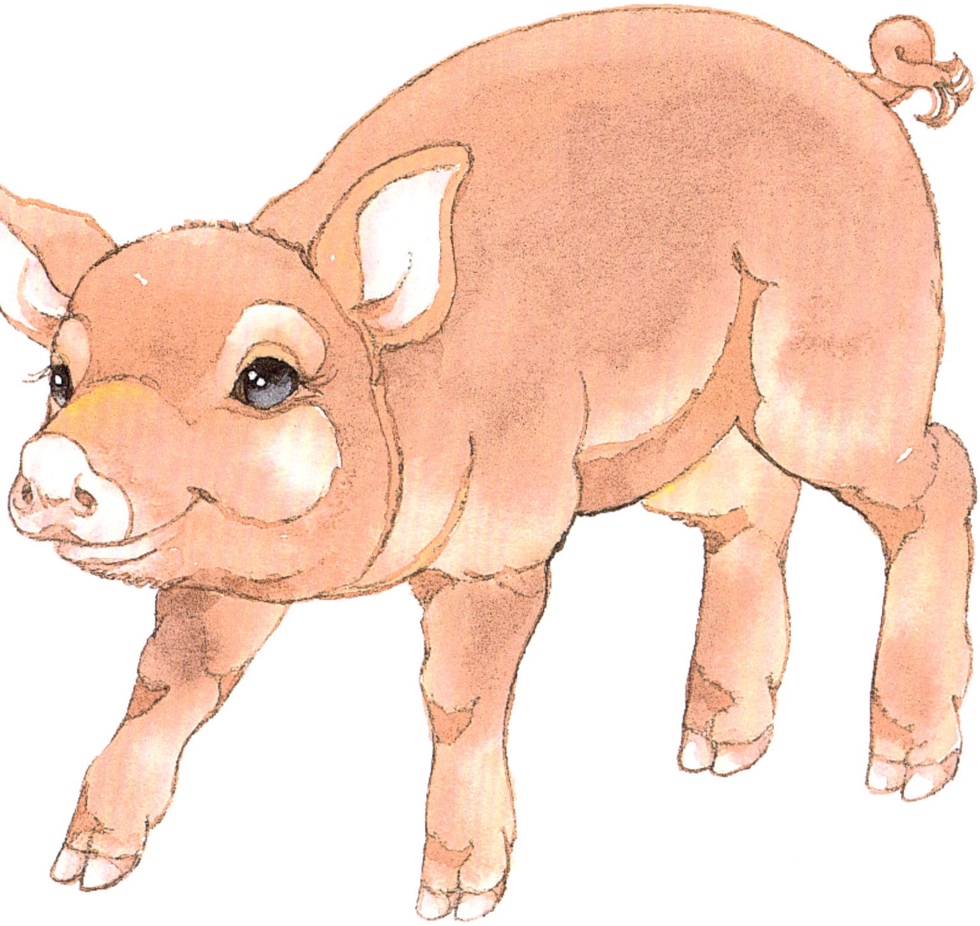

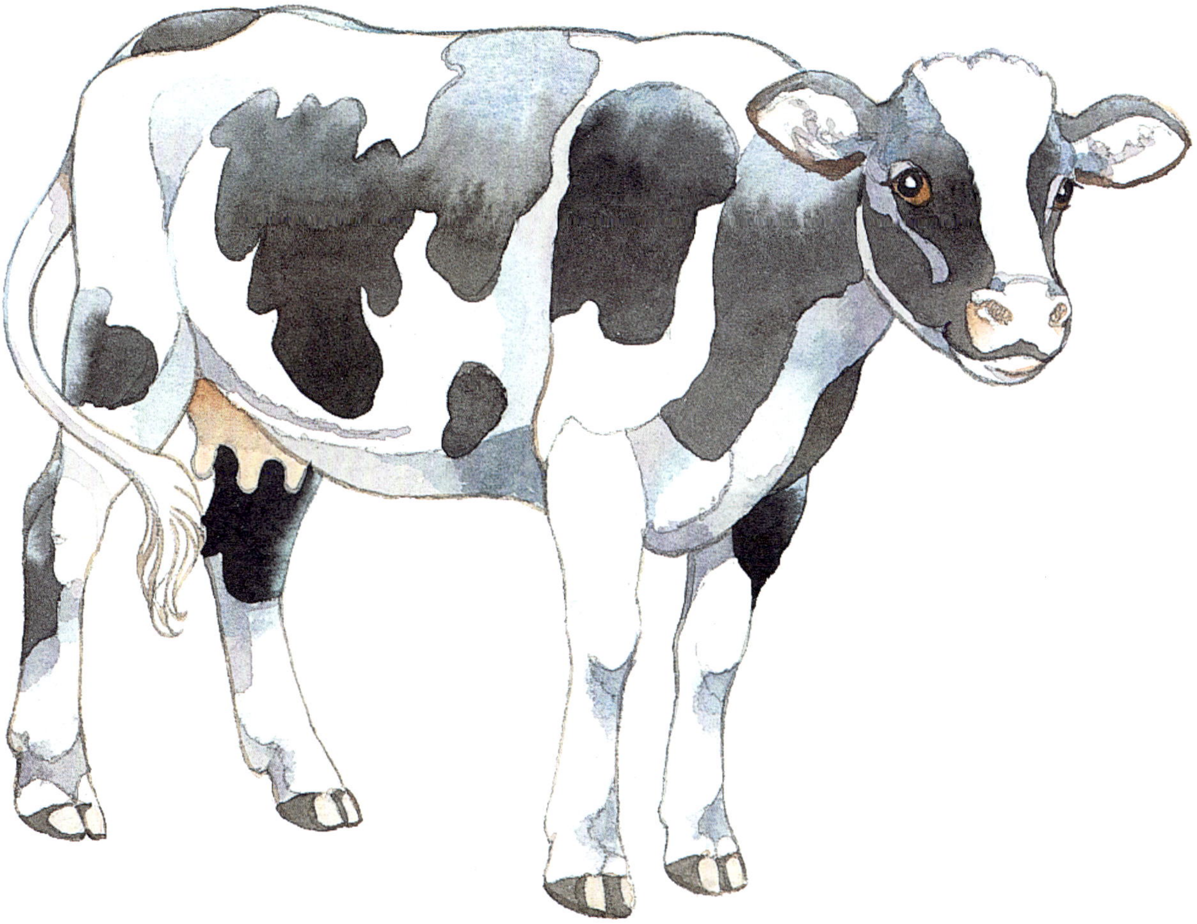

#14 pig

©LoyolaPress.

#15 cow

©LoyolaPress.

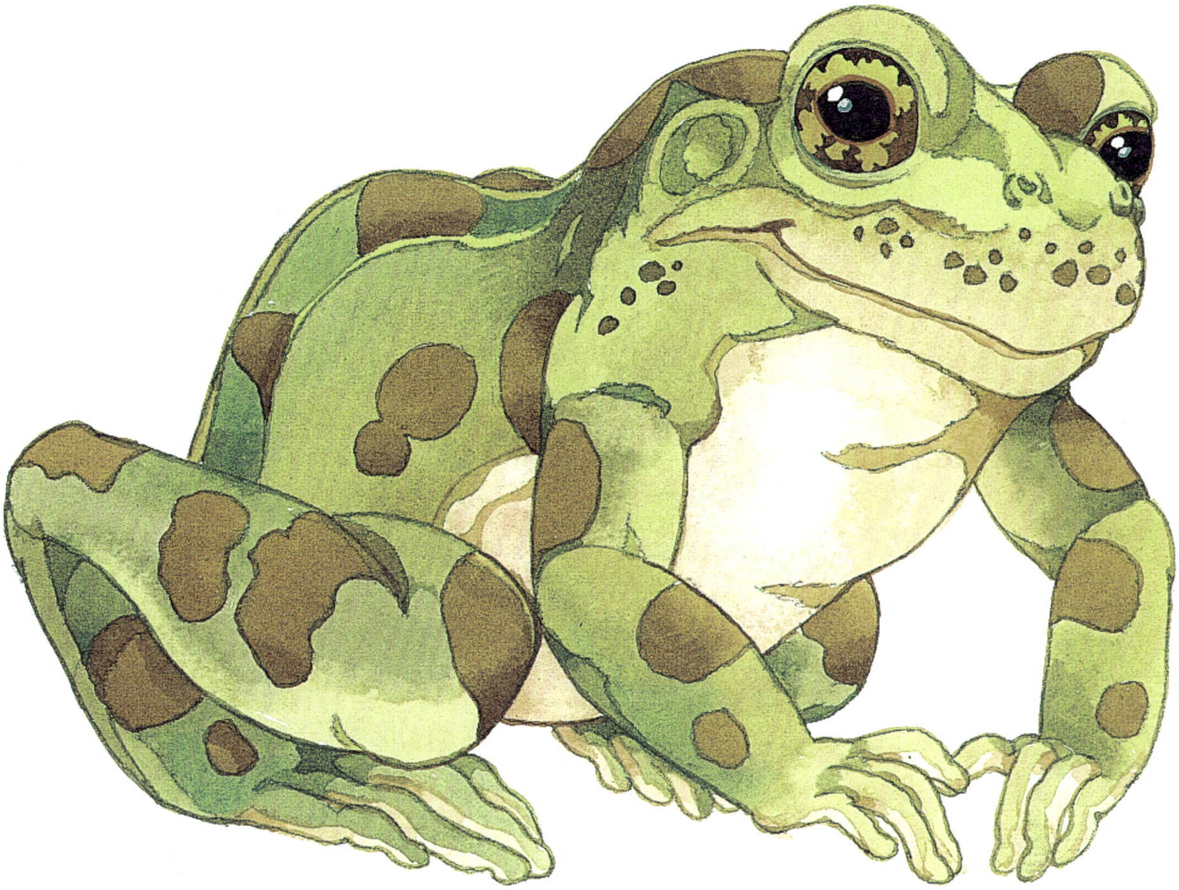

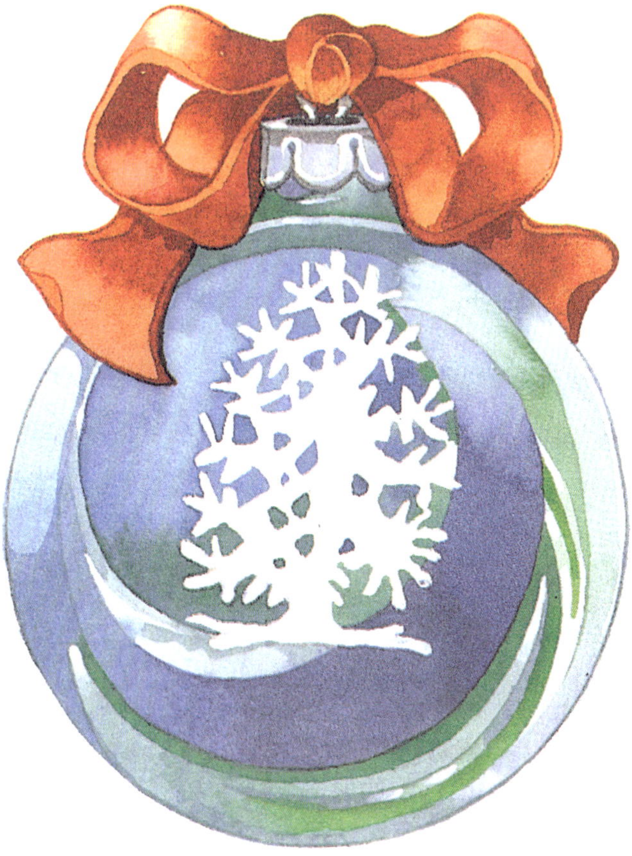

#16 frog

© LOYOLA PRESS.

#50 ornament

© LOYOLA PRESS.

UNITED STATES OF AMERICA
E PLURIBUS UNUM
ONE CENT

UNITED STATES OF AMERICA
E PLURIBUS UNUM
ONE CENT

UNITED STATES OF AMERICA
E PLURIBUS UNUM
ONE CENT

UNITED STATES OF AMERICA
E PLURIBUS UNUM
ONE CENT

UNITED STATES OF AMERICA
E PLURIBUS UNUM
ONE CENT

UNITED STATES OF AMERICA
E PLURIBUS UNUM
ONE CENT

#17 coin
(one of ten)
©LOYOLAPRESS.

#18 coin
(one of ten)
©LOYOLAPRESS.

#19 coin
(one of ten)
©LOYOLAPRESS.

#20 coin
(one of ten)
©LOYOLAPRESS.

#21 coin
(one of ten)
©LOYOLAPRESS.

#22 coin
(one of ten)
©LOYOLAPRESS.

UNITED STATES OF AMERICA
E PLURIBUS UNUM
ONE CENT

UNITED STATES OF AMERICA
E PLURIBUS UNUM
ONE CENT

UNITED STATES OF AMERICA
E PLURIBUS UNUM
ONE CENT

UNITED STATES OF AMERICA
E PLURIBUS UNUM
ONE CENT

#23 coin
(one of ten)
© LOYOLA PRESS.

#24 coin
(one of ten)
© LOYOLA PRESS.

#25 coin
(one of ten)
© LOYOLA PRESS.

#26 coin
(one of ten)
© LOYOLA PRESS.

#33 shamrock
(one of ten)
© LOYOLA PRESS.

#34 shamrock
(one of ten)
© LOYOLA PRESS.

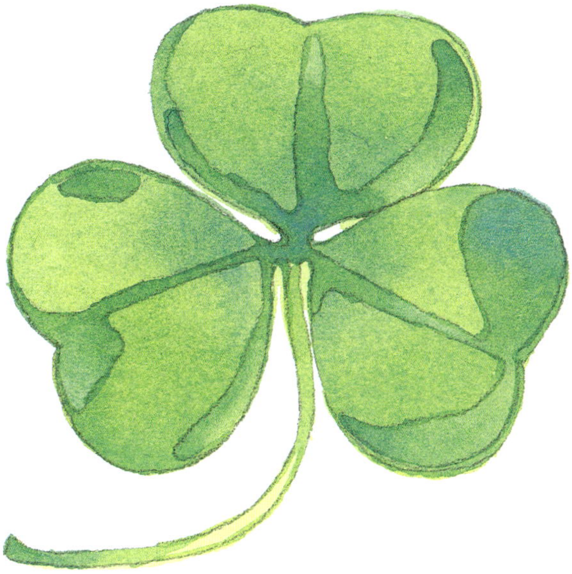
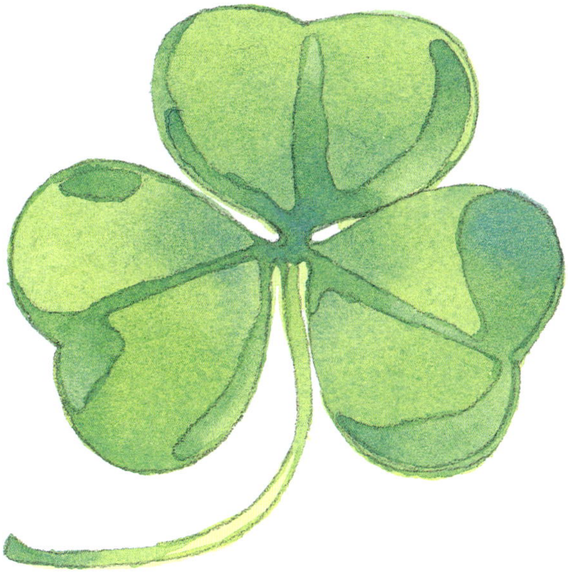
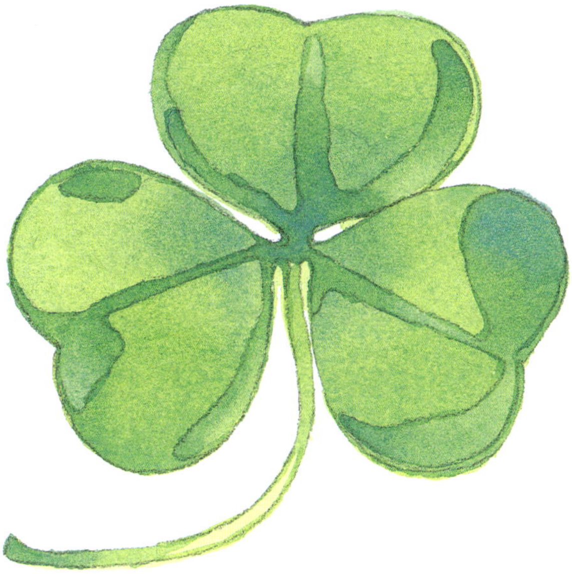
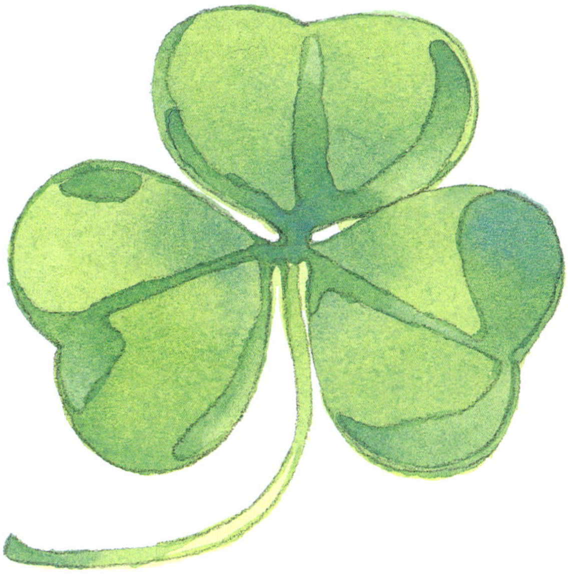
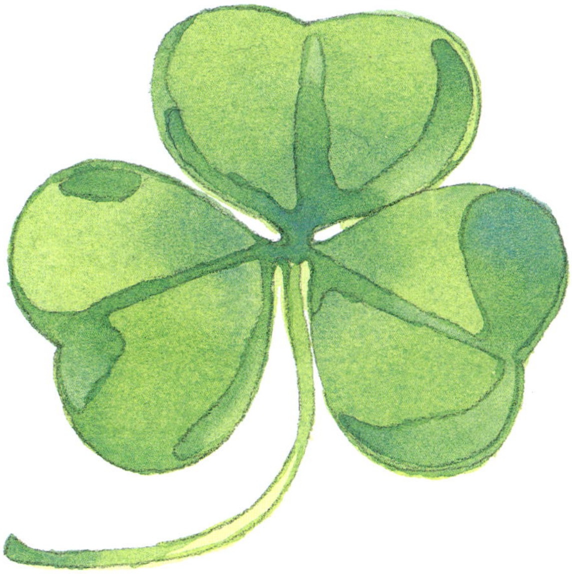
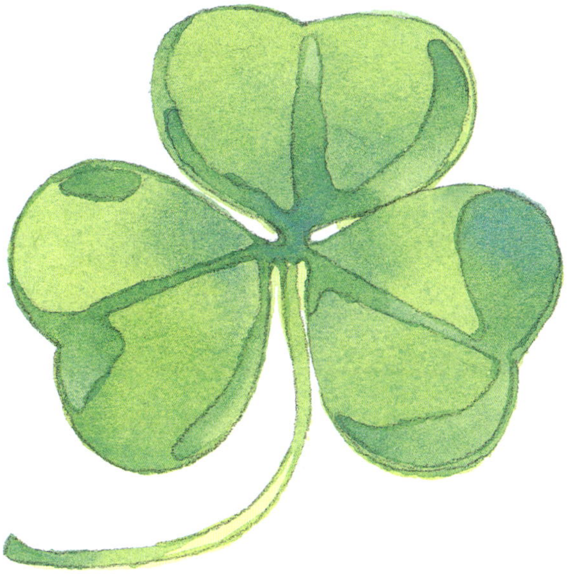

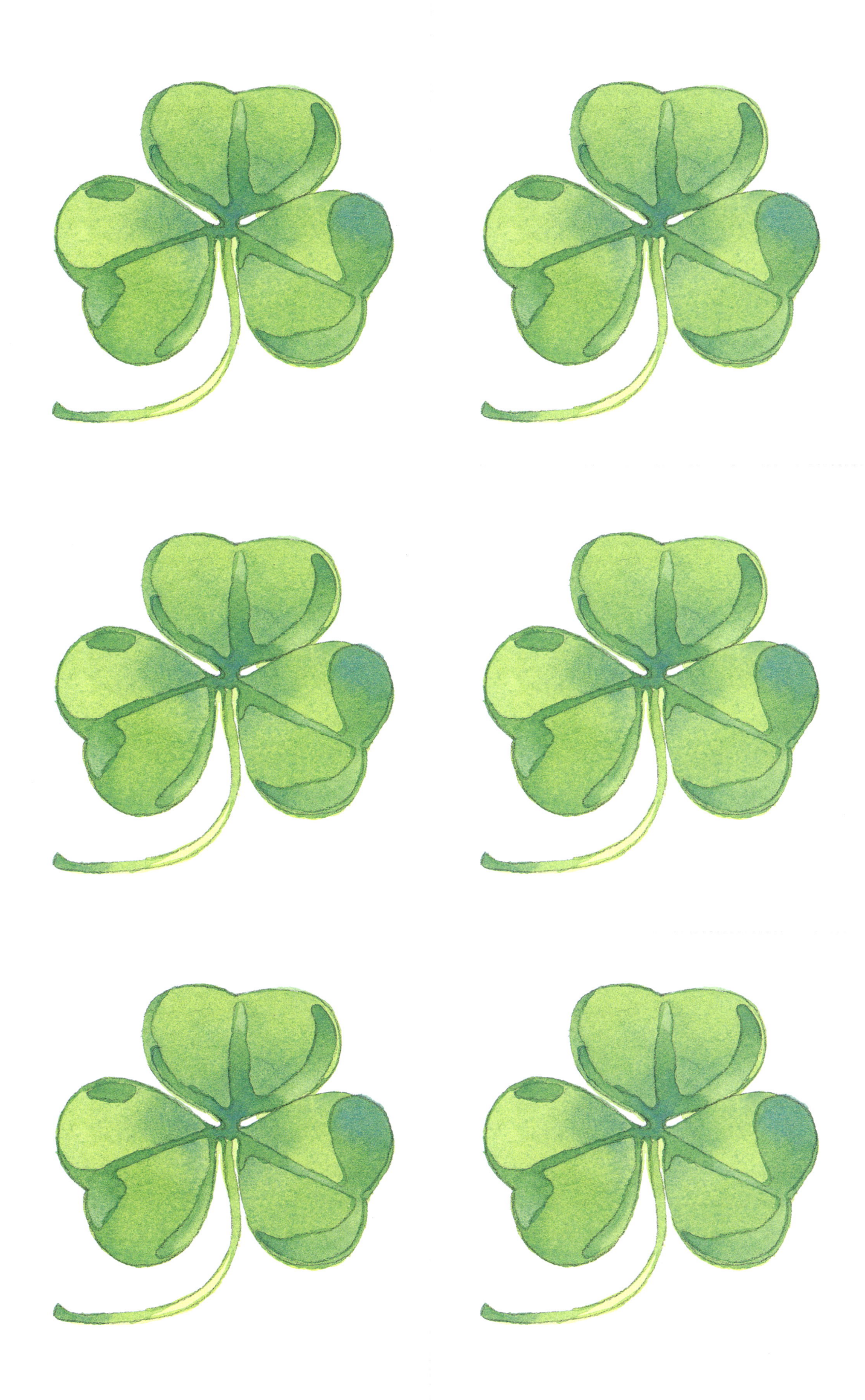

#35 shamrock
(one of ten)
©LoyolaPress.

#36 shamrock
(one of ten)
©LoyolaPress.

#37 shamrock
(one of ten)
©LoyolaPress.

#38 shamrock
(one of ten)
©LoyolaPress.

#39 shamrock
(one of ten)
©LoyolaPress.

#40 shamrock
(one of ten)
©LoyolaPress.

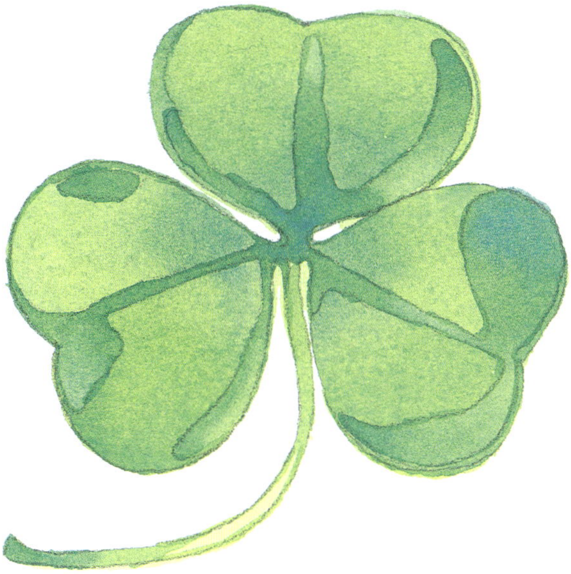
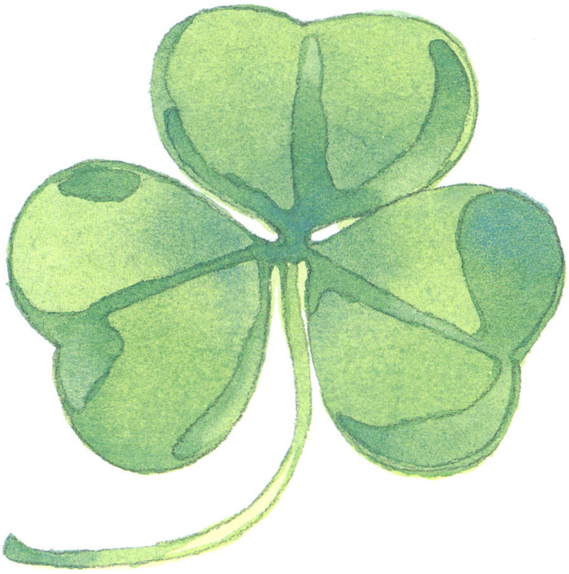

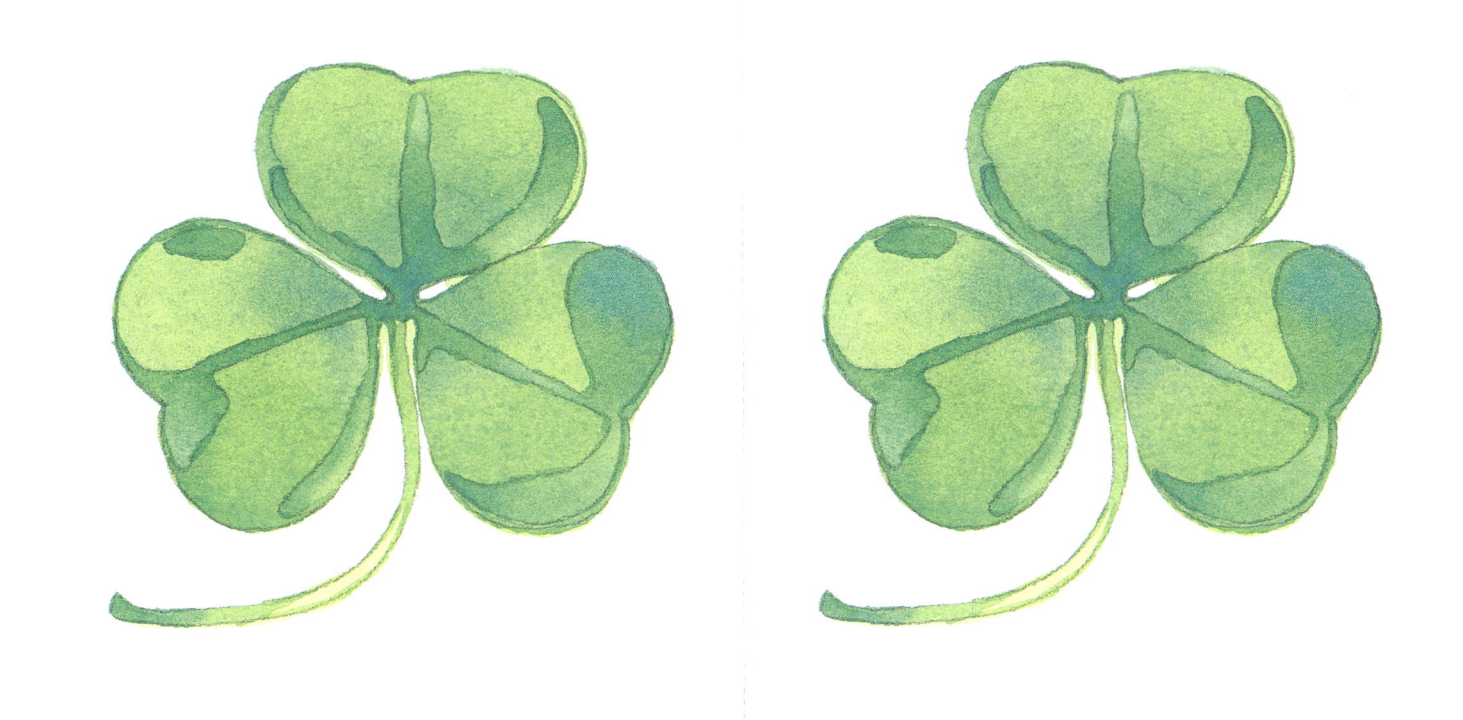

#41 shamrock
(one of ten)

© LOYOLA PRESS.

#42 shamrock
(one of ten)

© LOYOLA PRESS.

#29 heart

© LOYOLA PRESS.

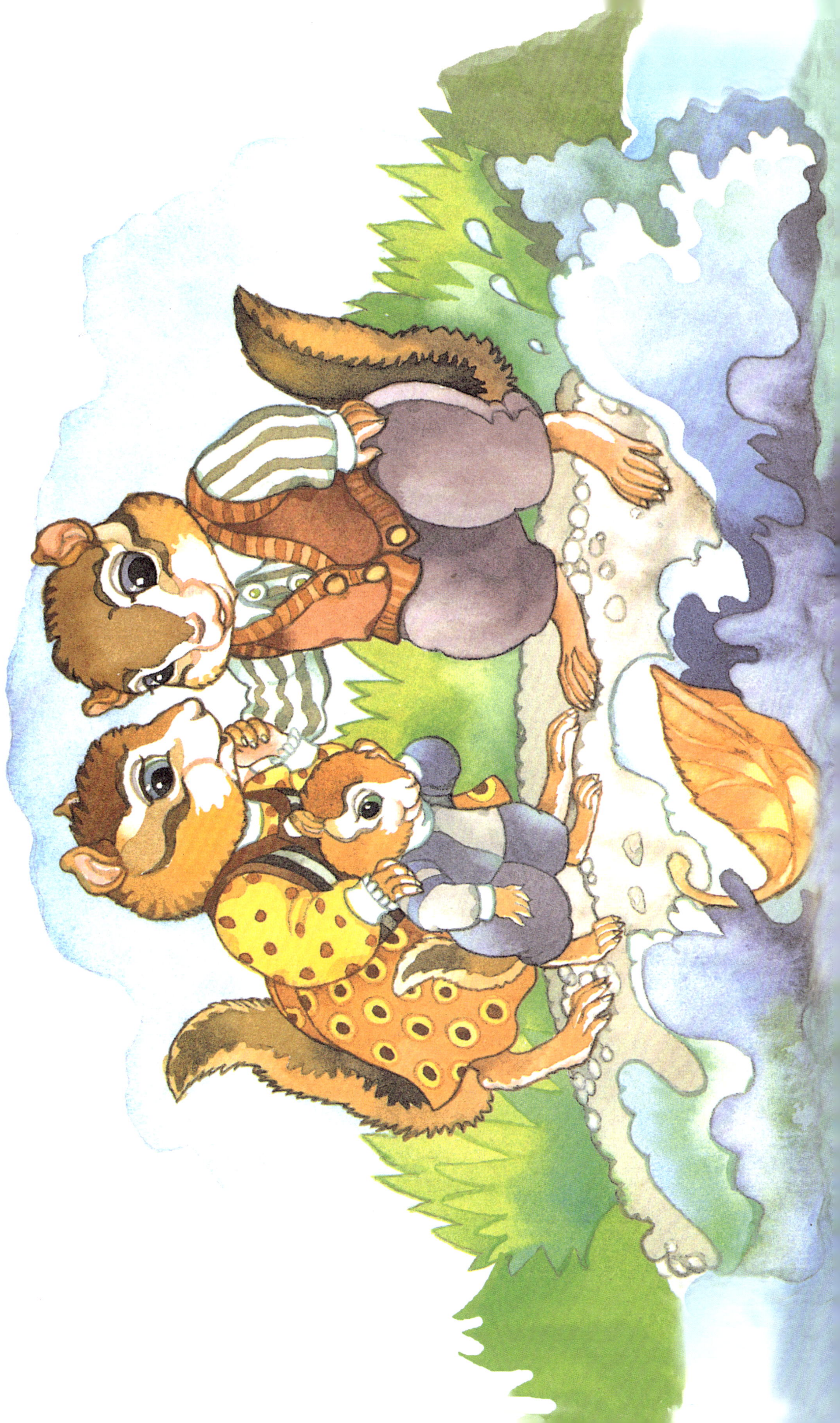

#27

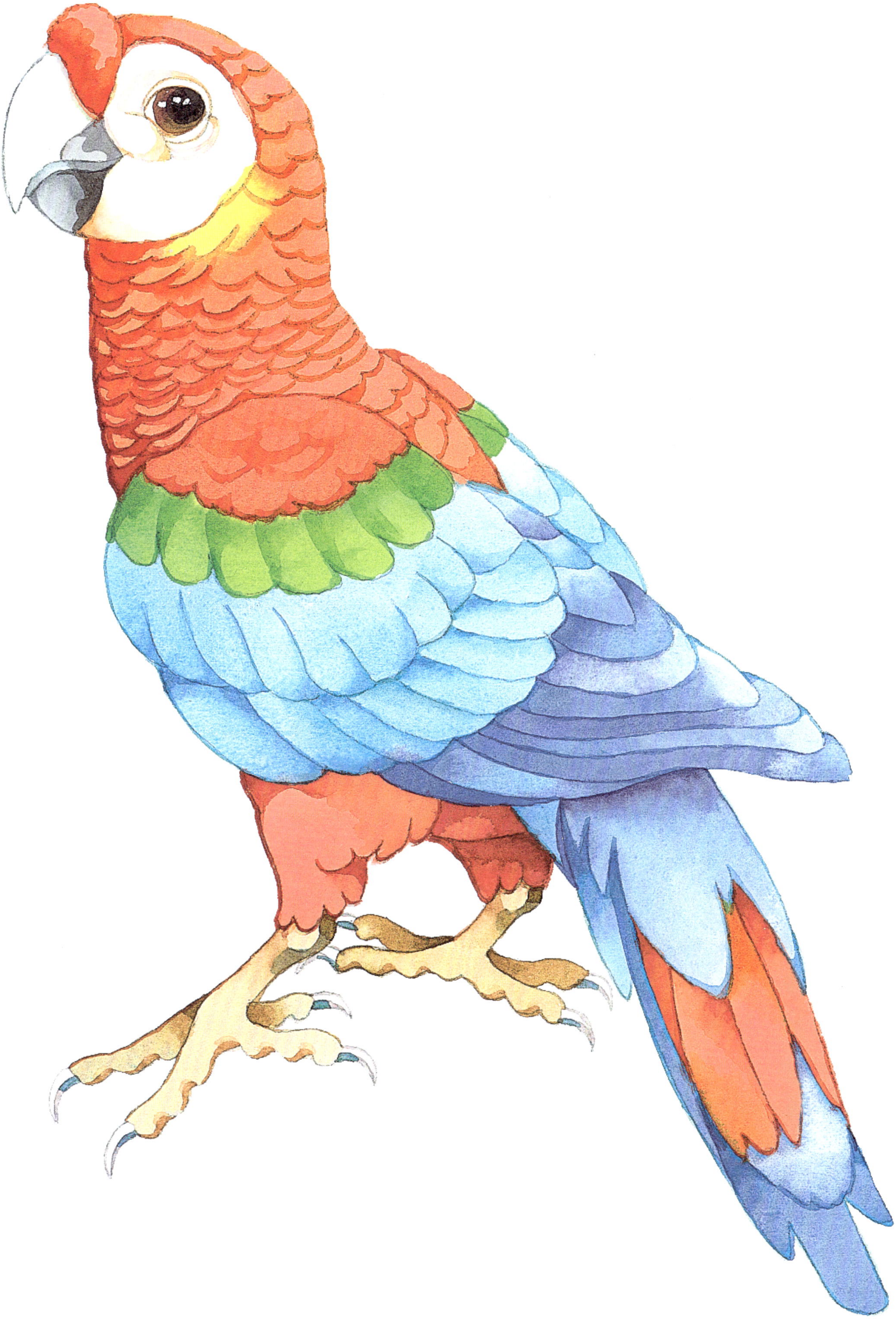

#28 Polly Parrot

© LOYOLAPRESS.

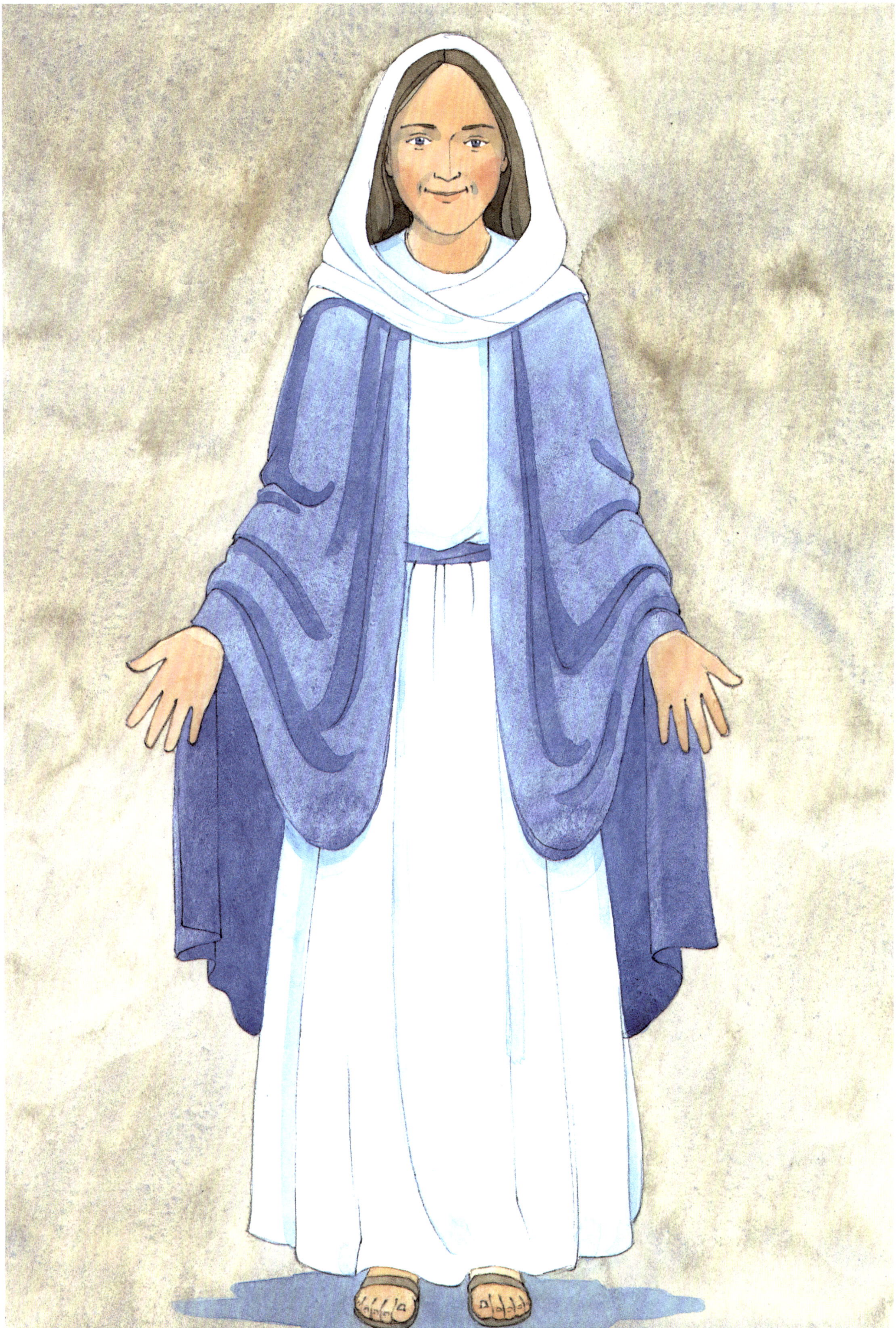

#30 Mary

© LOYOLAPRESS.

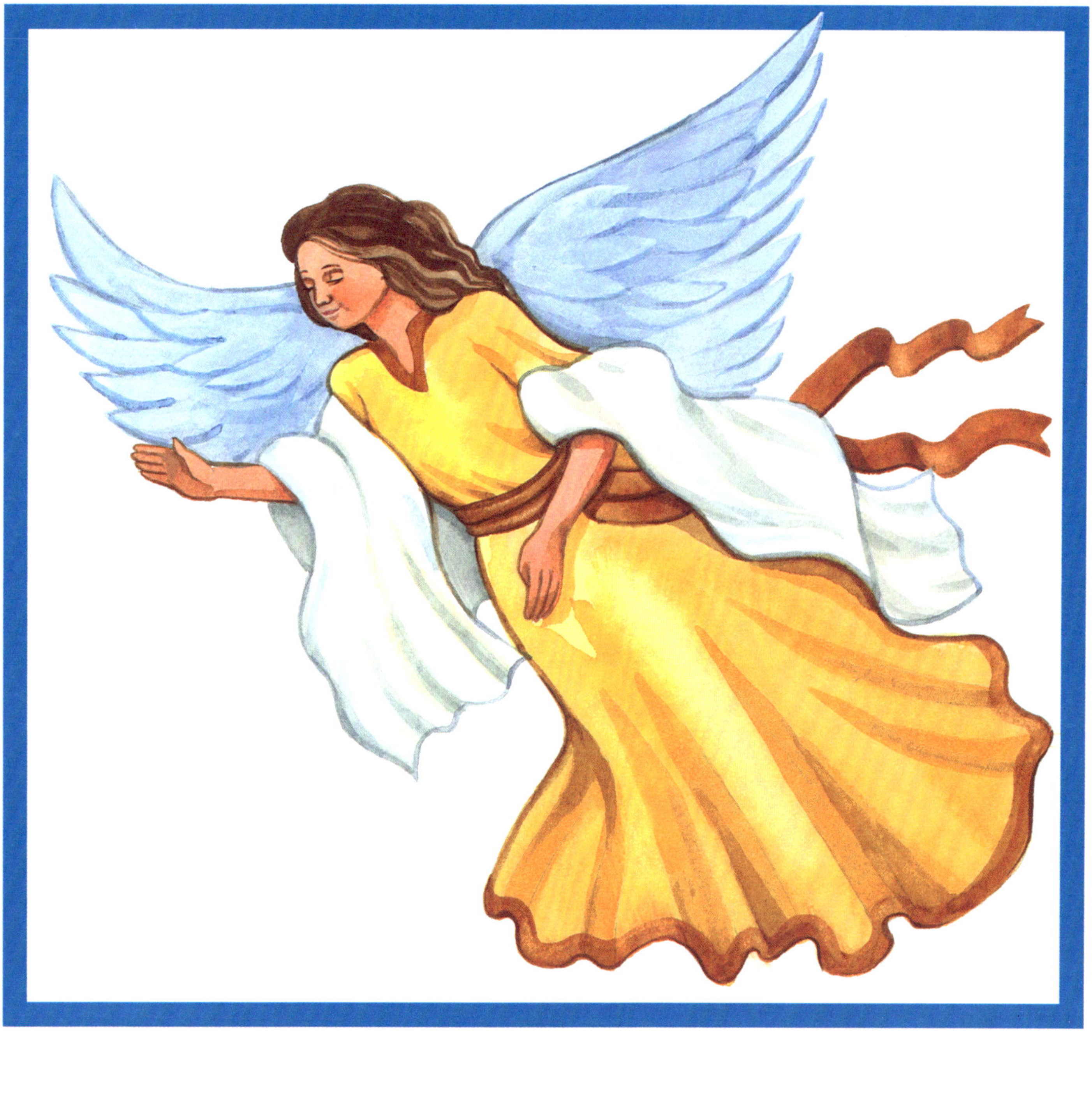

#31 angel
© LOYOLA PRESS.

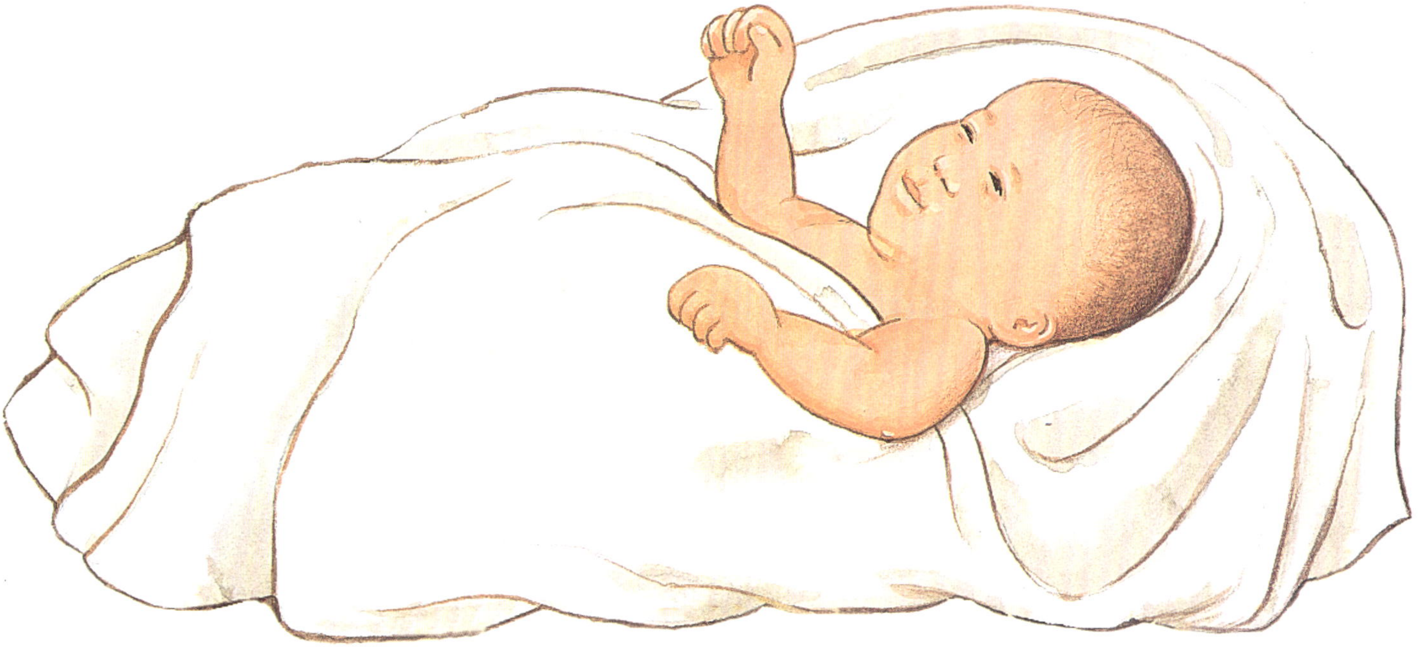

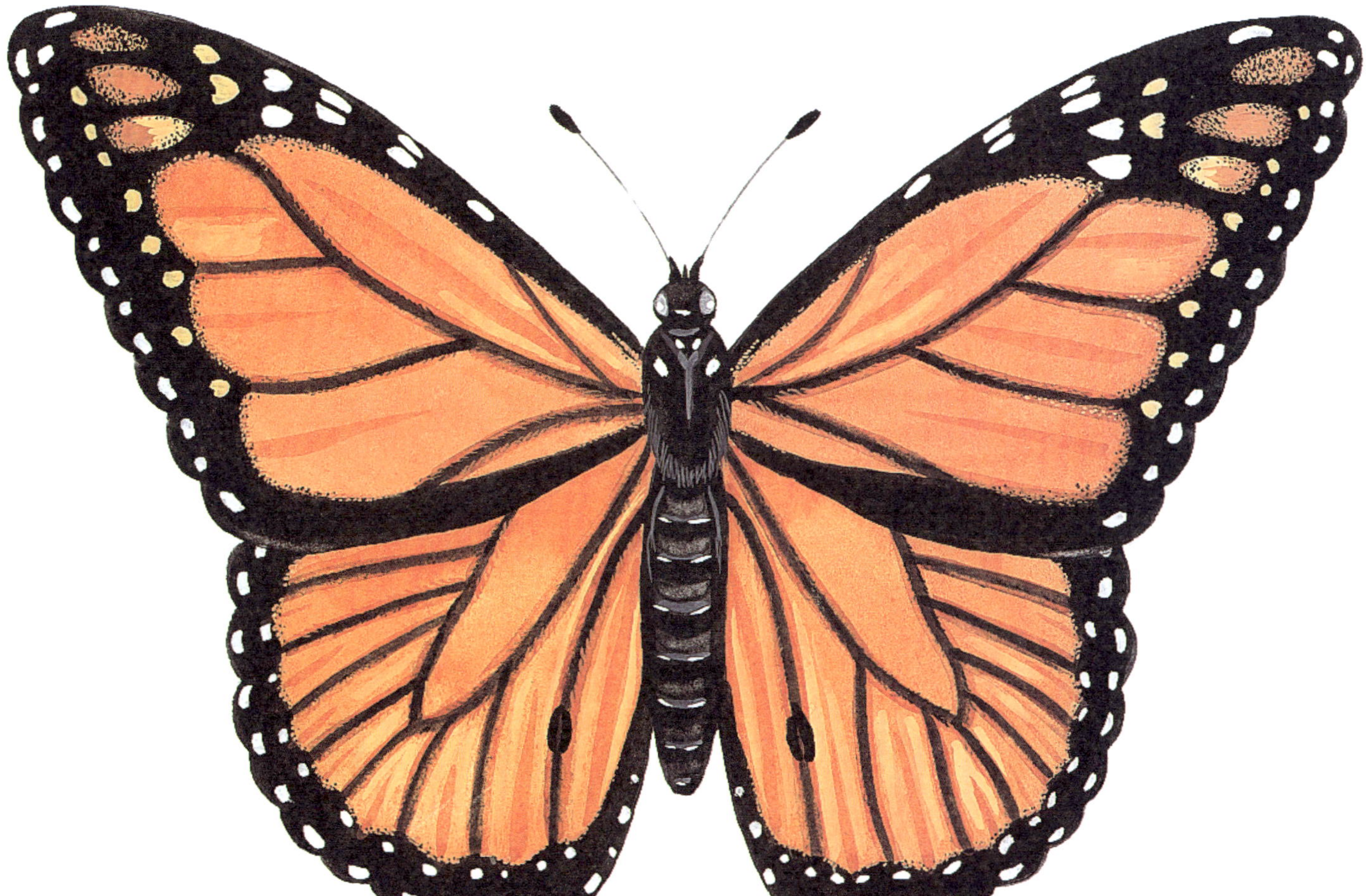

#32 baby

© LOYOLA PRESS.

#47 butterfly

© LOYOLA PRESS.

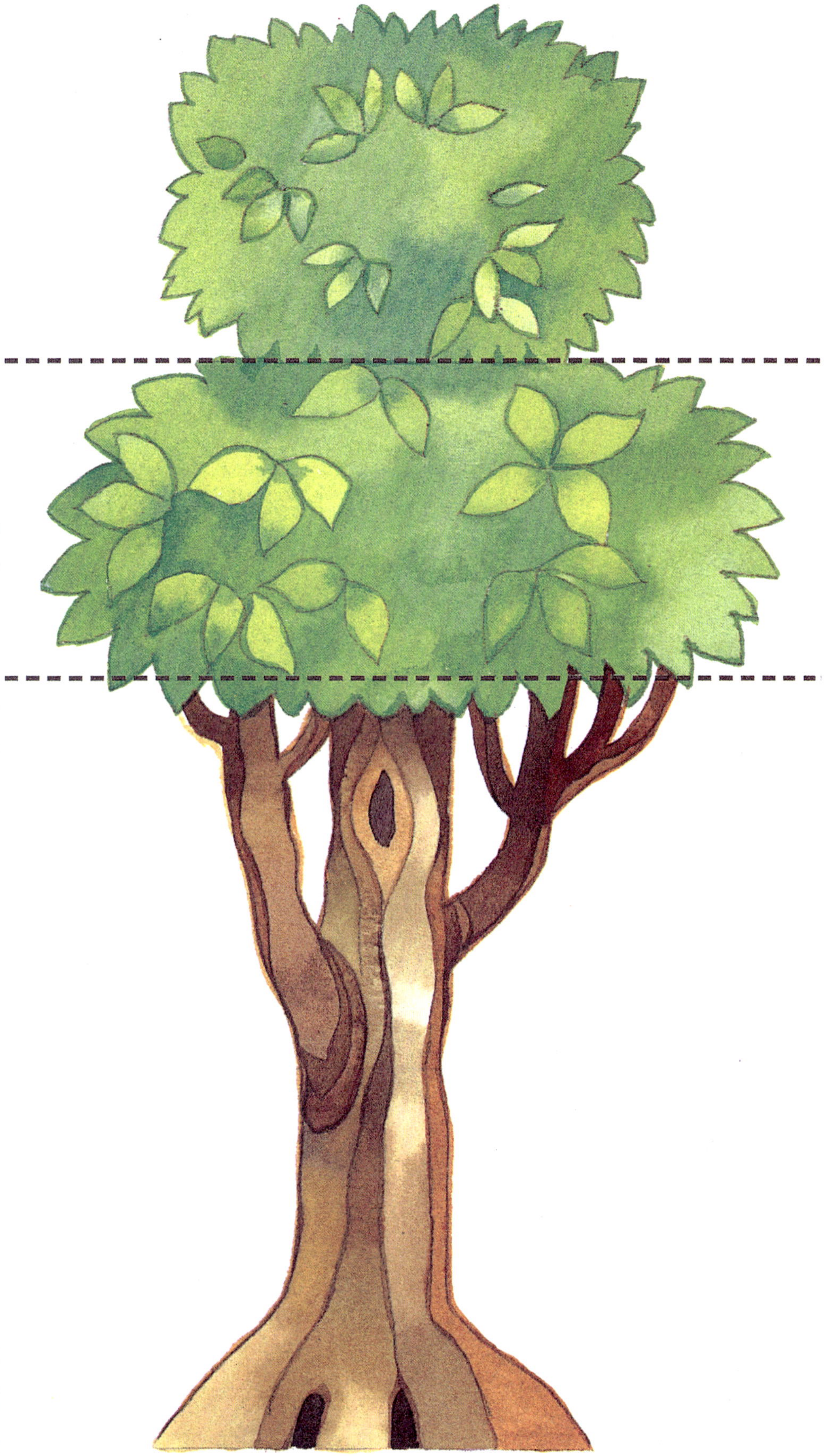

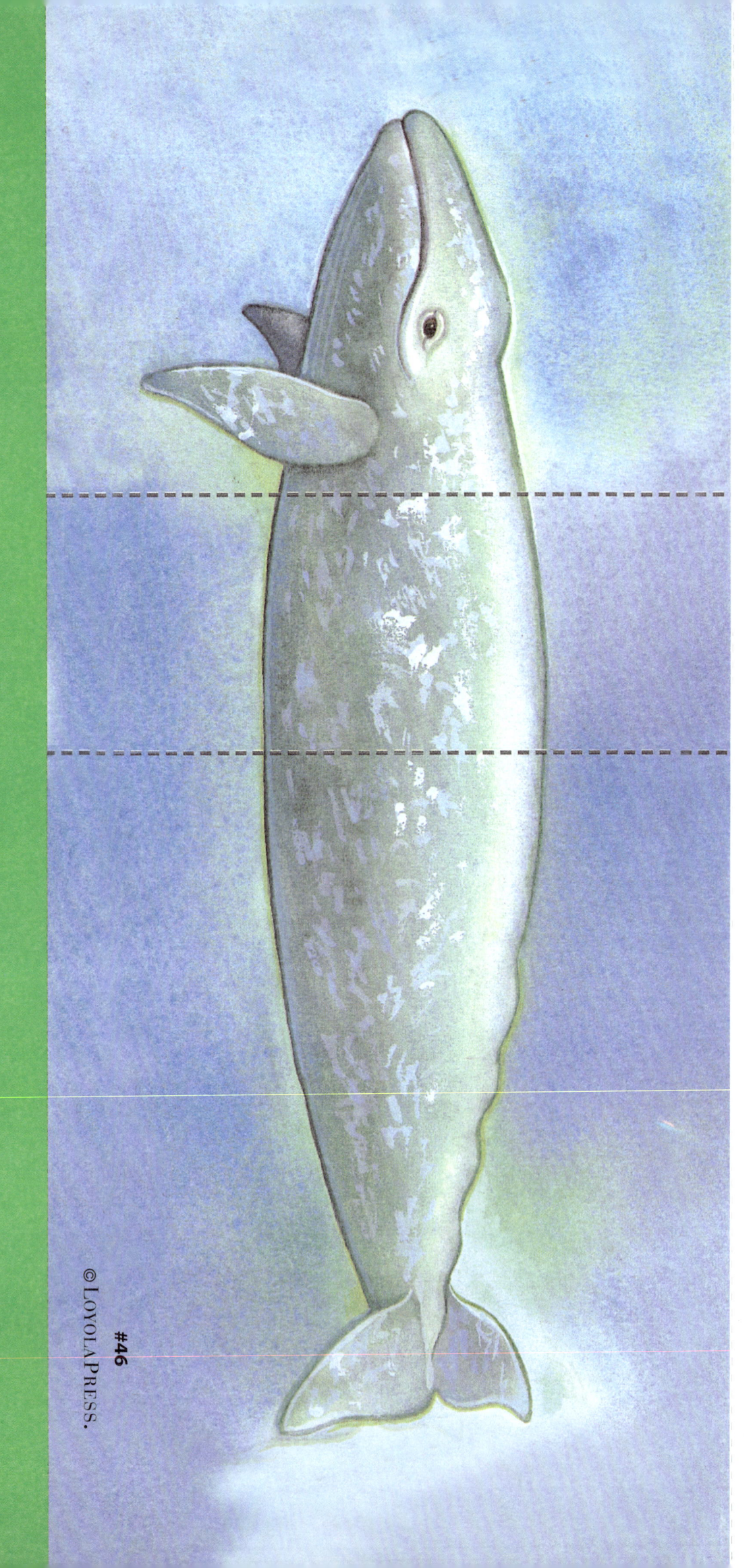

#43 strip for "Frog Hop"
© LoyolaPress.

#44 strip for "Frog Hop"
© LoyolaPress.

#46
© LoyolaPress.

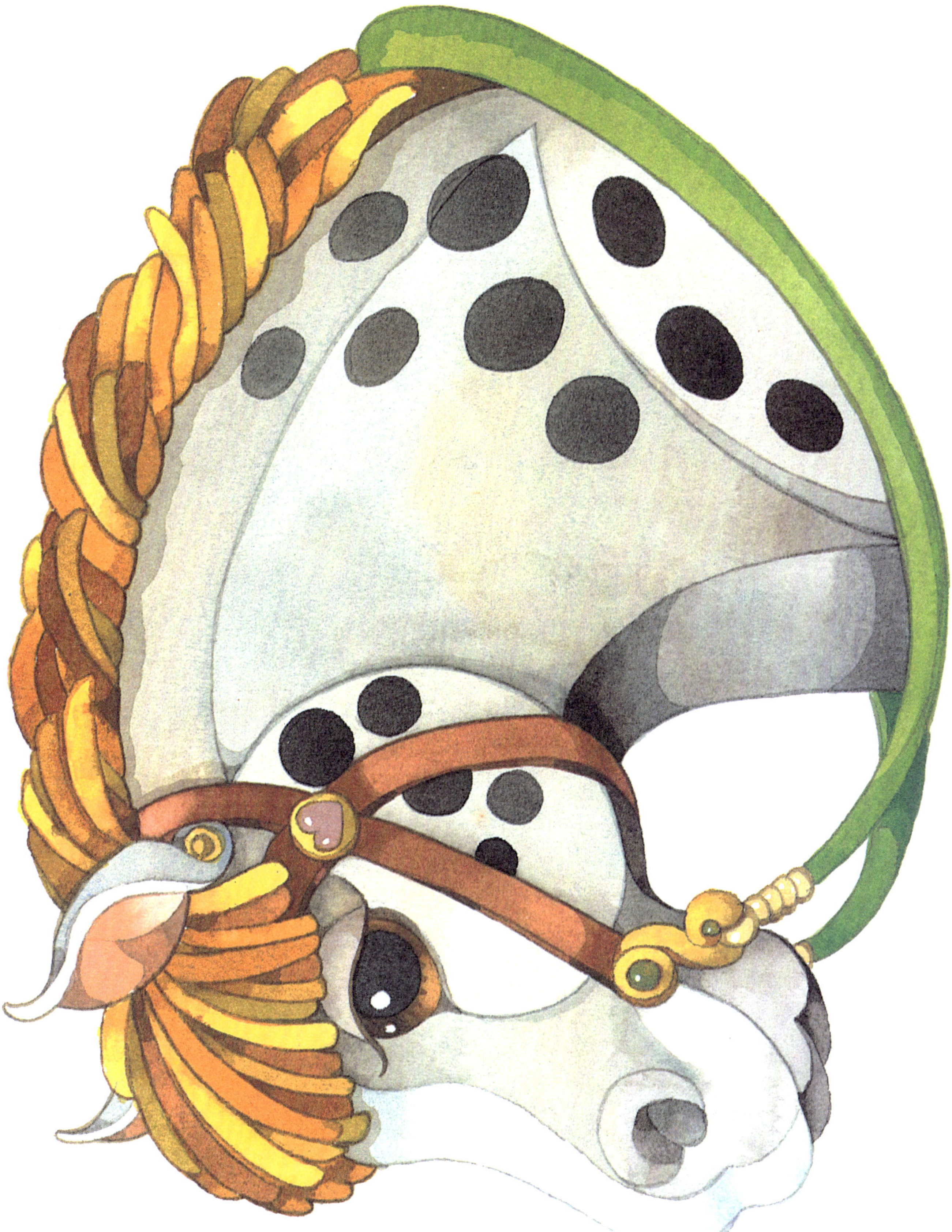

#45 hobby horse
© LOYOLA PRESS.

God is so good.

#48 God is so good.
© LOYOLA PRESS.

#49 heart
for "Love Bug Tag"
© LOYOLA PRESS.

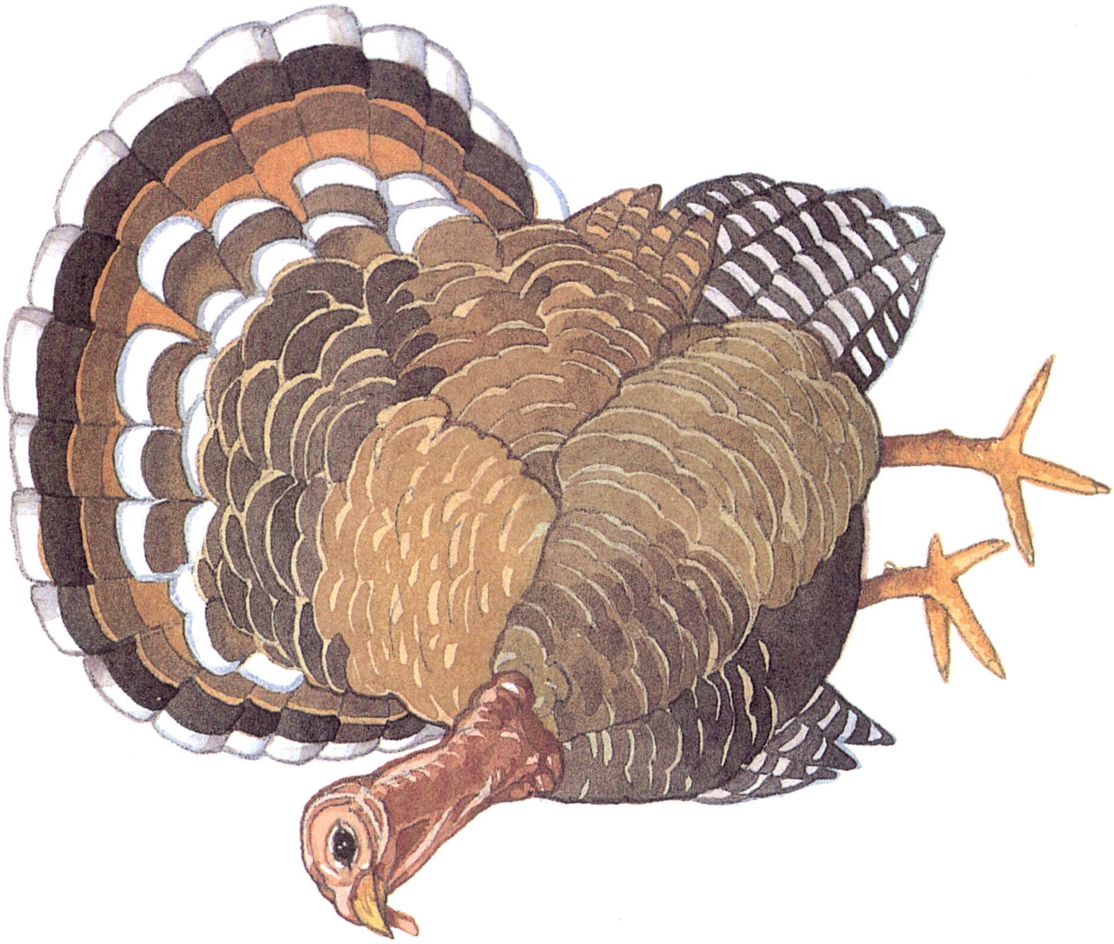

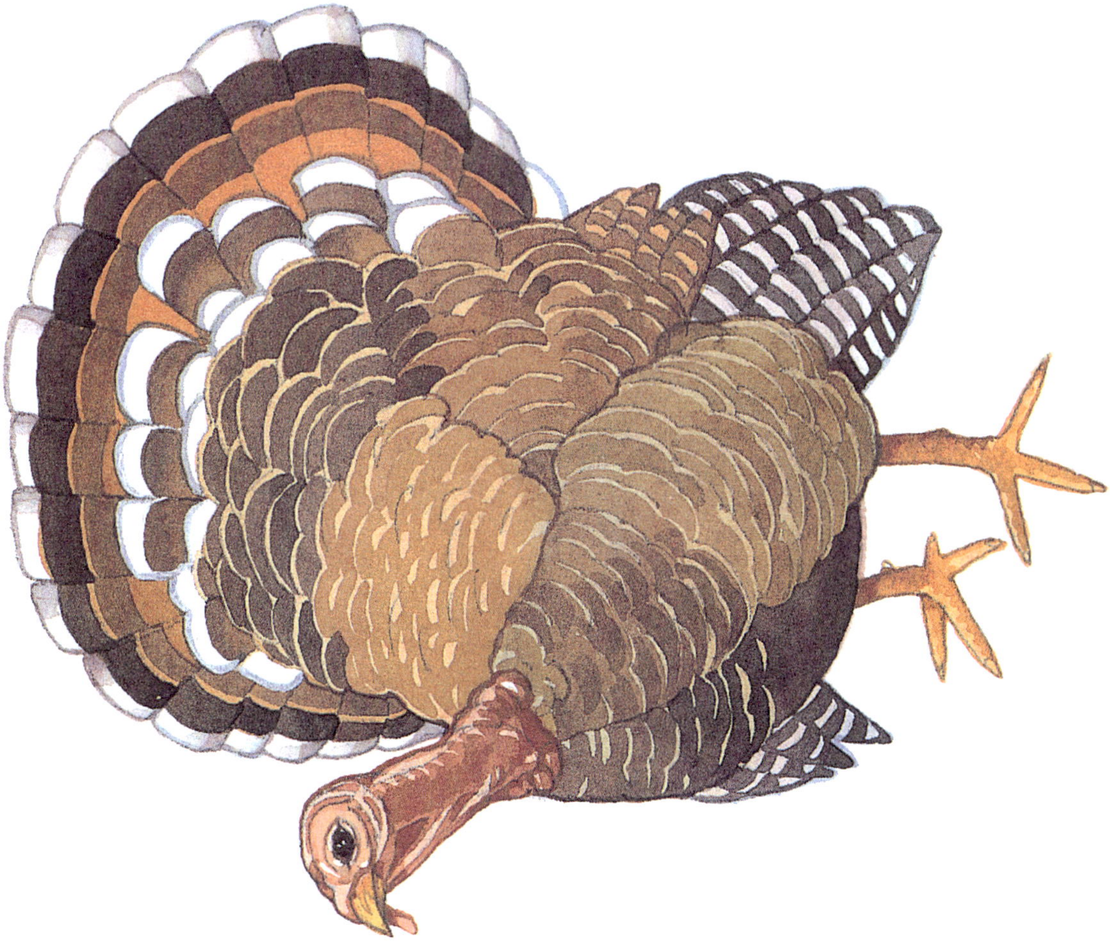

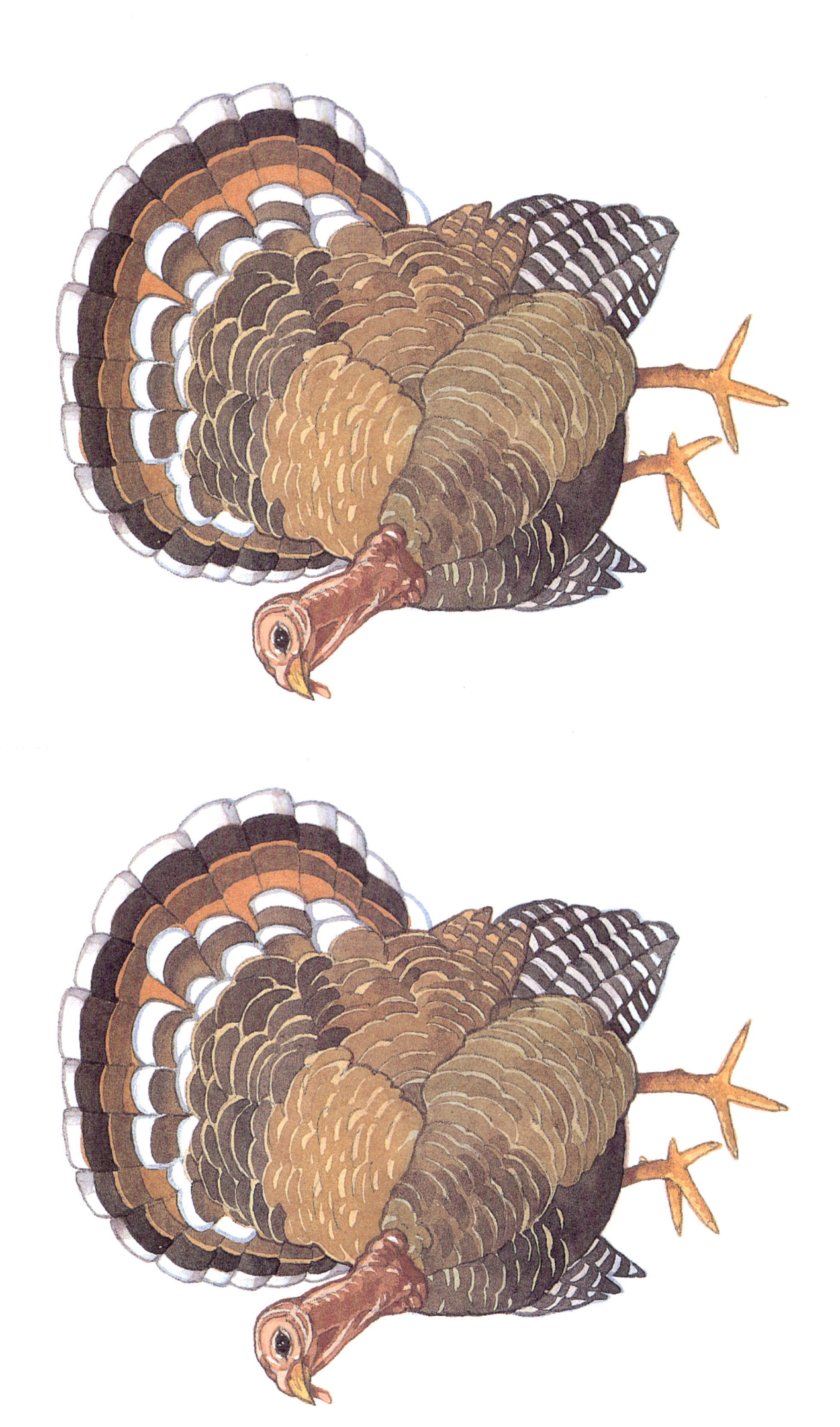

#51 turkey

©LoyolaPress.

#52 turkey

©LoyolaPress.

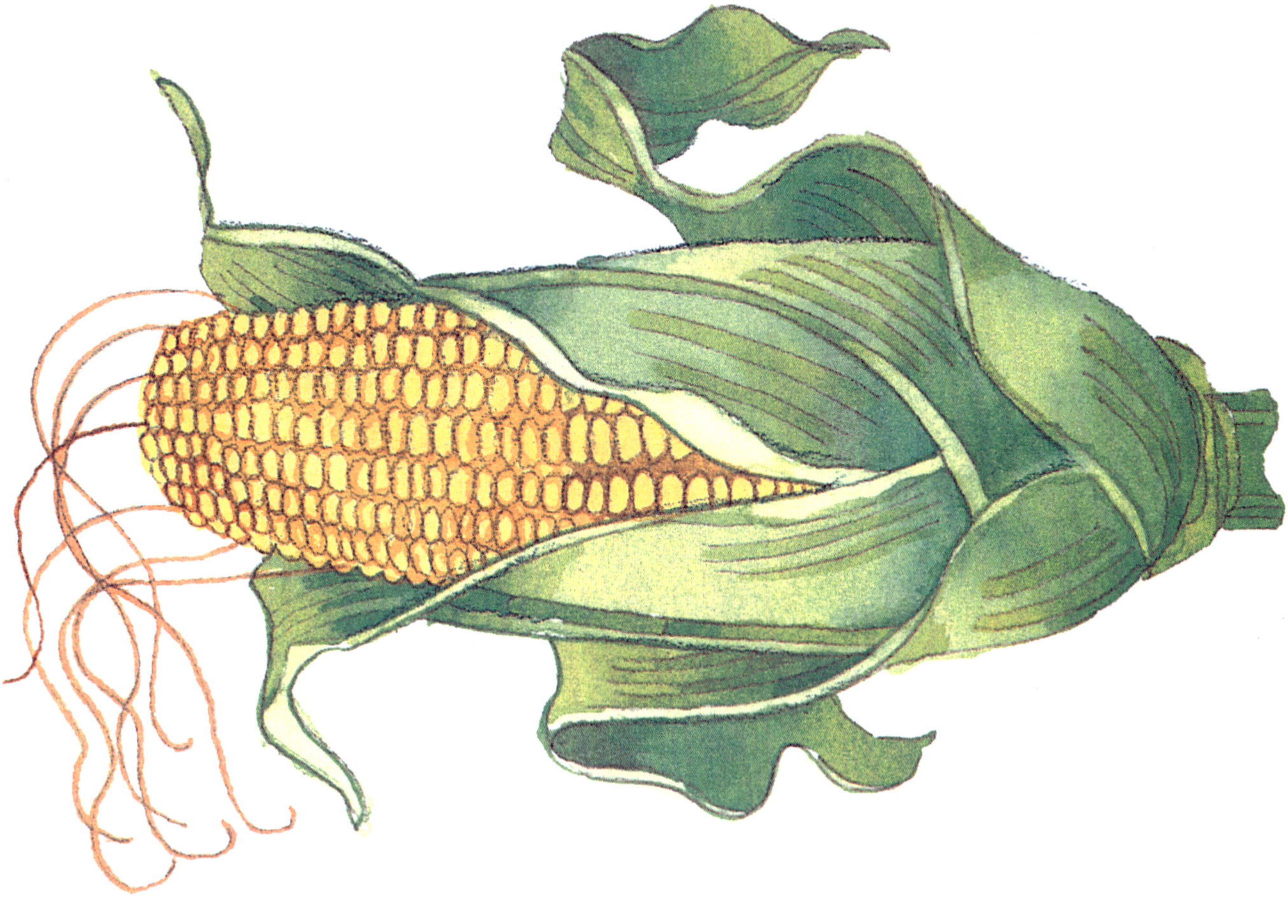

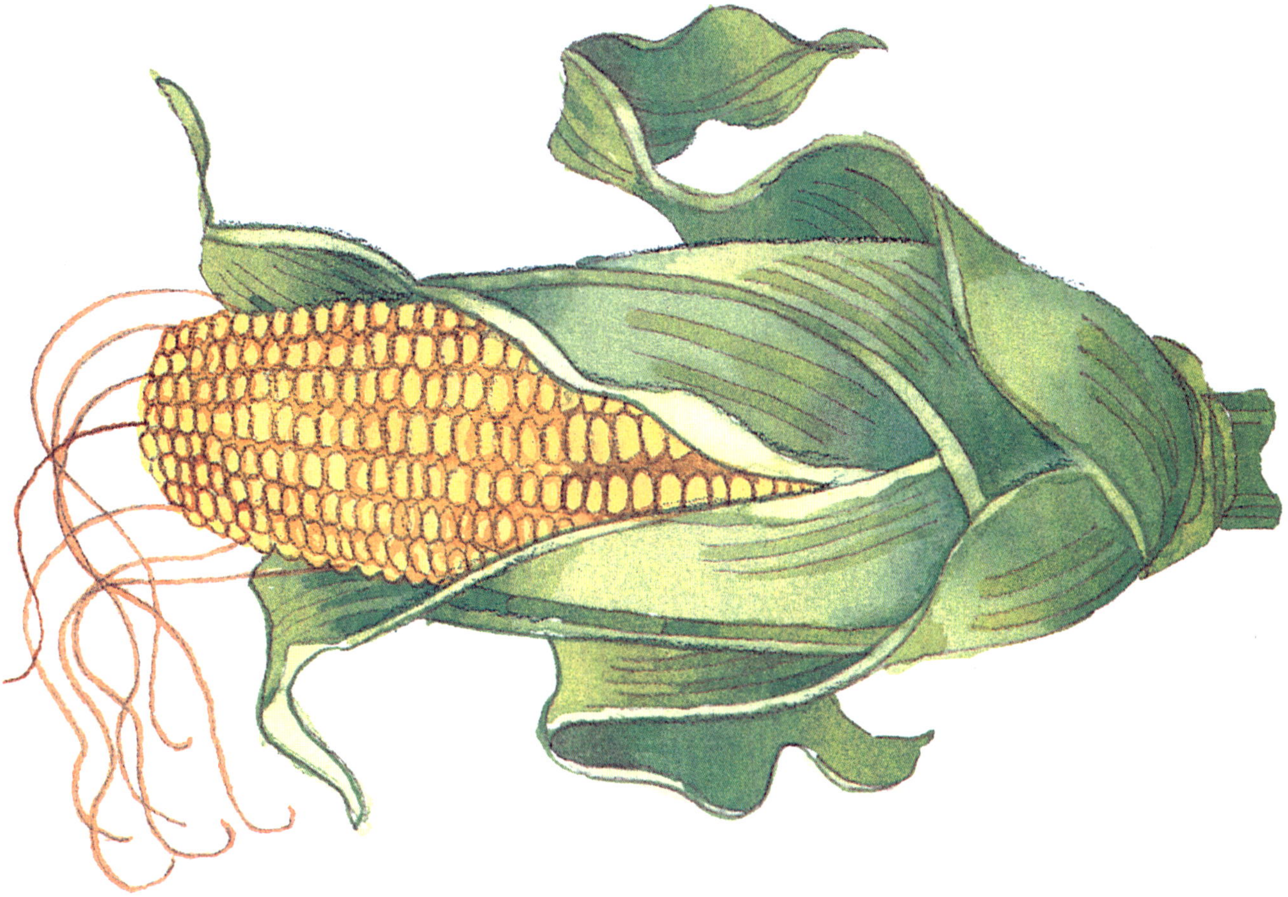

#53 corn

© Loyola Press.

#54 corn

© Loyola Press.

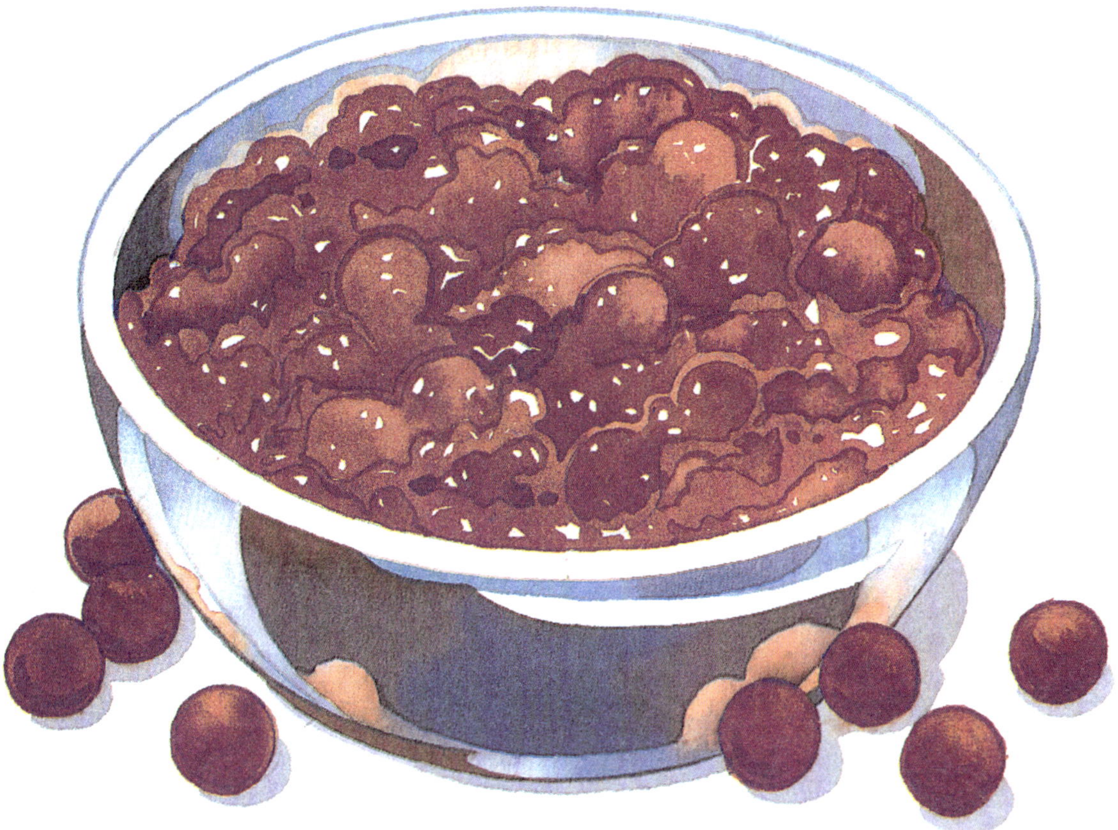

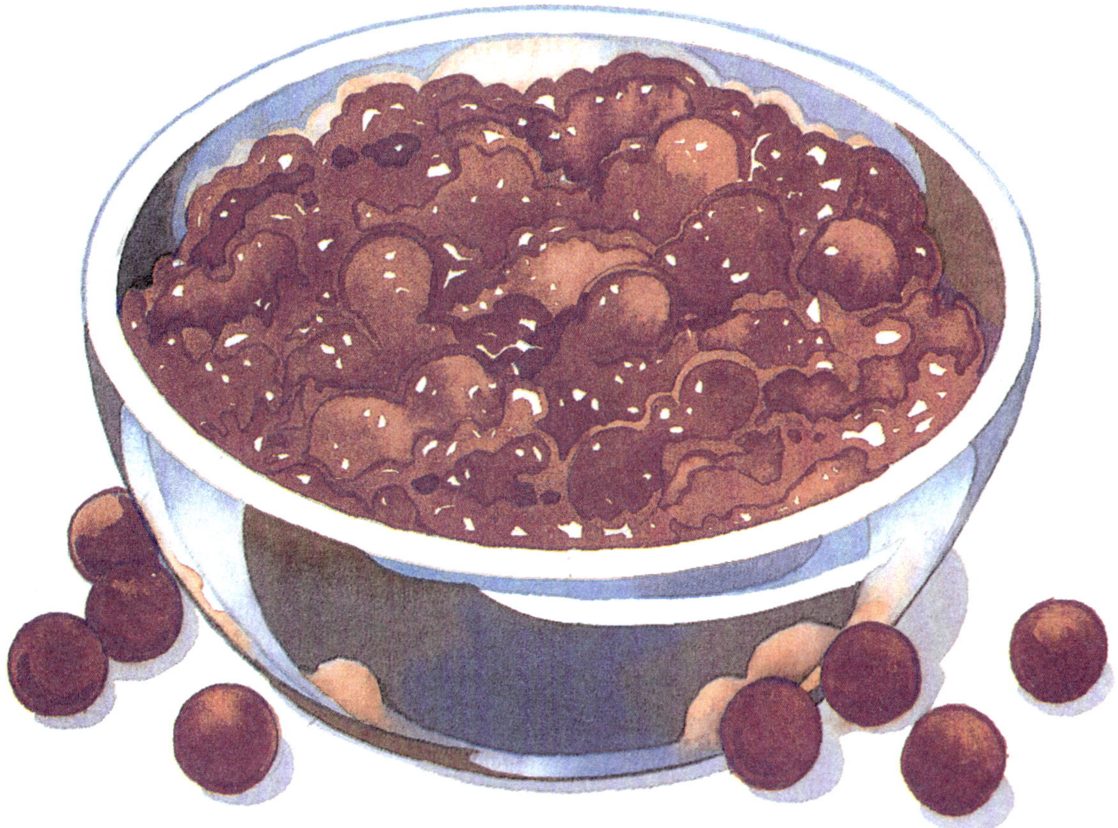

#55 cranberries
© LOYOLA PRESS.

#56 cranberries
© LOYOLA PRESS.

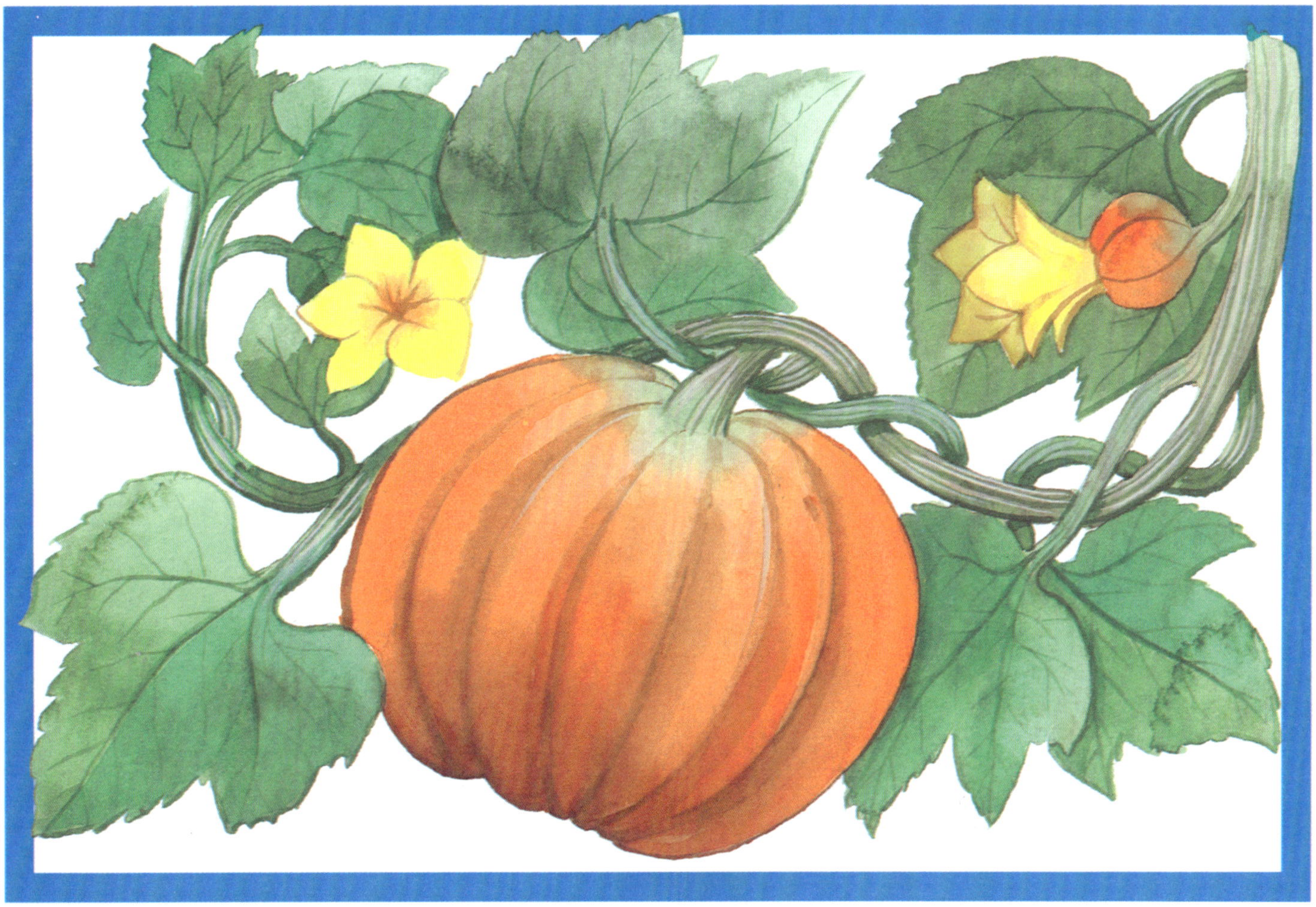

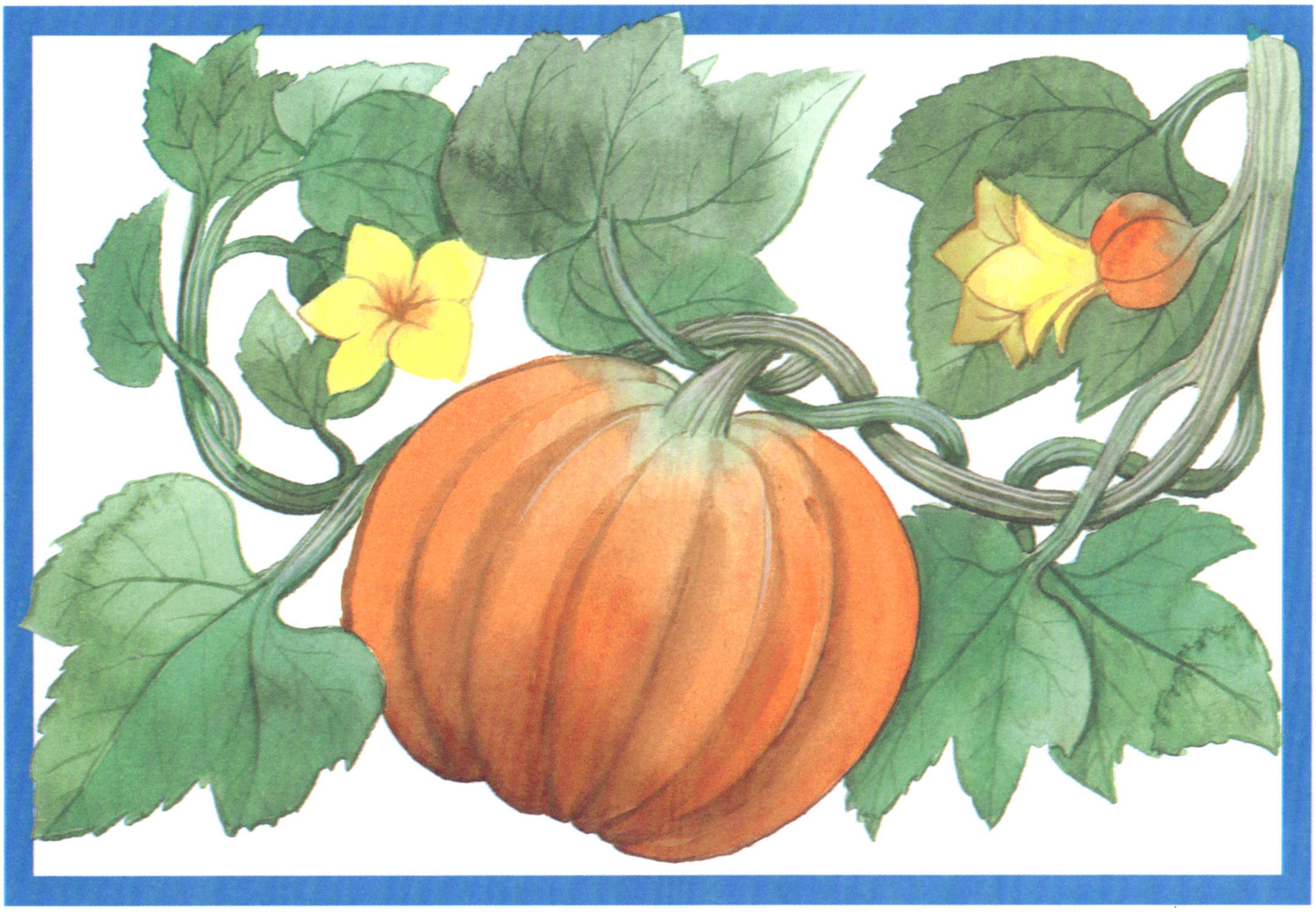

#57 pumpkin

©LoyolaPress.

#58 pumpkin

©LoyolaPress.

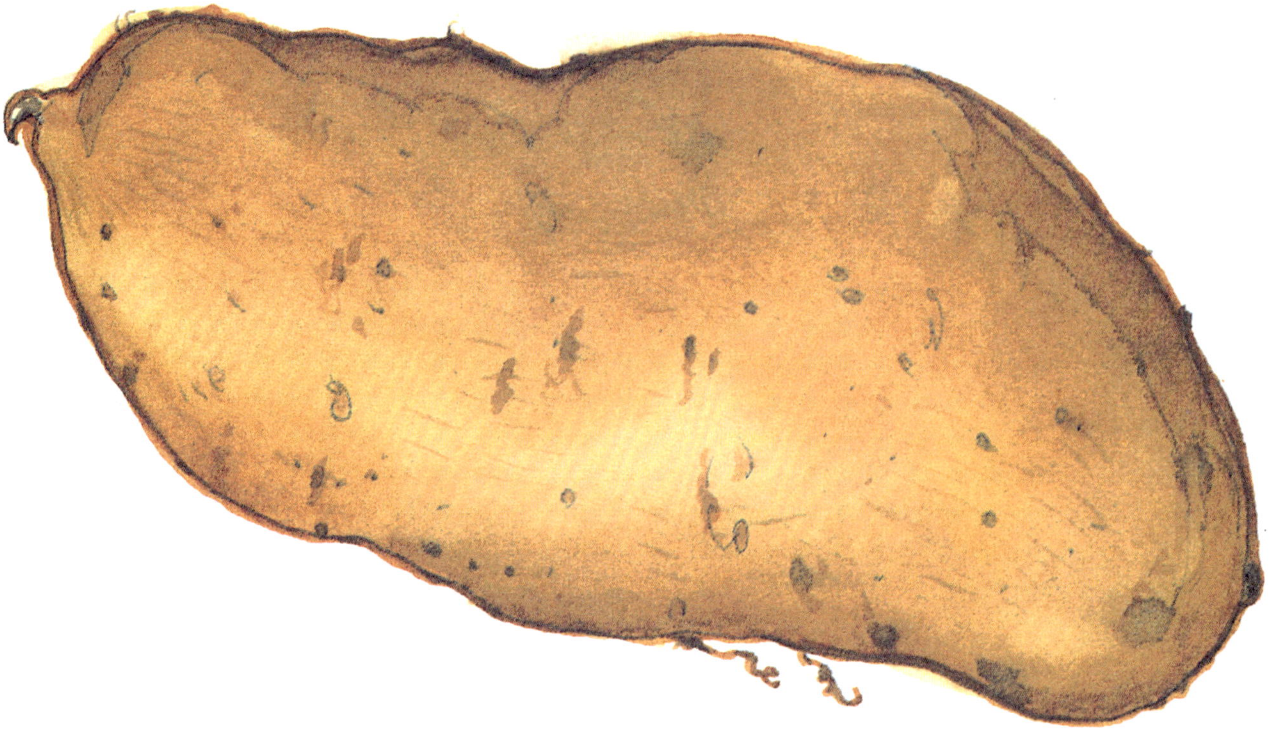

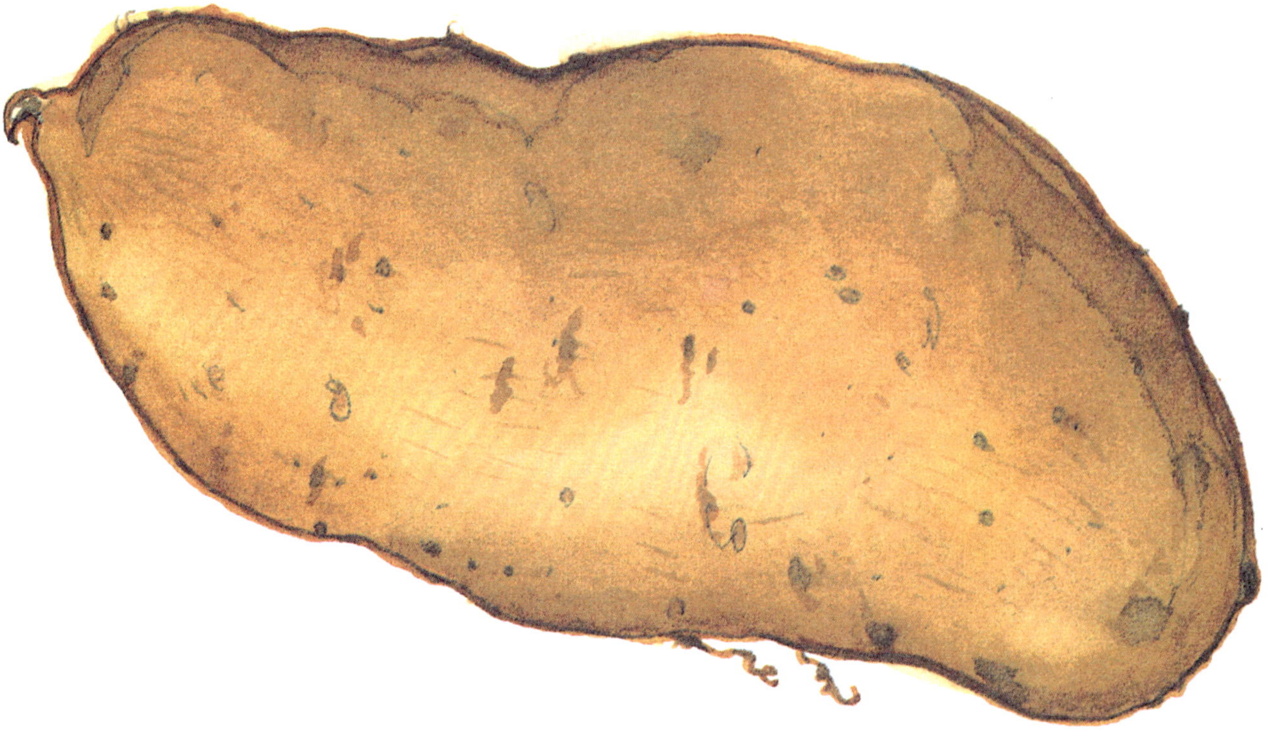

#59 sweet potato
© LOYOLA PRESS.

#60 sweet potato
© LOYOLA PRESS.

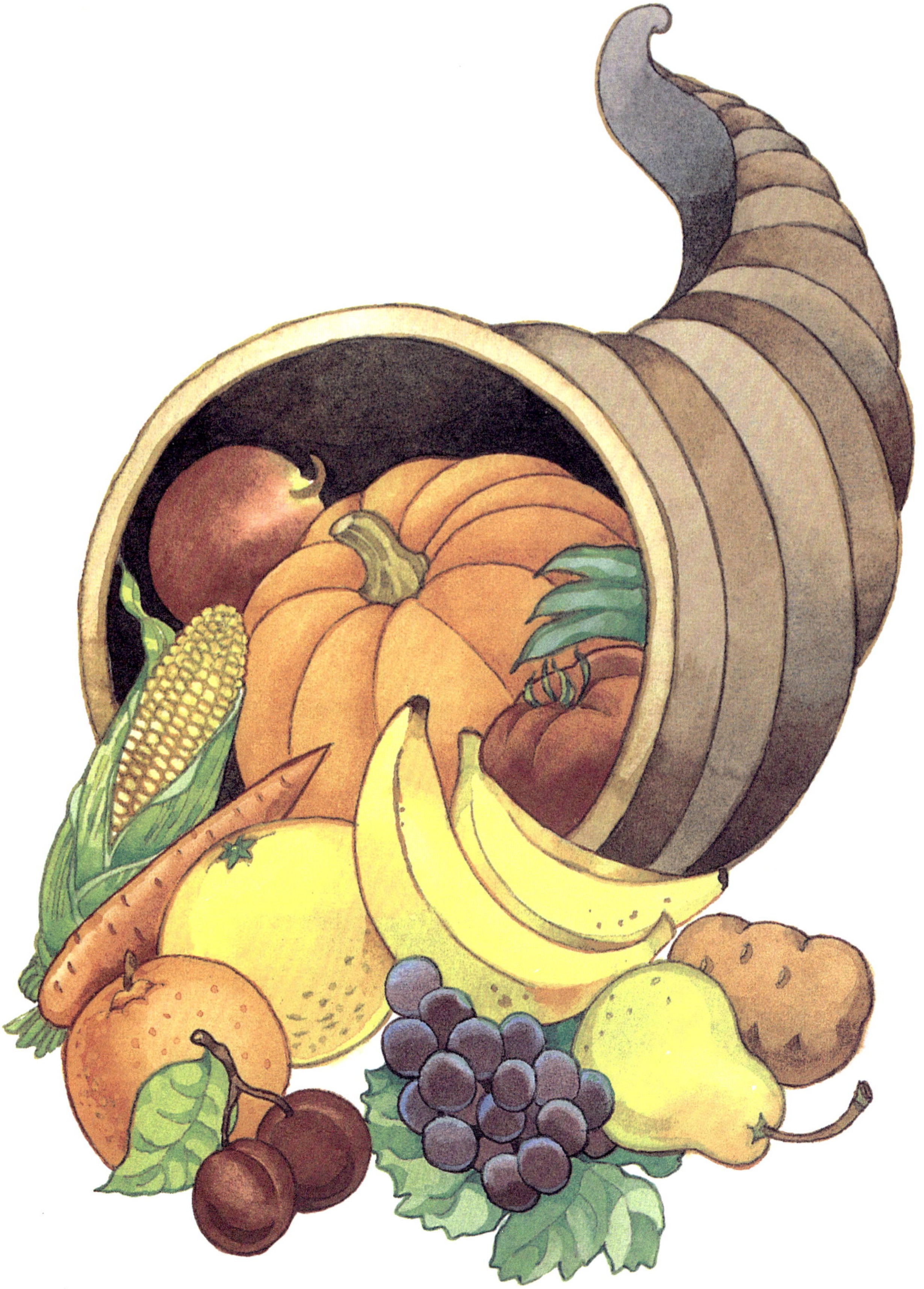

#61 cornucopia
©LoyolaPress.

Scripture Cards

You may wish to separate the Scripture cards and store them in a separate folder. Before presenting a lesson in which Scripture is quoted, place the corresponding card in your Bible.

As you read the card from the Bible during the lesson, you will be reinforcing for the children that the words are from "God's book."

Chapter 7

"God gives the earth rain. God makes grass grow. God gives food to birds and other animals."

adapted from Psalm 104:13–14

Chapter 5

"I give you food to eat."

adapted from Genesis 1:29–30

Chapter 1

"Jesus is my Son whom I love. Listen to him."

adapted from Matthew 17:5

Chapter 10

Sing joyfully to God, all people.

Live for God with gladness.

Come before God with joyful song.

adapted from Psalm 100:1–2

© Loyola Press.

Chapter 9

If someone is hungry, share your food.

If someone is thirsty, share your drink.

If someone has no clothes, share your clothes.

adapted from Matthew 25:35–36

© Loyola Press.

Chapter 8

"I will sprinkle clean water . . . to cleanse you . . ."

Ezekiel 36:25

© Loyola Press.

Chapter 13

"I sing praise to the Lord; I rejoice in God my savior."

adapted from Luke 1:46–47

"Glory to God in the highest . . ."

Luke 2:14

© Loyola Press.

Chapter 12

"Pray silently in your heart in secret.

Your Father will hear you."

adapted from Matthew 6:6

© Loyola Press.

Chapter 11

"God, I will speak words of praise to you."

adapted from Psalm 51:17

© Loyola Press.

Chapter 19

"God saw everything he had made and called it very good."

adapted from Genesis 1:31

Chapter 18

"May God bless us and bless the work that we do."

adapted from Psalm 90:17

Chapter 17

"I will praise the LORD with all my heart . . ."

Psalm 111:1

Chapter 24

"God, I praise you for making me so wonderful."

adapted from Psalm 139:14

Chapter 23

"[L]earn from me . . ."

Matthew 11:29

Chapter 20

"Jesus grew in age and wisdom."

adapted from Luke 2:52

Advent

"You will have a son and you shall name him Jesus. He will be great and will be called the Son of God."

adapted from Luke 1:31–32

Halloween/Feast of All Saints

"[B]e kind to one another . . ."

Ephesians 4:32

Chapter 25

"Love one another as I love you."

adapted from John 13:34

Pentecost

"The spirit of the Lord fills the whole world."

adapted from Wisdom 1:7

Easter

"I came to give you life."

adapted from John 10:10

Lent

"Unless a seed falls to the ground and dies, it remains just a seed; but if it dies, it produces much fruit."

adapted from John 12:24

© LoyolaPress.

Birthdays

"I have called you by name . . ."

Isaiah 43:1

Mother's Day

"Jesus went with Mary and Joseph to Nazareth and obeyed them. Mary remembered all these things in her heart."

adapted from Luke 2:51

Valentine's Day

"See, I have written your name on the psalms of my hands."

adapted from Isaiah 49:16

Last Class/Summer

"The Lord is kind and full of love."

adapted from Psalm 145:8